JOURNAL FOR THE STUDY OF THE NEW TESTAMENT SUPPLEMENT SERIES
188

Executive Editor
Stanley E. Porter

Sheffield Academic Press

'Servants of Satan', 'False Brothers' and Other Opponents of Paul

Jerry L. Sumney

Journal for the Study of the New Testament
Supplement Series 188

For
Elizabeth, Victoria and Margaret

May they and their father never need to argue
as Paul had to argue with his 'children'

Published by
Sheffield Academic Press Ltd
Mansion House
19 Kingfield Road
Sheffield S11 9AS
England

Typeset by Sheffield Academic Press
and
Printed on acid-free paper in Great Britain
by Bookcraft Ltd
Midsomer Norton, Bath

British Library Cataloguing in Publication Data

A catalogue record for this book is available
from the British Library

ISBN 1-84127-060-1

CONTENTS

PREFACE

I was prompted to undertake this study by two things: desire to understand the Pauline texts more clearly and an interest in understanding the shape of earliest Christianity. It is my belief that the two are interrelated. It is my hope that this work contributes to the clarification of both; this book tries to contribute to the scholarly discussion of early Christianity and the Pauline letters.

There are many people who need to be thanked for their contributions. Thanks goes to Ferrum College for their granting me funds to do research over several summers and a sabbatical. I also thank the Faculty Scholars Program of the University of Kentucky, through whom I received two James Still Fellowships (sponsored by the Mellon Foundation and the Bingham Foundation) to work on this book. I regret that this center of study is no longer available to scholars of the region. C.I. Dillon, Director of Library Services at Ferrum College and a supportive friend, read every chapter of the book and freely used his experience in teaching composition to help me clarify the language and keep an eye on the reading audience. He has saved subsequent readers much pain and deserves many thanks. John Bruton, chair of the Language and Literature Department of Ferrum College, also read sections of this book and offered helpful comments about its style. Diane, my wife, has constantly offered support and encouragement, and has taken on many responsibilities that have allowed me to pursue this interest. Thanks are also due to my daughters, to whom this book is dedicated. They supplied a delightful break from the arguments of the first century, even as they sometimes wondered why Dad needed to go to work when there were no students around.

ABBREVIATIONS

AB	Anchor Bible
AnBib	Analecta biblica
ANF	Anti-Nicene Fathers
ANRW	Hildegard Temporini and Wolfgang Haase (eds.), *Aufstieg und Niedergang der römischen Welt: Geschichte und Kultur Roms im Spiegel der neueren Forschung* (Berlin: W. de Gruyter, 1972–)
BETL	Bibliotheca ephemeridum theologicarum lovaniensium
Bib	*Biblica*
BJRL	*Bulletin of the John Rylands University Library of Manchester*
BNTC	Black's New Testament Commentaries
BT	*The Bible Translator*
BTB	*Biblical Theology Bulletin*
CBQ	*Catholic Biblical Quarterly*
CGTC	Cambridge Greek Testament Commentary
CNT	Commentaire du Nouveau Testament
ConBNT	Coniectanea biblica, Old Testament
EBib	Etudes bibliques
EKKNT	Evangelisch-Katholisher Kommentar zum Neuen Testament
ETR	*Etudes théologiques et religieuses*
ExpTim	*Expository Times*
FF	Foundations and Faces
FRLANT	Forschungen zur Religion und Literatur des Alten und Neuen Testaments
HNT	Handbuch zum Neuen Testament
HNTC	Harper's NT Commentaries
HTKNT	Herders theologischer Kommentar zum Neuen Testament
HTR	*Harvard Theological Review*
IB	*Interpreter's Bible*
ICC	International Critical Commentary
Int	*Interpretation*
IPQ	*International Philosophical Quarterly*
JBL	*Journal of Biblical Literature*
JETS	*Journal of the Evangelical Theological Society*
JRH	*Journal of Religious History*
JRS	*Journal of Roman Studies*

JSNT	*Journal for the Study of the New Testament*
JSNTSup	*Journal for the Study of the New Testament*, Supplement Series
JTS	*Journal of Theological Studies*
MeyerK	H.A.W. Meyer (ed.), Kritisch-exegetischer Kommentar über das Neue Testament
MNTC	Moffatt NT Commentary
NCB	New Century Bible
NICNT	New International Commentary on the New Testament
NIGTC	The New International Greek Testament Commentary
NovT	*Novum Testamentum*
NovTSup	*Novum Testamentum*, Supplements
NTD	Das Neue Testament Deutsch
NTS	*New Testament Studies*
PTMS	Pittsburgh Theological Monograph Series
RB	*Revue biblique*
RechBib	Recherche biblique
RevExp	*Review and Expositor*
RNT	Regensburger Neues Testament
RQ	*Restoration Quarterly*
RTR	*Reformed Theological Review*
SBL	Society of Biblical Literature
SBLDS	SBL Dissertation Series
SE	*Studia Evangelica I, II, III* (= TU 73 [1959], 87 [1964], 88 [1964], etc.)
SEÅ	*Svensk exegetisk årsbok*
SJT	*Scottish Journal of Theology*
SNTSMS	Society for New Testament Studies Monograph Series
ST	*Studia theologica*
SymBU	Symbolae biblicae upsalienses
TDNT	Gerhard Kittel and Gerhard Friedrich (eds.), *Theological Dictionary of the New Testament* (trans. Geoffrey W. Bromiley; 10 vols.; Grand Rapids: Eerdmans, 1964–)
TLZ	*Theologische Literaturzeitung*
TS	*Theological Studies*
TU	Texte und Untersuchungen
TZ	*Theologische Zeitschrift*
WBC	Word Biblical Commentary
WMANT	Wissenschaftliche Monographien zum Alten und Neuen Testament
WTJ	*Westminster Theological Journal*
WUNT	Wissenschaftliche Untersuchungen zum Neuen Testament
ZBK	Züricher Bibelkommentare
ZNW	*Zeitschrift für die neutestamentliche Wissenschaft*
ZTK	Zeitschrift für Theologie und Kirche

Chapter 1

INTRODUCTION

Few topics continually attract the attention of scholars and affect the interpretation of Pauline letters and early Christianity as much as the question of Paul's opponents. Nearly every thesis about both local Pauline congregations and Pauline Christianity more generally must presuppose or articulate a fairly specific understanding of the opposition Paul and his successors faced. Thus, hypotheses about Pauline opponents are legion.[1] However, most of these hypotheses are developed with little attention given to the use of appropriate methods,[2] that is, methods that conform to accepted canons of critical historical research and that conform to the genre of the documents involved.

Studies of Paul's opponents, especially those involving more than a single letter, have usually begun with presuppositions that significantly

---

1. A look at J.J. Gunther's listing of the hypotheses about opponents for each letter shows that there are hundreds (*St. Paul's Opponents and their Background* [NovTSup, 35; Leiden: E.J. Brill, 1973], pp. 1-7).

2. There are, of course, exceptions. Work on the opponents of Galatians has produced more discussion of method than any other Pauline letter. J.B. Tyson raised the issue of method in his 'Paul's Opponents in Galatia', *NovT* 10 (1968), pp. 241-54. Perhaps his essay has been the impetus for the discussions of method in relation to Galatians. Among others who discuss the issue in connection with Galatians are John M.G. Barclay, 'Mirror-Reading a Polemical Letter: Galatians as a Test Case', *JSNT* 31 (1987), pp. 73-93; Charles Cosgrove, *The Cross and the Spirit: A Study in the Argument and Theology of Galatians* (Macon, GA: Mercer University Press, 1988), pp. 31, 39-40; J. Louis Martyn, 'A Law-Observant Mission to Gentiles: The Background of Galatians', *SJT* 38 (1985), pp. 307-24 (310-13); *idem*, 'Events in Galatia: Modified Covenantal Nomism versus God's Invasion of the Cosmos in the Singular Gospel. A reponse to J.D.G. Dunn and B.R. Gaventa.', in J.M. Bassler (ed.), *Pauline Theology. I. Thessalonians, Philippians, Galatians, Philemon* (Minneapolis: Fortress Press, 1991), pp. 160-80 (160-63). For a listing of others who discuss method see below note 24.

influence their findings but are really appropriate only as conclusions. One of the most common of these presuppositions is that there was an organized and active anti-Pauline movement that sought to undermine Paul's authority or supplant his teachings or both. Such a presupposition is found in F.C. Baur's foundational work,[3] W. Schmithals's Gnostic thesis[4] and G. Lüdemann's more recent modification of Baur's thesis.[5] There is a growing dissatisfaction with such a simple scheme because it fails to account for the almost certain diversity of emerging Christianity. Furthermore, as I will argue below, this type of *presupposition* cannot be defended on methodological grounds.

Obvious and declared presuppositions of this sort are not the only ones that have hindered the search for Paul's opponents. Some identifications of his opponents relied on understanding them in terms of set theological categories (e.g. Christology or soteriology) and with a heresy/orthodoxy scheme, while others rely on a heteropraxy/orthopraxy scheme. But neither these schemes nor the theological categories can be assumed before the evidence is examined. We may find that some arguments between Paul and his opponents were about beliefs, others about practices, and some may not fit neatly into either category.

These controversies have been viewed in such a one-dimensional manner in part because little attention has been paid to sociological studies of the rise and functions of conflict within groups.[6] While such

---

3.   F.C. Baur, 'Die Christuspartei in der korinthischen Gemeinde, der Gegensatz des Petrischen und Paulinischen Christentum in der ältesten Kirche, der Apostel Petrus in Rom', *Tübingen Zeitschrift für Theologie* 4 (1831), pp. 61-206; *Paul, The Apostle of Jesus Christ: His Life and Work, his Epistles and Doctrine* (trans. E. Zeller; 2 vols.; London: Williams & Norgate, 2nd edn, 1876).

4.   W. Schmithals, *Paul and the Gnostics* (trans. John E. Steely; Nashville: Abingdon Press, 1972). Schmithals explicitly states that this is his presupposition as he approaches Galatians (*Paul and the Gnostics*, p. 17).

5.   Gerd Lüdemann, *Opposition to Paul in Jewish Christianity* (trans. M. Eugene Boring; Minneapolis: Fortress Press, 1989). Although Michael D. Goulder's *St. Paul versus St. Peter: A Tale of Two Missions* Louisville, KY: Westminster/John Knox Press, 1994) is not specifically a study of Paul's opponents, he describes early Christianity according to a scheme like that of Baur's and Lüdemann's with a Jerusalem mission defining itself as Paul's opposition.

6.   Unfortunately, few sociologists have addressed the topic at length, but the work of Lewis Coser, *The Functions of Social Conflict* (New York: Free Press, 1956), offers some helpful insights.

studies are not a focus of this work, insights from them can help us understand how or why some controversies developed and perhaps keep us from mistaken notions about what was happening in Paul's churches.[7]

Another prevalent inclination is to immediately identify Paul's opponents as heretics, whether defined as heterodoxy or heteropraxy. One result of this predilection is that we seldom envision the opponents outside a polemical context and so our view of them is skewed. Additionally, when we label them heretics, our investment in separating their views and practices as far as possible from Paul's and our own is increased.[8] Thus, most interpreters emphasize how different Paul is from his opponents. But it may well be that often very little separated them. This point warrants some expansion.

7.   While insights from sociological studies are essential, it would not be appropriate for a method which seeks initially to identify the opponents of specific situations to have a sociological approach as its primary emphasis because, as Gerd Theissen points out (*The Social Setting of Pauline Christianity* [ed. and trans. J.H. Schütz; Philadelphia: Fortress Press, 1982], pp. 176-77), sociological studies are 'less concerned with what is individual than with what is typical, recurrent, general' and 'less concerned with the singular conditions of a specific situation than with structured relationships which apply to several situations'. Thus, a sociological study which works with our findings would be more helpful than trying to identify these individual situations with a sociological analysis.

8.   Jonathan Z. Smith (*Imagining Religion: From Babylon to Jonestown*, [Chicago Studies in the History of Judaism; Chicago: University of Chicago Press, 1982], p. 6) writes that in 'the classification of religions, a dichotomous agenda of division has been most frequently employed…[in which] there are usually normative implications or the assignment of positive or negative valences which render the classification useless'. A rather extreme example of identifying with the 'orthodox' ancient writer which often hinders interpreters from understanding the opponents is found in A. Cleveland Coxe's 'Introductory Note to *Irenaeus Against Heresies*', in *The Apostolic Fathers with Justin Martyr and Irenaeus* (ANF; Grand Rapids: Eerdmanns, 1956), p. 309, where he writes of Irenaeus:

> He condescended to study these diseases of the human mind like a wise physician; and, sickening as was the process of classifying and describing them, he made this also his laborious task, that he might enable others to withstand and overcome them. The works he has left us are monuments of his fidelity to Christ.

One hardly expects such a perspective to produce a balanced understanding of those opposed.

Writers and conversation partners usually note differences only when something is at stake.[9] That is, only when the difference has some significance is it worth mentioning. We may take it for granted that the opponents addressed in the Pauline letters differed in ways that were considered important. That does not necessarily mean that the difference was very great, only that the difference's *importance* was perceived as great. Paul and the opponents of any Pauline letter probably agreed about more things than they disagreed about. If this were not the case, they would have been little threat to Paul's teaching or authority because they would have had no basis on which to establish their initial presence in his churches.

Besides this rather practical matter which requires that Paul's opponents be much like him, the probability that Paul and his opponents were much alike is borne out by both historical analogies and sociological theory. Jonathan Z. Smith notes that the other which is radically different is 'merely "other"', a curiosity, while the other which is more like the observer calls for more intense interest and concern.[10] A clear example of this principle is the interest the rabbis show in Gentiles as compared to fellow Jews considered aberrant. The rabbis show little interest in describing Gentiles or prescribing their behavior. Conversely, they give extensive treatment to those Jews who use and interpret Scripture differently from themselves.[11] For the rabbis the proximate deviations, those with which they shared the most, are of the greatest importance. Another example is the proliferation of protestant denominations almost immediately following Martin Luther's break with the Roman Church. The various protestant groups shared more (including a perceived common enemy) than they differed, and it seems that their similarity made their differences all the more important to them. So it is

9.   Jonathan Z. Smith, 'What a Difference a Difference Makes', in Jacob Neusner and Ernest S. Frerichs (eds.), *'To See Ourselves as Others See Us': Christians, Jews, 'Others' in Late Antiquity* (Studies in the Humanities; Chico, CA: Scholars Press, 1985) pp. 3-48 (4). See this entire insightful article for further discussion of how groups deal with 'otherness'.

10. Smith, 'What a Difference', p. 5. He notes examples of this from various fields including Robert Burns's use of Scottish and the taxonomy of parasites.

11. William S. Green, 'Otherness Within: Towards a Theory of Difference in Rabbinic Judaism', in Neusner and Frerichs (eds.), *'To See Ourselves as Others See Us'*, pp. 49-69 (58-59); Gary G. Porton, 'Forbidden Transactions: Prohibited Commerce with Gentiles in Earliest Rabbinism', in Neusner and Frerichs (eds.), *'To See Ourselves as Others See Us'*, pp. 317-35 (333-35).

those most like any group which evoke the group's more vehement responses. As Smith comments, 'While the "other" may be perceived as being either LIKE–US or NOT–LIKE–US, he is, in fact, most problematic when he is TOO–MUCH–LIKE–US, or when he claims to BE–US'.[12] When we find Paul combatting opponents, he and his churches have found themselves facing those most problematic 'others', those who claim to BE–US—the opponents were not merely like Christians, they claim to be Christians, perhaps even the true Christians. Thus they are a matter of great concern.

This understanding of relatedness/proximity in group conflict is supported by sociological analysis. Coser asserts that the closer two groups are to one another, the sharper the conflict is likely to be, and this is especially true for inter-group conflicts.[13] If the difference concerns an issue which threatens the unity or identity of the group, Coser argues, the conflict will be all the more intense.[14] If those who are different form a rival group, they are perceived as more dangerous than if they had simply joined the enemy[15] (in our case the enemy would be any non-Christian group). But the group perceives as even more dangerous the dissenter who does not separate him/herself from the group and so still claims to belong.[16] So again, the more the disputants are alike, the more necesary it seems to the group to expose and reject the difference that is deemed unacceptable.[17]

One final observation of Coser is immediately relevant. He notes that groups which expect outside opposition 'react violently against inner dissent' and the more acute the outside conflict is, the more violent the reaction is likely to be.[18] The apocalyptic outlook of the Pauline churches kept them in at least perceived conflict with the forces of evil.

---

12. Smith, 'What a Difference', p. 47.

13. Coser, *The Functions of Social Conflict*, p. 71.

14. Coser, *The Functions of Social Conflict*, p. 71.

15. Coser, *The Functions of Social Conflict*, p. 71.

16. Coser, *The Functions of Social Conflict*, p. 101.

17. Cf. Elizabeth A. Castelli, *Imitating Paul: A Discourse of Power* (Literary Currents in Biblical Interpretation; Louisville, KY: Westminster/John Knox Press, 1991), p. 22. She asserts here that often in Paul, 'difference is perceived as problematic, dangerous, threatening'. While she seems to have overstated the case by including, it seems, all difference, her essential point is on target.

18. Coser, *The Functions of Social Conflict*, p. 100; cf. p. 103: 'Groups engaged in continual struggle with the outside tend to be intolerant within.'

Thus we may expect them to react vehemently against any unacceptable difference.

While applying modern sociological theory to ancient societies and groups produces no certain conclusions, the convergence of elements of Coser's theory of conflict with the example of the rabbis indicates that we should not *presuppose* that the differences between Paul and his opponents were numerous and gaping.

One element of the function of conflicts bears mentioning here. Conflicts lead groups to produce a clearer self-image and to draw and reinforce group boundaries.[19] As J. Neusner and E. Frerichs comment, 'from center to frontier, societies discover themselves by signifying difference and stipulating what difference difference makes'.[20] Groups often need enemies to create and sustain their boundaries, that is to develop a self-identity. The issue of self-identity would be especially acute in new congregations of an emerging movement such as early Christianity. Within the process of developing a group self-understanding, differences may emerge which are not intended as opposition[21] and are only designated as such once they are more fully developed or reported to an authority. Gager asserts that 'it may well be among those in positions of leadership and power that the tendency to conceive of the world in terms of negative antitheses comes most readily to the fore'.[22] Thus a developing point of view may be interpreted as unacceptable more quickly by those in leadership roles than by the general membership. Following this lead, it is possible that in some instances where Paul identifies teachers or leaders as opponents, he is the first to perceive and label them such; he is the first to describe their differences in such sharp contrasts that it is possible to call them opponents.[23] Paul

19. Coser, *The Functions of Social Conflict*, pp. 72ff. Cf. John G. Gager, 'Jews, Christians and the Dangerous Ones in Between', in S. Biderman and B.-A. Scharfstein (eds.), *Interpretation in Religion* (Leiden: E.J. Brill, 1992), pp. 249-57 (251).

20. Jacob Neusner and Ernest S. Frerichs, 'Preface', in *idem*, *'To See Ourselves as Others See Us'*, pp. xi-xvi (xi).

21. Castelli (*Imitating Paul*, p. 86) notes that in Greco-Roman thought, sameness was valued over difference and linked with unity and harmony, while difference was associated with disunity and disorder. Furthermore, 'this treatment of difference has profound implications for processes of social formation, because it suggests that difference must be subversive of unity, harmony, and order'.

22. Gager, 'Jews, Christians and the Dangerous Ones in Between', p. 256.

23. Gerd Theissen (*Social Reality and the Early Christians: Theology, Ethics, and the World of the New Testament* [trans. M. Kohl; Minneapolis: Fortress Press,

may indeed have seen this as the necessary 'spin' to put on their difference (their otherness) to protect his churches from their, in his view, harmful influence. Furthermore, he may have thought it necessary for his churches to secure and reinforce their boundaries and identity by rejecting these 'others'. The tendency among leaders to construct antitheses may help explain why Paul draws such stark distinctions between himself and his opponents. Perhaps it was his concern for his churches' unity and fidelity rather than huge differences with his opponents which led him to emphasize the contrast between his positions and theirs.

We are, then, left with the possibility, perhaps the probability, that at least sometimes little separated Paul and his opponents. This is not to say that the differences that were present were of little importance. In fact, Paul often sees them to be of monumental importance. But this may indicate that Paul sees his opponents as dangerous precisely because they are so close, deceptively close for his churches, and yet distinctly 'other'. We must not rule out the possibility that the differences between Paul and his opponents are numerous, but we obviously cannot begin with this as a presupposition.

The detrimental effects these and other presuppositions have had on studies of Paul's opponents is evident in the many and radically different understandings of the opponents scholars have reached. Given the lack of consensus, the neglect of appropriate methods[24] and the use of unfounded presuppositions, it seems in order to approach this question again. These factors also indicate that the way to begin such a study is

---

1992], p. 255) notes that 'conflicts have an innovatory function' and often result in the creation of or movement beyond the current structures.

24. Among those who do discuss method we find Nils A. Dahl, 'Paul and the Church at Corinth According to 1 Corinthians 1:10–4:21', in W.R. Farmer, C.F.D. Moule and R.R. Niebuhr (eds.), *Christian History and Interpretation* (Cambridge: Cambridge University Press, 1967), pp. 313-35; C.J.A. Hickling, 'Is the Second Epistle to the Corinthians a Source for Early Church History?', *ZNW* 66 (1975), pp. 284-87; R.M. Wilson, 'How Gnostic were the Corinthians?', *NTS* 19 (1972), pp. 65-74; *idem*, 'Gnosis at Corinth', in M.D. Hooker and S.G. Wilson (eds.), *Paul and Paulinism* (London: SPCK, 1982), pp. 102-14; and K. Berger, 'Die implizten Gegner: zur Methode des Erschliessens von "Gegner" in neutestamentlichen Texten', in D. Lührmann and G. Strecker (eds.), *Kirche* (Tübingen: J.C.B. Mohr [Paul Siebeck], 1980), pp. 373-400. In addition, see those mentioned above in note 2. However, none of these discussions of method are sufficiently detailed or involve a sufficient number of issues to produce a relatively complete methodology.

by setting out a method that conforms to accepted principles of historical research.

The Method

The method I will employ to identify Paul's opponents was first proposed and supported in my *Identifying Paul's Opponents*. Since those arguments have already been made, I will primarily assert the method's procedures and supply only a few supporting arguments. It is important to recognize from the beginning that the purpose of this method is not to set out the entire occasion of a letter. Rather, the focus is on identifying opponents, if there are any, and on what made the Pauline author see them as opponents. Thus, there will be aspects of the occasion of many Pauline letters which are not discussed in this search for the identity of opponents.

The method set out here designates which materials are directly relevant for identifying a letter's opponents and then specifies how those materials can be used. To accomplish these tasks three broad topics must be addressed: the use of historical reconstructions, the use of sources other than the primary text, and the use of data within the primary text.

Many interpreters use reconstructions of early Christianity to identify Paul's opponents.[25] Some, like F.C. Baur and W. Schmithals, allow reconstructions to define in quite specific detail the opponents of particular letters. Others use them to a lesser extent, but still allow the reconstruction to be a determinative factor. We must reject all such uses of a reconstruction because they not only violate good historical method and what we know of early Christianity but also employ circular reasoning.

Using reconstructions to determine in any way the characteristics of a particular group of opponents violates good historical method by treating the *possibility* a reconstruction presents as a probability or as historical fact. Those who use reconstructions in these ways draw inferences about a particular situation from the conjecture about the broader situation which a reconstruction provides. Allowing reconstructions to

25. For a fuller discussion of this issue see Jerry L. Sumney, *Identifying Paul's Opponents* (JSNTSup, 40; Sheffield: JSOT Press, 1990), pp. 77-86.

serve in such ways also fails to recognize the diversity of early Christianity, a diversity necessarily implied by the spread of Christianity in its nascent state to so many widely scattered places by so many people in so short a time. Finally, allowing a reconstruction to determine elements of our portrait of opponents involves circular reasoning because the interpreter assumes what she or he sets out to prove, that is, the interpreter finds evidence for a particular type of opponent because that is the type the reconstruction posits.[26]

These problems indicate that our use of reconstructions must be strictly confined. Still, they can serve two important functions: (1) they provide a broad context in which to read our sources; and (2) they can supply a context that helps confirm a hypothesis by showing that such opponents can be integrated into the milieu of first century Christianity. At this point a reconstruction may suggest that a particular set of opponents belongs to a larger group (e.g. Gnostics). But even if this is the case, the reconstruction cannot add features to our characterization of that set of opponents because we cannot assume that all members of a group have identical views.

The two leading questions which involve documents other than the primary text are: (1) whether we should interpret letters individually or in conjunction with other letters in the same corpus, and (2) how we should use and identify parallels.

The letter genre requires us to interpret letters individually.[27] Letters are by their nature occasional and so we cannot assume that any two letters within a corpus address precisely the same or even related issues, problems, or opponents. Thus, we cannot allow matters discussed in one letter to determine the identity of another letter's opponents. This conclusion does not reflect a judgment that history is simple or that events

---

26. The extent to which they can function in this way reaches its extreme in Baur's remarks to the effect that even though 1 Corinthians yields no evidence of Judaizers, they must be the opponents in view because that is what the reconstruction allows ('Christuspartei', pp. 77-79) and in W. Schmithals who, in order to sustain his thesis that all of Paul's opponents are Gnostics, must resort to arguing that Paul does not understand his opposition (e.g. *Gnosticism in Corinth* [trans. John E. Steely; Nashville: Abingdon Press, 1971], pp. 102, 116, 144, 151-57; *idem*, *Paul and the Gnostics*, p. 247).

27. See the fuller discussion in Sumney, *Identifying Paul's Opponents*, pp. 87-88.

occur in a vacuum.[28] Rather, it acknowledges the complexity of history
and the unpredictability of changes which can occur within groups in a
brief period of time. Furthermore, this does not mean that we presuppose that every Pauline letter addresses different opponents, only that
each letter must be allowed to speak for itself as clearly as possible
without imposing opponents from outside. Only after a letter has been
thoroughly examined on its own are we in a position to compare its
opponents with those of another letter.

Most identifications of Paul's opponents rely in some measure on parallels identified on the basis of the same or similar terminology.[29] But
similar or identical terms are insufficient means for identifying parallels
because a single word can convey many different meanings, even within the same author.[30] Not only does this multivalent nature of language
disallow such a use of parallels, but so does the historian's rule of context. This rule states that the meanings of words and phrases can be
known only from the context.[31] Given these considerations, two conditions must be met to call a passage a parallel: (1) the two documents
must participate in the same conceptual framework; and (2) the words
must be shown within their contexts actually to carry the same meanings before identifying them as parallels.

Once we identify a parallel we must strictly limit its use because it
can do no more than present an analogy.[32] We cannot assume that just
because two documents use a particular word in the same way, the situations they address are identical or even similar. Once we have examined each text thoroughly, we may think the same opponents are in
view in both. If this is the case, a parallel may strengthen or confirm
this hypothesis. In addition, the parallel may illuminate the broad context and help us understand why some opponents argue as they do or
why they are concerned about particular issues. But even if this is the

28. In his review of *Identifying Paul's Opponents*, John Sieber asserts that limiting our investigation to individual letters demonstrates a 'limited view of history
[which] suggests that people, events, and ideas exist in a vacuum' (*Int* 45 [1991],
p. 426).

29. Schmithals (*Paul and the Gnostics*, p. 241) explicitly defends this procedure.

30. See the discussion in Sumney, *Identifying Paul's Opponents*, pp. 89-92.

31. See, e.g., Charles V. Langlois and Charles Seignobos, *Introduction to the
Study of History* (trans. G.G. Berry; London: Gerald Duckworth, 1898), p. 149.

32. For a fuller discussion see Sumney, *Identifying Paul's Opponents*, pp. 93-
94.

case, parallels cannot add features to our characterization of a particular letter's opponents, again, because we cannot assume that all members of a group have identical views on all topics.

Since other sources must be eliminated, the letter under consideration itself is the only primary evidence for its opponents. Thus, this method focuses on the primary text and how we use its data, ranking data within a letter according to two criteria: (1) How certain we can be that a statement refers to opponents; and (2) How reliable that statement is. To make these judgments we must distinguish among various types of statements and different kinds of contexts.[33]

To assess how certain we can be that a statement actually refers to opponents, our method distinguishes among explicit statements about opponents, allusions to them, and affirmations which seem to address them. This is necessary because we cannot assume that all statements in a letter address opponents or issues they raise. We must allow for the possibility, the almost certain probability, that an author addresses other matters. Explicit statements, those in which the author speaks directly about the opponents,[34] are our most certain references to opponents. Allusions are statements which seem to address opponents, but are indirect, and so more or less oblique references to them. We can identify a statement as an allusion only if it addresses an issue raised in explicit statements or other fairly certain allusions. For example, if explicit statements show that the opponents raise the issue of circumcision, a reference to circumcision would allow the passage in which it appeared to be considered an allusion. While we cannot be as certain that allusions refer to opponents, some statements do fairly clearly allude to them. Affirmations are statements which neither explicitly refer to opponents nor obviously allude to them. Since we must remain less certain that they actually refer to opponents, our use of affirmations must be strictly limited.

The characteristics of the context in which a statement appears helps us evaluate its reliability. The question of reliability does not concern how well the author understood the opponents, but how fairly or unfairly

---

33. The following assessments of the relative value of different types of statement in various contexts is directly depended on Sumney, *Identifying Paul's Opponents*, pp. 95-113. Those pages offer further defense of the positions taken here.

34. For example in 2 Cor. 10.10 Paul writes that 'they say' his letters are weighty but his presence is weak.

she or he represents what they believe their position to be. This judgment does not entail a claim to possess knowledge about authorial intent; rather, it is a statement about rhetorical function. It is an acknowledgment that context determines how authors present information. We cannot read all contexts as if they convey 'objective' information, especially when dealing with situations that include opponents. Therefore, we need to think of how various kinds of contexts should affect our use of statements about opponents. The types of contexts this method identifies include: polemical, apologetic, didactic and conventional epistolary periods (e.g. greetings, thanksgiving periods, etc.).

When classifying a passage we must take full advantage of the recent advances of rhetorical criticism. Recognizing that a section of text makes up a common rhetorical feature (e.g. a *narratio*) helps us decide what function it has within the letter as a whole and so whether it is more likely to be polemical, apologetic, etc. We must be careful, however, not to prescribe what an author must do in an argument based on assumptions about what rhetorical theory dictates. Rhetorical categories can primarily help us describe and understand Paul's argumentation.[35] So any use of rhetorical types must be done by reading a section in its literary context. Rhetorical criticism may also contribute to our search for opponents if a convincing case can be made that a letter belongs to a particular species (e.g. deliberative). However, caution is due here because the discovery (or presumption) that opponents form a central part of a letter's occasion (or conversely that they do not) may require us to modify our judgment about a letter's species. Furthermore, New Testament scholars are beginning to recognize the significant limits judgments about rhetorical types can make for interpretation, especially the interpretation of letters.[36]

---

35. See the careful distinctions and helpful comments on using rhetorical criticism in Jeffrey T. Reed, 'Using Ancient Rhetorical Categories to Interpret Paul's Letters: A Question of Genre', in S.E. Porter and Thomas H. Olbricht (eds.), *Rhetoric and the New Testament: Essays from the 1992 Heidelberg Conference* (JSNTSup, 90; Sheffield: JSOT Press, 1993), pp. 292-324, esp. pp. 313-14.

36. See C. Joachim Classen, 'St. Paul's Epistles and Ancient Greek and Roman Rhetoric', in Porter and Olbricht (eds.), *Rhetoric and the New Testament*, pp. 265-91, for a discussion of the use of rhetorical criticism with epistles. Also Stanley E. Porter, 'The Theoretical Justification for Application of Rhetorical Categories to Pauline Epistolary Literature', in Porter and Olbricht (eds.), *Rhetoric and the New Testament*, pp. 100-122. Porter points out many problems with the ways categories

To use the data of the primary text effectively, we must combine our two means of assessment (certainty of reference and reliability). We will do this by discussing each type of context and how statements within it may be used to identify opponents.

Polemical Contexts

In the Hellenistic era polemical remarks were often tendentious and partisan and included exaggerations and unsupportable charges about one's opponents. Early Christian anti-heretical writers commonly made exaggerated claims about their opponents and often accused them of deceit or immorality. Irenaeus's treatment of the Gnostics is a prime example. He disparages them every way he can and is willing to caricature and misrepresent them.[37] Since Irenaeus was not alone in his willingness to use any means available to discredit and defeat his opponents,[38] it seems probable that polemical contexts contain exaggerated claims about and partisan evaluations of opponents. Therefore, we must consider statements within polemical contexts to be somewhat unreliable and the more directly the opponents are mentioned, the less reliable the statement is likely to be.[39]

---

from oratorical rhetoric have been applied to epistles. These problems point clearly to the limits of rhetoric criticism in the study of Pauline letters.

37. Irenaeus writes in *Adv. Haer.* 1.31.4 that he wants not only to expose the Gnostics, but also 'from every side to wound the beast'. This comment, along with the writings we now have from Gnostics themselves, which present a very different picture to that Irenaeus gives, indicate that Irenaeus was willing to use all means at his disposal to defeat the Gnostics.

38. Those who comment on this characteristic of polemic include Kurt Rudolf, *Gnosis* (trans. and ed. R.M. Wilson; New York: Harper & Row, 1983), pp. 9-10; H. von Campenhausen, *The Fathers of the Greek Church* (trans. S. Godman; New York: Pantheon, 1959), pp. 23-25; Robert Grant, 'Charges of "Immorality" Against Various Religious Groups in Antiquity', in R. van den Broek and M.J. Vermaseren (eds.), *Studies in Gnosticism and Hellenistic Religions* (Leiden: E.J. Brill, 1981), pp. 161-70; and F. Wisse, 'The Use of Early Christian Literature as Evidence for Inner Diversity and Conflict', in C.W. Hedrick and R. Hodgson, Jr (eds.), *Nag Hammadi, Gnosticism, and Early Christianity* (Peabody, MA: Hendrickson, 1986), pp. 177-90. See Sumney, *Identifying Paul's Opponents*, pp. 97, 212-13. Also see Gager, 'Jews, Christians and the Dangerous Ones in Between', pp. 249-57 (250-51); Green, 'Otherness Within', p. 50; Sean Freyne, 'Vilifying the Other and Defining the Self: Matthew's and John's Anti-Jewish Polemic in Focus', in Neusner and Frerichs (eds.), *'To See Ourselves As Others See Us'*, p. 118.

39. See the discussion of Dennis L. Stamps, 'Rethinking the Rhetorical Situ-

Explicit statements are the least reliable statements in a polemical context because they speak directly of the opponents with the intent of defeating them and so often include exaggerations and misrepresentations. Allusions are probably a bit more reliable because they do not speak of the opponents as directly. Fairly certain allusions rank just below explicit statements in terms of certainty of reference. Less certain allusions cannot be grouped with the more certain references because they can produce evidence only if we use mirror exegesis (see below). Evidence gathered in this manner must be compatible with other more certain evidence about the opponents if it is to be used in our methodology.

We must establish that a passage relates directly to an issue already connected with the opponents to identify it as a relevant affirmation. Affirmations yield information about opponents only if we use 'mirror exegesis', a technique which assigns to one's opponents the opposite of whatever the text asserts. For example, if an author calls on the readers to abstain from sexual immorality, mirror exegesis claims that the opponents were advocating sexual license. Even though interpreters often use this technique, it is far too problematic[40] to be used without strict limitations. Since we can extract information about opponents from affirmations only by using mirror exegesis, they can never add a topic to the debate with opponents. Affirmations only clarify the opponents' views on previously identified issues and what is gained must be coherent with what we already know of them. Affirmations are more reliable than allusions because the opponents are not as directly in view, but we cannot be as certain that they refer to the opponents.

Apologetic Contexts
Statements in apologetic contexts are not completely reliable because the author is defending him- or herself. But since the tendentiousness is not aimed as directly at the opponents, each type of statement (ex-

ation: The Entextualization of the Situation in New Testament Epistles', in Porter and Olbricht (eds.), *Rhetoric and the New Testament*, pp. 193-210. Stamps notes here that authors embed within a letter a particular perspective on a historical situation to make their argument effective (see esp. pp. 198-204, 210). Such a perspectival presentation of one's opponents will be most prominent in polemical contexts.

40. See the discussion of the problems with this technique in Sumney, *Identifying Paul's Opponents*, pp. 98-100.

plicit statements, allusions and affirmations) in such contexts is probably somewhat more reliable than its counterpart in polemical sections.
Allusions in apologetic contexts must be closely related to an issue we
already know the opponents raise because the focus is not directly on
the opponents. They can only clarify those known issues and cannot
add a topic of debate to the opponents' agenda. Affirmations in apologetic contexts must tie directly to a known point of debate and can only
amplify that point.

Didactic Contexts

Didactic sections are among the most reliable parts of a letter when
identifying opponents because their immediate goal is to teach or inform rather than to defeat opponents or defend the writer. Explicit statements in didactic contexts are some of our best evidence for opponents
—they rank within the highest category for both our criteria. Supposed
allusions here are very reliable but we must strictly limit their use
because we must remain less certain that opponents are in view given
the nature of the section. Therefore, they must tie directly to a known
point of debate and can only add detail to this point. We cannot use
affirmations in didactic contexts because these sections often introduce
topics for their own sake, and things other than opponents may lead an
author to speak of such matters.

Epistolary Periods

The conventional epistolary periods we will discuss here are thanksgivings, greetings, closings and hortatory sections. Thanksgivings offer
reliable information about opponents because direct polemic is generally incompatible with such periods. So explicit statements here are extremely good data because they both certainly and reliably speak of the
opponents. The thanksgiving's nature also makes it less likely that there
will be allusions to opponents and so a statement must tie directly to an
issue we know they raise to be considered an allusion. Such allusions
rank as slightly less certain than affirmations in polemical contexts.
Individual affirmations in introductory thanksgiving/prayer periods cannot be used because we can be even less certain that they refer to opponents. However, a main theme of a thanksgiving may relate to arguments
with opponents and show that they are a leading problem. Still, these
themes cannot add particulars to our portrait of the opponents because
the thanksgiving is the author's thematic response to them, not direct

argument. So this evidence is primarily corroborative, though it may add some clarity.

Hortatory sections must be judged unreliable because, as we have seen, Hellenistic writers often accused their opponents of immorality. Since the most likely reference to opponents in such a section is some accusation about them and since defamation is the primary or only reason for mentioning them, this evidence is very unreliable, in fact the least reliable of any we encounter. Thus any remark made about opponents must be supported by more reliable statements to be admitted as evidence. We may use only explicit statements in these contexts because hortatory sections often include exhortations not directly demanded by the letter's occasion.

Greetings and closings are also unreliable because they are the author's first and last opportunities to make an impression about the opponents. We should expect the opponents to receive the same kind of treatment in these periods that they receive in polemical sections. Explicit statements about opponents in epistolary greetings are rare, in fact no Pauline greeting includes one. Allusions are difficult to identify and so rank very low in terms of certainty of reference, as well as being rather unreliable. Therefore they can only corroborate what we already know of the opponents from more certain and reliable references. Still, if a greeting alludes to opponents we can be sure that they are a major problem. Individual affirmations cannot be used to identify opponents, but if an extended greeting takes up a theme which ties directly to some part of the opponents' agenda, it may confirm that they are an important part of the letter's occasion. However, the author will probably frame this theme in his or her own way to begin to reject the opponents' perspective, as a result it will be of little help in identifying the opponents' views.

Similarly, statements in epistolary closings are likely to be unreliable because this is the last opportunity the author has to secure a judgment about them. Thus while explicit statements certainly refer to the opponents, they are as unreliable as those in greetings. Also like those in greetings, allusions can only be used to corroborate what we already know and affirmations cannot be used at all.

Ranking of Types of Passage for Use in Identifying Opponents

The results of my assessment of the various types of statements in various sorts of contexts are brought together in the chart on p. 29. This chart ranks types of statements in relation to one another and groups them with materials that we treat similarly. Those kinds of statements at the top of each column are ranked highest for that criterion; those in the lowest level of the certainty-of-reference column cannot be used at all.

Chart of Kinds of Passages according to
Certainty of Reference and Reliability

Certainty of reference	Reliability of reference
Explicit statements in all contexts	
	Explicit statements and allusions in Didactic contexts
Allusions in polemical contexts (that do not require the mirror technique)	Explicit statements, allusions and major themes in thanksgiving periods
Allusions in apologetic contexts	
	Major themes in greetings
Allusions in polemical contexts that require the mirror technique	Affirmations in apologetic contexts
	Affirmations in polemical contexts
Affirmations in polemical contexts	
Allusions in thanksgiving periods	Explicit statements and allusions in apologetic contexts
Main themes in extended greetings and thanksgiving periods	
	Allusions in polemical contexts
Individual non-explicit statements in greetings	Explicit statements in polemical contexts and epistolary greetings and closings
Individual affirmations in thanksgiving periods	
	Explicit statements in hortatory contexts
Non-explicit statements in epistolary closings and hortatory contexts	
Affirmations in didactic contexts	

A complicating element needs to be added here. We will discover that types of contexts are not always pure. For example, a passage which is primarily didactic may have a hint of apology. In such cases some moderation of our rules of usage is in order, with the degree of modification depending on the extent to which the passage is tinted.

One further point concerns the use of this method. We must begin our work with the clearest and most accessible evidence. Thus we begin with explicit statements and move to allusions, identifying them on the basis of evidence in the explicit statements. Then on the basis of explicit statements and allusions we identify affirmations. Similarly, within each category of statement we will also begin with the less difficult passages and move to the more difficult, interpreting the latter on the basis of the former.

Our method calls on the interpreter to make judgments about which category of statements a comment belongs in and what sort of context the statements are in. Inevitably there will be disagreements in these judgments which may affect some element of our understanding of the opponents. This method is not intended to resolve such interpretive disputes, though beginning with the less difficult materials may help settle some. These questions have to be argued on the basis of evidence, including perhaps what we have already learned about (or found absent from) the opponents. Still, the method provides a means for identifying which materials are directly relevant for our task and for assessing how those materials can be used appropriately.

Again, it is important to recognize that this method is *not intended to identify the full occasion of a letter, only its opponents*. Thus, if no opponents are found, we may know little about a letter's occasion and when they are found, we must acknowledge that they may not be the only reason for the letter's composition. Our focus on opponents is necessary to get as clear a perception as possible of one aspect of a letter's occasion, but it should not be assumed that it is the only aspect of that occasion.

Our portrait of the opponents of any particular letter may not be as detailed as that drawn by some other interpreters. Our method is minimalist in the sense that it seeks to establish what can be known with relative certainty. That is, it limits speculation about opponents by basing each assertion about them on the primary text. Thus, while we may not claim to know as much about the opponents as proponents of other hypotheses claim, what we claim will be more certain and so a more secure basis for exegesis and historical reconstruction.

In the following pages we will apply this method to every letter in the Pauline corpus except Philemon, Romans and Ephesians. The occasion of Philemon is the return of Onesimus and the assumed acceptance of the authority of Paul clearly indicates that no opponents are involved. Ephesians is not included because it seems that opponents are not a primary or even secondary concern of this letter, as most interpreters acknowledge. Indeed, one of the commonly recognized features of Ephesians is its general character. Still, a few interpreters have argued that it has opponents in view.[41] But such conjectures are based on extensive use of mirror exegesis and on reading the perceived problems of Colossians into Ephesians. Beyond this, Ephesians contains no explicit statements about opponents and the allusions to its audience and their situation remain quite general.[42] Since there is no evidence that Ephesians addresses opponents, further discussion of it is not necessary for this work. We exclude Romans, even though its purpose is still a matter of much debate, because the church at Rome was not a Pauline church in the sense that those in Corinth, Thessalonica and elsewhere were. Furthermore, since Paul had not been to Rome, anti-Pauline activity is not as probable. In addition, Romans was clearly not written as a response to anti-Pauline activity. We may take it, then, that the primary purposes of Romans do not involve opponents.

As a final introductory matter, this study will not take a stand on the authenticity of the disputed letters within the Pauline corpus. Such decisions are not necessary for the application of our method and have at times been used to identify the opponents of various letters. For example, some have argued that a date later than the life of Paul is important evidence that the opponents of the Pastorals are Gnostics. This type of

41. E.g. Hans-Friedrich Weiss ('Gnostische Motive und antignostische Polemik in Kolosser- und im Epheserbrief', in K.-W. Tröger [ed.], *Gnosis und Neues Testament* [Gütersloh: Gerd Mohn, 1980], pp. 311-24) thinks Ephesians combats Gnostics; M.D. Goulder ('The Visionaries of Laodicea', *JSNT* 43 [1991], pp. 15-39) finds Torah-obeying visionaries.

42. See Eph. 1.12-13; 2.2, 11; 3.1, 6; 5.8. Helmut Koester (*History and Literature of the New Testament. II. Introduction to the New Testament* [Hermeneia Foundations and Facets; Philadelphia: Fortress Press, 1982], p. 269) asserts that Ephesians addresses no 'specific problems of a particular church'. Cf. the comments of Ralph Martin, *Ephesians, Colossians, and Philemon* (Interpretation; Atlanta: John Knox Press, 1991), pp. 3-5.

presupposition improperly imposes a historical reconstruction into our task of identifying opponents. While we will not take a stand on authorship, our results may help date a letter and thus lend support to one view or another on this question.

Since we must treat each letter individually, a chapter is devoted to each canonical letter in the corpus except for those mentioned above, and the Pastorals are all in a single chapter. Within that framework, provision will be made to examine letters individually, including those found to be combined within a canonical letter.

This study will conclude with a sketch of those whom Paul and his successors found unacceptable. This reconstruction of Pauline opponents will find that Paul faced more than one type of anti-Pauline movement and, in addition, opposed other less organized teachers and teaching. Furthermore, this study concludes that the evidence of the Pauline letters does not support the notion that the Christianity based in Jerusalem defined itself to any significant extent by opposition to Paul or the Pauline mission.

Chapter 2

QUESTIONING THE EXTENT OF PAUL'S
AUTHORITY—1 CORINTHIANS

First Corinthians is a very practical letter that takes up specific problems and seems to reveal much about early Christian practices. While
the numerous remarks about Corinthian practices seem to have great
potential for clarifying the situation that 1 Corinthians addresses, the
staggering volume of publications on it has produced no consensus
about the identity of its opponents. Indeed, there is much doubt that 1
Corinthians has opponents in view. The majority of recent interpreters
contend that there are no opponents in the sense of a group of teachers
from outside who come to Corinth contesting either Paul's gospel or
apostleship.[1] Still, most see his authority and/or status under attack. For
example, Fee argues that the Corinthians have become decidedly anti-
Pauline under the influence of local leaders who contend that the Corinthians themselves are pneumatics and wise and so do not need Paul or
his gospel. These contentions are combined with an overrealized eschatology.[2] Other interpreters find an emphasis on wisdom understood in
terms of Hellenistic, sapiential Judaism.[3] Most interpreters find some

1. However, C.K. Barrett (*A Commentary on the First Epistle to the Corinthians* [HNTC; San Francisco: Harper & Row, 1968], pp. 44-45) and Walter Schmithals (*Gnosticism in Corinth*) are among those who do find intruders as the occasion
of 1 Corinthians. Gerd Lüdemann (*Opposition to Paul*, pp. 65-80) asserts that the
Cephas party was begun by Jewish–Christian missionaries who had left Corinth at
the time of 1 Corinthians.

2. Gordon D. Fee, *The First Epistle to the Corinthians* (NICNT; Grand Rapids:
Eerdmans, 1987), pp. 6-15. Similarly, but without the emphasis on a strong anti-
Pauline sentiment in the whole congregation, Nils A. Dahl, 'Paul and the Church at
Corinth', pp. 329, 332.

3. E.g. Birger A. Pearson, *The Pneumatikos-Psychikos Terminology in 1 Corinthians* (SBLDS, 12; Missoula, MT: SBL, 1973); Richard A. Horsley, 'Gnosis in
Corinth: 1 Corinthians 8.1-6', *NTS* 27 (1979), pp. 32-51; Gerhard Sellin, 'Das

emphasis on wisdom, an errant Christology, and pneumatism. First Corinthians is, of course, also the cornerstone of Schmithals's thesis that
Gnostics are Paul's constant opponents. Most of these views have tried
to identify the main body of opposition to Paul with one of the parties
mentioned in 1.12 (more on this below). In contrast to these various
views, it has been argued more recently that the real problem at Corinth
is competitiveness rather than particular theological viewpoints.[4]

Several interpreters have also questioned the integrity of 1 Corinthians. However, M. Mitchell has recently argued convincingly that it is
a unity.[5] She further demonstrates on the basis of themes, types of
appeals, types of proofs, and subject matter that the rhetorical species of
this letter is deliberative.[6] We can, then, treat 1 Corinthians as a single
letter, with the possible exceptions of some minor interpolations.

As we begin our investigation of 1 Corinthians, it is important to
keep in mind that the purpose of this investigation is to identify the
views and practices of Paul's opponents, not to determine the entire
occasion of the letter. This more narrow goal may mean that we do not
touch upon some significant aspects of the situation that prompts Paul
to write 1 Corinthians.

Explicit Statements

1.10-12

Our first explicit statement, 1.10-12, appears in the opening section of
the body of the letter, which comprises 1.10-17. This section directly

---

"Geheimnis" der Weisheit und das Rätsel der "Christuspartei" (zu 1 Kor 1–4)',
ZNW 73 (1982), pp. 70-71; James A. Davis, *Wisdom and Spirit: An Investigation of
1 Corinthians 1:18–3:20 Against the Background of Jewish Sapiential Traditions in
the Greco–Roman Period* (Lanham, MD: University Press of America, 1984), pp.
81, 144-45.

4.   E.g. Stephen M. Pogoloff, *Logos and Sophia: The Rhetorical Situation of
1 Corinthians* (SBLDS, 134; Atlanta: Scholars Press, 1992), p. 189; David W.
Kuck, *Judgment and Community Conflict: Paul's Use of Apocalyptic Judgment
Language in 1 Corinthians 3:5–4:5* (NovTSup 66; Leiden: E.J. Brill, 1992), p. 155;
Margaret M. Mitchell, *Paul and the Rhetoric of Reconciliation: An Exegetical
Investigation of the Language and Composition of 1 Corinthians* (HUT, 28; J.C.B.
Mohr [Paul Siebeck]; Louisville, KY: Westminster/John Knox Press, 1991), pp.
297-302.

5.   Mitchell, *Paul and the Rhetoric of Reconciliation*, pp. 184-92, 296-300.

6.   Mitchell, *Paul and the Rhetoric of Reconciliation*, pp. 23-63.

introduces the discussion of factionalism which extends through 4.21[7] and perhaps introduces the entire letter, as Mitchell suggests.[8] Schrage describes 1.10-17 as a *narratio* which describes the situation and carries on the exordium.[9] Thus, with most interpreters, he finds here Paul's statement of the facts[10] or of the problem.[11] These verses are by no means a straightforward or 'objective' statement of matters, rather they intend to increase 'the severity and ludicrousness' of the situation.[12] While Fee discerns some apologetic elements in this section, the rhetorical questions of v. 13[13] and the concluding reference to making the cross vain in v. 17 shows that the section is primarily polemical, even though it opens a deliberative letter.[14]

The λέγω δὲ τοῦτο (I say this) of v. 12 confirms that this description is Paul's interpretation of the report he has heard from Chloe's people.[15]

---

7. So most interpreters including William F. Orr and James A. Walther, Zürichor Bibelkommentare *1 Corinthians* (AB, 32; Garden City, NY: Doubleday, 1976), p. 147; August Strobel, *Der erste Brief an die Korinther* (ZBK; Zürich: Theologischer Verlag, 1989), p. 32; Fee, *First Epistle to the Corinthians*, p. 52.

8. Mitchell, *Paul and the Rhetoric of Reconciliation*, pp. 200-206. Mitchell begins the section with v. 11, separating v. 10 from the section because it is the thesis statement (*propositio*) of the letter and identifying vv. 11-17 as its expansion and explication. While this division is appropriate in terms of parts of speeches, it is not necessary for our purposes to separate the *propositio* from the following description of the situation (vv. 11-17).

9. Wolfgang Schrage, *Der erste Brief an die Korinther, 1 Kor 1,1–6,11* (EKK, 7.1; Zürich: Benziger, 1991), p. 134. Schrage sees 1.4-9 as the *exordium*.

10. So Mitchell, *Paul and the Rhetoric of Reconciliation*, p. 200; Strobel, *Der erste Briefe an die Korinther*, p. 32; Kuck, *Judgment and Community Conflict*, p. 154.

11. Fee, *First Epistle to the Corinthians*, p. 52.

12. Mitchell, *Paul and the Rhetoric of Reconciliation*, p. 201.

13. Kuck (*Judgment and Community Conflict*, p. 158 n. 34) identifies these questions about baptism and crucifuxion as a *reductio ad absurdum*. Cf. Schrage, *an die Korinther*, p. 137.

14. Strobel (*Der erste Brief an die Korinther*, p. 34) sees 1.10-17 as a strongly argumentative section.

15. So Mitchell, *Paul's Rhetoric of Reconciliation*, p. 86. C.K. Barrett ('Cephas and Corinth', in O. Betz, M. Hengel and P. Schmidt (eds.), *Abraham unser Vater: Juden und Christen im Gespräch über die Bibel* [Arbeiten zur Geschichte des Späatjudentums und Urchristentums; Leiden: E.J. Brill, 1963], p. 1) gives less place to the interpretive element that this phrase seems to introduce, commenting only that what follows is an explanation and expansion of what was said in v. 11.

Schüssler-Fiorenza may well be correct when she argues that the Corinthians do not see their 'debates, discussions, or competing claims' as party divisions.[16] The polemical edge of Paul's description is further evident in his exaggeration of the extent of the divisions when he claims that 'each' of the Corinthians is involved.[17]

In v. 11 Paul says the Corinthians are engaged in ἔριδες ('strifes', 'quarrels'). This language does not necessarily indicate that actual parties had formed and divided from each other, but only that there are disputes.[18] As Barrett points out, the fact that Paul addresses the church as a whole shows that no formal cleavage of the congregation had occurred.[19] Thus, all this description shows with certainty is that there are quarrels.[20] Paul's use of ἔριδες seems to begin his interpretation of the Corinthian situation because it is commonly used to describe political discord.[21] Thus, he already casts their behavior in an unfavorable light.

What makes it clear that 1.11-12 reflects opposition to Paul is the 'party slogans'. The presence of a Paul party indicates that Paul faces some competition or opposition since it is necessary for some to declare their allegiance to him.[22] Dahl seems to exceed the evidence when he claims that all the slogans except that of the Paul party are means of declaring independence of Paul.[23] Mitchell, on the other hand, contends that no such slogans were in use in Corinth and that Paul formulates these caricatures to portray their behavior as childish and slavish.[24] For us, it is of little importance whether these statements repeat actual slogans used in Corinth. More importantly, they indicate that quarrels have developed in which leaders other than Paul are cited as authorities over

---

16. Elizabeth Schüssler-Fiorenza, 'Rhetorical Situation and Historical Reconstruction in 1 Corinthians', *NTS* 33 (1987), p. 396. See also Henning Paulsen, 'Schisma und Häresie: Untersuchungen zu 1 Kor 11, 18.19', *ZTK* 79 (1982), p. 183.

17. See Orr and Walther, *1 Corinthians*, p. 148; Mitchell, *Paul and the Rhetoric of Reconciliation*, p. 86.

18. So Fee, *First Epistle to the Corinthians*, p. 54.

19. Barrett, *Commentary on the First Epistle to the Corinthians*, pp. 42-43. Cf. Davis, *Wisdom and Spirit*, p. 135.

20. So Dahl, 'Paul and the Church at Corinth', p. 318.

21. Mitchell, *Paul and the Rhetoric of Reconciliation*, p. 81.

22. So Fee, *First Epistle to the Corinthians*, p. 56; Barrett, *Commentary on the First Epistle to the Corinthians*, p. 43; Schrage, *an die Korinther*, p. 143; Dahl, 'Paul and the Church at Corinth', p. 322; Lüdemann, *Opposition to Paul*, p. 75.

23. Dahl, 'Paul and the Church at Corinth', p. 322.

24. Mitchell, *Paul and the Rhetoric of Reconciliation*, p. 83.

against Paul.[25] It seems much more likely that the names of Apollos and Cephas are being used in Corinth than that Paul chose them arbitrarily.[26] On the other hand, we should not limit the Corinthians' tendency to name authorities to the three or four names in this verse. These may only be representative or the most outstanding or outlandish examples of their citations.[27] It is also probable that Apollos and Cephas are not involved with or supportive of the groups which use their names[28] since they come under no attack themselves and Paul can cite Apollos as a colleague. Furthermore, as Fee points out, Cephas and Apollos are probably not involved with these groups because Paul and Christ clearly are not.[29]

There has been extended debate over how many factions v. 12 names. Some argue for four parties on the basis of the parallel structure in which the names appear.[30] Others doubt that there is a Christ party, arguing that its existence would contradict what Paul says in 1.13 and at the end of ch. 3[31] or that such a claim would have drawn Paul's heaviest criticism rather than being ignored. Thus, the Christ party was added to show the absurdity of having parties.[32] Still other interpreters find only two main parties, identifying others mentioned as sub-groups or exaggerations.[33] The parallel structure of the verse is *prima facie* evidence for four groups, but we must remember that Paul: (1) is giving his interpretation and so may indulge in exaggeration, as with the 'each' in v. 12a; (2) is perhaps not directly quoting the Corinthians; and (3) may

25. See the comments of Schrage *Brief an die Korinther*, p. 139, and Fee, *First Epistle to the Corinthians,* pp. 55-56.

26. Schrage, *Brief an die Korinther*, p. 139, asserts that this is beyond doubt.

27. David R. Hall ('A Disguise for the Wise: ΜΕΤΑΣΧΗΜΑΤΙΣΜΟΣ in 1 Cor. 4.6', *NTS* 40 [1994], pp. 143-44) contends that μετεσχημάτισα in 4.6 shows that the real leaders are not named. See my treatment of this passage below.

28. So Schrage, *Brief an die Korinther*, p. 139; Fee, *First Epistle to the Corinthians*, p. 55; Dahl, 'Paul and the Church at Corinth', p. 323.

29, Fee, *First Epistle to the Corinthians,* p. 55.

30. Fee, *First Epistle to the Corinthians*, p. 58; Sellin, 'Das "Geheimnis" der Weisheit und das Rätsel der "Christuspartei"', p. 73.

31. Antoinette Clark Wire, *The Corinthian Women Prophets: A Reconstruction through Paul's Rhetoric* (Minneapolis: Fortress Press, 1990), p. 42.

32. Schrage, *Brief an die Korinther*, p. 145.

33. Wire *The Corinthian Women Prophets*, p. 42; Pogoloff, *Logos and Sophia*, pp. 99, 178; Schmithals, *Gnosticism in Corinth*, pp. 199-206; Baur, *Paul, The Apostle of Jesus Christ*, pp. 259-65.

not have referred to all the factions in Corinth. The clearest point is that Paul views the actions of some during disputes at Corinth as challenges to his authority. Further clarity, if any can be gained, about the number and views of any parties must come from other passages. We certainly cannot claim on the basis of these names that any particular party emphasizes any particular theology as was often done earlier with Cephas and is, in more recent times, often done with Apollos.

3.3-4

Factions based on allegiance to teachers are discussed explicitly in 3.3-4. These verses appear in the section which serves as the transition between 2.6-16 and 3.5-17 (23);[34] 3.1-4 both applies the preceding comments to the Corinthians[35] and introduces the following discussion of apostleship.[36] Paul's reference to party-division in 3.1-4 is a rebuke[37] and is addressed (as always in chs. 1–4) to the whole church.[38] Since Paul is interpreting the Corinthians' behavior in a way that allows him to make a serious accusation against them, this section is polemical,[39] but mildly so. We have no evidence to support identifying 3.1-4 as an apology for either Paul's alleged lack of wisdom or some other lack.[40]

34. Fee, *First Epistle to the Corinthians*, pp. 121-22; Kuck, *Judgment and Community Conflict*, pp. 154-55. Benjamin Fiore ('"Covert Allusions" in 1 Corinthians 1–4', *CBQ* 47 [1985], p. 87) sees such a close connection between 2.6-16 and 3.1-4 that he includes the two as parts of one section. However, the vocative and Paul's reference to himself with κα'γώ in 3.1 indicates that a new section is beginning. So Strobel, *Der erste Brief an die Korinther*, p. 74; Schrage, *Brief an die Korinther*, p. 280.

35. So Hans Conzelmann, *A Commentary on the First Epistle to the Corinthians* (trans. J.W. Leitch; Hermeneia; Philadelphia: Fortress Press, 1975), p. 71; Schrage, *Brief an die Korinther*, p. 278.

36. Some interpreters see 3.1-4 as a sub-section within 3.1-17. E.g. Conzelmann, *First Epistle to the Corinthians*, p. 70; Strobel, *Der erste Briefe an die Korinther*, pp. 74-75, who extends the sub-section through v. 5.

37. So also Conzelmann, *First Epistle to the Corinthians*, p. 72; Barrett, *Commentary on the First Epistle to the Corinthians*, p. 81; Schrage, *Brief an die Korinther*, p. 283; Kuck, *Judgment and Community Conflict*, p. 159.

38. See Fee, *First Epistle to the Corinthians*, p. 123.

39. So also Fee, *First Epistle to the Corinthians*, p. 116.

40. Those who find an apology here find a defense of: Paul's possession of wisdom (Schmithals [*Gnosticism in Corinth*, pp. 142-43]); Paul's poor appearance (Strobel [*Der erste Brief an die Korinther*, pp. 74-75]); Paul's rhetorical ability (Dahl ['Paul and the Church at Corinth', p. 321]). Less specifically Richard A.

Even if Paul defends himself elsewhere in 1 Corinthians, the point of 3.1-4 is clearly to establish a judgment about the Corinthians, not to respond to some charge.

Paul's description of the Corinthians' behavior in v. 4 allows a bit less room for Paul's interpretive exaggeration than does 1.11-12. Paul expects them to recognize the behavior of some in their church who claim allegiance to a teacher. It may be that the limitation of this behavior to 'some' (τις) allows that the whole congregation is not implicated in the factious behavior.

The mention of only two teachers—Paul and Apollos—has been the object of much speculation. Some argue that the presence of only these two shows that the parties that claim them are the main problem.[41] Others assert that Paul mentions Apollos because there is clearly no competition between himself and Apollos and that this, in turn, indicates that the real problem is with the Cephas party.[42] Fee more cautiously comments that one should not make too much of the mention of Apollos here, but still asserts that most of the arguments to this point (and seemingly including this verse) are probably directed against the Apollos party.[43] But even this reads more into this text than we can be certain of. Schrage reflects a less predetermined view when he acknowledges that the mention of Apollos may be a sign of *either* tension or relaxed relations with him and so we can identify neither the Apollos nor the Cephas group as the main opposition on the basis of this verse.[44] The reference to the Paul and Apollos groups here does confirm that these teachers were among those for whom the Corinthians were claiming authority in contrast to or in competition with others.[45] Beyond that,

Horsley ('Wisdom of Word and Words of Wisdom in Corinth', *CBQ* 39 [1977], p. 238) says that 3.1-4 shows that Paul is being evaluated. Christian Wolff (*Der erste Brief des Paulus an die Korinther. II. Auslegung der Kapitel 8-16* [THNT, 7.2; Berlin: Evangelische Verlagsanstalt, 1982], p. 22) may see an apologetic element, commenting that these verses argue that the Corinthians are not Pneumatics and so cannot make judgments about Paul.

41. E.g. Pogoloff, *Logos and Sophia*, pp. 180, 213.

42. Barrett, *Commentary on the First Epistle to the Corinthians*, p. 82; Philipp Vielhauer, 'Paulus und die Kephaspartei in Korinth', *NTS* 21 (1975), p. 347.

43. Fee, *First Epistle to the Corinthians*, p. 127, see also p. 153, n. 12 where Fee says that the presence of Cephas in only 1.12 and 3.22 probably shows that he is less important in the Corinthian disputes.

44. Schrage, *Brief an die Korinther*, pp. 144, 284.

45. Conzelmann (*First Epistle to the Corinthians*, p. 72) remarks about 3.4 that

Paul may mention Apollos because the Corinthians are familiar with
him and know of his relationship with Paul, while it is doubtful that
Peter has been to Corinth.

Paul's judgment in 3.3 that the Corinthians are fleshly (σαρκικοί) has
been used to argue that they claim to be Pneumatics who espouse an errant pneumatology.[46] But the only basis for this conjecture is unsupported mirror reading. The meaning of σαρκικοί is explicated at the
end of the verse with 'living like [mere] humans' (κατὰ ἄνθρωπον περ-
ιπατεῖτε).[47] Paul's use of 'fleshly' advances his argument by allowing
him to add moral significance to their factiousness;[48] it contends that
they are not developing as they should and gives their strife as evidence. The Corinthians would certainly be offended at this evaluation.
It would be no extraordinary claim for someone in a Pauline congregation to claim to possess the Spirit and so be a Pneumatic. Such a
claim certainly does not entail some aberrant pneumatology, only that
they are experiencing the presence of God and developing in their lives
as Christians. We should expect no less an understanding of God's
presence from those making competitive claims to various authorities.
Thus, this passage yields no clear evidence of a faulty pneumatology.

Verses 3-4, then, add only confirmation that different groups at
Corinth have selected various leaders whom they invest with superior
authority in comparison with others.

3.21-22
The command not to boast about humans in 3.21 can be identified as an
explicit reference to the opposition Paul faces because Paul supports the
command in v. 22 by mentioning himself, Apollos and Cephas. It is

the use of only two slogans 'appears to be in keeping with the situation in Corinth
—but how?'

46. E.g. Conzelmann, *First Epistle to the Corinthians*, p. 72; Sellin, 'Das
"Geheimnis" der Weisheit und das Rätsel der "Christuspartei"', p. 82.

47. So also Schrage, *Brief an die Korinther*, pp. 283-84. However, Sellin ('Das
"Geheimnis" der Weisheit und das Rätsel der "Christuspartei"', p. 82) reads this
expression as evidence that the Corinthians claim to be more than human. But this
again rests totally on mirror reading. Additionally, nothing in this passage suggests
that σαρκικός carries a Gnostic designation of the substance of which one is composed, as Schrage (*Brief an die Korinther*, pp. 283-84) recognizes. To find opposition to such a Gnostic idea, one must presuppose the presence of a Gnostic Christology or pneumatology and we have seen no evidence of such.

48. Kuck, *Judgment and Community Conflict*, pp. 160-61.

generally agreed that 3.18-23 is a preliminary conclusion that reaches back to 1.18.[49] The section goes beyond moral exhortation to be a warning.[50] Given the sharp exhortation in 3.18 and its function of summarizing 1.18–3.17, this passage seems to be mildly polemical.

Verse 21 begins with another interpretation of the Corinthians' behavior with respect to leaders or teachers: they boast about them. This criticism indicates that they claim some superiority on the basis of the teacher they cite as most authoritative.[51] Verse 22 reveals this as the content of their boast when it returns to those teachers mentioned in 1.12. The mention of Cephas here after his absence throughout ch. 3 may, as Schrage asserts, show that Paul does not have the Apollos people in special focus when he thinks of the Corinthians over-valuing teachers.[52] It seems at least to demonstrate that Paul is conscious of a group that elevates Cephas.

Conzelmann identifies 3.21b, 'All things are yours', as a Stoic maxim used to describe the wise.[53] This maxim was also used more broadly, so much more broadly that Kuck identifies this belief as one of the 'common Hellenistic ideals'.[54] Thus we should not tie this claim to any specific school or understanding of wisdom. Indeed, at this point we cannot even claim that it reflects the Corinthians' views. All that is certain is that Paul sees this assertion as an effective means to combat their allegiances to teachers. It does seem to count against the presence of an overrealized eschatology in Corinth. After all, little could be more open to misinterpretation in the context of an overrealized eschatology than, 'all things are yours'.

49. So Conzelmann, *First Epistle to the Corinthians*, p. 39; Fee, *First Epistle to the Corinthians*, p. 150; Barrett, *Commentary on the First Epistle to the Corinthians 93; Schrage, Brief an die Korinther*, pp. 129, 311; Davis, *Wisdom and Spirit*, p. 87. Dahl ('Paul and the Church at Corinth', p. 327), however, sees it as a continuation of 3.15-17.

50. Strobel, *Der erste Brief an die Korinther*, p. 84. Kuck (*Judgment and Community Conflict*, p. 155) sees all of 3.5–4.5 as an attack on the Corinthians.

51. There is no basis in the text for limiting the reference of ἀνθρώποις to a single individual as Sellin ('Das "Geheimnis" der Weisheit und das Rätsel der "Christuspartei"', p. 96) does, identifying that person as Apollos.

52. Schrage, *Brief an die Korinther*, pp. 313-14.

53. Conzelmann, *First Epistle to the Corinthians*, p. 80.

54. Kuck, *Judgment and Community Conflict*, p. 190.

4.6-7

The references to Paul and Apollos and to being 'puffed up' because of
a relationship with one or the other teacher indicate that these verses
directly address opposition to Paul at Corinth. The section which includes these statements, 4.6-13, is again polemical, as seen by its use of
irony (vv. 8, 10) and piercing rhetorical questions (v. 7).[55] This section
attacks both the Corinthians' comparisons of teachers and their self-
evaluation.[56] Paul here applies to the Corinthian situation the points he
has been making since at least 3.5.[57]

As they do with 3.3-4, some interpreters have claimed that the mention of only Paul and Apollos in 4.6 shows that the main problem is
with Apollos,[58] while others claim that the absence of Cephas shows
that his group is the real problem and so not attacked directly.[59] But to
isolate the opposition to Paul to a particular group is to miss the point
of this verse and all that its ταῦτα ('these things') refers to. The meaning
of 4.6 hinges on giving sufficient weight to μετεσχημάτισα. The meaning of this term has been debated at length,[60] but whether it means Paul

55. Similarly Kuck, *Judgment and Community Conflict*, p. 210. Cf. Funk (*Language, Hermeneutics, and Word of God* [New York: Harper & Row, 1966], p. 287)
who describes 4.7-9 as 'direct and ironic speech'. However, Fee (*First Epistle to the
Corinthians*, p. 9) sees the section as apologetic. Schrage (*Brief an die Korinther*,
pp. 130, 331) identifies 4.6-13 as apologetic, even while regarding v. 6 as polemical. But there is no clear defense of Paul's authority or office in vv. 6-13 and vv. 6-
8 are clearly an attack on the Corinthians. The peristasis catalog in vv. 11-13 does
not necessarily show that Paul is defending himself here just because these catalogs
serve that purpose in 2 Corinthians.

56. Cf. Strobel, *Der erste Brief an die Korinther*, p. 87; Fiore, '"Covert Allusions"', p. 87.

57. Fee (*First Epistle to the Corinthians*, p. 166) and Kuck (*Judgment and
Community Conflict*, p. 210) see the ταῦτα of v. 6 to refer to 3.5–4.5. However,
Fiore ('"Covert Allusions"', pp. 93-94) takes it all the way back to 1.12 ,and Funk
(*Language, Hermeneutics, and Word of God*, p. 286) still further back to 1.10.
Whichever is the case, the most direct referent is the description of the functions of
Paul and Apollos in 3.5-17.

58. So Fee, *First Epistle to the Corinthians*, pp. 166-67; Strobel, *Der erste Brief
an die Korinther*, p. 87; Schrage, *Brief an die Korinther*, p. 334; Horsley, 'Wisdom
of Word', pp. 231-32; Sellin, 'Das "Geheimnis" der Weisheit und das Rätsel der
"Christuspartei"', p. 75; Pogoloff, *Logos and Sophia*, p. 214.

59. Barrett, *Commentary on the First Epistle to the Corinthians*, p. 106; Barrett,
'Cephas', p. 5; Vielhauer, 'Paulus und die Kephaspartei in Korinth', p. 347.

60. See, e.g., Fee, *First Epistle to the Corinthians*, pp. 166-67; Fiore, ' "Covert

used figures of speech or has substituted himself and Apollos for the real problem, it is clear that Paul's point is that he has used himself and Apollos 'to make a point that is of a more general application'.[61]

Unfortunately, what that point is is obscured by the immediately following ἵνα ('so that') clause. The meaning of 'not beyond what is written', has also been the subject of much discussion.[62] Even if a certain understanding of this phrase eludes us, we have a second and parallel ἵνα clause which depends on μετασχημάτισα,[63] 'that you might not be puffed up for one against the other'. This clause shows that Paul's point when using himself and Apollos is to exclude all claims of superiority based on who one identifies as their teacher.[64] Thus the problem he addresses is the Corinthians' relationship with one another, albeit caused by allegiance to teachers.

Allusions"', p. 89; Pogoloff, *Logos and Sophia*, p. 214; Kuck, *Judgment and Community Conflict*, pp. 210-12; F.H. Colson, 'Μετεσχημάτισα 1 Cor. iv6', *JTS* 17 (1915–16), pp. 379-84; Mitchell, *Paul and the Rhetoric of Reconciliation*, p. 54.

61. Orr and Walther, *1 Corinthians*, p. 177. Cf. Kuck, *Judgment and Community Conflict*, pp. 210-12; Colson, 'Μετεσχημάτισα 1 Cor. iv6', pp. 379-84.

62. See, e.g., Morna Hooker ('Beyond the Things that Are Written? St. Paul's Use of Scripture', *NTS* 27 [1981], pp. 295-309 [296]) who contends that it means that they are not to add philosophical notions to the gospel; Roger L. Omanson ('Acknowledging Paul's Quotations', *BT* 43 [1992], pp. 203-204) sees it as a Corinthian slogan; Dieter Georgi ('Der Kampf um die reine Lehre im Urchristentum als Auseinandersetzung um das rechte Verständnis der an Israel ergangenen Offenbarung Gottes', in W.P. Eckert, N.P. Levinson and M. Stöhr (eds.), *Antijudaismus im Neuen Testament*? [Munich: Chr. Kaiser Verlag, 1967], pp. 82-94 [84-85]) sees it as a reference to allegorical interpretation of Scripture; Barrett ('Cephas', p. 5) asserts that it refers to what the Hebrew Bible says about ministers; and Wire (*The Corinthian Women Prophets*, p. 44) argues that it means that they do not accept the limitations of subordination. The more plausible interpretations are those of Peter Marshall ('Hybrists Not Gnostics in Corinth', *SBLSP* 23 [1984], pp. 275-87 [279-80), who sees it as a reference to a well-known maxim against excessive behavior; Kuck (*Judgment and Community Conflict*, pp. 213-14), who finds an allusion to tracing the letters of a school master and so interprets it as a call to imitation; and L.L. Wellborn ('A Conciliatory Principle in 1 Cor. 4:6', *NovT* 29 [1987], pp. 320-46 [322, 343-45]), who believes it is a well-known saying used in the context of the resolution of conflicts which could encourage one to abide by an agreement.

63. So also Schrage, *Brief an die Korinther*, p. 336.

64. Fee (*First Epistle to the Corinthians*, pp. 169-70) narrows this phrase too much when he allows it to refer to only two particular teachers. Even if it does single out two teachers, the verse does not designate Paul and Apollos as the two since at least Cephas and Christ have also been mentioned in 3.22.

Verse 7 continues this attack on competitiveness with its rhetorical questions and makes it clear that the Corinthians are claiming positions of status based on allegiance to their chosen leader. The διακρίνει (judges) of this verse implies that they set themselves apart from one another and Paul's use of it in this rhetorical question is a sharp rebuke. Paul also calls their claim to status 'boasting', another condemnatory judgment like 'puffed up' in v. 6. Verse 7 accuses those Corinthians who engage in competitive citation of leaders of arrogance.[65]

However much this reveals the deterioration of community relations because of the competition among the Corinthians, it tells us nothing about the theological content of the disputes the teachers are used to settle. All Paul is concerned about in 4.6-7, and by his statement in 4.6 his primary concern from 3.5, is their discord and their claims to superior status.

4.18-19

Another explicit statement appears in 4.18-19 where Paul speaks of those who have become 'puffed up'. These verses are part of a section comprising 4.14-21[66] that concludes the argument begun in 1.10 and may begin a transition to 5.1-13. There is a clear division in this conclusion at v. 18. While 4.14-17 is more conciliatory and milder than most of chs. 1–4, v. 18 renews the more characteristic polemic. Still, the section fits together because its various parts reflect the different arguments Paul has used in the preceding chapters. Verses 18-21 particularly pick up on those who are puffed up in 4.6-7, and at the same

---

65. Cf. Marshall, 'Hybrists', p. 281. Fee (*First Epistle to the Corinthians*, p. 171) comments that v. 7 describes them as ungrateful.

66. So most interpreters. However, Kenneth Bailey ('The Structure of I Corinthians and Paul's Theological Method with Special Reference to 4:17', *NovT* 25 [1983], pp. 160-65) constructs an interesting argument which insists that 4.17 begins a new major section which extends through 7.40. Thus, 4.17-18 introduces the section on sexual ethics. In spite of the strength of some of his argument, especially his relating of the puffed up of 4.17-18 with those in 5.2, the close connection between the call to imitation in 4.16 and the reminder of the example of Titus make this thesis untenable. Still, there may be some connection between the puffed up here and those in 5.2. Barrett (*Commentary on the First Epistle to the Corinthians*, p. 117) makes this connection without identifying 4.17-18 as part of a paragraph separated from 4.14-16. Bailey's case would be more compelling if he began the section at v. 18, but then the section on sexual ethics would not fit the pattern he finds in all major sections of 1 Corinthians.

time may prepare for the reference to those puffed up in 5.2. Overall, 4.14-21 seems best described as hortatory[67] since its point is to call them to a particular sort of behavior based on their relationship to Paul.

Although Paul's judgment that some are 'puffed up' is not sufficient cause to label them opponents, their reason for taking this attitude (i.e. they think he is not returning) shows that they do represent a challenge to, or at least a turning away from, Paul. Verse 18 indicates that those who tend to disregard Paul are from within the congregation rather than intruders.[68] This verse also shows that Paul is aware of a group within the congregation which disregards him and which he can distinguish from the rest of the congregation.[69] We do not know how much influence this group had had on the rest of the church but it is sufficient to require the response of chs. 1–4 which includes some apologetic statements.[70] Furthermore, while it is tempting to use 4.18 to claim that the arguments at Corinth are related to questions about Paul's return, as Dahl and Wire do,[71] the verse's obscurity renders it useless for that purpose. As Conzelmann notes, it is not clear whether they *claim* Paul is not coming back or *act* (in Paul's view) as if he were not returning.[72] Given Paul's earlier 'interpretive' description of the Corinthian situation, it seems equally probable that he reads their behavior as evidence of this assumption in 4.18. However, v. 19 may indicate that their 'talk' (λόγον) is involved. Perhaps it was both. Perhaps some behavior or view in some matter (there is a host to choose from in this letter) prompted a disapproving fellow-Christian to comment that Paul might not approve of their action, to which they responded, 'So what? He's never coming back anyway!' This takes us beyond the evidence of these verses, but hopefully serves to show how opposition to Paul or disregard for him could develop within his congregation after an absence of several years which probably included much change at Corinth, in-

---

67. Schrage (*Brief an die Korinther*, p. 351) sees the section as a concluding exhortation. Cf. Fiore, '"Covert Allusions" ', p. 87.

68. See also Fee, *First Epistle to the Corinthians*, pp. 189-90.

69. Fee, *First Epistle to the Corinthians*, pp. 189-90; Dahl, 'Paul and the Church at Corinth', pp. 318-19.

70. Fee (*First Epistle to the Corinthians*, p. 190) has perhaps gone too far when he asserts that they had swayed the majority.

71. Dahl, 'Paul and the Church at Corinth', pp. 318-19; Wire, *The Corinthian Women Prophets*, p. 42.

72. Conzelmann, *First Epistle to the Corinthians*, p. 93.

cluding the development of their own leaders, without starting from a rejection of his apostolic office.

That Paul does not draw in the names of Cephas and Apollos here may indicate that we cannot limit the 'puffed up' to the members of either or both of the parties which cite them as authorities.[73] The absence of any names may indicate that the basic issue for Paul here at the conclusion of the argument is the competitiveness about status which has been the main subject up to this point.[74] It may also be the case that the reference to being puffed up links those who question Paul's authority with those who allow the sexual behavior described in ch. 5. However, in ch. 5 the 'puffed up' seem to include the whole congregation, not just a segment of it as in 4.18-19.

All we can say, then, from 4.18-19 is that the behavior of some group at Corinth leads Paul to think they believe he is never returning. It may well be that they assert this, but we cannot be certain. Their behavior necessarily entails, at least in Paul's view and probably in that of those devoted to him, a questioning of or challenge to, if not outright opposition to, Paul's authority.

4.3

In 4.3 Paul asserts that the Corinthians' evaluation of him is unimportant. This verse appears in the section that stands between the concluding summary of chs. 1–3 in 3.18-23 and the application of that material to the Corinthians in 4.6-13. Verses 1-5 seem to be Paul's application of 3.18-23 to Christian leaders and so focuses those conclusions on the issue at hand, even as it prepares for the broader and polemical application of those conclusions in 4.6-13.[75] This section is primarily an apology in response to some evaluation of Paul.[76] This is

---

73. Some interpreters do, however, identify the 'puffed up' as members of one of these parties; e.g. Schrage (*Brief an die Korinther*, p. 361) and Wire (*The Corinthian Women Prophets*, p. 42) identify them as members of the Apollos party.

74. So Pogoloff, *Logos and Sophia*, p. 222.

75. Funk (*Language, Hermeneutics, and Word of God*, p. 285) argues that 4.1-5 is more closely related to the preceding major section. However, the already noted parallel function of 4.1-5 and 6-13 counts against this view. Furthermore, Mitchell (*Paul and the Rhetoric of Reconciliation*, pp. 219-20) asserts that 4.1-13 is a comparison of Paul and the Corinthians.

76. Schrage (*Brief an die Korinther*, p. 318) sees this as one aspect of the section. Cf. Horsley, 'Wisdom of Word', p. 238 n. 30.

not its only function, but it seems to be its dominant function. Even as Paul gives himself as an example,[77] he is rejecting their evaluation of him. That Paul does not try to show that he is faithful is not proof that he is not defending himself[78] but only that he takes a different tack, that is, he argues that those judging him do so illegitimately.

Verse 3 removes any doubt that some Corinthians are evaluating Paul.[79] Interestingly, Paul does not respond to any particular in which he might have been found wanting. His strategy is rather to reject the Corinthians' right to make judgments about him; both their position (they are not his master) and timing (before the parousia) make any evaluation of him by them illegitimate. Thus, whatever conclusions they reach are inconsequential for Paul, but, as vv. 6-13 show, their act of judging is not inconsequential for his evaluation of their spiritual well being.

Paul has been challenging their status assumptions about themselves, Christian leaders, and relationships between the two throughout chs. 1–3. Verses 1-6 continue that challenge both directly and indirectly. Directly it removes them from the position of those qualified to evaluate teachers. Paul acknowledges that it is important for him to be found trustworthy, it is just not important that *they* find him so. Verse 3 seems intended to be a bit of a slap in the face (the 'by you' is in an emphatic position) and implies that they have usurped a position appropriate only to God. Paul challenges their assumptions indirectly by identifying himself as an οἰκονόμους ('servant', v. 1). This image conveys much of what Paul wants to assert; it leaves Christian leaders in a low status position but also invests them with authority as they are the servants in charge of the household.[80] Thus, they are not figures to identify oneself by (since they are only slaves) but they do have to be obeyed.

77. Mitchell (*Paul and the Rhetoric of Reconciliation*, pp. 54-55) and Kuck (*Judgment and Community Conflict*, p. 202) contend that Paul is not defending himself but only giving himself as an example.

78. Contra Kuck, *Judgment and Community Conflict*, p. 198.

79. Kuck (*Judgment and Community Conflict*, pp. 198-99) argues that since ἀνακρίνειν has the broader meaning of forming an opinion, its use here does not necessarily imply a criticism of Paul. While this may be philologically correct, our other explicit statements require that some negative conclusions about Paul are being reached at Corinth.

80. Pogoloff, *Logos and Sophia*, p. 221.

Verse 4.3 indicates that some Corinthians have been evaluating Paul. He responds to no specific questions they raise[81] but simply rejects their right to judge him or any Christian leader. Since Paul seems to give himself as an example in v. 4, the passage signals that we should not overestimate the amount or severity of the judgment Paul rejects. If he is still able to give himself as an example, their judgments do not include a complete rejection of his position or authority, at least among the majority.

9.4-6

Our final explicit statement, 9.4-6, mentions a criticism of Paul to which he says he gives the defense which follows. The nature of the section in which this statement occurs is both greatly debated and extremely important. How we understand ch. 9 significantly influences our understanding of Paul's opposition at Corinth. Many interpreters find the primary purpose of this section to be a defense of Paul's apostleship.[82] Others, however, see it more integrally related to the surrounding discussion of food sacrificed to idols and thus contend that its primary function is to give Paul's conduct as an example of what he recommends in ch. 8.[83] An important key to discerning its purpose may be found in setting the limits of the passage in question. Most interpreters see all of ch. 9 as a separate section within Paul's discussion of idol meat. But it seems more likely that this larger section ends at 9.23.[84] Verses 24-27 introduce the examples of 10.1-13 by beginning the discussion of not losing one's contest after having begun, as those Israelites mentioned in 10.1-10 did. Not only is 9.24-27 an excellent introduction to those examples, but the conclusion in 9.19-23 is parallel to 8.9-13, the conclusion of 8.1-8. Just as 8.9-13 gives the results of

---

81. Lüdemann (*Opposition to Paul*, p. 261 n. 54) comments that no 'concrete attacks against Paul' are visible in 4.1-13.

82. E.g. Conzelmann, *First Epistle to the Corinthians*, pp. 151-53; Fee, *First Epistle to the Corinthians*, pp. 392-94; Wire, *The Corinthian Women Prophets*, p. 195; Lüdemann, *Opposition to Paul*, pp. 65-67.

83. E.g. Orr and Walther, *1 Corinthians*, p. 240; Barrett, *Commentary on the First Epistle to the Corinthians*, p. 197; Strobel, *Der erste Brief an die Korinther*, p. 141; Wolff, *Der erste Brief des Paulus an die Korinther*, II, p. 16; Mitchell, *Paul and the Rhetoric of Reconciliation*, pp. 130, 245-47; Willis, 'An Apostolic Apology: The Form and Function of 1 Corinthians 9', *JSNT* 24 (1985), pp. 34-35.

84. Similarly Orr and Walther (*1 Corinthians*, p. 235) identify 9.1-22 as an excursus.

participating at temple meals without regard for fellow-Christians, 9.19-23 gives the result of Paul's altering his behavior for the sake of those around him.[85] Thus we have two sections which spell out the contrasting results of contrasting behaviors. Lüdemann has noted that the discussion of freedom in 9.19-23 returns to the first question of 9.1: 'Am I not free?'[86] This offers some confirmation that 9.19-23 serves as a conclusion. Verse 1 also picks up the theme of ἐξουσία ('right') struck in 8.9. This, in turn, strengthens our view that 9.19-23 is an inverted parallel to 8.9-13. If this is correct, there is a direct and intimate relationship between chs. 8 and 9. Furthermore, Wolff asserts that the personal reference in 8.13 prepares for the personal example of 9.1-23.[87] These points strongly suggest that the main purpose of 9.1-23 is to give an example of what Paul asks the strong to do. This view is further supported by the conclusion of the whole discussion of idol meat (10.31–11.1) in which Paul returns to the substance of 9.19-23 and explicitly calls the Corinthians to follow his example.

The dominant function of 9.1-23, then, makes it didactic or hortatory rather than polemic or apologetic. As support for Paul's appeal not to eat at temples, the passage seems more didactic, even though it has the hortatory aim of convincing the Corinthians to live in a particular way. This does not mean that Paul does not respond to criticism,[88] but that this response is not the passage's primary purpose. Identifying 9.1-23 as a didactic section limits our use of what is said there to explicit statements and other statements that are directly a part of an issue already known to be under discussion. This eliminates much of what some interpreters find about opponents in ch. 9.

The sub-section that our explicit statement appears in is 9.3-14. Verses 3-6 introduce the topic of Paul's renunciation of the right of support.

---

85. Even the results listed in each paragraph may have opposing parallels: 8.9-13 has wounding, destroying and causing one's brother to fall and so sinning against Christ as results of the rejected behavior; 9.19-23 has winning some for the gospel, saving some, and sharing in the blessings of the gospel (perhaps the opposite of sinning against Christ).

86. Lüdemann, *Opposition to Paul*, p. 68.

87. Wolff, *Der erste Brief des Paulus an die Korinther*, II, p. 16. This is contra Fee (*First Epistle to the Corinthians*, p. 394) who thinks Paul begins a defense in 9.1 that is distinct from 8.9-13.

88. Barrett (*Commentary on the First Epistle to the Corinthians*, p. 200) links the issue of opposition to Paul and idol meat by suggesting that Paul thinks his advice about limiting freedom would provoke some to question his authority.

Verses 7-14 then set out an elaborate justification for the *principle* of receiving support.[89] Verses 3-6 seem to take a bit of an apologetic tone while serving a different primary purpose.

Paul is clearly responding to what he perceives as criticism in 9.3 when he refers to those who judge him,[90] even though the larger section is not primarily apologetic. Some interpreters contend that this judging is done by people outside Corinth,[91] but the rhetorical questions which follow in vv. 4-6 show that some Corinthians[92] have questions about Paul's means of support.[93] It is possible that they mention his refusal of congregational support as a reason to question his status or authority, but 9.3-6 gives no basis for this conjecture.[94] Paul only distinguishes his (and Barnabas's) practice from that of other apostolic figures. The emphatic negative rhetorical question of 9.4 indicates that Paul expects the Corinthians to acknowledge that he has this right, as does the concluding question of v. 6. The specific inquiry he is responding to may well ask why he does not take pay rather than whether he has the right to it. Either interpretation depends on mirror reading and thus goes beyond secure evidence.

Verses 3-6 confirm that Paul perceives some criticism at Corinth and indicate that such judgments include questions about his means of support. This criticism is significant enough that he feels a need to respond directly, even if in a rather off-handed way. On the other hand, it is not so severe or successful that it keeps him from giving himself as an example using this very topic. Thus, he must not perceive the criticism as widespread or as very effective.

Summary of Explicit Statements
Explicit statements in 1 Corinthians reveal that Paul perceives some challenges to his authority. Not only are some Corinthians evaluating

89. See Willis, 'Apostolic Apologia?', p. 35.

90. Mitchell (*Paul and the Rhetoric of Reconciliation*, pp. 130, 245-47) however sees this as a 'mock defense speech'.

91. E.g. Conzelmann, *First Epistle to the Corinthians*, p. 153.

92. Most commentators see 9.3 as a response to critics. So e.g. Barrett, *Commentary on the First Epistle to the Corinthians*, p. 202; Wolff, *Der erste Brief des Paulus an die Korinther*. II, pp. 21-22; Fee, *First Epistle to the Corinthians*, p. 401.

93. As Fee (*First Epistle to the Corinthians*, p. 404) comments, v. 6 may show that their problem is not just Paul's refusal of support but also his working at a trade.

94. Neither is it clear that Paul is touchy about this topic as Fee (*First Epistle to the Corinthians*, pp. 398-99) contends.

and so questioning his authority because of his extended absence, but some also call upon other Christian leaders, including at least Cephas and Apollos, as authorities in competition with Paul. These comparative and competitive authority claims seem to arise in congregational disputes, but we have no information about the issue(s) involved. Those who cite the various authorities also express some allegiance to them and on this basis assert some superiority for themselves. So there seem to be certain recognizable groups that favor various leaders. Still, these dissensions are not yet so severe that they keep the groups from mutual recognition and common worship.

Among the questions raised about Paul, the issue of his means of support is the only one explicitly mentioned. Finally, we should note that comparisons and evaluations do not necessarily entail complete rejection. Those who ally themselves with other leaders do not necessarily reject Paul's apostolic status and deny all authority to him, especially if these comparisons are with other apostolic figures. Such questionings may only challenge some exclusivist claims on the Corinthians made by either Paul or the Pauline loyalists. Indeed, since Paul believes his example will be an effective sanction for his appeals in both chs. 4 and 9, he must believe that the majority still accord him some significant status.

Again, it is important to remember that our method seeks to identify opponents, not describe the entire occasion of a letter. Thus descriptions of the Corinthians themselves or their problems are not automatically relevant to our search. Only passages that mention things related to the issues discovered in explicit statements can be identified as allusions to *opposition*.

Allusions

3.5-9

Statements in 3.5-9 unmistakably allude to the Corinthians' arguments about leaders, including Paul's position. These verses form a sub-section of 3.5-17[95] that is directly related to 3.1-4.[96] As we noted in connec-

---

95. Interpreters who divide the text this way include Fee, *First Epistle to the Corinthians*, p. 128; Davis, *Wisdom and Spirit*, p. 132; Dahl, 'Paul and the Church at Corinth', p. 327. Other interpreters (e.g. Kuck, *Judgment and Community Conflict*, p. 155; Fiore, ' "Covert Allusions" ', p. 87) see 3.5–4.5 as the larger section into which 3.5-17 fits while still recognizing 3.5-17 as a sub-section. It seems more

tion with 3.3-4, 3.1-4 is a transition to 3.5-17 and thus introduces what
3.5-17 applies. Verses 5-17 give one reason why it is wrong to claim
allegiance to leaders, including Paul and Apollos. Since these verses
support the polemic of 3.1-4 in this way, we identify 3.5-17 as a didactic section.

As we have seen with other passages that mention Paul and Apollos,
some argue that these verses support the contention that the major
problem at Corinth is with the Apollos group.[97] But again the evidence
is ambiguous and may signal the opposite, that there is very little trouble with the Apollos group so that Paul can easily use Apollos as an
example.[98] Apart from either assumption, Paul may simply use himself
and Apollos because they are the apostolic figures known best to the
Corinthians.[99] So we can claim nothing about the place of Apollos[100] or
the Apollos party on the basis of these verses.

The theme of 3.5-9 is the proper evaluation of ministers and their
varying functions. As Fee notes, v. 5 sets out the thesis that vv. 6-9 elaborate.[101] Verse 5 asserts that both Apollos and Paul are merely and
equally servants, but that they have different functions. Identifying these
leaders as servants takes away any honor or status accruing to those
who claim allegiance to them.[102] This evaluation of teachers supports

likely, however, that 3.18-23 serves as a polemical conclusion to chs. 1–3 and 4.1-5
as transition to 4.6-13. See further the above discussion of 3.21-22 and 4.3.

96. Fee (*First Epistle to the Corinthians*, p. 129) comments that 3.5-9 picks up
directly from the rhetorical questions of 3.3-4.

97. E.g. Pogoloff, *Logos and Sophia*, p. 180; Horsley, 'Wisdom of Words', pp.
231-32.

98. So Kuck, *Judgment and Community Conflict*, p. 161.

99. Hall ('A Disguise for the Wise', p. 145) makes a strong argument that 3.4-
20 makes better sense if the real leaders causing problems are Corinthians and that
Paul uses himself and Apollos as examples to make the status of servant easier to
accept when applied to local leaders. But while the rivalries at Corinth must have
had local leaders, there still seem to be claims connected with apostolic figures or
they would not appear as often as they do throughout chs. 1–4.

100. Fee (*First Epistle to the Corinthians*, p. 130) seems to go beyond the evidence when he claims that the farm analogy absolves Apollos of any responsibility
for the problems at Corinth. This passage addresses primarily how the Corinthians
are to evaluate leaders, not how particular leaders act.

101. Fee, *First Epistle to the Corinthians*, p. 131.

102. This is similar to the strategy Paul uses in 4.1-3 (see above). Pogoloff
(*Logos and Sophia*, p. 213) finds here a direct opposition to the Corinthians' view
of Paul and Apollos as wise rhetors with this figure of a servant.

the rebukes of 3.3-4 which condemn the Corinthians' attachments to teachers and makes those attachments ludicrous, almost making Paul's assessment of their lack of spiritual discernment seem kind.

Verses 3.5-9 emphasize that Paul and Apollos have distinct functions even while they both work as servants of God. This is Paul's indirect way of addressing the differences the Corinthians perceive among leaders and their use of leaders as a basis for choosing sides. Paul subordinates the functions of both himself and Apollos to the working of God (v. 7) and thereby reduces the importance of their differences and simultaneously makes them equally subordinate to God's working.[103] This common subordination to God is again raised in v. 9 as Paul and Apollos are called 'fellow-workers for God'.[104] Paul also reduces the status of leaders by explicitly placing their work under the judgment of God.

Verses 5-9, then, confirm that, in Paul's view, the Corinthians inappropriately value relationships with particular leaders and that they compare leaders.

1.13-17

The rhetorical questions that open 1.13 follow up the interpretive description of the Corinthian situation in vv. 11-12 and the subsequent comments in vv. 14-17 on how few Paul baptized at Corinth allude to the Corinthians' allegiances to various teachers. We have already identified 1.10(11)-17 as polemical. In this highly polemical section we may expect statements that exaggerate and make ridiculous the problem described. We are not disappointed. This should caution us about using vv. 13-17 to fill in details about the opposition to Paul.

Verse 13 begins with a rhetorical question that renders the Corinthians' claims to leaders absurd ('Is Christ divided?').[105] While it may

103. Paul will assign more significance to their different functions in 3.10-17, but here he wants to establish that the differences cannot be used to elevate one teacher over another.

104. See Victor P. Furnish ('"Fellow Workers in God's Service"', *JBL* 80 (1961), pp. 364-70 [368-69]) for arguments in favor of this interpretation, the strongest of which is that this understanding best fits the context. If placing 3.8b in a parenthesis so that v. 8a attaches directly to 9a means that 8b is of little importance, then the analysis of Kuck (*Judgment and Community Conflict*, pp. 155-56), which finds 3.5-17 to be placing leaders and the church in eschatological perspective, counts against Furnish's view of 3.8b.

105. It is quite possible that v. 13a is not a question at all but a statement ('Christ

be possible that this interrogation is aimed at a Christ party as Fee contends,[106] it seems much more likely that it, along with the next two questions, should be understood as a *reductio ad absurdum*.[107] In spite of how obvious this is for the second question ('Paul wasn't crucified for you was he?'), many read a description of the opposition's theology into the third question ('You weren't baptized into the name of Paul were you?'), that is, they claim the Corinthians hold some aberrant view about baptism. But as it usually happens with unsupported mirror reading, what interpreters claim the reference proves about the Corinthian situation differs: Wilson asserts that 1.14-17 reflects sacramentalism, perhaps to the point of seeing the sacraments as magic,[108] Horsley contends that the Corinthians' problems with baptism stem from Apollos's wrong understanding of the rite as reported in Acts,[109] Dahl thinks it possible that Paul was criticized for not baptizing enough people,[110] Fee finds a magical view of baptism that leads them to emphasize the baptizer,[111] and Conzelmann says that it reflects an understanding of baptism similar to that in the mysteries where a special relationship exists between the baptized and the baptizer.[112] But there is no evidence to base any mirror reading on here. The issue of this passage is rivalries, not baptism.[113] One point of dwelling on baptism after raising it in the absurd question in v. 13 is to demonstrate that their experience of baptism renders such rivalry unacceptable, indeed ludicrous.

Paul's remarks in v. 13 are probably quite sarcastic, particularly the second question. This supports Conzelmann's translation of the εὐχαρ-ιστῶ in v. 14a as 'Thank God!'[114] Paul thus mocks their attachments to

is divided') which defines the result of the Corinthians' attachments to teachers. See the mention of this translation in Fee, *First Epistle to the Corinthians*, p. 60 n. 62.

106. Fee, *First Epistle to the Corinthians*, p. 60.

107. Fee (*First Epistle to the Corinthians*, p. 60) recognizes this function for the second two questions but separates them from the first equally absurd question.

108. Jack H. Wilson, 'The Corinthians Who Say There Is No Resurrection of the Dead', *ZNW* 59 (1968), pp. 90-107, 99.

109. Horsley, 'Wisdom of Word', p. 232.

110. Dahl, 'Paul and the Church at Corinth', p. 322.

111. Fee, *First Epistle to the Corinthians*, pp. 61-63.

112. Conzelmann, *First Epistle to the Corinthians*, p. 35. Conzelmann (*First Epistle to the Corinthians*, p. 35 n. 35) also thinks it is possible that this question is a 'polemical *ad hoc* statement'.

113. See the comments of Pogoloff, *Logos and Sophia*, pp. 106-108.

114. Conzelmann, *First Epistle to the Corinthians*, p. 36. The translation of the

teachers by somewhat artificially separating himself from the Corinthians and their entrance into Christianity. It is *Paul* who draws in the subject of baptism, not the Corinthians, and he gives their baptism as clear evidence that their strife in the name of leaders is unsuitable, even impossible, if they recognize the meaning of belonging to Christ and of having been baptized into Christ's name. I find no evidence here that the Corinthians are concerned about a relationship with the one who baptized them—after all, if this were the basis of their commitments, the Paul group would be so small as to be insignificant and we should expect Silas and Timothy groups since they participated in Paul's founding visit.

Comments about baptism yield to the topic of Paul's gospel in v. 17. As Paul concludes this opening section of the body of the letter he sets 'wise words' in opposition to the cross and thus begins his treatment of the theme that will dominate the next two chapters. Both the contrast with the cross and the pervasiveness of the theme suggest that Paul has referred to an issue they raise: σοφίᾳ λόγου ('wisdom of word').[115] This use of mirror reading in a polemical section is permissible but still does not produce conclusive evidence. Unfortunately, even if we are correct that the Corinthians speak favorably of σοφίᾳ λόγου, this passage supplies no hints about the meaning of the expression except that Paul sees it as the opposite of the cross.

Thus, while it contains an extended rebuke in a sarcastic tone, 1.13-17 reveals little about those challenging Paul. It does not indicate that the Corinthians focus their attention on baptism or their baptizer. These verses do suggest, though not conclusively, that they are concerned about wisdom of word.

2.1-5
In 2.1-5 Paul discusses his preaching, both its style and its content. We identify this passage as an allusion because of its references to wise speech. Verses 1-5 are a supporting argument for the thesis set out in 1.17 and elaborated throughout the rest of ch. 1. Fee finds 2.1-5 to have 'strongly apologetic overtones',[116] but it seems to function more as a

---

sentence would then be: 'Thank God I didn't baptize any of you except Crispus and Gaius!' Conzelmann focuses the absurdity of the statement on Paul's rejection of the role of a savior, but it is more likely a denial of any connection to any partisans.

115. So Fee, *First Epistle to the Corinthians*, p. 64.

116. Fee, *First Epistle to the Corinthians*, p. 89. At the opposite end of the

parallel to the example in 1.26-31,[117] which gave the Corinthians as examples of the opposition between the cross and human wisdom. To this point we have no direct evidence that 'wisdom of words' plays a role in the judging of Paul referred to in 4.1-5 and 9.4-6, but its connection with Paul's presentation of the gospel in 2.1-5 makes it hard to deny that it has some connection with the comparisons being made among leaders.[118] Moreover, it precisely concerns the issue of wisdom when Paul reproaches the Corinthians in 3.1-4 for being worldly and infantile. So, there may be an apologetic element in 2.1-5 even though this is not its primary function. Overall it seems best to identify 2.1-5 as a didactic section which gives Paul's preaching as an example of the contrast between human wisdom and the cross, though with a slight apologetic tinge.

Some interpreters think Paul is discussing two elements of his ministry in 2.1-5; vv. 1-2 are on his preaching, vv. 3-5 on his life.[119] Schrage acknowledges a similar distinction but then comments that such alternatives are misguided.[120] The inseparability of these two things is well known in Paul and their conjunction in the thought of the Corinthians seems probable. The cultural context also makes such a separation unlikely because many in the Hellenistic world posited a relationship between wisdom, one's character and oratorical ability.[121]

This brings us to the meaning of σοφία λόγου ('wisdom of word') and similar expressions in 1 Corinthians. There is a growing recognition that Paul's use of σοφία ('wisdom') language here and elsewhere in 1 Corinthians is related to its use in the rhetorical tradition.[122] Mar-

---

spectrum Kuck (*Judgment and Community Conflict*, p. 159) argues that there are no 'concrete references to the Corinthian situation' in all of 1.18–2.16.

117. So Schrage, *Brief an die Korinther*, p. 222. Cf. Barrett (*Commentary on the First Epistle to the Corinthians*, p. 62) who says that 2.1-5 applies the principle from the end of ch. 1 to Paul's ministry. Similarly A. Robertson and A. Plummer, *A Critical and Exegetical Commentary on the First Epistle of St. Paul to the Corinthians* (ICC; Edinburgh: T. & T. Clark, 1911), p. 29.

118. There is, however, no basis for claiming that these verses show that some say that Paul lacks wisdom, as Davis (*Wisdom and Spirit*, p. 133) argues.

119. So Conzelmann, *First Epistle to the Corinthians*, pp. 53-54; Fee, *First Epistle to the Corinthians*, p. 92.

120. Schrage, *Brief an die Korinther*, p. 224.

121. This is seen particularly among the Stoics.

122. E.g. Fee, *First Epistle to the Corinthians*, p. 89 n. 4, following Lars Hartman, 'Some Remarks on 1 Cor. 2:1-5', *SEÅ* 34 (1974), pp. 109-20.

shall argues that both καθ' ὑπεροχὴν...σοφίας ('according to superior wisdom', v. 1) and ἐν πειθοῖς σοφίας (λογοίς) ('in persuasive wise words', v. 4) imply eloquence which is 'the substance of rhetorical *dynamis*'.[123] Similarly Pogoloff finds the use of πειθοῖς ('persuasive') with 'wise words' to be a clear reference to rhetoric. Furthermore, Paul's distinction between persuasive speech and demonstration (vv. 4-5) reflects discussions of types of arguments in Aristotle and the succeeding tradition. Pogoloff concludes that 2.4 shows decisively that the wisdom at issue is rhetoric.[124] This understanding has the advantage of fitting most easily into the cultural milieu at Corinth and, more directly connected with evidence we have found, helps make sense of the competitiveness among the Corinthians. What is being compared is not some esoteric knowledge but widely accepted (and often compared) 'social and cultural qualities' which included speech, education and physical appearance.[125] Paul here purports to eschew the values such comparisons are made on and presents himself, as good rhetors did, as an 'anti-rhetor',[126] even as he makes use of rhetorical terminology, concepts and tradition. So the 'wisdom of word' referred to in 1.17 is the eloquence (and all that that included) which established one's social position. Paul's use of it in contrast to the cross is a rebuke of the Corinthians' comparisons and competitiveness about teachers.[127]

Verses of 2.1-5 then continue Paul's rejection of the Corinthians' standard of measurement for status. By saying that he rejects these standards in favor of the cross, Paul seems to set himself completely outside the realm of rhetoric, but then in v. 4 he claims the more substantial type of argument, a demonstration, for himself. This allusion does not show that Paul's weak demeanor is being singled out for examination, but rather that Paul presents his demeanor as one aspect of his rejection of their standards. Given the common bases of competition for status in Hellenistic culture, it does seem likely that Paul's weakness is one

123. Peter Marshall, 'Invective: Paul and his Enemies in Corinth', in E.W. Conrad and E.G. Newing (eds.), *Perspectives on Language and Text* (Winona Lake, IN: Eisenbrauns, 1987), pp. 359-73 (365).

124. Pogoloff, *Logos and Sophia*, pp. 137-38.

125. Marshall, 'Invective', p. 366.

126. So Hartman, 'Remarks', pp. 117-18.

127. Johannes Munck (*Paul and the Salvation of Mankind* [trans. F. Clarke; Atlanta: John Knox Press, 1977], p. 157) writes that 2.1-5 and 1.26-31 show that the Corinthians boast of leaders only to boast about themselves.

aspect of his ministry that they examine. But we should not separate this issue from the manner and content of his preaching.

9.1-2, 11-12

We may tentatively identify 9.1-2 and 11-12 as allusions to the opposition to Paul because the former discusses Paul's apostolic qualifications and the latter deals with his rejection of support, both of which are raised in explicit statements. We have already identified 9.1-23 as a didactic section. This is further confirmed by the opening question of 9.1 which has to do with freedom,[128] not apostleship. The remarks about apostleship that follow this first question are supporting evidence for Paul's claimed freedom rather than beginning a discussion of apostleship.[129] Verse 2 is an *ad hominem* elaboration of Paul's second proof of his apostleship—his work.[130] Many interpreters argue that v. 2 shows that Paul's apostleship is under attack,[131] but this gives too little weight to the role v. 2 plays in securing and elaborating Paul's claim on the Corinthians[132] which he will exploit to make the point about his renunciation of freedom in vv. 11-23. Verse 2 certainly refers to some who question Paul's apostolic status. That these 'others' are non-Corinthians seems obvious.[133] Some assert that these 'others' have been to

---

128. Even Fee, who argues that ch. 9 is a strong apology, acknowledges that the issue of ch. 9 is authority and freedom (*First Epistle to the Corinthians*, p. 394).

129. Lüdemann (*Opposition to Paul*, p. 67) sees the last two questions in 9.1 as support for the second question—'Am I not an Apostle?' This is certainly correct. What Lüdemann seems to miss, as do all those who see these verses as primarily an apology for Paul's apostleship, is the role that this second question plays as a subsidiary of the first question, that about freedom.

130. Fee, *First Epistle to the Corinthians*, p. 396; Robertson and Plummer, *First Epistle of St. Paul to the Corinthians*, p. 178.

131. Fee, *First Epistle to the Corinthians*, p. 396; Conzelmann, *First Epistle to the Corinthians*, p. 152; Lüdemann, *Opposition to Paul*, p. 66; Wolff, *Der erste Brief des Paulus an die Korinther*, II, p. 20. Willis ('Apostolic Apology', p. 34) comments that Paul's remarks here are too short to be a real defense and that vv. 1-2 are a collection of 'obvious truths, with no particular opponents in view'.

132. It is to support his superior claim on them that Paul makes 'you' emphatic in 9.1 rather than because his apostleship is under attack (contra Strobel, *Der erste Briefe an die Korinther*, p. 143).

133. So also most commentators, including: Robertson and Plummer, *First Epistle of St. Paul to the Corinthians*, p. 185; Strobel, *Der erste Brief an die Korinther*, p. 143; Wolff, *Der erste Brief des Paulus an die Korinther*, II, p. 21.

Corinth in the past and go on to identify them with some particular type of presupposed broader anti-Pauline movement.[134] While it is *possible* that some intruders have been to Corinth and had challenged Paul's apostleship, there is no evidence for this here and, as we will see below, no real support for it in vv. 11-12 or elsewhere in 1 Corinthians. Thus, any identification of these 'outsiders' with any particular group or theology is without basis.

The function these verses have in introducing the topic of Paul's rights as an apostle and particularly identifying v. 2 as an elaboration of Paul's claim on the Corinthians casts doubt on our identification of 9.1-2 as an allusion to opposition. After all, we have found no evidence that the Corinthians question Paul's apostleship, only his relative authority in comparison with other leaders, particularly apostolic figures. Still, the immediate reference to being judged in v. 3 lets us see that the evaluations some Corinthians are making are not far from his mind in vv. 1-2. We cannot claim, as some do, that these verses demonstrate that Paul's apostleship was challenged in Corinth. The only basis for this claim is insufficiently supported mirror reading. Since we are in a didactic context, no mirror reading is permissible, but these verses do seem to go beyond the mere assertion of Paul's apostolic status. So perhaps they respond indirectly to criticisms of which Paul knows that center on his renunciation of support, because he immediately turns to that issue. Thus the claims about his apostleship take on a supporting role—they ground his claim to the right of support.

At 9.11 Paul turns from a general argument supporting the principle of the right of support for apostles to his own right to it from the Corinthians in particular. Verses 11-12 perhaps confirm that some questioned Paul's renunciation of support, but the main purpose of these verses is to establish Paul's right to maintenance from the Corinthians so he can reject that right categorically. What has interested interpreters is the mention of 'others' who have received pay from the Corinthians (v. 12). Interpreters identify them in a multitude of ways including: Apollos and Peter,[135] Jewish-Christian missionaries who founded the

---

134. So Lüdemann, *Opposition to Paul*, pp. 68-71; Robertson and Plummer, *First Epistle of St. Paul to the Corinthians*, p. 185. Fee (*First Epistle to the Corinthians*, p. 396) thinks it is possible that these 'others' have been to Corinth, but notes that Paul's concern is not with those outsiders here.

135. Fee, *First Epistle to the Corinthians*, pp. 409-410.

Cephas-party[136] and Judaizers.[137] Since there is nothing in the text that characterizes these 'others', we have no basis for any identification of them.[138] We cannot even claim they are non-Corinthians, they may be native Corinthian leaders.[139] The only two necessarily excluded from this group of 'others' are Paul and Barnabas (v. 6). It seems quite likely that Apollos would be among them, but Paul is not concerned with who has accepted pay, only that the Corinthians recognize his superior claim to it. There is no reason to identify these others as sources of opposition to Paul just because their practice with respect to maintenance is different from his. Paul's mention of them here contains no hint that they opposed him.

So while 9.11-12 emphatically asserts Paul's right to maintenance, it adds nothing new to our understanding of opposition to him in Corinth. At most it confirms that some at Corinth raise questions about why he does not accept pay as others do. Similarly, though 9.1-2 seemed likely to produce helpful information, it does not because the subordination of the topic of apostleship to that of freedom and Paul's right to support and the role of v. 2 as supporting evidence for his claim on the Corinthians do not allow us to say that these verses respond to challenges to Paul's apostolic status.

4.8-13

The statements in 4.8-13 comprise an allusion because the reference to Paul's work with his hands in v. 12 relates to the issue of Paul's maintenance. The surrounding verses, which sarcastically describe the Corinthians, can be included as allusions because they continue Paul's description of their being puffed up (v. 6). We have already identified 4.6-13 as polemical. In 4.8-13 Paul opposes the Corinthians' competing claims to status with apostolic existence as he understands and experiences it. So the passage functions to defeat their self-assigned importance by describing apostolic existence as the opposite of what they wanted to claim about themselves through identifying with particular

136. Lüdemann, *Opposition to Paul*, p. 80.
137. Robertson and Plummer, *First Epistle of St. Paul to the Corinthians*, p. 185.
138. Similarly, Conzelmann, *First Epistle to the Corinthians*, p. 155.
139. Paul's right to maintenance would be supported all the more strongly if these 'others' included non-apostolic figures.

apostles.[140] At the same time these verses correct their improper view of apostleship.[141] Furthermore, its irony certainly exaggerates the Corinthians' claims about themselves.[142] As others have noted, vv. 8-10 are *ad hominem*[143] and ironic support for the implicit accusations contained in the questions of v. 7.[144] Verses 8-10, then, attack the Corinthians' rivalrous competition for exalted spiritual status[145] and their conception of apostleship which fuels the competition.

Most interpreters see 4.8-13 as evidence of an overrealized eschatology, particularly the 'already' of v. 8.[146] However, claims to advanced spiritual status, pneumatic enthusiasm or spiritual superiority do not necessarily entail an overrealized eschatology.[147] Our interpretation must not presume such an eschatology since to this point we have discovered no evidence for it. Moreover, other explanations for the language of this text lie closer to hand. First, claims to being full, rich and rulers are not unique to the Christian movement or movements with an apocalyptic eschatology. Such claims are found not only in Stoic and Cynic descriptions of the wise person[148] but also quite widely in Hel-

---

140. So also Fee, *First Epistle to the Corinthians*, p. 156; Fiore, ' "Covert Allusions" ', p. 87. Cf. Schmithals, *Gnosticism in Corinth*, p. 182; Pogoloff, *Logos and Sophia*, p. 222.

141. Cf. Fee, *First Epistle to the Corinthians*, p. 165; Schrage, *Brief an die Korinther*, p. 350.

142. So also Fee, *First Epistle to the Corinthians*, p. 165.

143. So Fee, *First Epistle to the Corinthians*, p. 165, and Barrett, *Commentary on the First Epistle to the Corinthians*, p. 110.

144. See Schrage, *Brief an die Korinther*, p. 350.

145. Cf. Pogoloff, *Logos and Sophia*, p. 222. Wire's contention that 'without us' in 4.8 refers to the time when Apollos was in Corinth and so shows that Apollos was part of the problem at Corinth (*The Corinthian Women Prophets*, p. 44), is completely unsupported by this text.

146. E.g. Fee, *First Epistle to the Corinthians*, p. 178; Schrage, *Brief an die Korinther*, p. 334; Barrett, *Commentary on the First Epistle to the Corinthians*, p. 109; Conzelmann, *First Epistle to the Corinthians*, pp. 87-88; Robertson and Plummer, *First Epistle of St. Paul to the Corinthians*, p. 84; Munck, *Paul and the Salvation of Mankind*, p. 165.

147. Neither do they necessarily indicate a connection between the emphasis on the Spirit and opposition to Paul, as Lüdemann (*Opposition to Paul*, p. 84) recognizes.

148. See Conzelmann, *First Epistle to the Corinthians*, p. 87 who also notes its use in Gnosticism and then goes on to find an overrealized eschatology. See also

lenistic culture, so widely that Kuck argues that the influence of no particular school needs to be presupposed for either Paul's or the Corinthians' use of them.[149] Grant contends that Paul's response to the Corinthians draws on philosophers' critique of this Stoic ideal.[150] Alternatively,
Marshall relates this language more closely to the Greek traditional
criticism of hybris which included characterizing the haughty as sated,
rich and tyrants.[151] Since these verses are an exaggerated and ironic
description of the Corinthians' claims, there is no certain, direct connection between the language of these verses and the claims they actually make. Nothing beyond a spirit of competition and rivalry is needed
to account for Paul's characterization of their behavior in vv. 8-10.[152]
Furthermore, even if the 'already' of v. 8 and the 'up to this moment' of
v. 11 point to eschatology, this would indicate only that Paul frames the
discussion in this way,[153] not that the Corinthians hold some aberrant
eschatology. Thus, these verses do not demonstrate that the Corinthians' claims to status are rooted in an overrealized eschatology.

Paul's description of apostolic weakness and dishonor in the tribulation catalog of vv. 11-13 tells us little about opposition to him. It does
show that Paul sees a connection between his plying a trade and the
other low-status markers that characterize his apostleship. This is not
evidence that the Corinthians make such a connection to question his
apostolic status. So this description of Paul's apostleship seems directed
at the criteria the Corinthians use to evaluate all apostles, not just their
evaluation of him in particular. Indeed, it seems most appropriately

Pogoloff, *Logos and Sophia*, p. 222; Robert M. Grant, 'The Wisdom of the Corinthians', in Sherman E. Johnson (ed.), *The Joy of Study: Papers on New Testament and
Related Studies Presented to Honor Frederick Clifton Grant* (New York: Macmillan, 1951), pp. 51-59 (51-52); A.J.M. Wedderburn, 'The Problem of the Denial of
the Resurrection in 1 Corinthians XV', *NovT* 23 (1981), pp. 229-41 (234-35).

149. Kuck, *Judgment and Community Conflict*, pp. 217-18.

150. Grant, 'The Wisdom of the Corinthians', pp. 52-53.

151. Peter Marshall, 'Hybrists', pp. 280-82.

152. See the discussion of Kuck (*Judgment and Community Conflict*, pp. 210-
19), where he argues that Paul is discussing their advances in morality, not eschatology.

153. Conzelmann (*First Epistle to the Corinthians*, p. 87) comments in connection with v. 8 that 'for Paul, the eschatological sense is a matter of course'. But he
still goes on to see a problem with overrealized eschatology without, it seems, considering the possibility that it was *only* Paul, operating within his eschatological
presuppositions, who frames the discussion in this way.

aimed at his supporters who enter him into competition with other lead-ers. But there is no textual basis for limiting its scope of application to any single group. This description is not even good evidence that the Corinthians have a problem with Paul's apostleship.[154] All it clearly does is oppose, in very strong terms, the Corinthians' self-assigned status by describing apostolic existence as the opposite of what they claim. So it remains a matter of inter-community relations, of their being puffed up because of their allegiance to a particular leader.

So 4.8-13 yields no new information about opposition to Paul. It is unjustified to mirror read an overrealized eschatology into the 'already' of v. 8. Instead, the passage employs well-known claims about the wise and perhaps criticisms of the proud to reject the Corinthians' claims to status.

15.(8)9-11

Our next possible allusion to opposition to Paul appears in 15.(8)9-11 where Paul speaks of his witnessing of Christ's resurrection and in connection with it his apostleship. As was the case with ch. 9, the na-ture of the section significantly influences our understanding of the state-ments contained in it. A number of interpreters identify 1 Cor. 15.1-11 as an apology for Paul's apostleship, contending that the purpose of the references to resurrection witnesses and their extension to include Paul is to establish Paul's equality with the other witnesses.[155] But more commentators identify all of ch. 15 as a discussion of the resurrection of Christians[156] and so see the remarks on Christ's resurrection as a reestablishment of common ground from which Paul can launch his argument about the resurrection of Christians.[157] Our difficulty in deter-mining the section's purpose is exacerbated by how different its begin-ning is from most sections of chs. 5–15, where Paul usually announces

154. Contra Fee, *First Epistle to the Corinthians*, p. 176.

155. So, e.g., Peter von der Osten-Sacken, 'Die Apologie des Paulinischen Apos-tolats in 1 Kor 15_{1-11}', *ZNW* 64 (1973), pp. 254-56; Lüdemann, *Opposition to Paul*, pp. 72-74.

156. So Fee, *First Epistle to the Corinthians*, p. 713; Conzelmann, *First Epistle to the Corinthians*, pp. 248-49; Robertson and Plummer, *First Epistle of St. Paul to the Corinthians*, pp. 329-30; Barrett, *Commentary on the First Epistle to the Corin-thians*, p. 335.

157. See Fee, *First Epistle to the Corinthians*, pp. 713-14; Conzelmann, *First Epistle to the Corinthians*, p. 249.

the subject at the start.[158] But he nowhere states the subject in 15.1-11. Still, the smooth flow from v. 11 to v. 12 and its introduction of the topic of the resurrection of the dead strongly indicates that vv. 1-11 in some way address this question. Furthermore, the resurrection of Christ is used as evidence for Paul's view in vv. 12-23. Thus vv. 1-11 set out Christ's resurrection as evidence for the Christians' resurrection. The Corinthians do not seem to question Christ's resurrection because Paul can use it to support his contention that Christians are raised. Thus, 15.1-11 is a didactic section;[159] it sets out a point of Christian teaching which is not in dispute but will be used for other ends. Identifying this section as didactic does not keep us from examining it for evidence of opposition to Paul, but it does prohibit any use of mirror reading to identify such opposition.

Verses 15.9-10 are an explanation of Paul's identification of himself as an ἐκτρώματι ('miscarriage') with respect to his witnessing of Christ's resurrection.[160] Paul's use of this unusual metaphor has given rise to speculation about its use by his opponents.[161] But unsupported mirror reading is the only basis for finding such a use. Verse 8 does seem to include Paul as a witness of this special type and to close the door behind him. The first half of v. 8 ('And last of all to me') makes it more likely that the meaning of ἔκτρωμα ('miscarriage') is related to the time of the revelation to Paul, not his lack of appropriate preparation for such a call[162] or some other deficiency.[163] Since v. 8 sets Paul apart from non-apostolic persons and includes him among the apostolic witnesses, it is possible that it reflects the criticism he faced in Corinth. At

158. This difference is noted by many commentators including Barrett, *Commentary on the First Epistle to the Corinthians*, p. 335.

159. This is especially the case if Wilson ('The Corinthians Who Say There Is No Resurrection of the Dead', pp. 102-104) and others are correct that Paul had not taught about the resurrection of Christians while in Corinth but only about the parousia.

160. So also Fee, *First Epistle to the Corinthians*, pp. 716, 733-34; Robertson and Plummer, *First Epistle of St. Paul to the Corinthians*, p. 342.

161. Those who attribute it to the opponents include Barrett, *Commentary on the First Epistle to the Corinthians*, p. 344 and Fee, *First Epistle to the Corinthians*, pp. 733-34.

162. Contra Robertson and Plummer, *First Epistle of St. Paul to the Corinthians*, p. 339; Barrett, *Commentary on the First Epistle to the Corinthians*, p. 344.

163. Contra Fee, *First Epistle to the Corinthians*, p. 716; Barrett, *Commentary on the First Epistle to the Corinthians*, p. 344.

most, v. 8 may possibly reflect that the criticism he faced included questions about his apostolic credentials, possibly questioning his experience of the risen Christ, but we cannot be certain of either. Some mirror reading could also suggest that Paul cuts off competition with local leaders by excluding them from apostolic status. This latter possibility must be considered more improbable because it finds no clear support from other texts, while the suggestion that Paul's apostolic credentials are being examined receives some support in 9.1-2, 11-12.[164] Thus, 15.9-11 perhaps relates to the types of criticism of Paul we have seen, but they shed no clear light on them. Furthermore, nothing in ch. 15 indicates that the problem with the resurrection originated in some group opposed to Paul. It seems at least equally probable that some Corinthian Christians[165] have developed their own thoughts about the afterlife without consulting the absent Paul and have come to a position which Paul now opposes for the first time.[166]

2.13-16

We claim 2.13-16 as an allusion because it mentions both σοφίας λόγοις ('wise words') and the matter of passing judgment. These verses appear in a section comprising 2.6-16 which develops the antithesis between human wisdom and the cross which has been the leading theme since 1.17. It follows the two examples—the Corinthians themselves in 1.26-31 and Paul's own preaching in 2.1-5—Paul gives of the apparent foolishness of God's wisdom. The latter example demonstrates that Paul's preaching rejects the common cultural and rhetorical standards used for judging wisdom and denigrates those standards as human in comparison with the divine wisdom. 2.6-16 continues this theme by further distinguishing these wisdoms and by claiming that Christians (at

164. These verses in ch. 9 do not support Lüdemann's claim (*Opposition to Paul*, pp. 73-74) that there were questions specifically about the appearance of Jesus to Paul. Rather, 9.1-2 takes these experiences as accepted by the Corinthians and so counts against seeing this as an issue raised in Corinth.

165. Lüdemann (*Opposition to Paul*, p. 381) thinks this 'some' is the majority of the congregation, but Conzelmann (*First Epistle to the Corinthians*, p. 262) thinks it refers to only a few. There is no sufficient basis to make either claim with certainty.

166. See Wilson ('The Corinthians Who Say There Is No Resurrection of the Dead', pp. 102-104) who takes this position and argues that Paul had preached only about the parousia and not about the resurrection. Also see the discussion of this problem in Dale Martin, *The Corinthian Body* (New Haven: Yale University Press, 1995), pp. 104-36.

least the pneumatics) possess divine wisdom. Since its primary purpose is to explicate the antithesis between human and divine wisdom which Paul himself introduces, it seems best to identify the 2.6-16 as a didactic section[167] which sets up the polemic of 3.1-4.[168]

Verses 2.6-16 have been used extensively by many interpreters to identify opposition in Corinth. Schmithals argues that the passage directly opposes Gnostic ideas.[169] Those who find an abherrant Christology or soteriology based on Hellenistic Jewish philosophical mysticism also use this passage extensively.[170] But all attempts to use this passage so extensively not only ignore its function as support for the antithesis between the two types of wisdom that Paul himself introduces, but also rely almost totally on unsupported mirror reading[171] combined with terminological parallels from non-Pauline sources.[172] These techniques make such identifications of opponents' views at best uncertain. Furthermore, as Funk points out to oppose Wilckens, there is no evidence

167. Others see the passage as either polemic (Schmithals, *Gnosticism in Corinth*, pp. 142-43; perhaps also Fee, *First Epistle to the Corinthians*, pp. 98, 114) or apologetic (J. Bradley Chance, 'Paul's Apology to the Corinthians', *Perspectives* 9 [1982], pp. 145-55 [153]).

168. Similarly Schrage, *Brief an die Korinther*, p. 242; Strobel, *Der erste Brief an die Korinther*, p. 61; Pogoloff, *Logos and Sophia*, p. 140; Fiore, '"Covert Allusions"', p. 87; Conzelmann, *First Epistle to the Corinthians*, pp. 58-59. W. Willis ('The "Mind of Christ" in 1 Corinthians 2,16', *Bib* 70 [1989], pp. 110-22 [119-22]) sees the section as paraenesis. While the ultimate goal of all of 1.17–2.16 is exhortation, as is appropriate for a deliberative composition, the immediate purpose seems more didactic with the exhortation becoming more explicit in 3.1-4. E. Earle Ellis ('Traditions in 1 Corinthians', *NTS* 32 [1986], pp. 481-502 [490]) identifies 2.6-16 as preformed material which Paul has adapted for this context. But this seems to unnecessarily remove the basic structure of the passage from the Corinthian situation for which it seems ideally suited.

169. Schmithals, *Gnosticism in Corinth*, pp. 151-52.

170. E.g. Horsley, 'Wisdom of Word', pp. 230-39; Strobel, *Der erste Brief an die Korinther*, p. 62; Georgi, 'Der Kampf um die reine Lehre im Urchristentum', p. 84; Sellin, 'Das "Geheimnis" der Weisheit und das Rätsel der "Christuspartei"', pp. 79-96; Pearson, *Pneumatikos-Psychikos Terminology*, esp. pp. 27-90.

171. E.g. Chance ('Paul's Apology to the Corinthians', pp. 153-54) cites 7 polemical contrasts in 2.6-16; Fee (*First Epistle to the Corinthians*, pp. 102, 117) cites at least 5 uses of the opponents' language; Pearson (*Pneumatikos-Psychikos Terminology*, pp. 4-5, 27-28, 31-38) finds no less than 8.

172. E.g. Pearson, *Pneumatikos-Psychikos Terminology*, pp. 28-30.

in this text of any christological debate. Disallowing these mirror readings and parallels does not remove 2.6-16 from Paul's argument against the Corinthians' divisiveness, it only limits how we use it to locate their views.

Paul further defines the 'words of wisdom' (σοφίας λόγοις) in v. 13 by calling them ἀνθρωπίνης ('human') and in this way denigrates those wise words by opposing them with the things of the Spirit. So Paul uses v. 13 to further separate himself from the cultural expectations the Corinthians employ.[173] Verse 13 also brings together the antithesis between types of wisdom and the Corinthians' passing of judgment and thus, along with vv. 14-16, provides strong confirmation that these judgments involve the 'words of wisdom'.

The theme of judging/discerning dominates vv. 14-16. Ἀνακρίνω ('to judge') appears in both vv. 14 and 15 (as well as eight other times in 1 Corinthians) and so may come from the Corinthians' usage, as Fee claims,[174] but we cannot be certain. If they do use this term, it adds further confirmation that they are comparing leaders and making some judgments about them.

Paul claims here that the non-pneumatic person cannot receive, know or discern the spiritual things of God. This assertion forces the reader to either accept Paul's view or place themselves among the ψυχικοί ('natural ones', i.e. without God's Spirit), which no Christian would want to do. There is no support in this text for proposing that ψυχικοί is a Corinthian catchphrase, even though it appears only here among Paul's letters.[175] Just because Paul uses it as the opposite of πνευματικοί ('pneumatics'), it does not mean that the Corinthians did. This is not impossible, but there is no evidence to support it. It is probably correct that the Corinthians identified themselves as pneumatics, as many have noted.[176] Chapter 12 clearly indicates that they exercised gifts of the Spirit and so could appropriately call themselves pneumatics. But that claim does not necessarily entail some errant pneumatology or indicate that they divide Christians into pneumatics and non-pneumatics (or psychics). Rather it is the expectation that all Christians

173. Horsley ('Wisdom of Word', pp. 230-31) argues that 2.13 shows that the Corinthians include eloquence as part of their spiritual achievement.

174. Fee, *First Epistle to the Corinthians*, p. 117.

175. Contra Pearson, *Pneumatikos-Psychikos Terminology*, pp. 4-5.

176. E.g. Pearson (*Pneumatikos-Psychikos Terminology*, p. 38) identifies both πνευματικοῖς and πνευματικὰ as part of the opponents' vocabulary.

are pneumatics; this is what gives 3.1 its force. There is no basis in 1 Corinthians for identifying these comments in 2.14-15 as a polemic against a Gnostic or Hellenistic philosophical anthropology.

What Paul has done in 2.13-14 is call upon the Corinthians to pass judgment on themselves. Then in v. 15 he rejects their right to judge him, explaining in v. 16 that the spiritual person cannot be judged because those who would attempt to judge him or her do not know the mind of the Lord. Thus, it seems, Paul grounds his claim that the Corinthians' judgment of him is illegitimate in the assertion that such judgment is the prerogative of God alone, as he will explain further in 4.3-13.

Finally in 2.16 Paul claims to possess the mind of Christ. Sellin identifies v. 16 as a polemical–apologetic remark which is the culmination of vv. 6-16 and shows that Paul has been challenged on precisely this point.[177] But again, this thesis requires too much mirror reading and does not sufficiently take into account the place 2.6-16 has in the overall argument about the appropriate wisdom. It is much more probable that Paul's claim to possess the mind of Christ means, following vv. 13-15, that he possesses the wisdom of God and it implicitly questions the pneumatic status of those who question him. For, according to his argument, only the spiritual can discern the spiritual possessions he now claims. Verse 16 may also prepare for the judgment of the Corinthians Paul makes in 3.1, which he can now make as one who has the mind of Christ.

Verses 13-16 unquestionably address the issues of 'wise words' and evaluating leaders. It denigrates the 'wise words' as human in comparison with the divine wisdom and it explicitly makes illegitimate any judgment of Paul by the Corinthians. But beyond confirming that these are issues and that they are related, this much over-read passage adds nothing to our knowledge of the opposition Paul faces.

1.18-25

The first development of Paul's antithesis between 'wise words' and the cross appears in 1.18-25.[178] We identify these verses as allusions to the questioning Paul faces because they address the standards (the wisdom)

177. Sellin, 'Das "Geheimnis" der Weisheit und das Rätsel der "Christus-partei"', p. 89.

178. So also Fee, *First Epistle to the Corinthians*, p. 66. Similarly, Pogoloff (*Logos and Sophia*, p. 130) sees 1.18-25 as support for 1.17.

the Corinthians use to compare leaders. Schmithals identifies all of 1.17-25 as polemic against the Corinthians' Gnostic ideas.[179] Others see 1.18-25 as an apology either for Paul's apostleship and his 'refusal to promote himself'[180] or for not speaking wisdom.[181] However, it seems more likely that the section is didactic because its purpose is to draw out the distinction Paul makes between human and divine wisdom.[182] Paul is here establishing some fundamentals on which he will base his more direct comments,[183] that is, Paul must create some common ground for himself and the Corinthians so that his critique of their practice of comparing leaders will be heeded.[184] This does not mean that there are no polemical intentions or remarks. Rather, this element is muted and postponed while Paul develops what is, for him, a central point of his preaching.[185] Paul then resumes his polemic in ch. 3. Thus, while the ultimate goal is to support an explicit polemic, 1.18-25 is more directly an explication of a point of teaching.

Since we are in a didactic context, we must closely limit mirror reading. But even if this were an apologetic section, there is no sufficient basis for mirror reading v. 22 to show that the problem is between Jews and Gentiles,[186] or v. 24 to indicate that Paul must overcome a sophia soteriology,[187] or to read vv. 18-25 as a whole as a defense against the

---

179. Schmithals, *Gnosticism in Corinth*, pp. 136, 142. Though Davis identifies the opponents differently, he also understands the section to be polemic (*Wisdom and Spirit*, p. 81).

180. So Chance ('Paul's Apology to the Corinthians', pp. 148, 150) who extends this apology through 1.31.

181. Wire, *The Corinthian Women Prophets*, p. 47; Troels Engberg-Pedersen, 'The Gospel and Social Practice According to 1 Corinthians', *NTS* 33 (1987), pp. 557-84 (562).

182. So also Fiore, '"Covert Allusions"', p. 87.

183. Similarly Conzelmann, *First Epistle to the Corinthians*, p. 41; Munck, *Paul and the Salvation of Mankind*, p. 166.

184. Kuck (*Judgment and Community Conflict*, pp. 154-55), following Bünker, seems to assert that this common ground already existed and that Paul is simply bringing it into view in 1.18-31. But Paul must present arguments for his point of view throughout chs. 1–2, so his position on this matter is not common ground at the beginning.

185. See Schrage, *Brief an die Korinther*, p. 40.

186. Contra Mitchell, *Paul and the Rhetoric of Reconciliation*, pp. 87-88.

187. Contra Horsley, 'Gnosis', pp. 46-47.

charge that Paul does not preach wisdom. All these conjectures go beyond a prudent use of mirror reading by adding topics or issues to the opposition's agenda which have not arisen in statements more certainly referring to them. A more defensible allusion to them is the reference to a 'disputant' in v. 20.[188] But this reference does not expand our knowledge of the issues being disputed, much less how those involve judgments about Paul. Additionally, Paul's calling the wisdom of the Corinthians worldly is a polemical evaluation,[189] but again this tells us nothing about the wisdom's content. If the wisdom of the Corinthians is to be equated with the cultural, social and rhetorical qualities expected in a wise person, then 1.18-25 attacks no specific group but rather the standards all the disputants use to assess various leaders.

Summary of Allusions

Allusions to opposition to Paul confirm that the Corinthians compare leaders and claim allegiance to different ones. Paul's apostolic credentials are being examined, but there is no evidence that anyone has denied his apostolic status. Paul's rejection of support raises questions as the Corinthians compare him with other leaders. The most important addition that allusions contribute to understanding the Corinthians' comparisons of leaders is that 'wise words' play an important part in them. Allusions show that these 'wise words' refer to the demeanor, speech, education and appearance expected of the wise by Hellenistic culture.[190] This perhaps implies that the examination of Paul's apostleship has more to do with his manner of speech and life, both of which receive significant attention in 1 Corinthians, than with doctrinal issues. Interestingly, we have discovered no connection between the opposition to Paul and the issues addressed in chs. 5–15.

---

188. Mitchell (*Paul and the Rhetoric of Reconciliation*, p. 87) identifies this as a reference to all those arguing at Corinth.

189. So also Sellin, 'Das "Geheimnis" der Weisheit und das Rätsel der "Christus-partei"', p. 80.

190. This may support Dale Martin's contention that the opposition to Paul comes from the higher-status members of the congregation because they would be most likely to emphasize these values (*The Corinthian Body*). However, this is not certain. Furthermore, our evidence does not support Martin's contention that all the issues raised in 1 Corinthians stem from this group.

Affirmations

2.6-12

Paul's comments in 2.6-12 refer to the issues raised in explicit state-ments and allusions as they expand the antithesis of human wisdom and the cross that has been the leading theme since 1.17. We have already identified 2.6-16 as a didactic section.

Verse 6 begins to turn the practice of judging leaders back onto the Corinthians as Paul implicitly excludes them from the τελείοις ('mature/perfect'),[191] as he will explicitly judge them to be non-pneumatic in 3.1. Several interpreters use 2.6 to argue that those who oppose Paul claim the title τελείος and thus identify them with a particular theology on this basis.[192] This identification relies solely on mirror reading which is not permissible in a didactic context. Moreover, other understandings make equal or better sense in the context. Munck asserts that it carries the general meaning of mature, as opposed to being children.[193] Willis proposes the interesting suggestion that it functions in a fashion similar to terms like 'saint', 'faithful' and 'called' and in this context serves as 'a polemic puncturing of the elitist Corinthians' self-esteem'.[194] Pogoloff's reading gives the term a similar function. He argues that the term means one is accomplished at a task, citing ἰδιώτης as its opposite. From this he argues that τελείος singles out the well-educated as those referred to here.[195] While it seems more likely that τελείος is intended to exclude all the Corinthians, not just those of higher status, Pogoloff's attention to the broader usage of the term is important. This wider use shows that mirror reading of this term cannot be used to find a par-

---

191. Chance ('Paul's Apology to the Corinthians', p. 153) asserts that 2.6-16 denies the Corinthians the status of pneumatics.

192. E.g. Pearson, *Pneumatikos-Psychikos Terminology*, p. 27; Schmithals, *Gnosticism in Corinth*, pp. 151-52; Sellin, 'Das "Geheimnis" der Weisheit und das Rätsel der "Christuspartei"', p. 82.

193. Munck, *Paul and the Salvation of Mankind*, p. 159. Similarly Barrett (*Commentary on the First Epistle to the Corinthians*, p. 68) who also excludes reference to a Gnostic dichotomy.

194. Willis, 'Mind', pp. 114, 112.

195. Pogoloff, *Logos and Sophia*, pp. 141-42.

ticular theology here because, as Willis notes, the point is to pass a negative judgment on the Corinthians' evaluations of leaders.[196]

Paul goes on from v. 6 to claim that the wisdom of God he has is unknown to the 'rulers of this age' (vv. 7-9).[197] He introduces a new point in vv. 10-12, claiming that the wisdom of God can only be understood by those who possess the Spirit of God and are thus πνευμάτικοι (pneumatics), among whom he includes himself and, at least initially, the Corinthians as the 'we' in v. 12 shows. This assertion, however, becomes a judgment on the Corinthians in 3.1. So 2.10-16 prepares for that judgment.

The only basis for identifying any word or expression in 2.6-12 as a catch-phrase of the Corinthians is that it does not appear elsewhere in Paul's writings. This is insufficient evidence because Paul may introduce these terms and expressions to address this (perhaps unique) situation even though he does not use them in other settings. As he seeks ways to turn the Corinthians from their present standards of judging leaders, he would want to make the contrast as clear as possible, identifying what he rejects as repugnant and making his view as attractive as possible. No Pauline Christians would have allowed that they did not possess the Spirit, but Paul leaves this as the only option to not agreeing with his definition of God's wisdom.

So 2.6-12 develops Paul's own antithesis between the Corinthians' standards of judgment and God's wisdom and prepares for his judgment of the Corinthians in 3.1-9. But when we properly limit mirror reading, this passage reveals no new information about the opposition at Corinth.

1.26-31

The comments in 1.26-31 relate to the questioning of Paul because they have to do with wisdom, status, and the antithesis between the world's standards and God's in these matters. These verses expand this antithesis by means of an example; the Corinthians themselves exemplify the point Paul is arguing. 1.26-31 builds directly on 1.25 which resumes the

196. Willis, 'Mind', pp. 110-22.
197. For our purposes it does not matter whether these rulers are cosmic powers as many argue (e.g. Barrett, *Commentary on the First Epistle to the Corinthians*, p. 70; Conzelmann, *First Epistle to the Corinthians*, p. 61) or human rulers as Fee (*First Epistle to the Corinthians*, pp. 103-104) asserts. Either way it adds nothing to our knowledge of the opposition since there is no good evidence that they use this term.

foolish/wise motif and introduces a weakness/strength theme. Verses 26-31 take up both, explicitly extending the latter into the area of social status. Since this section is supporting evidence for the thesis of 1.18-25[198] it is a didactic section. According to our method, we may add no information to our sketch of opponents from affirmations in didactic sections. Still, we can observe that Paul's continuing treatment of the antithesis between human and divine wisdom demonstrates that he sees this as a key point that he must establish to set things right in Corinth.

16.12

The reference to Apollos introduces the possibility that 16.12 refers to the opposition to Paul. This verse appears in a section comprising 16.5-12[199] that informs the Corinthians about the travel plans of Paul, Timothy and Apollos.[200] This section is didactic because its purpose is to pass on information. This reference to Apollos adds nothing to our knowledge of the Corinthian opposition to Paul. At the most it may confirm that some were claiming allegiance to Apollos and comparing Paul to him. Paul may include this reference to Apollos to indicate that there is no rivalry between them and that they are genuinely colleagues. But even this requires mirror reading in a didactic context and so goes beyond what we can say with certainty. This collegiality does seem to indicate that Apollos is not responsible for the use of his name at Corinth.[201]

16.15-18

An interesting affirmation that may relate to the Corinthians' questioning of Paul's authority appears in 16.15-18, where Paul exhorts the Corinthians to recognize and submit to Stephanas and others like him. The section these verses appear in, 16.13-18, is clearly hortatory and

---

198. Similarly Conzelmann, *First Epistle to the Corinthians*, p. 39; Fee, *First Epistle to the Corinthians*, pp. 50, 78.

199. So also Barrett, *Commentary on the First Epistle to the Corinthians*, p. 388.

200. Fee's separation of v. 12 from the other travel plans is unwarranted. His reason for doing this seems to be that it begins with περί (concerning) and so answers a question that the Corinthians had asked (*First Epistle to the Corinthians*, p. 823). However, as Ernst Baasland ('Die περί-Formel und die Argumentation-(ssituation) des Paulus', *ST* 42 (1988), pp. 77, 81-82) and Mitchell (*Paul and the Rhetoric of Reconciliation*, pp. 229-56) have shown, περί does not always indicate that a question is being answered, only that a new topic is being introduced.

201. So also Fee, *First Epistle to the Corinthians*, p. 824.

forms a fitting conclusion to Paul's argument about divisiveness as it urges recognition of a particular leader.[202] It is tempting to use these passages to clarify the arguments going on in Corinth, but our method does not allow us to use affirmations in hortatory sections to describe opponents. These verses do indicate that Stephanas (whom Paul says in 1.16 that he baptized), along with Fortunatus and Achaicus, have been loyal to Paul in the comparisons of leaders[203] and that Paul thinks the trouble would be eased by recognition of and submission to these leaders. So this passage suggests a practical solution to the Corinthian arguments about leaders, but it provides no insight into how the arguments were carried on or what other issues were involved.

Excursus on 10.30

Fee[204] and Bailey[205] contend that Paul's question in 10.30 ('Why am I blasphemed for that which I give thanks?') reflects a charge about Paul's eating of food sacrificed to idols. Though such an interpretation seems unlikely to this reader, it requires some comment.

Verses 10.23–11.1 form the conclusion to the discussion of food sacrificed to idols that began at 8.1. This section draws in many themes used in chs. 8–10,[206] and gives practical advice based on the arguments marshaled for Paul's view that Christians should usually not eat such meat.[207] Its primary thrust is hortatory;[208] Paul instructs the Corinthians to behave in specific ways in differing circumstances. Identifying the section as hortatory means that only explicit statements can be used to identify opponents.

---

202. Similarly Schüssler-Fiorenza, 'Rhetorical Situation and Historical Reconstruction in 1 Corinthians', p. 393 and Mitchell, *Paul and the Rhetoric of Reconciliation*, p. 294. Dahl ('Paul and the Church at Corinth', p. 324) supports this understanding of the section's function by citing the παρακαλῶ (I beseech/ask) of v. 15.

203. So also Fee, *First Epistle to the Corinthians*, pp. 827-29.

204. Fee, *First Epistle to the Corinthians*, pp. 9, 476.

205. Bailey, 'The Structure of 1 Corinthians', p. 166.

206. These themes include limiting oneself for the good of fellow Christians, the affirmation that the sacrificed food itself is not tainted, and Paul's use of himself as an example.

207. Wolff, *Der erste Brief des Paulus an die Korinther*, II, p. 57.

208. Mitchell (*Paul and the Rhetoric of Reconciliation*, p. 256) also seems to understand it as hortatory, calling it an appeal and she extends its function so that it serves as the conclusion and summary for all of 5.1–11.1.

It appears possible that 10.30 is an explicit statement with which Paul responds to a charge since its question uses the first person singular. But, given the context, it seems much more probable that it is a rhetorical device. Paul here affirms the principle cited by those who eat sacrificed meat (i.e. idols have no reality, 8.4), a principle already alluded to in 10.26, but at the same time tries to alter their behavior. Stylistically it also prepares nicely for the insertion of Paul's example in the first person singular in v. 33.

Even if 10.30 reflects some comment of the Corinthians, we cannot be certain it is a criticism of Paul. Omanson identifies it as a question from the strong which asks why their freedom should be limited.[209] This fits the context better than a surprise insertion of criticism of Paul. But both these interpretations rely on mirror reading in a hortatory context. Even if we allow that this is a polemical section, mirror reading 10.30 as a criticism of Paul receives no support from chs. 8–10. Thus we cannot include it as one of the criticisms Paul faces at Corinth.

Summary of Affirmations

Our examination of affirmations which relate to the questions being raised about Paul has not dealt with a number of passages which speak of the Corinthians' boasting, being arrogant, and not being wise, even though these assessments of their behavior surfaced in explicit statements and allusions. These passages include 5.2, 6; 6.5; 8.1-3. These general descriptions of the Corinthians' behavior are directly connected to specific actions on their part but have no perceivable relationship to the judgments they make about Paul. Thus, these descriptions are an insufficient basis on which to establish a connection between them and the comparisons of leaders. Neither have we discussed those passages which quote the slogan 'All things are permitted for me' because there is no evidence that connects those who use it with the opposition to Paul, though it does reflect some Corinthians' views. Another passage that some think may refer to the views of some opposition is 7.40 where Paul says that he *too* has the Spirit. We exclude it because the context of ch. 7 includes nothing that would lead us to think Paul is dealing with some denial of his possession of the Spirit and because it can be understood well as support for his opinion.[210] Finally, even though

---

209. Omanson, 'Acknowledging Paul's Quotations', pp. 210-11.
210. So Fee, *First Epistle to the Corinthians*, pp. 356-57. Conzelmann (*First*

12.14-26 discusses community relations and the importance of unity, its place within the argument about spiritual gifts focuses its application on developing a proper use of those gifts at Corinth and we have found no connection between that issue and the judgments being made about leaders.[211]

The affirmations which do seem to relate to the questions being raised about Paul confirm that his antithesis between human and divine wisdom is a key element in his rejection of the Corinthians' practice of comparing leaders. It is possible that the mention of Apollos in 16.12 confirms that some are claiming allegiance to him and opposing Paul in doing so.

Conclusion

As we synthesize our results, we need to remember that we have not tried to describe the full occasion of 1 Corinthians but only to determine what we can about opposition to Paul. Our search for opponents has yielded no evidence that the problems in Corinth are the result of intruders who are attempting to take Paul's place. Rather, the questions raised about Paul come from the Corinthians themselves. There are clearly challenges to his authority as he is compared to other leaders, specifically at least Cephas and Apollos. The Corinthians place these and perhaps other leaders in competition as various groups choose one or another of them as their authority. These comparisons include an examination of Paul's apostolic credentials. The evidence indicates only that his credentials are being entered into the competition among leaders, not that anyone denies his apostolic status. This makes it more probable that the other leaders are apostolic figures and that what those who cite other leaders deny is that Paul has an exclusive claim to authority in Corinth. While Paul acknowledges the importance of the work of others at Corinth, particularly that of Apollos, he does assert a sort of primacy of authority as their father in 4.14-15. We have also seen that the issue of Paul's means of maintenance plays a role in these comparisons, with some questioning his rejection of support.

We have found that the primary standard the Corinthians use to compare leaders is summed up with σοφίᾳ λόγου ('wise words/wisdom of

---

Epistle to the Corinthians, p. 136) and Lüdemann (*Opposition to Paul*, pp. 264-65 n. 88) also fail to find any reference to such a charge in 7.40.

211. Similarly, Lüdemann, *Opposition to Paul*, p. 84.

word'). The most probable (and least speculative) meaning for this expression is the broadly held cultural expectations of what a wise person would be like. This model expects a wise person to be eloquent and educated with a specific and impressive demeanor and appearance. This understanding of the Corinthians' standards has the advantage that it is found among philosophers and rhetoricians and in the broader culture. Moreover it fits excellently with the obvious competitiveness the Corinthians demonstrate in their choosing of a figurehead. This competition for superior placement of one's own wise person is also a common part of higher Hellenistic culture. This is important for the followers because their own status is tied to the status of the wise person with whom they identify themselves.

We have found no evidence that the questions about Paul's authority stem from any specific theological agenda. We have found no evidence for the presence of Gnostic thought or a modified Hellenistic sophia theology or soteriology. Evidence for even some aberrant pneumatology or overrealized eschatology is also completely absent from the remarks which involve challenges to Paul. It is also important to observe that nearly all the evidence about opposition to Paul comes from chs. 1–4 which are almost entirely taken up with this question and the Corinthians' divisiveness. The few references to this opposition that do appear in chs. 5–15 give no indication that the questions about Paul's authority have given rise to the issues dealt with there. So these issues seem to be distinct from the opposition to Paul. While it is an insufficiently supported conjecture, it rings true to experience that the questions about Paul's authority were first raised in, and perhaps were limited to, the debates at Corinth over various issues, especially those referred to in chs. 5–15. The problem appears to have escalated from that point so that the question of authorities and how one evaluates them had become a separate issue. This allows that there may be some relationship between these issues and the challenge to Paul's authority; it simply acknowledges that there is no evidence that they are the result of such a challenge or that they reflect an organized and coherent theology which is tied to both challenging Paul and the issues of chs. 5–15.

First Corinthians, then, yields no evidence of opponents in the usual sense of intruders who reject either Paul's gospel or apostolic status. Not only are these questioners of Paul's authority not outsiders and so far as the text speaks without the support of the outside authorities they claim, but neither do they reject Paul's apostleship or gospel. Our evidence allows only that they challenge the level of authority claimed for Paul by his supporters in Corinth. The questioners' examinations of various leaders do find Paul lacking in comparison with other apostolic figures and so their challenge to Paul may be interpreted as opposition. But this opposition is of a very different sort from what we find in 2 Corinthians and other letters where Paul's apostolic status is rejected and his gospel found to be deficient.

Chapter 3

POWERFUL PNEUMATIC APOSTLES AND PAUL'S
WEAKNESS—2 CORINTHIANS*

Hypotheses about the opponents of 2 Corinthians fall into four basic categories. Following F.C. Baur, a number of interpreters argue that Paul has been attacked by Judaizers.[1] Walter Schmithals rejects the Baur thesis and uses the Corinthian correspondence as the foundation for his view that all the Pauline letters oppose Gnostics.[2] Other interpreters follow Georgi, who argues that the opponents are 'divine men' like those he finds in Hellenistic Judaism.[3] Finally, Käsemann identifies the opponents of 2 Corinthians as Pneumatics whose fundamental con-

---

* This chapter is directly dependent on chs. 11–13 in Sumney, *Identifying Paul's Opponents*. The material here has been shortened significantly and revised to reflect new publications on 2 Corinthians.

1. F.C. Baur, *Paul, the Apostle of Jesus*; D.W. Oostendorp, *Another Jesus: A Gospel of Jewish–Christian Superiority in II Corinthians* (Kampen: Kok, 1967); C.K. Barrett, 'Paul's Opponents in II Corinthians', *NTS* 17 (1971), pp. 233-54; J.J. Gunther, *Paul's Opponents and their Background*; G. Lüdemann, *Paulus, der Heidenapostel*. II. *AntiPaulinismus in frühen Christentum* (FRLANT, 130; Göttingen: Vandenhoeck & Ruprecht, 1983); John M. Court, 'The Controversy with Adversaries of Paul's Apostolate in the Context of his Relations to the Corinthian Congregation (2 Corinthians 12,14–13,13)', in E. Lohse (ed.), *Verteidigung und Begründung des apostolischen Amtes (2 Kor 10–13)* (Rome: Abtei St. Paul vor den Mauern, 1992), pp. 87-106. Similarly, Scott Hafemann, 'Corinthians, Letters to the', in G.F. Hawthorne and R.P. Martin (eds.), *Dictionary of Paul and his Letters* (Downers Grove, IL: IVP, 1993), pp. 177-78.

2. Schmithals, *Gnosticism in Corinth*.

3. Dieter Georgi, *Die Gegner des Paulus im 2. Korintherbrief: Studien zur religiösen Propaganda in der Spätantike* (WMANT, 11; Neukirchen–Vluyn: Neukirchener Verlag, 1964), ET: *The Opponents of Paul in Second Corinthians* (trans. H. Attridge *et al.*; Philadelphia: Fortress Press, 1986).

cern is the legitimacy of Paul's apostleship. According to him, these
opponents both reject the authenticity of Paul's authority and claim to
possess authority from the Jerusalem apostles, but do not impose requirements from the Law.[4]

Identifying these opponents is complicated by questions about the
integrity of 2 Corinthians. Nearly all interpreters recognize that canonical 2 Corinthians contains at least two letters, with chs. 10–13 making
up a well-defined and independent literary unit. Some see chs. 1–9 as a
single letter, while others break them into as many as four different letters plus an interpolation at 6.14–7.1. Chapters 8 and 9, which concern
the collection for Jerusalem, and are sometimes seen as two separate
letters,[5] are of little importance for our study because they contain nothing about opponents. So a decision about the literary relationship between chs. 8–9 and chs. 1–7 does not affect our investigation. Thus, the
significant question for us is whether 2.14–7.4 is a separate letter from
1.1–2.13 plus 7.5-16.

In addition to the clear break at 2.14, many perceive a difference in
tone and content between 2.14–7.4 and 1.1–2.13 plus 7.5-16 which
indicates that the two sections address different stages in the dispute
with the Corinthians. Verses 2.14–7.4 are often seen as a harsh apology
written in contrast to the milder text that precedes it.[6] Besides the
change in tone, 7.5 seems to resume the report of Titus's return begun
in 2.12.[7]

However, the many connections between 2.14–7.4 and 1.1–2.13 plus
7.5-16 suggest that they are parts of a single letter. First, these latter
sections are not all joy and reconciliation. Paul is on the defensive in

---

4.   Ernst Käsemann, 'Die Legitimität des Apostels. Eine Untersuchung zu II
Korinther 10–13', *ZNW* 41 (1942), pp. 33-71.

5.   There are however some significant connections between chs. 7 and 8 and
chs. 8 and 9. See Victor P. Furnish, *II Corinthians* (AB, 32A; Garden City, NY:
Doubleday, 1984), pp. 35-36; Schmithals, *Gnosticism in Corinth*, pp. 96-101; W.H.
Bates, 'The Integrity of II Corinthians', *NTS* 12 (1965–66), pp. 56-69 (59).

6.   See Willi Marxsen, *Introduction to the New Testament: An Approach to its
Problems* (trans. G. Buswell; Philadelphia: Fortress Press, 1968), p. 80; Helmut
Koester, *Introduction to the New Testament. II. History and Literature of Early
Christianity*, pp. 127-28; G. Bornkamm, *Die Vorgeschichte des sogenannten zweiten
Korintherbriefes* (Sitzungsberichte der Heidelberger Akademie der Wissenschaften;
Heidelberg: Carl Winter, 1961), pp. 16-23, esp. 23.

7.   Marxsen, *Introduction*, p. 78.

ch. 1 when he speaks of the change in his travel plans. So the change in tone at 2.14 is not as pronounced as it is sometimes claimed. Furnish acknowledges that 2.14–7.4 is functionally distinct, but asserts that the break is not severe enough to require a separate letter hypothesis.[8] Furthermore, Kümmel contends that the switch from first person singular in 2.13 to first person plural in 7.5 and from πνεῦμα ('spirit') to σάρξ ('flesh') is intolerable for Paul.[9] George Kennedy's rhetorical analysis also supports including 2.14–7.4 as part of the same letter as 1.1–2.13 plus 7.5-16.[10] He identifies 7.2-16 as

> an epilogue which recapitulates Paul's defense (7.2), rounds out the letter by completing the narrative of Paul's experience since arriving in Macedonia (7.5-7), builds on the three topics of the proem, and projects the pathos of Paul's afflictions onto the Corinthians with a considerable amount of pleonasm. The letter is rhetorically complete at this point. All of its topics and headings have been fully explored, and the end has been linked with the beginning.[11]

This analysis links 7.4 with 7.5 and 7.2-16 to various parts of both 2.14–7.4 and the other parts of 2 Corinthians 1–7. In light of these considerations, we will treat chapters chs. 1–7 as a single letter.[12]

Since our method requires letters to be examined individually, we must identify the opponents of chs. 1–7 and those of chs. 10–13 independently. Once we have completed this task, we may search for commonalities to determine whether the two letters address the same opponents.

---

8. Furnish, *II Corinthians*, p. 35.

9. W.G. Kümmel, Introduction to the New Testament (trans. H.C. Kee; Nashville, TN: Abingdon, rev. edn, 1975), p. 291.

10. George A. Kennedy, *New Testament Interpretation through Rhetorical Criticism* (Studies in Religion; Chapel Hill: University of North Carolina Press, 1984), pp. 88-89. He thinks that 6.14–7.1 is an interpolation (Kennedy, *New Testament Interpretation*, p. 91).

11. Kennedy, *New Testament Interpretation*, p. 91.

12. It is not necesary for us to determine which letter was written first to procede with our study. However, it seems more likely that chs. 1–7 were written before chs. 10–13. See the arguments of F.F. Bruce, *1 and 2 Corinthians* (NCB; London: Oliphants, 1971), p. 168 and Furnish, *II Corinthians*, pp. 37-38. So also Ralph P. Martin, *2 Corinthians* (WBC; Waco, TX: Word Books, 1986), pp. xlv-xlvi.

THE LETTER OF CHAPTERS 1–7

Most of chs. 1–9 is apologetic.[13] Even those with different views on the opponents agree with Käsemann that the point of the letter is to defend Paul's apostleship.

Explicit Statements

2.17

In this letter's first explicit statement about other preachers, Paul accuses them of being hucksters. Verses 2.14–3.6[14] contain some polemical aspects,[15] but their purpose is broadly a defense of Paul's ministry,[16] as

---

13. So also Margaret E. Thrall, 'Salvation Proclaimed: Part 5. 2 Corinthians 5^{18-21}: Reconciliation with God', *ExpT* 93 (1981–82), p. 227; John Howard Schütz, *Paul and the Anatomy of Apostolic Authority* (SNTSMS, 26; Cambridge: Cambridge University Press, 1975), p. 165; Hans Windisch, *Der zweite Korintherbrief* (Göttingen: Vandenhoeck & Ruprecht, 1924), p. 95.

14. Furnish, *II Corinthians*, pp. 173, 185-86; Martin, *2 Corinthians*, p. 45. Windisch isolates vv. 14-16a as a separate section and then identifies 2.16b–3.6 as a section (*Der zweite Korintherbrief*, p. 95). A. Plummer separates 3.1-3 as the introduction to 3.4–6.10 (*A Critical and Exegetical Commentary on the Second Epistle of St. Paul to the Corinthians* [ICC; Edinburgh: T. & T. Clark, 1915], p. 75). However, James I. McDonald divides the text more satisfactorily. He holds that 2.14–3.3 is the introduction to 2.14–7.1 ('Paul and the Preaching Ministry: A reconsideration of 2 Cor. 2.14-17 in its context', *JSNT* 17 [1983], pp. 35-50 [45]). Furnish also identifies 2.14–3.6 as an introductory section (*II Corinthians*, p. 191).

15. Georgi asserts that 2.16 begins a massive polemic (*Die Gegner*, p. 248). Schmithals considers 2.17–3.3 to be polemical (*Gnosticism in Corinth*, p. 185). Scott Hafemann also sees 2.14–3.6 as polemical (*Suffering and Ministry in the Spirit: Paul's Defense of his Ministry in II Corinthians 2.14–3.3* [Grand Rapids: Eerdmans, 1990], p. 180).

16. Windisch, *Der zweite Korintherbrief*, p. 112. R. Bultmann thinks that 2.14-17 has opponents in view (*The Second Letter to the Corinthians* [trans. Roy A. Harrisville; Minneapolis: Augsburg, 1985], p. 70). Martin asserts that Paul is offering a rationale for his ministry in the larger section of 2.7–4.6 (*2 Corinthians*, p. 46). However, as Furnish reads 2.14–3.6, Paul does not think that the problem is serious enough to warrant sustained polemic or 'full-scale defense' (*II Corinthians*, p. 191). In a similar vein, Barrett notes that this passage is not one of 'passionate invective, but is one where the reference to other preachers arises incidentally' (C.K. Barrett, *A Commentary on the Second Epistle to the Corinthians* [*2 Corinthians*] [HNTC; New York: Harper & Row, 1973], p. 103).

his use of rhetorical questions (3.1 and perhaps 2.16c) and comments on competence for ministry (3.5-6) demonstrate.[17] Within this apologetic section, 2.17 is polemical.[18]

Verse 17 shows that these preachers accept pay for their preaching, but they probably do not see themselves as 'hucksters' or as dishonest —this is Paul's polemical evaluation. Verse 16c suggests that the opponents link accepting pay and apostolic legitimation.[19] While 2.17 does not explicitly state that the opponents make complaints against Paul, the repetition of ἀλλ' ὡς ('but as') which emphasizes the distinction Paul makes between himself and these preachers, may point to some criticism of Paul.[20]

3.1b

Still within the apologetic section 2.14–3.6, 3.1 shows that the opponents have come to Corinth with letters of recommendation[21] which they use as evidence of apostolic status. Some interpreters have argued that such letters could only come from Jerusalem because no other church exercised enough authority to commend ministers to another church.[22] But there is no indication in this passage that the letters were

17. Martin contends that Paul's concern in 2.14–3.6 is 'to demonstrate (as far as possible) the validity of his apostolic ministry in a context where it is under suspicion' and so sees the section to be apologetic (*2 Corinthians*, p. 55). Windisch asserts that we have an apologetic motif in 2.16b–3.6 (*Der zweite Korintherbrief*, pp. 95, 99, 112).

18. Plummer, *Commentary*, p. 73. Furnish also lists this as the first explicit comment about opponents (*II Corinthians*, p. 50). So also S. Davies, 'Remarks on the Second Epistle to the Corinthians 4:3, 4', *BSac* 25 (1968), pp. 23-30 (28); Earl Richard, 'Polemics, Old Testament, and Theology: A Study of II Cor. III,1–IV,6', *RB* 88 (1981), pp. 340-67 (344). Barrett lists this verse as a 'historical notice' (*2 Corinthians*, p. 15).

19. Schütz, following Georgi (*Die Gegner*, pp. 234-37), argues that the opponents see pay as 'a positive affirmation of their pneumatic endowment' and Paul's refusal of pay as an admission of his lack of that endowment (*Paul and the Anatomy of Apostolic Authority*, p. 172).

20. See the discussion of the repetition of ἀλλ' ὡς in Hafemann, *Suffering and Ministry*, p. 165.

21. See William Baird, 'Letters of Recommendation: A Study of II Cor 3:1-3', *JBL* 80 (1961), pp. 166-72 (169).

22. E.g. Käsemann, 'Die Legitimität des Apostels', pp. 45-47; Barrett, *2 Corinthians*, pp. 40-41.

from authorities, much less from Jerusalem.[23] In fact, a decisive argument against the letters being from authorities is that the Corinthians could write as well as receive them.[24] So, we cannot say who wrote these letters, only that they gave these preachers a favorable hearing upon their arrival.

Paul's incredulous question about his need for a letter and his identification of the Corinthians as his letter (vv. 2-3) imply that the opponents demand proof of Paul's apostleship. Even though 3.1-5 is more apologetic than polemical,[25] it shows that the opponents make claims about apostolic status at Corinth.[26]

5.12

A third explicit statement about opponents appears within the section comprising 5.11-19. The recurrence of the matter of the Corinthians' misunderstanding of Paul (raised previously in 1.13-14) signals a return to apology.[27] While defending himself, Paul asserts in 5.12 that he is not commending himself and that the opponents take pride in appearances.[28] This is Paul's evaluation of their conduct or teaching. They do not, of course, claim to do this.

'Boasting' seems to be part of the opponents' means of evaluating ministries. The repetition of forms of καυχάομαι ('to boast') in this verse and the frequency of cognates in this letter suggest that 'the matter of legitimate versus illegitimate boasting was an important part of the dispute between Paul and his Corinthian rivals'.[29] Paul's use of

23. Bultmann, *The Second Letter to the Corinthians*, p. 71.

24. Furnish, *II Corinthians*, p. 193; Schütz, *Paul and the Anatomy of Apostolic Authority*, p. 171 (following R. Bultmann, *Exegetische Probleme des zweiten Korintherbriefes* [SymBU, 9; Uppsala: Wretman, 1947], p. 21).

25. Richard, 'Polemics', p. 344.

26. Furnish, *II Corinthians*, p. 191.

27. So Plummer, *Commentary*, pp. 166-67. Martin classifies 5.11-15 and 5.16-21 as apologetic (*2 Corinthians*, pp. 118-19, 136). Similarly, Hafemann asserts that 5.12 reflects a charge against Paul ('"Self-Commendation" and Apostolic Legitimacy in 2 Corinthians: A Pauline Dialectic?', *NTS* 36 [1990], pp. 66-88 [66]).

28. Furnish asserts that 'judging by externals' means that the opponents boast of spiritual displays (*II Corinthians*, p. 323). But this is not clear from this passage. Linda Belleville ('A Letter of Apologetic Self-Commendation: 2 Cor. 1:8–7:16', *NovT* 31 [1989], pp. 142-63 [154]) notes that 5.12a has 'condemnatory intent'.

29. Furnish, *II Corinthians*, p. 307.

these terms shows that the opponents compare ministries and qualifications for ministry.

Summary of Explicit Statements

The three explicit statements about opponents reveal that they accept pay for their ministerial service and may question Paul's refusal of pay. Furthermore, they arrived in Corinth with letters of recommendation as evidence of their authority or authenticity and probably also demand similar proof (perhaps written) of Paul's apostleship. Finally, Paul and these opponents evaluate apostolic behavior differently. The opponents also believe it is proper to compare ministries and qualifications for ministry. Paul calls this boasting.

Allusions

1.12, 13-14, 17

Statements in 1.12-14 refer explicitly to the situation at Corinth, but not directly to the opponents.[30] In 1.12–2.2 (4)[31] Paul defends his recent actions, saying that he has been misunderstood and hopes that, after this letter, the Corinthians will understand him completely. Thus, the section is apologetic.[32] Paul asserts in 1.12 that he has not behaved in a worldly fashion (ἐν σοφίᾳ σαρκικῇ) toward the Corinthians. In 1.17 he says that he does not make his plans κατὰ σάρκα (according to the flesh). These assertions within the apologetic section 1.12–2.2 enclose

---

30. We will not discuss other explicit statements about the situation at Corinth (6.12; 7.7-23; 13-16) because they are not directly relevant for identifying the opponents. As Barrett comments, all 'historical notices' in 2 Corinthians do not help to unravel Paul's relationship with that community (*2 Corinthians*, p. 15).

31. Plummer continues the section to 2.4 saying that the discussion of the offender and the effect of the tearful letter begins in v. 5 (*Commentary*, p. xx). But Furnish makes a better division. He begins the next section at 2.3 (see *II Corinthians*, pp. 141, 153-68). This is where Paul begins to discuss the painful letter.

32. So Plummer, *Commentary*, p. 23. Those who see these verses as apologetic include G. Lüdemann, *Paulus, der Heidenapostel. I. Studien zur Chronologie* (FRLANT, 123; Göttingen: Vandenhoeck & Ruprecht, 1980), p. 94; Martin, *2 Corinthians*, pp. 29, 31; Windisch, *Der zweite Korintherbrief*, pp. 52, 59; Jean Héring, *The Second Epistle of Saint Paul to the Corinthians* (trans. A.W. Heathcote and P.J. Allcock; London: Epworth Press, 1967), p. 9 and Bultmann, *The Second Letter to the Corinthians*, p. 32.

the discussion of the Corinthians' misunderstanding of Paul. We identify these comments as allusions[33] because they relate to evaluating
ministers. Additionally, 1.12 mentions 'boasting'.

Verses 15-22 show that the Corinthians' misunderstanding of Paul
involves the change in his travel plans. Windisch thinks that in 1.12-14
Paul is answering the charges that he lives κατὰ σάρκα ('according to
the flesh') and that his letters show self-interest.[34] Plummer contends that
the strong appeals of 1.18 (as well as those in 3.1; 4.2 and 5.11) 'are
evoked by his opponents' charges of untrustworthiness and timidity'.[35]
However, the evidence so far does not support finding charges of self-
interest or timidity, but some in Corinth are questioning Paul's reliability. Furnish more accurately speaks of 'criticisms' in connection with
1.17 to refer to the Corinthians' remarks which prompt this section.[36]
These verses do not reveal whether their misunderstanding is malicious
(at least on the part of some instigators) or innocent.[37] However, the
questions about Paul's reliability may have lead the opponents to accuse
Paul of acting in an unspiritual manner.

2.16b

Within the apologetic section 2.14–3.6 Paul asks rhetorically in 2.16b,[38]
'Who is sufficient?' This question not only relates to evaluating ministries, it also immediately precedes the explicit statement of 2.17
which offers a preliminary response[39] and thus connects the matters of
pay and sufficiency. So we may securely identify v. 16b as an allusion.

The close proximity of the issue of pay to the initial reference to
sufficency suggests that Paul and his opponents are debating the relationship between them, with the opponents connecting legitimate apostleship and accepting pay.

33. Furnish states that Paul is also dismissing criticism in 1.17 (*II Corinthians*,
p. 145).

34. Windisch, *Der zweite Korintherbrief*, pp. 52-53. Bultmann agrees that Paul
is answering charges in 1.15–2.4 and subtitles the section, 'The reproach of the
unreliability of his promises' (*The Second Letter to the Corinthians*, p. 37).

35. Plummer, *Commentary*, p. 42.

36. Furnish, *II Corinthians*, p. 145.

37. Martin, *2 Corinthians*, p. 31.

38. Martin identifies this as a rhetorical question (*2 Corinthians*, p. 49).

39. Cf. Hafemann, *Suffering and Ministry*, p. 178.

Paul's extended discussion of his ministry indicates that he asks this rhetorical question because his sufficiency is being questioned.[40] Since the opponents assert[41] their own authority, we hear a polemical note as well. Thus, 2.16b is both polemical and apologetic; Paul is rejecting the opponents' claims and answering questions about his qualifications.

3.1a
In 3.1a Paul asks the Corinthians if they think he is again commending himself to them. Since the issue of self-commendation arose in explicit statements, and is related to the issue of proof of apostleship, we may identify 3.1a as an allusion.

Most commentators identify 3.1a as a response to the charge that Paul engages in improper self-commendation.[42] But while the opponents are calling on Paul to show proof of his apostleship, it is not clear that they accuse him of self-commendation, as he accuses them of boasting.[43] Interpreters must rely on mirror exegesis to argue that the opponents charge Paul with self-commendation. Verse 12 lends some credence to this view, but it is more likely that Paul wants to distance himself from their tactics. They commend themselves, that is, they legitimate their apostleship by comparing their ministries with others; Paul rejects this as a proper way to manifest or prove his apostleship. When the subject of commendation arises in 3.1, 5.12, 4.2 and 6.4, Paul contrasts himself

---

40. Bultmann, *The Second Letter to the Corinthians*, p. 69. He cites 3.1-2 and 3.5-6 as supporting evidence for this view.

41. Martin, *2 Corinthians*, p. 49. Martin adds that the term ἱκανότης was obviously being used at Corinth.

42. So Plummer, who cites 4.5; 5.12 and 6.4 as supporting evidence (*Commentary*, p. 77); Bultmann, who cites 4.2 and 5.12 as other evidence (*The Second Letter to the Corinthians*, p. 70); Philip E. Hughes (*Paul's Second Epistle to the Corinthians* [NICNT; Grand Rapids: Eerdmans, 1962], p. 85); Barrett (*2 Corinthians*, pp. 105-106); Hafemann, *Suffering and Ministry*, p. 182; and Furnish, who cites 4.2; 5.12; and 6.4 as further evidence (*II Corinthians*, p. 192). Martin does not explicitly reject this view, but he does assert that 3.1-3 serves to justify 2.16-17. Martin does not mention charges against Paul in connection with this verse (*2 Corinthians*, p. 50).

43. If they are charging Paul with improper self-commendation, the comments of Goudge describe Paul's problem well. He says: 'Self-defense is almost impossible without self-commendation. St. Paul's opponents at Corinth made the former necessary, and then blamed him for the latter' (quoted by Barrett, *2 Corinthians*, p. 106).

with the opponents and separates himself from their methods. So this is probably a polemical rather than an apologetic statement. Whichever it is, the opponents' behavior makes self-commendation an issue.

3.5-6a

Paul's remarks on competence in 3.5-6a allude to the discussion of sufficiency and proof of apostleship. Here Paul indirectly answers the question, 'Who is sufficient?'[44] His answer is, only those whom God makes sufficient. Even within an apologetic section, v. 5 could be rejecting the opponents' claims[45] to competence. But, Paul may be responding to charges that he does not offer proof of his apostleship. Verse 5 is broad enough to encompass a polemical and an apologetic aspect, but the focus narrows to apology in v. 6. So Paul is probably responding to complaints that he does not present evidence for apostleship.[46] He says simply that his sufficiency is secured by God (vv. 4-6) and evidenced by the Corinthian Christians themselves (vv. 2-3), so he does not need confirmation through letters.

4.2-3

Another allusion in an apologetic section (4.1-6) appears in 4.2-3. Paul claims in v. 2b that he sets forth the truth plainly. His contention in 4.3 that his gospel is only veiled to unbelievers links this passage with Paul's concern to be understood fully.[47] Morna Hooker sees the strong language of v. 2 as a sign that Paul is defending himself,[48] but Schütz and Martin see the verse as polemical. According to them, Paul suggests that the opponents' recommendation depends on adulterating God's word.[49] The reference to commendation may again point to elements of

44. So Baird, 'Letters of Recommendation', p. 72. Richard ('Polemics', pp. 349-50) and Thomas A. Provence ('"Who is Sufficient for These Things?" An Exegesis of 2 Corinthians ii15–iii18', *NovT* 24 [1982], pp. 54-81 [61]) say that 3.4-6 is directly connected with 2.15-16; See also Hafemann, *Suffering and Ministry*, p. 98.

45. Richard, 'Polemics', p. 350.

46. The discussion of letters of recommendation in 3.1-3 confirms the apologetic function of these verses.

47. Martin asserts that Paul is responding to a charge in v. 3 (*2 Corinthians*, p. 78).

48. Hooker, 'Beyond the Things that Are Written?', p. 302.

49. Schütz, *Paul and the Anatomy of Apostolic Authority*, p. 172; Martin, *2 Corinthians*, p. 77.

both polemic and apology.[50] While Paul would not be averse to accusing the opponents of distorting the word of God, 4.2-3 is probably apologetic[51] because 4.1-6 resumes the points discussed in 3.1-6, an apologetic section.

There is some talk in Corinth that Paul's message has not been clear enough. This has led some to question his apostleship or perhaps his integrity. Paul's statement in v. 2 that he has renounced secret and shameful ways may point to the issue being raised in the latter way.

4.7-9

Within 4.7–5.10, the main point of the sub-section 4.7-15[52] is that ministers of the gospel are weak to demonstrate that the power of the gospel comes from God.[53] The section's orientation shows that the opponents question Paul's apostleship because of his inglorious life. Thus the sub-section is apologetic.[54]

Verses 7-9 allude to the discussion of the sufficiency of apostles,[55] as Paul asserts that a glorious life is not part of sufficiency for apostleship.[56] This assertion may counter the opponents' contention that Paul's weakness in body and speech discredits his authority.[57] Even if it is not

50. Martin identifies v. 2 as polemic and v. 3 as apology (*2 Corinthians*, pp. 77-78). Barrett suggests that v. 2 has two implications: (1) Paul has been accused of being deceptive; and (2) there are preachers who falsify the gospel (*2 Corinthians*, p. 128). So Barrett understands v. 2 as both apologetic and polemical. On the basis of v. 3 Barrett suggests that the opponents charge Paul with preaching a veiled gospel.

51. Furnish suggests that 4.2 may be either apologetic or polemical (*II Corinthians*, p. 246). He seems to favor apology. See also the comments of Hafemann (*Suffering and Ministry*, pp. 106-125) on the term 'huckster'.

52. Plummer (*Commentary*, xxi, p. 125) and Furnish (*II Corinthians*, pp. 252-53, 277-78) outline the text in this way.

53. Plummer, *Commentary*, p. 125; Barrett, *II Corinthians*, pp. 137-38.

54. Furnish (*2 Corinthians*, p. 277) suggests that in the whole of 4.7–5.10 Paul is concerned 'to counteract misunderstandings and complaints about his own apostolic service'. We must agree with Furnish that Windisch (*Der zweite Korintherbrief*, p. 141) is incorrect when he asserts that this section has no apologetic intent.

55. Furnish identifies 4.8-9 as an allusion (*II Corinthians*, p. 52).

56. Bultmann suggests that the vessel figure emphasizes the 'contradiction between status and appearance' seen in Paul's ministry (*The Second Letter to the Corinthians*, p. 112). Plummer asserts that Paul is affirming in 4.7 that preachers should not preach themselves (*Commentary*, pp. 125-26).

57. So Hughes, *Paul's Second Epistle to the Corinthians*, p. 135.

responding to such a charge, Paul is rejecting the idea that a powerful presence is evidence that God is with a person.

5.11

At the beginning of the apologetic section 5.11-19, Paul returns to the theme of misunderstanding. Since he has dealt with misunderstanding and truthful behavior in conjunction with each other before (1.12-14; 4.2-3), v. 11a is probably a response to some charge of improper behavior.[58] So the opponents question Paul's integrity, perhaps in the context of their evaluation and comparison of ministers.[59] Paul responds by saying that he conducts his ministry in 'the fear of the Lord'. Therefore[60] the Corinthians can trust him.

5.16[61]

Paul says in 5.16 that he knows no one, not even Christ, κατὰ σάρκα (according to the flesh). This passage, especially the meaning of κατὰ

58. Similarly, Bultmann, *The Second Letter to the Corinthians*, pp. 147-48; Barrett, *2 Corinthians*, p. 163. Barrett adds that this is not necessarily the case (*2 Corinthians*, p. 164). See Furnish's discussion of 'persuade' (*II Corinthians*, pp. 322-23).

59. See Martin, *2 Corinthians*, p. 122; Furnish, *II Corinthians*, pp. 322-23.

60. Hughes notes that the 'Therefore' of v. 11a ties the verse to the judgment referred to in v. 10 (*Paul's Second Epistle to the Corinthians*, p. 186).

61. Schmithals contends that 5.16 is a Gnostic gloss (*Gnosticism in Corinth*, pp. 302-18). But nearly all interpreters accept 5.16 as Pauline and think it is in its original position. Many see vv. 16 and 17 as parallel. E.g. E.B. Allo, *St. Paul, seconde épître aux Corinthiens* (EBib; Paris: Librarie Lecoffre, 1956), pp. 167-68. Cf. John W. Fraser, 'Paul's Knowledge of Jesus: II Cor. 5:16 Once More', *NTS* 17 (1971), pp. 293-313 (297); Frank C. Porter, 'Does Paul Claim to Have Known the Historical Jesus?', *JBL* 47 (1928), pp. 257-75 (260); Floyd V. Filson, '2 Corinthians', *IB* X, p. 338. Many also see v. 16 as the conclusion from 5.14-15. E.g. Dikran Y. Hadidian, 'A Case Study: 2 Corinthians 5:16', in *idem* (ed.), *From Faith to Faith* (PTMS, 31; Pittsburgh: Pickwick Press, 1979), p. 107; Hughes, *Paul's Second Epistle to the Corinthians*, p. 201; Charles B. Cousar, 'II Cor. 5:17-21', *Int* 35 (1981), pp. 180-83 (181); J. Louis Martyn, 'Epistemology at the Turn of the Ages: 2 Corinthians 5:16', in W.R. Farmer, C.F.D. Moule and R.R. Niebuhr (eds.), *Christian History and Interpretation* (Cambridge: Cambridge University Press, 1967), pp. 269-88 (274). Some who feel the same kind of tension that moves Schmithals to declare the verse a gloss view the passage as a parenthesis. So Plummer (*Commentary*, p. 175) and J. Cambier ('Connaissance charnelle et spirituelle de Christ dans 2. Cor 5.16', A. Descamps (ed.), *Littérature et théologie pauliniennes* [RechBib, 5; Paris: Desclee de Brouwer, 1960], pp. 72-92 [76]).

σάρκα, has been quite important for some who identify the opponents as Judaizers[62] and Divine Men.[63]

To understand κατὰ σάρκα correctly, we must determine how it functions in the sentence, that is, whether it is adverbial or adjectival. The phrase appears twice in v. 16, once in v. 16a and again in v. 16b. Since these parts of v. 16 are parallel, Paul probably uses the phrase in the same way in both parts.[64] The structure of v. 16a points to an adverbial usage.[65] Thus in v. 16b, κατὰ σάρκα modifies 'we know' (ἐγνώκαμεν).[66] So 5.16 is not a statement about Christology,[67] but about the proper way to perceive others. Paul wants the Corinthians to evaluate others, all others, in the light of the dawning of the eschatological era, as the opening words of v. 16 ('From now on') demonstrate.[68] Since the issue is how to judge others, the question of the proper evaluation of ministers has come up again. Therefore, 5.16 is an allusion.[69]

62. Baur, 'Christuspartei', pp. 89-98; Baur, *Paul, an Apostle of Jesus*, pp. 271-72; Oostendorp, *Another Jesus*, pp. 52-58.

63. Georgi, *Die Gegner*, pp. 254-57, 290-92.

64. Schmithals grants that 16a and 16b are 'in perfect parallelism', but denies that the phrase should go with the same part of speech in the parallel parts of the verse (*Gnosticism in Corinth*, pp. 307-308). He contends that when Paul uses κατὰ σάρκα adverbially it always has an 'ethical sense', meaning 'in a sinful way' (*Gnosticism in Corinth*, p. 309). Rejecting this meaning here, Schmithals concludes that the phrase is adjectival and so a reference to the historical Jesus. So the verse must be non-Pauline because Paul thinks the historical Jesus is important for salvation-history (*Gnosticism in Corinth*, pp. 309-310).

65. J.H. Bernard, *Second Epistle to the Corinthians* (The Expositor's Greek Testament; Grand Rapids: Eerdmans, repr. edn, 1974 [1847–1910], pp. 566-71 [571]. See further the fairly conclusive arguments of Paul Schubert ('New Testament Study and Theology', *Religion in Life* 14 [1945], p. 566) and Furnish (*II Corinthians*, p. 312).

66. The adverbial use of this phrase in Paul always has a negative connotation. So Schmithals, *Gnosticism in Corinth*, p. 309; Eduard Schweizer, 'σάρξ', TDNT VII,, pp. 119-51 (127). Schweizer interprets κατὰ σάρκα here to mean, to know 'by human standards' ('σάρξ', p. 131).

67. Schubert, 'New Testament Study', p. 566. See Furnish, *II Corinthians*, pp. 312, 330. Cf. Hadidian, 'Case Study', p. 119.

68. On the relationship between v. 16 and Paul's discussion of eschatology in vv. 14-15, see Plummer, *Commentary*, p. 176; Bultmann, *The Second Letter to the Corinthians*, p. 154; Furnish, *II Corinthians*, pp. 321, 329; Martin, *2 Corinthians*, pp. 135-36, 151.

69. Baur, 'Christuspartei', pp. 89-98; Baur, *Paul, the Apostle of Jesus*, pp. 271-72; Oostendorp, *Another Jesus*, pp. 52-58; Georgi, *Die Gegner*, pp. 254-57, 290-92;

The point of v. 16 is that Christians cannot judge others 'on the basis of externals, as his rivals do'.[70] Perceiving things κατὰ σάρκα is the equivalent of boasting in appearances;[71] perceiving Christ κατὰ σάρκα is the extreme case.[72]

Since Paul gives v. 16b as an example, we learn little about the opponents except that he thinks their standards are inappropriate for Christians.[73] Some who acknowledge that κατὰ σάρκα is adverbial and that the main issue concerns viewing things in an eschatological perspective still maintain that Paul is discussing the opponents' Christology here.[74] But there is no discussion of Christology in this context, or the rest of the letter.[75] Furthermore, this view misses the point of the example. The point is, as Bultmann writes, that 'not even Christ may be regarded as he can be met with in the world'.[76] The entire verse is about the correct way to perceive others.[77]

Paul engages in this discussion because he wants the Corinthians to judge his apostleship by standards other than those offered by his opponents. So this passage confirms that Paul and his rivals have different standards for evaluating apostles.

Plummer, *Commentary*, p. 178; Barrett, *2 Corinthians*, p. 170; Hughes, *Paul's Second Epistle to the Corinthians*, pp. 200-201; Furnish, *II Corinthians*, p. 330.

70. Furnish, *2 Corinthians*, p. 329.

71. Schweizer, 'σαρξ', p. 127; Georgi, *Die Gegner*, p. 256.

72. Bultmann, *The Second Letter to the Corinthians* 153; Georgi, *Die Gegner*, pp. 255-56. Furnish comments that 16b functions as a support for 16a (*II Corinthians*, p. 330). Barrett asserts that 16b is almost parenthetical and is a special case of 16a, but then also identifies 16b as polemical (*2 Corinthians*, pp. 170-71).

73. Furnish, *II Corinthians*, p. 330.

74. E.g. Georgi, *Die Gegner*, pp. 254, 290-92; Martin, *2 Corinthians*, p. 151.

75. Bultmann, *The Second Letter to the Corinthians*, p. 156.

76. Bultmann, *The Second Letter to the Corinthians*, p. 156.

77. Discussions of the Christology of this passage have a long history which centers on Paul's view of the historical Jesus. See John W. Fraser, 'Paul's Knowledge of Jesus', pp. 293-97, for a survey of the ways this verse has been used to speak of Paul's view of the historical Jesus. Also see his survey of how 'Christ according to the flesh' has been interpreted (Fraser, 'Paul's Knowledge of Jesus', pp. 310-13). This verse is a favorite passage for many to use when identifying opponents because it is vague enough to be taken many ways. See Furnish, *II Corinthians*, pp. 330-31 for a discussion of Georgi's position on this passage.

6.3-4

Another allusion appears in 6.3-4. The whole of 5.20–6.10 is an apology[78] for Paul's ministry that supports his appeal[79] for the Corinthians to be reconciled to him. Allusions to the issues of self-commendation and proper apostolic behavior surface as 6.3-4 introduces the *peristasis* catalog of vv. 4b-10 which Paul gives as evidence of his apostleship.[80] Some see Paul's claim in v. 3 that his behavior has not discredited his ministry as a response to charges that he is unreliable or weak.[81] Others contend that he is answering a reproach of self-commendation in v. 4a.[82] But Paul is more likely resorting to commendation of his ministry (under protest) in the face of charges that he presents no evidence of his apostleship. He now commends himself, but in a manner, he says, that befits servants of God.[83] With this remark, he is attacking the way the opponents commend themselves rather than defending himself against a charge of excessive self-commendation.

The stumbling-block that Paul does not place in anyone's way (v. 3) is improper self-commendation. When he must finally give proof of his apostleship, his evidence—his self-commendation—is not what the opponents or the Corinthians expect. Paul's proof of apostleship is his weakness and he presents the *peristasis* catalog as evidence of this weakness.[84] The particulars of the *peristasis* catalog, however, cannot

---

78. Plummer, *Commentary*, p. 189. Bultmann states that 6.3-10 is written in 'apologetic-polemical fashion' (*The Second Letter to the Corinthians*, p. 163). Martin also suggests that 6.3-10 is an apologetic section (*2 Corinthians*, p. 160). Furnish allows that the section has an 'apologetic hint' (*II Corinthians*, p. 186). Hafemann (*Suffering and Ministry*, pp. 72-73) comments that 6.1-10 is 'an appropriate capstone for Paul's self-defense as an apostle'.

79. Furnish thinks 5.20 begins a major section devoted to appeals (*II Corinthians*, p. 186).

80. Furnish, *II Corinthians*, p. 353; Martin, *2 Corinthians*, p. 171.

81. Martin (*2 Corinthians*, p. 171) thinks they charge that Paul has brought disrepute on himself and his ministry, possibly because of his change in travel plans and certainly because of his frailty and proneness to suffering.

82. Plummer, *Commentary*, p. 192; Bultmann, *The Second Letter to the Corinthians*, p. 170.

83. See Hughes, *Paul's Second Epistle to the Corinthians*, p. 222; Martin, *2 Corinthians*, p. 171.

84. See Bultmann, *The Second Letter to the Corinthians*, p. 169; Gerhardt Friedrich, *Amt und Lebensführung: Eine Auslegung 2 Kor, 6,1-10* (Biblische Studien, 39; Neukirchen–Vluyn: Neukirchener Verlag, 1963), p. 24.

serve as evidence about the opponents because of its stylized form.[85]

We learn from 6.3-4a, then, that the opponents may contend that Paul's life discredits his ministry. The immediate context points to his weakness as the purported cause of this disrepute. Paul is being forced to commend himself in the face of charges that he offers no proof of his apostleship. But he commends himself in a qualified manner: 'in every way, as a servant of God should'.[86] So Paul and his rivals disagree about what commends apostles. Paul contrasts his weakness with their views and their practice of self-commendation.

4.5

Within the apologetic section 4.1-6 Paul says in 4.5 that he does not preach himself. This statement alludes to the issues of self-commendation, the proper kind of commendation, and the evaluation of ministers. Unfortunately, we must use mirror exegesis to gain information about the opponents from it.

Several meanings are possible for this verse when we use the mirror technique. These include: (1) the opponents claim that Paul preaches himself;[87] (2) Paul thinks that the opponents' conduct shows that they preach themselves; and (3) the opponents purposefully emphasize their own ministry in their preaching.[88] We cannot tell what Paul is responding to here. Still, this verse reinforces the idea that the opponents emphasize self-commendation and the necessity of giving proof of apostleship.

7.2

Paul's vehement claim in 7.2 that he has acted properly toward the Corinthians appears within a section comprising 6.11–7.3. In this section Paul asserts that the Corinthians are the cause of the problems in

---

85. See the study of Michael L. Barré, 'Paul as "Eschatological Person"': A New Look at 2 Cor. 11:29', *CBQ* 37 (1975), pp. 523-26. See especially the vocabulary chart on his p. 526.

86. This is the translation of Furnish, *II Corinthians*, p. 338.

87. So Plummer, *Commentary*, p. 79; Bultmann, *The Second Letter to the Corinthians*, pp. 106-107; Barrett, *2 Corinthians*, p. 133; Hughes, *Paul's Second Epistle to the Corinthians*, p. 130.

88. Furnish acknowledges that the verse may be either apologetic or polemical (*II Corinthians*, p. 249).

his relationship with them.[89] His tone is pastoral,[90] but he is still defending himself. The immediate purpose of this apology is to support the appeal that the Corinthians renew their love for him (7.2a).

Most interpreters identify 7.2 as a response to charges, or at least insinuations.[91] Even if that is correct, we cannot discern what those charges are,[92] only that Paul is still afraid of being misunderstood. This fear is his impetus for emphasizing that he had not wronged, corrupted or exploited the Corinthians. Though it is tempting to link the charge of exploitation and the Jerusalem collection (see 12.16-18),[93] there is no evidence for this connection in chs. 1–7.

Since Paul says in 7.3 that he is not accusing anyone of wrongful behavior, his comments are apologetic.[94] His opponents have helped the Corinthians misunderstand him, but that is not the focus here. Paul only entreats his church to trust and accept him.

Summary of Allusions

Allusions indicate that these opponents exacerbate the strained relations between Paul and the Corinthians, using the change in his travel plans to question his reliability. This allows the opponents to question his integrity and accuse him of being unspiritual. Thus, they also question his apostleship.

The opponents set out and, of course, meet their own criteria for apostleship as they engage in self-commendation (boasting) to prove their apostolic status. They seem to present self-commendation itself as evidence of their legitimacy. They demand proof of apostleship from Paul and question his legitimacy because he has not given sufficient evidence. They further challenge his apostleship because of his inglorious life and assert that he discredits the ministry by being weak. So his improper behavior includes both his lack of integrity (evidenced by his change in travel plans) and his manner of life. Perhaps in connection

89. Martin, *2 Corinthians*, p. 216.
90. Furnish, *II Corinthians*, p. 368.
91. Plummer, *Commentary*, p. 213; Bultmann, *The Second Letter to the Corinthians*, p. 203; Hughes, *Paul's Second Epistle to the Corinthians*, p. 260; Barrett, *2 Corinthians*, p. 203; Furnish, *II Corinthians*, p. 369; Martin, *2 Corinthians*, p. 217.
92. Plummer, *Commentary*, p. 213.
93. Among those who make this connection are: Bultmann (*The Second Letter to the Corinthians*, p. 178), Furnish (*II Corinthians*, p. 369), and Martin (*2 Corinthians*, p. 217).
94. Furnish, *II Corinthians*, p. 369.

with questions about his integrity, they also claim that Paul's message is not clear.

So the opponents challenge Paul's apostleship because they understand apostolic existence differently. They believe apostles' lives should be marked by strength and the ability to rise above human weakness. For them, suffering and an unimpressive life show a lack of spirituality and so demonstrate the illegitimacy of Paul's apostleship. They charge that Paul's change of travel plans demonstrates his weakness and thus disqualifies him from being an apostle. They also believe apostles should emphasize their powerful way of life as part of their message.

Appended Note

I have not discussed 3.7-18, one of the most controversial passages in 2 Corinthians 1–7. Purported allusions to opponents in this section are decisive for many who identify the opponents as Judaizers[95] or divine men.[96]

Before drawing information about the opponents from 3.7-18, we must determine the nature of the section. Baur, Oostendorp, Georgi and Friedrich identify it as polemical.[97] But the sections on each side of it (i.e. 2.14–3.6 and 4.1-6) are apologetic. So Paul composes 3.7-18 in the context of a defense of his ministry. Some interpreters maintain that Paul defends his ministry in 3.7-18 by comparing the two *covenants*.[98] If so, this is an unexpected turn. Given that discussions of Paul's apostleship frame 3.7-18, we would expect the topic to be Paul's ministry rather than covenants. The διὰ τοῦτο ('for this reason') of 4.1,[99]

95. E.g. Baur, *Paul, the Apostle of Jesus*, pp. 259-60; Baur, 'Christuspartei', pp. 77-79; Oostendorp, *Another Jesus*, pp. 31-47.

96. E.g. Georgi, *Die Gegner*, pp. 258-82, and Friedrich, 'Die Gegner', pp. 184, 202-205.

97. Plummer, who identifies the opponents as Judaizers, also sees this as a polemical section (*Commentary*, p. 84).

98. E.g. Edmund Hill, 'The Construction of Three Passages of St. Paul', *CBQ* 23 (1961), pp. 296-301 (300-301); Bernardin Schneider, 'The Meaning of St. Paul's Antithesis "The Letter and the Spirit"', *CBQ* 15 (1953), pp. 163-207 (193-96). E. Richard seems to hold this view ('Polemics', p. 353). See also Heikki Räisänen, *Jesus, Paul, and Torah* (trans. D.E. Orton; JSNTSup, 43; Sheffield: JSOT Press, 1992), p. 247.

99. C.J.A. Hickling, 'The Sequence of Thought in 2 Corinthians, Chapter Three',

and a careful reading of vv. 7-11 show that the main topic is in fact Paul's ministry.[100]

The comparison of the ministries of the two covenants rises out of the contrast Paul makes in 3.3 and builds on in 3.6.[101] Fitzmyer observes that ch. 3 moves along by 'catchword bonding'.[102] Paul begins with letters of recommendation (3.1) and moves to letters on the heart (3.2).[103] This reminds him of Jeremiah 31 and the contrast between the law on tablets of stone and on the hearts of the people (3.3).[104] There is no apparent polemical motive to this contrast.[105] This same contrast leads Paul to speak of himself as a minister of the 'new covenant' (3.6). From this point he expounds the significance of being a minister of this new covenant[106] by comparing his ministry with the ministry of Moses (vv. 7-18).

NTS 21 (1975), pp. 380-94 (395); Jan Lambrecht, 'Structure and Line of Thought in 2 Cor 2,14–4,6', *Bib* 64 (1983), pp. 344-80 (350).

100. So Bultmann, *The Second Letter to the Corinthians*, p. 79; Provence, '"Who is Sufficient for These Things?"', p. 68; Schmithals, *Gnosticism in Corinth*, p. 318; Morna Hooker, 'Beyond the Things that are Written? St. Paul's Use of Scripture', NTS 27 (1981), pp. 295-309 (296-97); Hickling, 'Sequence of Thought', pp. 384-87; Lambrecht, 'Structure and Line of Thought', pp. 346, 364, 378; Furnish, *II Corinthians*, pp. 226, 243. Héring, *The Second Epistle of Saint Paul to the Corinthians*, p. 22; Hafemann, *Suffering and Ministry*, p. 232.

101. Windisch identifies 3.7-18 as a midrash composed at an earlier time and then inserted into 2 Corinthians (*Der zweite Korintherbrief*, pp. 95, 112). Joseph A. Fitzmyer agrees that the passage was composed before its insertion into 2 Corinthians ('Glory Reflected on the Face of Christ [2 Cor 3:7–4:6] and a Palestinian Jewish Motif', *TS* 42 [1981], pp. 630-44 [632]).

102. Fitzmyer, 'Glory Reflected on the Face of Christ', p. 635.

103. Räisänen (*Jesus, Paul, and Torah*, p. 247) acknowledges that Paul is not discussing the Law at this point.

104. See Räisänen, *Jesus, Paul, and Torah*, pp. 634-36; Furnish, *II Corinthians*, p. 197 Héring, *The Second Epistle of Saint Paul to the Corinthians*, pp. 21-22. Hafemann (*Suffering and Ministry*, pp. 197-98) is not convinced that this motif echoes any particular passage. Rather, the contrast was so widespread in the first century that it is not possible to isolate a specific source. Still, he notes that Paul's use of this motif is the transition to imagery from the Hebrew Bible.

105. Hickling, 'Sequence of Thought', p. 386.

106. Hickling, 'Sequence of Thought', p. 384; Schmithals, *Gnosticism in Corinth*, p. 287; Furnish, *II Corinthians*, pp. 226, 243. See also Hafemann, *Suffering and Ministry*, p. 222.

The whole of 3.7-18 almost seems to be an excursus on 3.6.[107] Perhaps this is saying too much, but it is clearly an explication of the meaning of being a *minister* of the new covenant. Therefore it is best to identify this passage as didactic. It springs from comments of Paul rather than accusations or teachings of opponents. Paul is explaining the significance of the claim he makes for himself in 3.6. This didactic section serves Paul's apology for his apostolic office, but it is not directly apologetic and it is certainly not polemical.

Hafemann disputes this understanding of 3.7-18.[108] He asserts that 3.7-18 shows the opponents contend that their experience of the Spirit is dependent on observing the Law.[109] But Hafemann's view relies on mirror exegesis and a prior reconstruction which he imposes on 2 Corinthians. Even if Paul's ministry is constantly troubled by opponents who assert that keeping the Law and participation in the Spirit through the gospel are inseparable, as Hafemann conjectures,[110] that does not mean they are present in Corinth at the time of this letter. Such a presumed reconstruction cannot be the basis for identifying the opponents of this letter or for determining what sort of passage we have in ch. 3. Nothing in the rest of 2 Corinthians indicates that there were problems with the Law, and this comparison of ministries is an insufficient basis for such a view.

Even if 3.7-18 is apologetic or polemical, we are hard-pressed to find allusions to the opponents. Verse 12, where Paul says that he is bold, is the leading possibility.[111] This may be an oblique reference to the discussion of the proper means of self-commendation or proper way of life for apostles, but we cannot be certain. If it is an allusion, we must still use mirror exegesis to learn anything about the opponents. Even though we have no evidence that boldness (παρρησία) per se has a role in their

107. Lambrecht identifies 3.7-18 as an excursus ('Structure and Line of Thought', p. 378).

108. Hafemann, Review of *Identifying Paul's Opponents* (Sumney) in *JBL* 111 (1992), p. 350.

109. Hafemann, *Suffering and Ministry*, p. 223; Hafemann, 'Corinthians', p. 178.

110. See Hafemann, *Suffering and Ministry*, p. 223; Hafemann, 'Paul and His Interpreters', in Hawthorne and Martin (eds.), *Dictionary of Paul and His Letters*, p. 671. Hafemann asserts that the same type of opponent caused problems for Paul in Galatia, Antioch and Jerusalem, as well as in Corinth. This takes us back to something like Baur's reconstruction.

111. Plummer (*Commentary*, p. 95) and Martin (*2 Corinthians*, pp. 66-67) identify v. 12 as an allusion.

view of ministry, it does complement their rejection of weakness. The most, then, that we can learn from this passage is that it is *possible*[112] (we could not say probable even in a polemical section) that the opponents express their view of apostleship with bold speech.

Affirmations

1.24[113]

When Paul says, in 1.24,[114] that he does not 'lord it over' the Corinthians, he may be addressing the issue of proper apostolic behavior, with Paul rejecting the propriety of the relationship between apostle and congregation that the opponents advocate.[115] However, it seems to read best as a safeguard against misunderstanding 1.23.[116] Since Paul is in the midst of an explanation of his conduct necessitated by misunderstanding, it is only natural to try to ensure that the Corinthians understand him correctly now.

While we cannot rule out the possibility that 1.24 refers to the opponents, it seems less likely because no other evidence points to a discussion of the *use* of authority. Even if we accept it as an affirmation, it could not add the use of authority as an issue between Paul and the opponents.

112. Since we are in a didactic context, we can properly not even go this far because the only legitimate use of mirror exegesis here is to confirm something we already know.

113. We will not discuss statements found in 4.16–5.10 that might be identified as affirmations because that is a didactic section. Verses 4.16–5.10 are an elaboration of the preceding discussion of Paul's weakness (see Sumney, *Identifying Paul's Opponents*, pp. 142-43). We cannot, of course, use affirmations in didactic sections to identify opponents.

114. Some interpreters see 1.24 as an allusion rather than an affirmation, e.g. Bultmann, who suggests that it is apologetic (*The Second Letter to the Corinthians*, p. 44); Oostendorp, who identifies it as polemical (*Another Jesus*, pp. 30, 49); Plummer, *Commentary*, p. 45.

115. Oostendorp (*Another Jesus*, pp. 30, 49) thinks the exercise of authority is a central issue at Corinth and that the opponents contend that apostles must exercise strong control over a congregation. But the issue of exercising authority did not surface in the explicit statements or allusions.

116. So Hughes, *Paul's Second Epistle to the Corinthians*, p. 48; Furnish, *II Corinthians*, p. 151.

5.13

Commentators are almost unanimous in identifying 5.13 as an allusion to opponents.[117] Within the apologetic section 5.11-19, v. 13 follows an explicit statement about the opponents, in which Paul accuses them of boasting in externals (v. 12b). In v. 13 Paul refers to his own behavior, saying that if 'we are out of our minds' (ἐξέστημεν) it is for God and if 'we are wise' (σωφρονοῦμεν) it is for the Corinthians. Most exegetes hold that ἐξέστημεν means ecstatic behavior[118] and conclude that the opponents make ecstatic gifts of the Spirit an issue.

But instead of alluding to the opponents' behavior, these remarks flow out of Paul's distinction between ways of judging apostles. Verse 13 may be an example that clarifies v. 12—an apt example given the Corinthians' past problems with spiritual gifts (see 1 Cor. 12–14). Paul would then be saying that apostolic legitimacy cannot be judged on the basis of appearance, even if that appearance includes ecstatic gifts or what seems to be nonsense, if ἐξέστημεν does not mean ecstatic behavior.

Sine v. 13 contains the only possible reference to problems with ecstatic gifts of the Spirit in chs. 1–7, we cannot claim that the opponents make an issue of such gifts.[119] Even if it relates to the opponents, an affirmation cannot add a topic to our portrait of opponents.

Conclusion

In 2 Corinthians 1–7 Paul faces opponents who claim to be apostles and emphasize evaluating and comparing ministries and ministers. Contend-

---

117. E.g. Plummer, *Commentary*, pp. 171-72; Bultmann, *The Second Letter to the Corinthians*, p. 150; Héring, *The Second Epistle of Saint Paul to the Corinthians*, p. 41; Hughes, *Paul's Second Epistle to the Corinthians*, pp. 190-91; Furnish, *II Corinthians*, pp. 51, 322-23; Martin, *2 Corinthians*, pp. 126-27. Also see its use in Oostendorp, *Another Jesus*, pp. 56, 80; Schmithals, *Gnosticism in Corinth*, pp. 189-90, 303; Georgi, *Die Gegner*, pp. 255, 296.

118. So Windisch, *Der zweite Korintherbrief*, pp. 179-80; Bultmann, *The Second Letter to the Corinthians*, pp. 149-50; Barrett, *2 Corinthians*, pp. 166-67; Furnish, *II Corinthians*, pp. 324-25; Martin, *2 Corinthians*, pp. 126-27. However, Plummer suggests that its meaning is simply madness (*Commentary*, p. 172). The evidence which supports both of these positions is drawn from chs. 10–13 and so is not permissible here. Paul speaks of spiritual powers in 12.1-10 and of being out of his mind in 11.23.

119. Georg Strecker ('Die Legitimität des Paulinischen Apostolates nach 2 Korinther 10–13', *NTS* 38 [1992], pp. 566-86 [571]) notes that there is no clear evidence of tongues speaking in 2 Corinthians.

ing that apostles must present evidence of their status, these opponents bring letters of recommendation and make claims about their qualifications as part their evidence. Comparing ministries is itself a part of their presentation of evidence of apostolic status. So they see both their presentation of evidence of apostleship and their comparisons as part of the proper apostolic manner of life. They also interpret receiving pay from churches as evidence of apostolic status.

In conjunction with comparing ministries, presenting claims about themselves and accepting pay, these opponents contend that apostles' lives should be characterized by a strong presence and, perhaps, a successful ministry. This powerful demeanor, they argue, shows that God is with them. There is insufficient evidence to claim that ecstatic gifts play a role in their claims.[120]

Beyond setting out criteria for apostleship, these opponents challenge Paul's apostleship. They fault him for not presenting the proof of his apostleship. They also contend that his unimpressive demeanor is inappropriate for apostles. They go so far as to equate his weakness with living 'according to the flesh' and thus charge that he lacks the spirituality needed for apostolic status. They use his change of travel plans as further evidence of this lack of spirituality, evidence of both his weakness and his own recognition that he lacks power. Thus, they also question his integrity because he claims apostolic status.

We know little about the teachings of these opponents beyond what they think apostles' lives should be like and what they think of Paul's claim to apostolic status, given his failure to measure up to their criteria. Their view of apostles' lives may indicate how they understand Christian existence generally, but we cannot be sure. These opponents may be pneumatics in the sense that they cite ecstatic manifestations of the Spirit as evidence of apostleship, but this remains uncertain.

The entire debate between Paul and his opponents centers on the proper manifestation of divine power in apostles' lives. The opponents believe that apostles should be impressive figures who are successful and demonstrate the power of God in their lives by means of this manner of life, this bearing and demeanor. Paul, on the other hand, contends that apostles can be unimpressive to the average observer—so unimpressive that their lives are seemingly disgraceful. According to Paul,

---

120. If there were evidence that the opponents called for demonstrations of ecstatic gifts, there would be some sense in which we could call them pneumatics. But the evidence from the text of chs. 1–7 is too weak to support this thesis.

apostles show God's power by enduring trials and hardships (i.e. being 'weak') with faith and, in the process, bring others to the gospel.

THE LETTER OF CHAPTERS 10–13

Chapters 10–13 are more polemical than apologetic; Paul is on the attack.[121] This allows us to see more of what Paul thinks about the opponents,[122] but also increases the probability that his perspective will be skewed.

Explicit Statements

10.10-11

In 10.10-11 Paul acknowledges that 'they say' his letters are forceful, but his presence unimpressive. All of 10.7-18[123] deals with Paul's conduct as an apostle, particularly his use of authority.[124] Though there is an apologetic aspect here, this section, especially vv. 12-18,[125] is polemical.

The quotation from the opponents in 10.10[126] shows that they complain that Paul's presence is inconsistent with the style of his letters. If

121. Baur comments that Paul openly attacks his opponents in the last part of 2 Corinthians (*Paul, the Apostle of Jesus*, p. 271).

122. Ellis remarks that 2 Cor. 10–13 gives the most detailed picture of opponents in a Pauline letter ('Paul and his Opponents: Trends in Research', in J. Neusner [ed.], *Christianity, Judaism, and Other Greco–Roman Cults: Part 1* [Leiden: E.J. Brill, 1975], pp. 264-98 [285]).

123. So Barrett, *2 Corinthians*, p. 254; Furnish, *II Corinthians*, p. 459. Bultmann (*The Second Letter to the Corinthians*, p. 181) and Martin (*2 Corinthians*, p. 297) make the section 10.1-11.

124. Furnish (*II Corinthians*, p. 459) makes these verses a section.

125. So Barrett, *2 Corinthians*, p. 262, *idem*, 'Christianity at Corinth', *BJRL* 46 (1964), pp. 269-97 (291-92) 'Cephas and Corinth', pp. 9-11 and Eric Fuchs, 'La Faiblesse Glorie de l'Apostolat selon Paul; Etude sur 2 Corinthiens 10–13', *ETR* 55 (1980), pp. 231-53 (233). Plummer notes that Paul is satirical throughout vv. 12-18 (*Commentary*, p. 284). Christopher Forbes ('Comparison, Self-Praise and Irony: Paul's Boasting and the Conventions of Hellenistic Rhetoric', *NTS* 32 [1986], pp. 1-30 [16]) asserts that 10.12 is similar to what rhetoricians recommend when one is attacked. This lends support to identifying the section as polemical. However, Windisch suggests that vv. 5-12 are more apologetic and vv. 13-15 more polemical (*Der zweite Korintherbrief*, p. 329).

126. So Hans Dieter Betz, *Der Apostel Paulus und die Sokratische Tradition*

their assessment of Paul's letters is positive, as seems likely,[127] the opponents are paying him a backhanded compliment. They say that Paul is bold, but only at a safe distance; in person he does not live up to his powerful letters.[128] Verse 11 shows that the criticism is that Paul's presence is not impressive. These verses yield no evidence that the opponents criticize Paul for lacking the Spirit[129] or its visible manifestations.[130] Verses 10-11 do show that the opponents believe Paul's demeanor is inappropriate for an apostle.

10.12-18

Paul begins the polemical sub-section 10.12-18 with a sarcastic rejection of comparing himself with his opponents.[131] After acknowledging that the opponents compare ministries, Paul ironically presents his refusal to make comparisons as weakness. In reality he is contending that such comparisons are inappropriate for ministers.

(BHT, 45; Tübingen: J.C.B. Mohr [Paul Siebeck], 1972), p. 44 (also *idem, Paul's Apology 2 Corinthians 10–13 and the Socratic Tradition* [Protocol of the Second Colloquy; Berkeley: Center for Hermeneutical Studies, 1975], p. 5); T. Fahy, 'St. Paul's "Boasting" and "Weakness"', *ITQ* 31 (1964), pp. 214-27; Oostendorp, *Another Jesus*, p. 20; Plummer, *Commentary*, p. 282; Barrett, *2 Corinthians*, p. 260. Bultmann identifies φησίν as a 'customary quotation formula, used especially of opponents' objections' (*The Second Letter to the Corinthians*, p. 190).

127. So Plummer, *Commentary*, p. 282; Oostendorp, *Another Jesus*, p. 20; Betz, *Apostel Paulus*, pp. 44-45 (*idem, Paul's Apology*, p. 5). Forbes ('Comparison, Self-Praise and Irony', p. 16) comments that they view his letters as the sort that come from a real leader. But Barrett (*2 Corinthians*, p. 260) and Furnish (*II Corinthians*, p. 478) think the description of the letters is derogatory. Verse 11, however, shows that the problem is not powerful letters, but an unimpressive presence.

128. Martin, *2 Corinthians*, p. 311. Furnish (*II Corinthians*, p. 478) notes that overall vv. 10-11 reflect criticism. Court ('The Controversy with Adversaries', p. 89) asserts that the Corinthians dislike both Paul's weak presence and his strong letters and Romano Penna ('La presence des adversaires de Paul en 2 Cor 10–13: Approche litteraire', in Lohse [ed.], *Verteidigung und Bregründung des apostolischen Amtes*, pp. 7-41 [26]) argues that this antithesis was formulated by the opponents.

129. As Schmithals conjectures (*Gnosticism in Corinth*, p. 177).

130. As Oostendorp conjectures (*Another Jesus*, pp. 14, 17, 20).

131. Bultmann, *The Second Letter to the Corinthians*, p. 192; Plummer, *Commentary*, p. 286; Furnish, *II Corinthians*, p. 480; Martin, *2 Corinthians*, p. 318.

The issue in 10.12-18 is self-recommendation,[132] as references to it in both v. 12 and v. 18 show.[133] The opponents have recommended themselves to the Corinthians on the basis of the qualifications for apostles which they themselves have proposed. Now Paul confronts their claims by rejecting their standards.[134]

It is not clear whether the opponents' objections involve Paul's coming to Corinth[135] or whether Paul raises the issue of jurisdiction to answer questions about his apostleship.[136] In either case the opponents are questioning Paul's apostleship.

Verses 12-18 suggest that they criticize Paul for not engaging in self-commendation, that is, for not presenting proof of his apostleship. The irony of v. 12 loses its edge and the comments of v. 18 are incomprehensible if Paul is being accused of boasting.[137] The opponents recommend themselves in order to demonstrate their apostolic status and they contend that Paul must do the same.

11.18

An explicit statement appears in 11.18, which is a part of the prologue of the 'Fool's Speech' (11.1-21a). This prologue has three sections. The first section, vv. 1-4,[138] defends Paul's presentation of the 'Fool's Speech', and so is apologetic.[139] The second section, vv. 5-15,[140] defends

---

132. Barrett, *2 Corinthians*, p. 262; Martin, *2 Corinthians*, pp. 318-19; Hafemann, ' "Self-Commendation" ', p. 76.

133. Martin, *2 Corinthians*, p. 324.

134. See also Oostendorp, *Another Jesus*, p. 21; Barrett, *2 Corinthians*, pp. 262-63; Martin, *2 Corinthians*, p. 319.

135. See the discussions of possible meanings of this reference to jurisdiction in Oostendorp, *Another Jesus*, p. 22; Barrett, *2 Corinthians*, p. 265; Furnish, *II Corinthians*, p. 481; Penna, 'La presence des adversaires de Paul', pp. 27-28; Strecker, 'Die Legitimität des Paulinischen Apostolates', p. 571. Furnish rejects the idea that this verse refers to the Jerusalem accord, noting that Paul reports in Gal. 2.9 that the Jerusalem agreement was based on the Jerusalem apostles' recognition of God's grace to Paul (*2 Corinthians*, p. 481).

136. See the comments of Käsemann, 'Die Legitimität', pp. 49-51.

137. Plummer (*Commentary*, p. 286) argues that Paul is being accused of boasting.

138. So Windisch, *Der zweite Korintherbrief*, p. 315; Furnish, *II Corinthians*, p. 498. However, Plummer (*Commentary*, p. 291) and Bultmann (*The Second Epistle to the Corinthians*, p. 199) identify the first section as vv. 1-6.

139. Cf. Furnish, *II Corinthians*, p. 499; Bultmann, *The Second Epistle to the*

Paul's apostolic status. Verses 16-21a, which comprise the final section of the prologue, renew Paul's appeal for the Corinthians to accept the 'Fool's Speech',[141] but the tone is polemical, as the irony of several verses (vv. 16, 19, 20, 21a) indicates.[142] Here Paul is on the offensive.

Within this polemical context, Paul says in v. 18 that 'many' are boasting 'according to the flesh' (κατὰ σάρκα). Paul uses this evaluation of the 'many' (i.e. his rivals) to distinguish himself from them. Furthermore, this oblique 'many' may be calculated 'to diminish their stature in the eyes of the Corinthians'.[143]

Interpreters understand the κατὰ σάρκα (according to the flesh) of v. 18 in different ways, often depending on how they have identified the letter's opponents.[144] But the context must determine the meaning of this phrase here. Furnish notes that κατὰ σάρκα stands in opposition to κατὰ κύριον (according to the Lord) in v. 17.[145] With this contrast Paul asserts that he and the opponents operate with different and opposing standards. Verse 18 shows that Paul includes 'boasting' (their self-commendation) as part of the other standard. Since this is a polemical evaluation, all we can see is that Paul objects to the manner and content of their claims.

11.20-21a
Still within the polemical section (11.16-21a) of the prologue to the 'Fool's Speech', Paul chides the Corinthians for accepting his rivals in

---

Corinthians, p. 199. Windisch (*Der zweite Korintherbrief*, p. 315) goes too far when he asserts that these verses are primarily polemical.

140. Windisch (*Der zweite Korintherbrief*, p. 317) and Furnish (*II Corinthians*, p. 502) make this division.

141. Windisch, *Der zweite Korintherbrief*, p. 344; Bultmann, *The Second Epistle to the Corinthians*, p. 209; Furnish, *II Corinthians*, p. 511.

142. Cf. Penna, 'La Presence des Adversaires de Paul', pp. 15, 20.

143. Furnish, *II Corinthians*, p. 511. Furnish is citing the dissertation of P. Marshall, now published as *Enmity in Corinth: Social Conventions in Paul's Relations with the Corinthians* (WUNT, 23; Tübingen: J.C.B. Mohr, 1987).

144. E.g. Oostendorp *Another Jesus*, p. 80) contends that they boast about Israel's primacy over Gentiles; Martin (*2 Corinthians*, p. 363) and E. Schweizer ('σάρξ', p. 128) take it to mean that they behave like 'the race of sinful creatures'; Plummer (*Commentary*, p. 315) suggests pride in one's ethnic background and position in life; and Barrett (*2 Corinthians*, p. 291) asserts that it means evaluating things 'on a scale of values that leaves God out of account'.

145. Furnish, *II Corinthians*, p. 496.

v. 19 and describes the opponents' treatment of the Corinthians in v. 20, saying that they enslave, exploit, take advantage of, and slap them in the face. Then, in v. 21a, he admits ironically[146] that he was 'too weak' to treat them in that way.

Many interpreters assign doctrinal significance to the terms Paul uses to describe the opponents' behavior.[147] However,[148] the continuing irony[149] suggests that we take these terms 'with a grain of salt'. Still, as a group, they seem to refer to the opponents' acceptance of maintenance and their attitudes,[150] which Paul interprets as abusive and tyrannical.[151] By ironically confessing his failure to meet these standards, Paul is in reality discrediting the opponents' criteria for apostleship.[152]

So 11.20-21a shows that the opponents assume a commanding and superior demeanor in their relations with the Corinthians. Verse 18 indicates that they make claims about themselves to support this superiority.

11.21b-23a

Paul matches his opponents' claims to Jewish heritage in 11.21b-23a.[153] These verses open the body of the 'Fool's Speech' (11.21b–11.33[154]).

146. Aida B. Spenser, 'The Wise Fool (and the Foolish Wise): A Study of Irony in Paul', *NovT* 23 (1981), pp. 349-60 (355); Bultmann, *The Second Epistle to the Corinthians*, p. 292; Plummer, *Commentary*, p. 317; Martin, *2 Corinthians*, p. 366.

147. See, e.g., Barrett, *2 Corinthians*, p. 291. Cf. the more restrained use of λαμβάνω by Furnish (*II Corinthians*, p. 512) and Martin (*2 Corinthians*, p. 365).

148. See Bultmann's refusal to do this here (*The Second Epistle to the Corinthians*, p. 212). Penna ('La presence des adversaires de Paul', p. 20) notes that the accumulation of verbs in v. 20 shows that the verse has polemical intent and that it is not an objective description.

149. Martin, *2 Corinthians*, p. 364.

150. Bultmann, *The Second Epistle to the Corinthians*, pp. 211-12. Cf. Plummer, *Commentary* p. 316; Furnish, *II Corinthians*, p. 512.

151. Cf. Jorge Sànchez Bosch, 'L'apologie apostolique: 2 Cor 10–11 comme réponse de Paul à ses adversaires', in Lohse (ed.), *Verteidigung und Begründung des apostolischen Amtes*, pp. 42-61 (62).

152. Betz, *Der Apostel*, pp. 67, 96-97, 99 (*idem, Paul's Apology*, p. 14); Martin, *2 Corinthians*, p. 366. According to Plummer, this ironical confession is also a rebuke to the Corinthians (Plummer, *Commentary*, p. 317).

153. Furnish identifies 11.21b–12.10 as 'The Fool's Speech Proper' (*II Corinthians*, pp. 512-13). Martin agrees with his assessment (*2 Corinthians*, p. 368). However, Barrett (*2 Corinthians*, p. 288) and Plummer (*Commentary*, pp. 311-18) begin the section at 11.16. Plummer then separates vv. 16-21 as a sub-section.

154. Most interpreters see a break at v. 33. E.g. Plummer, *Commentary*, pp. 311-

This section is polemical because Paul's primary purpose is to reject the criteria that the opponents use to make their claims.

After again expressing his discomfort with making claims for himself, Paul proceeds to make comparisons. The titles 'Hebrews', 'Israelites' and 'Seed of Abraham' show that Paul is comparing himself with other Jews. Barrett contends that Paul moves beyond his immediate rivals with the 'anyone' (τις) of v. 21b[155] and begins speaking of the Jerusalem Apostles.[156] According to Barrett, these titles point to Palestinian Jews with knowledge of the earthly Jesus. But, as Friedrich[157] and Georgi[158] have demonstrated, these titles do not necessarily point to Palestinians, much less those who knew Jesus. Furthermore, it is unlikely that Paul momentarily turns his attention from his immediate rivals at this point,[159] particularly since he uses τις throughout v. 20 to refer to them. It is improbable that now in v. 21b, without warning, Paul has changed the referent of his pronoun without some signal. So the context favors identifying Paul's rivals at Corinth as the object of his comparisons in v. 21b.[160] Even though the titles of v. 22 are probably somewhat synonymous,[161] together they show that the claimants emphasize being Jewish to the fullest extent, including the ethnic and religious implications of that identity.[162]

The final comparison Paul makes in vv. 21b-23a involves being a 'servant of Christ'. He does not simply say, 'So am I' as he did with the Jewish titles. He says, claiming to speak like a person who is out of his mind, 'I am more'.[163] The opponents probably use the title 'servants of Christ' because Paul uses it only here in this series of claims.[164]

13; Barrett, *2 Corinthians*, p. 288; Bultmann, *The Second Letter to the Corinthians*, p. 214; Martin, *2 Corinthians*, p. 366.

155. Barrett, *2 Corinthians*, p. 292.

156. Barrett, *2 Corinthians*, pp. 292-94. So also Court, 'The Controversy with Adversaries', pp. 96-97.

157. Friedrich, 'Die Gegner', pp. 181-82, cf. 185-86.

158. Georgi, *Die Gegner*, pp. 63-81.

159. Martin, *2 Corinthians*, p. 373.

160. Furnish, *II Corinthians*, p. 533.

161. Plummer, *Commentary*, p. 319.

162. Plummer, *Commentary*, pp. 319-20; Bultmann, *The Second Letter to the Corinthians*, p. 214; Furnish, *II Corinthians*, p. 534.

163. Furnish (*II Corinthians*, p. 535) and Martin (*2 Corinthians*, p. 375) suggest that the opponents may deny Paul this status.

164. Furnish, *II Corinthians*, p. 535.

Those who think Paul is comparing himself with the Jerusalem apostles often contend that Paul could not call the same persons false apostles and servants of Christ. However, Paul 'admits' they are servants of
Christ only for the sake of argument.[165] Furthermore, if, as Martin suggests, the 'I am more' of v. 23 has an exclusive force,[166] Paul is not
allowing that they are his equals or servants of Christ; he is claiming
superiority.[167] Cumulatively, the evidence clearly indicates that Paul is
comparing himself with the rivals at Corinth who make claims about
being Jewish and about being 'servants of Christ'.

The hardship catalog that Paul gives as evidence for his claim to
being a servant of Christ shows the kind of evidence the opponents
marshal to support their claim to the title. Paul employs encomiastic
conventions in vv. 23b-33, but reverses their effect.[168] He mentions experiences that show the *inglorious* nature of his life and interprets them
as evidence of his weakness (v. 30). This is not the proof the Corinthians expect. The opponents claim powerful, glorious lives as evidence
of apostleship. Paul has agreed to compare himself with them, but his
evidence *for* the legitimacy of his ministry is their evidence *against*
him. So he is rejecting their criteria of legitimacy.

This passage shows that the opponents claim the title servant of
Christ, an equivalent of apostle,[169] and support that claim by pointing
to their glorious lives and Jewish heritage. This latter claim does not
necessarily mean they are Judaizers.[170] Jews could claim special com-

165. Plummer, *Commentary*, p. 321. Forbes ('Comparison, Self-Praise and Irony',
p. 17) asserts that Paul allows this equality only in indignation and irony.

166. Martin (*2 Corinthians*, p. 374) argues that ὑπέρ has this force.

167. Bultmann, *The Second Letter to the Corinthians*, p. 215.

168. S.H. Travis, 'Paul's Boasting in 2 Corinthians 10–12', *SE* 6 (1969), pp. 527-
32 (529); Betz, *Der Apostel*, p. 141 (*idem, Paul's Apology*, pp. 11-12). Forbes
('Comparison, Self-Praise and Irony', pp. 18-19) sees 11.23-29 as a 'ruthless parody' of the opponents.

169. So also Eduard Lohse, 'Das kirchliche Amt des Apostels und das apostolische Amt der Kirche', in *idem* (ed.), *Verteidigung und Begründung des apostolischen Amtes*, p. 133.

170. So Lohse, 'Das kirchliche Amt'. C. Forbes sees the arrival of these Jewish
opponents as a manifestation of 'resurgent Jewish national and religious pride',
which was on the rise and was influencing Jews outside of Palestine in the middle
part of the first century. Thus, the claims about their Jewish heritage do not necessarily entail the preaching of Jewish doctrines ('Paul's Opponents in Corinth',
Buried History 19 (1983), pp. 19-23 [21-22]).

petence as teachers based on their more extensive exposure to Scripture. They could claim a fuller understanding of Scripture because of this exposure, and thus a better understanding of Christian doctrine. Such an emphasis on being Jewish is possible no matter what teaching they espouse.

10.2

In 10.2 we learn that some are saying Paul lives 'according to the flesh' (κατὰ σάρκα). This statement appears in the first extant section of this letter, 10.1-6.[171] If only the greeting is missing (as seems to be the case),[172] this letter begins with an appeal for obedience,[173] combined with a defense of Paul's conduct in his dealings with the Corinthians.[174]

Since it comes at the beginning of the letter, Paul perceives the charge that he lives 'according to the flesh' as a serious and central problem.[175] Whether 'those who think' Paul lives in this way are the opponents (as seems more likely)[176] or the members of the Corinthian congregation,[177] the charge originated with the opponents and plays a role in their evaluation of ministers.

The general context of this letter and the discussion of Paul's demeanor in 10.1-10 suggest that the opponents use κατὰ σάρκα (according to the flesh) to evaluate his way of life, asserting that it is not suitable for an apostle.[178] This interpretation of his manner of life seems

171. So Plummer, *Commentary*, p. 270; Barrett, *2 Corinthians*, pp. 243-44; Furnish, *II Corinthians*, p. 459; Abraham J. Malherbe, 'Antisthenes and Odysseus, and Paul at War', *HTR* 76 (1983), pp. 143-73 (148, 170). But Martin makes the section 10.1-11 (*2 Corinthians*, p. 297).

172. So Barrett, *2 Corinthians*, p. 245. Cf. Robert W. Funk, *Language, Hermeneutic, and Word of God*, pp. 273-74. Funk rightly compares this beginning with the beginning of Galatians.

173. Furnish, *II Corinthians*, pp. 459-61.

174. Malberbe, 'Paul at War', p. 172. Martin calls vv. 1-11 'Paul's Self-vindication' (*2 Corinthians*, p. 297). Penna ('La presence des adversaires de Paul', p. 26 n. 58) follows Betz (*Der Apostel Paulus*, p. 52) in finding apology here.

175. Bultmann asserts that this is the main charge against Paul (*The Second Letter to the Corinthians*, p. 184).

176. Martin, *2 Corinthians*, p. 304.

177. Plummer, *Commentary*, p. 274.

178. This is the interpretation of Georgi (*Die Gegner*, p. 232, n. 1). Others include this as a major feature in their interpretation of κατὰ σάρκα. E.g. Barrett,

to imply that he does not possess a sufficient measure of the Spirit to be an apostle. However, this accusation is not sufficent evidence to connect the issues of manner of life and the presence of the Spirit in the form of charismata. All we can say about the meaning of κατὰ σάρκα in 10.2 is that the opponents use it to reject Paul's way of life as inconsistent with possessing apostolic status. Paul's use of the phrase to describe the opponents' behavior in 11.18 contributes nothing to our understanding of the opponents because Paul and the opponents use it to mean different things.

13.2b-3
According to 13.3, the Corinthians are demanding proof that Christ speaks through Paul. This statement comes in the final section of the letter's body, 13.1-10.[179] In this section Paul is no longer defending himself or arguing against his opponents, but calling the Corinthians to repent and warning them about the consequences if they do not.[180] So it is best described as didactic.

13.2b-3 indicates that the Corinthians rather than the opponents are demanding proof that Christ speaks through Paul. But in light of what we know about the opponents we cannot doubt that this demand comes indirectly from them.[181] The context suggests that questions about Christ

2 Corinthians, p. 250; Furnish, *II Corinthians*, p. 461. For other interpretations of the phrase see Schmithals, *Gnosticism in Corinth*, pp. 164-65; Friedrich, 'Die Gegner', p. 184; Barrett, *2 Corinthians*, p. 250; Furnish, *II Corinthians*, p. 461; Martin, *2 Corinthians*, p. 304; Fuchs, 'La Faiblesse', p. 243. See also Malherbe ('Paul at War', pp. 170-72) who shows that the section is about Paul's way of life.

179. Many interpreters (e.g. Plummer, *Commentary*, pp. 365-66, 371; Bultmann, *The Second Letter to the Corinthians,* p. 236) see 13.1-10 as a sub-section of 12.19–13.10. Martin divides 13.1-10 into two parts (*2 Corinthians*, pp. 452, 454-56). Barrett simply identifies 12.19–13.10 as a single large section (*2 Corinthians*, pp. 326-27). Others see 13.1-10 a sub-section of 12.14–13.10 (e.g. Furnish, *II Corinthians*, pp. 557-58). Windisch identifies 12.14–13.13 as the concluding section of the letter (*Der zweite Korintherbrief*, p. 398).

180. Plummer, *Commentary*, pp. 367, 371; Furnish, *II Corinthians*, p. 574; Martin, *2 Corinthians*, pp. 452, 454-55. Cf. David Alan Black, *Paul, Apostle of Weakness: Astheneia and its Cognates in the Pauline Literature* (American University Studies, Theology and Religion Series, 3; New York: Peter Lang, 1984), p. 160.

181. See the discussion of 12.12 below. Oostendorp (*Another Jesus*, p. 17), Schmithals (*Gnosticism in Corinth*, pp. 193-94), Bultmann (*The Second Letter to the Corinthians*, p. 242), and Barrett (*2 Corinthians*, p. 335) see 13.3 as an allusion to charges of the opponents.

speaking through Paul center on his weakness, his unimpressive, unassertive behavior.[182] Verse 3b focuses on this issue when Paul says he will not be weak among them because Christ is not. In v. 4 he contends that his past behavior has exhibited Christ and that his change in demeanor will also reflect Christ. This reference to weakness near the end of the letter confirms that the appropriate way of life for apostles is a central issue.

10.7

We find out in 10.7 that the opponents[183] claim to be 'of Christ'. The Χριστοῦ ('of Christ') in v. 7 has received a great deal of attention,[184] but most commentators recognize that there is no warrant for identifying these opponents with the Christ-party of 1 Corinthians.[185] Neither is there reason to suspect that being 'of Christ' entails knowledge of the earthly Jesus.[186] No references to the earthly Jesus appear in the context and we have seen no discussion of such knowledge in this letter. Legitimating apostleship is the main issue in 10.7.[187]

182. However, it has been interpreted many different ways. See, e.g., the very different interpretations in Oostendorp, *Another Jesus*, pp. 17-25; Schmithals, *Gnosticism in Corinth*, pp. 193-95.

183. Barrett argues that the τις of v. 7 singles out a particular individual whose identity Paul never discloses. Still, says Barrett, the figure is seen occasionally (*2 Corinthians*, pp. 256-57; 'Cephas', pp. 8-9). This view is necessary for Barrett to argue that Cephas is an important part of the debate in Corinth. But the singular τις is not proof that Paul has a particular individual in mind. Paul is more likely using the singular to personalize the reference. See also Plummer, *Commentary*, p. 280; Martin, *2 Corinthians*, p. 307; Penna, 'La presence des adversaires de Paul', pp. 14-15.

184. See its use in the hypotheses of Schmithals (*Gnosticism in Corinth*, pp. 197-98), Baur (*Paul, the Apostle of Jews*, p. 285), and Oostendorp (*Another Jesus*, pp. 17-20).

185. Plummer, *Commentary*, p. 280; Bultmann, *The Second Letter to the Corinthians*, p. 187; Furnish, *II Corinthians*, p. 476. See especially the discussion of Furnish. Only unsupported mirror reading can justify a connection between these opponents and the problems in 1 Corinthians.

186. Barrett (*2 Corinthians*, p. 257), Furnish (*II Corinthians*, p. 476), and Martin (*2 Corinthians*, pp. 307-308) include knowledge of the earthly Jesus as a part (at least possibly) of the meaning of Χριστοῦ (of Christ).

187. Barrett, *2 Corinthians*, p. 257; Plummer equates 'of Christ' here with 'servant of Christ' in 11.23 (*Commentary*, p. 280).

Therefore, the argument in 10.7 is over who has the spiritual relationship to Christ which gives authority over churches. The opponents claim this relationship as the basis for their claims to apostleship and authority. Paul wants this discussion to include the proper use of authority, because he thinks that they abuse the authority they claim.

11.5-6; 12.11c

As Paul begins the apologetic second section of the prologue of the 'Fool's Speech' (11.5-15), he asserts that he is not inferior to the 'superlative apostles' (ὑπερλίαν ἀποστόλοι) and that while he may be a novice (ἰδιώτης) in speech he nevertheless has knowledge. We will deal with 12.11c here because it contains the other reference to the superlative apostles. 12.11 stands within the epilogue of the 'Fool's Speech' (12.11-13). Here Paul again justifies his presentation of the speech and defends his apostolic status. So that section is also apologetic.

Käsemann, Barrett and Martin argue that the 'super-apostles' of 11.5 and 12.11 are the Jerusalem Twelve.[188] Martin cannot believe Paul could acknowledge the apostolic status of a group (11.5) and almost simultaneously call them false apostles (11.13-14).[189] Barrett asserts that Paul would not merely claim that he is not inferior in the face of 'servants of Satan'.[190] Barrett and Käsemann argue that since the irony of 'superlative' is parallel to the irony of calling the Jerusalem Apostles 'Pillars' in Gal. 2.14, Paul is dealing with the Jerusalem Apostles in 2 Cor. 11.5 and 12.11.[191] Perhaps the strongest argument for identifying the 'super-apostles' with the Jerusalem Twelve is that Paul mentions pay immediately after both references to the 'super-apostles'. This is significant because he discusses the Jerusalem apostles in connection with support in 1 Corinthians 9.[192]

Using the mention of support to identify the super-apostles with the Jerusalem apostles is, however, an illegitimate use of parallels.[193] An-

---

188. Käsemann, 'Die Legitimität', p. 45; Barrett, *2 Corinthians*, pp. 31, 277-78; Martin, *2 Corinthians*, p. 342. They are followed by Court, 'The Controversy with the Adversaries', pp. 96-97.

189. Martin, *2 Corinthians*, p. 342.

190. Barrett, *2 Corinthians*, pp. 277-78; Cf. Barrett, 'Paul's Opponents', pp. 252-53.

191. Barrett, *2 Corinthians*, p. 31, 278; Käsemann, 'Die Legitimität', p. 45.

192. Barrett, 'Paul's Opponents', pp. 244, 252; Käsemann, 'Die Legitimität', p. 46.

193. As my method argues, such an easy identification and use of parallels can show possibilities, but not probabilities.

other problem with using 1 Corinthians 9 as Barrett and Käsemann do is that it violates the principle that letters must be interpreted individually. Thus, this argument cannot serve as primary evidence that the super-apostles are the Jerusalem apostles.[194]

The immediate context strongly favors identifying the super-apostles with the Corinthian intruders. In 1.4 Paul chides the Corinthians for accepting teachers who bring a different Jesus, Spirit and gospel. Calling them 'superlative' (v. 5) fits the 'satirical vein of the passage, and is also germane to his immediate concern which is with these imposters rather than with any of the Twelve'.[195] Further, Paul's only references to the super-apostles appear in the prologue (11.5) and epilogue (12.11c[196]) of the 'Fool's Speech'. Thus, equality with them is a fundamental theme of the speech.[197] Since Paul's argument throughout 11.1–12.13 is clearly not against the Jerusalem apostles, it would be strange to mention them in the prologue and epilogue as though they were a central part of the intervening discussion.

The connection between 11.5 and 6 also supports identifying the intruders with the 'super-apostles'. It makes no sense for Paul to call himself a 'novice in speech' (ἰδιώτης τῷ λόγῳ) in comparison with the Jerusalem apostles.[198] Martin recognizes this and designates v. 5 a parenthesis, asserting that Paul returns to his discussion of the opponents at Corinth in v. 6.[199] However, it is more likely that v. 5 begins a new section and is the topic sentence for vv. 6-12.[200] So, vv. 5 and 6 are

194. If proper evidence demonstrated the point, 1 Cor. 9 might possibly serve as corroborative evidence.

195. Hughes, *Paul's Second Epistle to the Corinthians*, pp. 379-80. Cf. Furnish, *II Corinthians*, p. 503. Similarly Schmithals, *Gnosticism in Corinth*, p. 280; Georgi, *Die Gegner*, pp. 48, 288 n. 4; Forbes, 'Comparison, Self-Praise and Irony', p. 16. Furnish suggests that 'super-apostles' is like the comparisons of 11.21b-22 (*II Corinthians*, p. 502). Cf. P.W. Barnett, 'Opposition in Corinth', *JSNT* 22 (1984), pp. 3-17 (4-5). See further the contrasts noted by Bultmann (*The Second Letter to the Corinthians*, p. 203), Lohse ('Das kirchliche Amt des Apostels', p. 134), and Penna ('La presence des adversaires de Paul', pp. 23-24) between the ways Paul treats the 'superlative apostles' and the Jerusalem Apostles.

196. Furnish contends that the context of 12.11c shows that the 'super-apostles' are the opponents (*II Corinthians*, p. 504).

197. Furnish, *II Corinthians*, p. 502.

198. Furnish, *II Corinthians*, p. 504.

199. Martin, *2 Corinthians*, p. 342.

200. Furnish, *II Corinthians*, p. 502.

closely related; v. 6 explains v. 5. Thus the 'super-apostles' are in view in both v. 5 and v. 6.[201]

The weight of the arguments falls decisively on the side of identifying the super-apostles with the Corinthian intruders. So Paul ironically[202] claims in 11.5 that he is his opponents' equal to support his appeal for the Corinthians to bear with him in some foolishness (11.1), just as they extend this courtesy to his rivals.[203]

In v. 6 Paul defends his equality with the opponents while allowing that he is a 'novice in speech'. Even though this phrase is used in the tradition of true philosophers conceding poor speech while arguing with Sophists,[204] we have seen that Paul's manner of speaking is being discussed (10.10). Therefore, Paul is probably answering a charge that involves his rhetorical skills.[205] This makes it especially appropriate for him to make his opponents look like Sophists.

The immediate context does not support the common view that v. 6 shows Paul is faced with pneumatic/ecstatic speakers.[206] The reference could simply be to rhetorical skills. It is not even evident here that the opponents attribute their rhetorical skills to the Spirit. Paul defends himself by denying that rhetorical skills are a true measure of apostleship and by proposing knowledge, probably supernatural knowledge, as a proper criterion.[207]

---

201. Furnish, *II Corinthians*, p. 504. See also the grammatical argument of Margaret E. Thrall, 'Super-Apostles, Servants of Christ, and Servants of Satan', *JSNT* 6 (1980), p. 45.

202. See Lohse, 'Das kirchliche Amt des Apostels', p. 134.

203. Bultmann maintains that the γάρ (for) of v. 5 goes back to v. 1 (*The Second Letter to the Corinthians*, p. 203).

204. Betz, *Der Apostel*, pp. 60, 66, 69 (*idem, Paul's Apology*, p. 7).

205. E.g. Georgi, *Die Gegner*, p. 228; Käsemann, 'Die Legitimität', p. 35; Oostendorp, *Another Jesus*, p. 17; Schmithals, *Gnosticism in Corinth*, pp. 142-45; Hughes, *Paul's Second Epistle to the Corinthians*, p. 380; Martin, *2 Corinthians*, p. 342.

206. Held by Oostendorp, *Another Jesus*, pp. 11-12, 17; Schmithals, *Gnosticism in Corinth*, pp. 142-45; Käsemann, 'Die Legitimität', p. 35; Georgi, *Die Gegner*, p. 22; Friedrich, 'Die Gegner', pp. 182-83; Bultmann, *The Second Letter to the Corinthians*, p. 204. However, Strecker ('Die Legitimität des Paulinischen Apostolates', p. 571) sees that there is no clear evidence of tongues-speaking in 2 Corinthians.

207. Furnish, *II Corinthians*, p. 505; Friedrich, 'Die Gegner', pp. 182-83. However, Barrett (*2 Corinthians*, p. 280) suggests that knowledge is a criterion of the opponents rather than of Paul.

So 11.5-6 shows that the opponents' understanding of apostolic demeanor requires apostles to be impressive speakers. They contend that Paul lacks the necessary rhetorical skills and so question his apostleship. Paul accepts their criticism, but says it is insignificant; it does not bear on the issue of legitimate apostleship.

When Paul claims equality with the super-apostles in 12.11c, he has just concluded his main argument for himself and against them. Though we learn nothing new about the opponents there, the connection with the 'signs of an apostle' (v. 12) indicates that the super-apostles perform such signs.

11.12, 13-15

The polemical remarks of 11.12-15[208] conclude the apologetic second section of the prologue of the 'Fool's Speech'. In v. 12 we see that the opponents compare themselves with Paul, particularly on the matter of accepting support. They accept pay and cite it as evidence of their apostleship. Inversely, they question Paul's apostleship because he refuses it (see 11.7),[209] perhaps suggesting that he does not accept pay because he knows he does not have a right to it. The opponents want Paul either to admit that he does not have a right to support or to accept it from the Corinthians. Either way they gain ground. If he renounces the right, they are shown to be his superiors. If he accepts support, he puts himself on their level, and thus, they can assert, admits they are his equals.

In 11.13-15 Paul calls his opponents false apostles, deceitful workers and servants of Satan. The polemical tone indicates that they claim the titles apostle, worker and servant.[210] 'Worker' (ἐργάται) is a technical term for missionaries in early Christianity.[211] The term 'servant' (διάκονος), which is also used in 11.23, seems to be a rough equivalent of apostle here[212] and is equivalent to 'servant of God' because it stands in

208. Fuchs, 'La Faiblesse', p. 234; Furnish, *II Corinthians*, p. 509.

209. So Oostendorp, *Another Jesus*, p. 76; Plummer, *Commentary*, p. 307; Bultmann, *The Second Letter to the Corinthians*, p. 207.

210. So Georgi, *Die Gegner*, pp. 31-50, esp. 31, 39, 49; Martin, *2 Corinthians*, pp. 350-51. Cf. Penna, 'La presence des adversaires de Paul', pp. 22-23; 32-33.

211. Georgi, *Die Gegner*, pp. 49-50; Furnish, *II Corinthians*, p. 510.

212. Georgi, *Die Gegner*, p. 31; Oostendorp, *Another Jesus*, p. 11. Oostendorp also contends that the opponents use 'servants of righteousness' (v. 15) to claim that they are promoters of righteousness by promoting the Law (*Another Jesus*, p. 11). But the text does not warrant this specialized understanding of 'servants of righteousness'.

opposition to servants of Satan.[213] So, the opponents claim the titles apostle, missionary and servant of God (or Christ; see 11.23). They also demand support from the congregation, probably on the basis of their possession of these offices.

Summary of Explicit Statements

Explicit statements in chs. 10–13 demonstrate that the central issue is the appropriate way of life for apostles. The opponents contend that true apostles are impressive individuals with commanding demeanors and persuasive speaking skills. This impressive way of life includes the power to rise above troubles. Paul's rivals have taken up this way of life in Corinth and act as superiors toward the Corinthians. These rivals also believe apostles must present their qualifications to the community. Afterward, they use those qualifications to assume special authority and rights, including financial support.

The opponents question Paul's apostleship because he does not possess this powerful demeanor. For them, his lack of a powerful personality, glorious life and impressive rhetorical skills are evidence that he is not an apostle. They even accuse him of living 'according to the flesh'. These rivals also want Paul either to accept support or to give up the right to it because they understand receiving pay as evidence of apostolic status. They further complain that Paul refuses to present his apostolic credentials.

Paul's rivals recommend themselves on the basis of being Jewish. They seem to assert that Jewish teachers are in the best position to understand and teach the Christian message. These Jewish teachers claim to be 'servants of Christ', a title that designates a special relationship with Christ and appears to be an equivalent of 'apostle', another title they claim. Additionally, this special relationship with Christ supports their use of the title 'missionary'.

Allusions

10.1

Paul begins the apologetic section 10.1-6, by describing himself as 'humble' when present, but 'bold' when away. This ironic self-descrip-

---

213. Plummer, *Commentary*, p. 310; Georgi, *Die Gegner*, p. 249; Furnish, *II Corinthians*, p. 510. Cf. Bultmann who equates 'servants of righteousness' with angel of light (*The Second Letter to the Corinthians*, p. 209).

tion responds to the charge that Paul is inconsistent.[214] While 10.1b is not necessarily a quotation from the opponents,[215] as many interpreters hold,[216] it does allude to their criticisms of Paul's manner of life.[217]Paul ironically accepts the charge,[218] but then cites the 'meekness and gentleness of Christ' as the source and model for his behavior[219] and to demonstrate the foolishness of the charge.[220]

This parallel with Christ's demeanor (which he makes again in 13.3-4) shows how important the issues of Paul's 'weakness' and apparent inconsistency are in the dispute. If Malherbe is correct that Paul's use of ταπεινός ('humble/lowly') here alludes to his manual labor and so points to the issue of maintenance,[221] Paul raises three of the major issues of the letter in what is perhaps the first sentence of this letter's body. The tack he chooses is also evident; he begins with irony.

10.9

Within the polemical section 10.7-11, Paul says in v. 9 that he does not want to seem to be trying to scare the Corinthians too much with his letters. The compound, intensive verb ἐκφοβεῖν ('to scare') demostrates the ironical tone of the verse.[222] Verse 9 alludes to the contrast the opponents draw between the tone of Paul's letters and his demeanor when present.

214. Malherbe, 'Paul at War', p. 168; Schmithals, *Gnosticism in Corinth*, p. 177.

215. Malherbe, 'Paul at War', p. 168.

216. E.g. Plummer, *Commentary*, p. 273; Schmithals, *Gnosticism in Corinth*, p. 176.

217. Bultmann, *The Second Letter to the Corinthians*, p. 183; Oostendorp, *Another Jesus*, p. 30; Barrett, *2 Corinthians*, p. 247; Furnish, *II Corinthians*, p. 460; Martin, *2 Corinthians*, p. 303.

218. Betz, *Paul's Apology*, pp. 5-6. Most interpreters see irony in this verse. E.g. Kennedy, *New Testament Interpretation through Rhetorical Criticism*, p. 93; Bultmann, *The Second Letter to the Corinthians*, p. 183; Furnish, *II Corinthians*, p. 460. Malherbe identifies this kind of 'self-deprecating irony' as Cynic in character ('Paul at War', p. 168).

219. Bultmann, *The Second Letter to the Corinthians*, p. 183; Barrett, *2 Corinthians*, pp. 247-48; Martin rightly comments that Paul 'cites their estimate, while retaining in a double entendre his own self-estimate based on the model of the incarnate Lord' (*2 Corinthians*, p. 303).

220. Furnish, *2 Corinthians*, p. 460.

221. Malherbe, 'Paul at War', p. 168.

222. Plummer, *Commentary*, p. 281; Hughes, *Paul's Second Epistle to the Corinthians*, p. 361; Barrett, *2 Corinthians*, p. 259; Furnish, *II Corinthians*, p. 468.

This allusion may indicate that some complained about the tone of Paul's letters.[223] But the real criticism centers on the contrast between his letters and his way of life.[224] As Oostendorp comments, the opponents charge Paul with trying to frighten the Corinthians with his letters, while having no intention of carrying out his threats.[225] In v. 9, as a prelude to his more direct statements in vv. 10-11, Paul alludes to the complaint that his letters and behavior are inconsistent.

11.7-11

Paul alludes to the criticism of his refusal of support at the beginning of this apologetic paragraph by asking ironically[226] if he has sinned against the Corinthians by not charging them for his preaching.[227]

Four factors necessitate Paul's defense about pay.[228] First, his work as an artisan is the means of support for teachers and itinerant preachers that his contemporaries found least acceptable.[229] Second, since Paul took money from other churches, the opponents could charge him with inconsistency.[230] Third, the opponents may portray his refusal of pay as a refusal to enter a client/patron relationship with the Corinthians.[231]

223. Barrett, *2 Corinthians*, pp. 259-60.

224. Hughes, *Paul's Second Epistle to the Corinthians*, pp. 361-62; Oostendorp, *Another Jesus*, p. 20.

225. Oostendorp, *Another Jesus*.

226. Friedrich, 'Die Gegner', p. 188; Plummer, *Commentary*, p. 302; Barrett, *2 Corinthians*, p. 281; Furnish, *II Corinthians*, pp. 506-507; Martin, *2 Corinthians*, p. 344.

227. Windisch, *Der zweite Korintherbrief*, p. 333; Oostendorp, *Another Jesus*, p. 75; Plummer, *Commentary*, p. 302; Bultmann, *The Second Letter to the Corinthians*, p. 199; Barrett, *2 Corinthians*, pp. 281-82; Furnish, *II Corinthians*, p. 506; Martin, *2 Corinthians*, p. 344. It is unlikely that Friedrich is correct in saying that the opponents actually accuse Paul of sinning against the Corinthians by not accepting support. Friedrich contends that ἁμαρτία is a catchphrase of the opponents ('Die Gegner', p. 188). Bultmann explicitly rejects the idea that the opponents say that refusing pay is a sin (*The Second Letter to the Corinthians*, p. 205).

228. Furnish cites all 4 of these. See his discussion at *II Corinthians*, pp. 506-508.

229. Ronald Hock, *The Social Context of Paul's Ministry* (Philadelphia: Fortress Press, 1980), pp. 56-65; Windisch, *Der zweite Korintherbrief*, p. 334; Plummer, *Commentary*, p. 302; Furnish, *II Corinthians*, pp. 506-507; Martin, *2 Corinthians*, p. 344.

230. Furnish, *II Corinthians*, p. 507; Martin, *2 Corinthians*, p. 345.

231. Furnish, *II Corinthians*, pp. 507-508. Cf. Oostendorp, *Another Jesus*, p. 76.

Thus he denies them the status of patron.[232] The opponents may also interpret this refusal as evidence that Paul does not really care about the Corinthians (see 11.11).[233] We will discuss the fourth factor, the collection for Jerusalem,[234] in connection with 12.14-18.

As we have already seen, the opponents see pay as both a right of apostles and evidence of their legitimacy. 11.7-11 shows that they want Paul to accept support from Corinth, complain that he does not, and perhaps say that his refusal demonstrates a lack of love for the Corinthians.

12.13

Paul again speaks of his refusal of pay in the apologetic epilogue of the 'Fool's Speech' (12.11-13). In 12.13 Paul asks how he had demeaned the Corinthians except by not being a burden, and ironically[235] requests forgiveness for this injustice. This discussion of support as one of the 'signs of an apostle' (12.12[236]) confirms that the opponents understand receiving maintenance as evidence of apostolic status.[237] Since they

For a discussion of the privileges and demands of this relationship see Ramsay MacMullen, *Roman Social Relations: 50 BC to AD 284* (New Haven: Yale University Press, 1974), pp. 112-13, 124-25; E.A. Judge, 'The Social Identity of the First Christians: A Question of Method in Religious History', *JRH* 11 (1980), pp. 201-17 (213-17).

232. Furnish, *II Corinthians*, p. 508. The suggestion of Friedrich that the Corinthians believe that Paul is wronging them by not accepting pay may find some support here. They may hold that Paul humiliates them when he humiliates himself in this way ('Die Gegner', p. 188). But that they term this a sin seems extremely doubtful.

233. Oostendorp, *Another Jesus*, p. 76; Windisch, *Der zweite Korintherbrief*, p. 338; Barrett, *2 Corinthians*, p. 284; Martin, *2 Corinthians*, p. 345; Hafemann, *Suffering and Ministry*, p. 152. Plummer sees this as a possibility (*Commentary*, p. 306).

234. Furnish, *II Corinthians*, p. 508.

235. Windisch, *Der zweite Korintherbrief*, p. 398; Plummer, *Commentary*, p. 360; Furnish, *II Corinthians*, p. 556; Martin, *2 Corinthians*, p. 439; Demetrias Trakatellis, 'Power in Weakness: Exegesis of 2 Cor. 12,1-13', in Lohse (ed.), *Verteidigung und Begrundigung des apostolischen Amtes*, p. 83. Barrett comments that 12.13 is 'cutting sarcasm' (*2 Corinthians*, p. 323).

236. See the discussion of this point in Plummer, *Commentary*, p. 360; Barrett, *2 Corinthians*, p. 323; and especially Martin, *2 Corinthians*, pp. 438-39.

237. Plummer, *Commentary*, p. 360; Barrett, *2 Corinthians*, pp. 323, 438-39. Georgi suggests that the opponents see Paul's rejection of pay as a sign that he is no

interpret accepting support in this way, they may construe Paul's rejection of pay as an admission that he lacks apostolic status. So they may use it to accuse him of not being a true apostle.[238] The apologetic context, combined with repeated attention to the topic, allows us to find such an accusation.

12.15b-18

The material in 12.14-18 is an apologetic sub-section[239] of 12.14-21[240] in which Paul defends his refusal of maintenance.[241] After explaining that it is only natural for him, as their parent in Christ, to spend for them rather than have them spend for him (vv. 14-15a), Paul responds in 12.15b to the charge that his refusal of support shows a lack of love for the Corinthians by interpreting that refusal as an act of abundant love.

Verse 16 continues the discussion of pay with Paul ironically admitting that he has beguiled the Corinthians. Since this ironical statement appears in an apologetic context, we may identify it as an allusion to a charge of duplicity. Perhaps the best explanation of vv. 16-18 is that the opponents charge that Paul refuses support, but then embezzles funds from the Jerusalem collection.[242] It is possible that they say he refuses pay to avoid the obligations of a client/patron relationship, but gets the benefits (i.e. the money) by taking funds from the collection.[243] This scenario makes the charge of deception feasible.[244]

longer willing to give all of his spiritual gifts in relation to the Corinthians (*Die Gegner*, p. 240).

238. Cf. Court, 'The Controversy with Adversaries', p. 90.

239. Furnish, *II Corinthians*, pp. 563-64. The most common place to break the section is v. 18. So Plummer, *Commentary*, pp. 356-57; Bultmann, *The Second Letter to the Corinthians*, p. 233. Barrett, *2 Corinthians*, pp. 318-19; Martin, *2 Corinthians*, pp. 425-29.

240. See this division of the text in Windisch, *Der zweite Korintherbrief*, p. 398; Furnish, *II Corinthians*, p. 557.

241. Bultmann, *The Second Letter to the Corinthians*, pp. 233, 235; Barrett, *2 Corinthians*, p. 324; Oostendorp, *Another Jesus*, p. 75; Furnish, *II Corinthians*, pp. 563-64. Plummer (*Commentary*, pp. 363-64) and Martin (*2 Corinthians*, pp. 439, 444, 449) assert that the section is not apologetic, but still acknowledge that Paul is answering charges.

242. Georgi, *Die Gegner*, p. 240; Oostendorp, *Another Jesus*, p. 75; Schmithals, *Gnosticism in Corinth*, p. 108; Barrett, *2 Corinthians*, p. 324; Furnish, *II Corinthians*, p. 565; Martin, *2 Corinthians*, p. 449.

243. Furnish, *II Corinthians* p. 508. Cf. Barrett, *2 Corinthians*, p. 324.

244. Martin identifies Paul's use of πανοῦργος and ἔλαβον as polemical (*2 Corin-*

Thus, 12.15b-18 indicates that these opponents accuse Paul of deceit, possibly in connection with the collection. Even if the collection is not involved, they probably extend the charge of deceit to Paul's presentation of himself as an apostle because they see a relationship between accepting support and legitimate apostleship. So they contend that his refusal of support and his deception demonstrate that he is, at best, an inferior apostle.[245] They may also charge that Paul does not love the Corinthians.

12.1-10
The infamous passage in which Paul tells of a vision and of his 'thorn in the flesh', is a major section of the 'Fool's Speech'. The irony and parody[246] of 12.1-10 as well as Paul's rejection of the procedure (12.5), show that the section is polemical.[247] Paul is not defending himself as much as he is repudiating a point of view.[248] Verses 1-10 allude to the opponents' 'boasting'. The 'It is necessary to boast' of 12.1 may be a quotation from the opponents. It at least describes Paul's perception of their mode of operation.[249]

Paul apparently agrees to match his opponents' claims to 'visions and revelations of the Lord' in 12.1.[250] This is the first clear evidence that spiritual experiences are important for the opponents; the polemical context allows us to infer that they claim to receive visions and revelations.[251] The 'it is not beneficial, but...' of v. 1 and the focus of debate on legitimate apostleship confirm that this is an allusion.[252]

thians, pp. 445-46). Plummer sees πανοῦργος as the opponents evaluation of Paul (*Commentary*, p. 363).

245. Martin, *2 Corinthians*, p. 449.

246. Betz identifies parody as a polemical device which Paul uses a great deal in the 'Fool's Speech' (*Der Apostel*, pp. 84-85 [*idem, Paul's Apology*, pp. 9-10]).

247. Martin, *2 Corinthians*, p. 390.

248. The polemical nature of the other major section of the 'Fool's Speech' supports this view of the section.

249. Oostendorp, *Another Jesus*, p. 14; Furnish, *II Corinthians,* p. 543; Martin, *2 Corinthians*, p. 395.

250. Furnish (*II Corinthians*, p. 532) comments that Paul adopts the opponents' tactics in the 'Fool's Speech'.

251. So Schmithals, *Gnosticism in Corinth*, pp. 209-210; Georgi, *Die Gegner*, pp. 296-98; Friedrich, 'Die Gegner', p. 13; Oostendorp, *Another Jesus*, p. 14; Furnish, *II Corinthians*, p. 543; Martin, *2 Corinthians*, p. 396.

252. Georgi, *Die Gegner*, p. 296; Furnish, *II Corinthians*, p. 543; Martin, *2 Corinthians*, p. 395.

Paul relates a vision of a 'person in Christ' in 12.2-4, and so distances himself from the required recounting by using the third person. This strategy contributes to his rejection of the opponents' criteria for apostleship. We may not use mirror exegesis to identify particulars about the opponents' visions,[253] as Schmithals does.[254] Even a polemical context does not allow such extensive use of this technique. Furthermore, vv. 2-4 emphasize the foolishness of relating visions at all, as Paul parodies the opponents' *use* of visions.[255] In v. 5 he explicitly states the point of the parody and his use of the third person: he does not care to ground his apostolic status on such claims. He claims only weakness as evidence of his apostleship.[256]

What we find in 12.1-10, then, indicates that the opponents use visionary experiences as evidence of their apostleship. Paul's reference to his weakness in this context implies that they claim the Spirit as the source of their powerful lives. Since Paul's 'thorn' keeps him from leading the life they claim is appropriate for apostles, they may also claim that he does not have the Spirit in the measure required for apostolic status. Perhaps this is part of what they mean when they say that he lives 'according to the flesh'.

12.12

The apologetic epilogue of the 'Fool's Speech', 12.11-13, contains Paul's assertion (12.12) that he performed the 'signs of an apostle' among the Corinthians. Whether 'signs of an apostle' is a slogan of the opponents[257] or a phrase the Corinthians use to assume the role of judge of apostles,[258] it alludes to comparing ministries[259] and giving evidence of apostolic status.

253. So also Oostendorp, *Another Jesus*, p. 14.

254. Schmithals, *Gnosticism in Corinth*, pp. 211-18.

255. Betz, *Der Apostel*, pp. 93-94 (idem, *Paul's Apology*, pp. 9-10); Furnish, *II Corinthians*, p. 543.

256. Furnish, *II Corinthians*, p. 544.

257. Oostendorp, *Another Jesus*, p. 15; Käsemann, 'Die Legitimität', p. 35; Friedrich, 'Die Gegner', p. 13; Bultmann, *The Second Letter to the Corinthians*, p. 231; Martin, *2 Corinthians*, p. 435. Furnish allows that this may be the case (*II Corinthians*, p. 555). Windisch simply states that it is a 'Corinthian slogan', without indicating its origin (*Der zweite Korintherbrief*, p. 396).

258. Barrett, 'Paul's Opponents', p. 245; idem, *2 Corinthians*, pp. 320-21.

259. The fact that comparing ministries is a part of the opponents' mode of operation supports the view that the phrase is their slogan.

These 'signs of an apostle', which are miraculous deeds ('signs, won-ders, and powers'), are criteria that one must satisfy to be considered a legitimate apostle. Paul's rivals seem to criticize him for not performing such signs.[260] Paul does not concede here; he says he gave this proof. However, as Georgi notes, the question is not just about visions and miracles, but about how much they are characteristic of Paul.[261]

The source of such 'signs of an apostle' can only be the Spirit. This second reference to manifestations of the Spirit in the 'Fool's Speech' confirms that the opponents contend that the Spirit shows itself in spe-cial ways in apostles' lives. This in itself is not strange—Paul would even agree with them to this point. Paul and these rivals share, with most people of their time,[262] the belief that manifestations of divine power accompany religious truth. Paul and his rivals differ on what that man-ifestation looks like: the opponents believe divine power shows itself in the glorious lives of apostles; Paul believes it is seen more clearly when the apostle is weak and inglorious.[263] So the primary difference between Paul and his rivals stems from their different understandings of the proper manifestation of the Spirit in apostles' lives.

11.4

Our final and most difficult allusion, 11.4, is the last verse in the apolo-getic first section of the prologue of the 'Fool's Speech'. Some see 11.4 as a key to understanding the opponents of chs. 10–13.[264] However, since it does not explicitly mention the opponents we cannot accord it this status. Paul says in v. 4 that *if* someone comes preaching another Jesus, different Spirit, or different gospel, the Corinthians accept it readily. We identify the verse as an allusion to actual rivals because the

260. Furnish, *II Corinthians*, p. 555. Cf. Hughes, *Paul's Second Epistle to the Corinthians*, p. 456.

261. Georgi, *Die Gegner*, p. 297.

262. Furnish, *II Corinthians*, pp. 553, 555. See especially the references to the ancient literature on p. 553.

263. The 'in all patience' of v. 12 may point to Paul's 'weak' demeanor. So Bar-rett, *2 Corinthians*, p. 321; Furnish, *II Corinthians*, p. 555; Martin, *2 Corinthians*, pp. 435-36.

264. E.g. Käsemann, 'Die Legitimität', p. 37; Oostendorp, *Another Jesus*, p. 7. Oostendorp comments, 'No clearer introduction to the problems of 2 Corinthians can be found than 11:4' (*Another Jesus*, p. 7).

main reason Paul writes this letter is that the Corinthians are accepting his rivals.[265]

Some interpreters use the three 'others' in 11.4 to identify specific problems at Corinth. Thus, they contend, Paul's rivals had an aberrant Christology and pneumatology.[266] Several identify Christology as a major issue because Paul uses 'Jesus' rather than 'Christ'.[267] However, as Bultmann and others point out, Paul can use the terms 'Jesus' and 'Christ' without distinction. So 'another Jesus' does not necessarily indicate problems with Christology.[268] Furthermore, Paul does not discuss Christology in explicit statements or other, clearer, allusions to opponents or anywhere else in chs. 10–13 (or all of 2 Corinthians). Therefore, we cannot conclude that it is a major issue.

There has been some discussion of the Spirit in this letter, but it addressed only the Spirit's manifestations in apostles and no other points. Since the reference to Jesus does not point to problems with Christology and since 'gospel' is too general to reveal anything about the opponents, 'other Spirit' is not a reference to a heretical pneumatology. Rather, 11.4 is a general list like that in Gal. 1.6-9.[269] So we cannot attach specialized significance to any of the three 'others' of 11.4. They simply show that the opponents have a 'wrong-headed perception of the entire Christian Kerygma as Paul understands it'.[270]

---

265. In addition, 11.4 takes the form of a conditional question, which most scholars rightly see as a real rather than a hypothetical (contrary-to-fact) condition. So Käsemann, 'Die Legitimität', pp. 37-38; Barrett, 'Paul's Opponents', p. 277; Oostendorp, *Another Jesus*, p. 8; Schmithals, *Gnosticism in Corinth*, pp. 132-33; Georgi, *Die Gegner*, p. 284; Bultmann, *The Second Letter to the Corinthians*, p. 201; Furnish, *II Corinthians*, p. 488; Martin, *2 Corinthians*, p. 335.

266. E.g. Oostendorp, *Another Jesus*, pp. 7, 9; Schmithals, *Gnosticism in Corinth*, pp. 132-34; Georgi, *Die Gegner*, pp. 284-85; Friedrich, 'Die Gegner', p. 188; W. Bieder, 'Paulus und seine Gegner in Korinth', *TZ* 17 (1961), pp. 319-33 (324-25).

267. Oostendorp, *Another Jesus*, p. 7; Schmithals, *Gnosticism in Corinth*, p. 134; Georgi, *Die Gegner*, pp. 284-85; Friedrich, 'Die Gegner', pp. 188-89; Bieder, 'Paulus und seine Gegner', pp. 324-25; Martin, *2 Corinthians*, p. 336.

268. Bultmann, *The Second Letter to the Corinthians*, pp. 202-203; Barrett, 'Paul's Opponents', p. 241; Furnish, *II Corinthians*, p. 501. Bultmann cites 2 Cor. 10.7; 11.23; 4.10-11; and 4.4-6 as evidence of this in 2 Corinthians (*The Second Letter to the Corinthians*, pp. 202-203). Cf. Rom. 3.26.

269. Furnish, *II Corinthians*, p. 501.

270. Martin, *2 Corinthians*, p. 341. Martin is following Bultmann (*The Second*

Thus 11.4 demonstrates that Paul perceived these opponents as a serious threat to the community and that he thinks they represent an aberrant understanding of the Christian message. This verse reveals nothing more specific.

Summary of Allusions

Two issues dominate allusions to opponents: accepting support and the proper apostolic manifestation of the Spirit. The many references to receiving support (11.12; 11.7-11; 12.13; 12.15b-18) indicate that the opponents understand it as evidence of legitimate apostleship. Pay is more than an apostolic right to them; it is a 'sign of an apostle'. They interpret Paul's refusal of pay as evidence that he is not a true apostle and as an indication that he does not love the Corinthians. They may also accuse Paul of fraud, asserting that while he refuses overt support, he takes money from the Jerusalem collection fund.

Allusions also show that Paul's rivals identify the Spirit as the source of the powerful lives of apostles. They believe visionary experiences demonstrate spiritual power or a special measure of the Spirit and thus are evidence of apostleship.

The question of the proper manifestation of the Spirit in apostles takes us to the heart of the problems at Corinth. Even the question of accepting pay is related to the issue of the apostolic way of life. Since the opponents believe that the Spirit enables them to live powerful lives, they question Paul's apostleship because he does not live this sort of life.

Affirmations

10.8[271]

Within the polemical section composed of 10.7-11, Paul says in v. 8 that even if he were to boast more than he does, he would be telling the truth. He then identifies the purpose of his authority as building up, not tearing down. This comment about boasting is an affirmation, not an

---

Letter to the Corinthians, pp. 202-203) here. So also Furnish, *II Corinthians*, pp. 501-502. However, Martin does make 'Jesus' refer to problems with Christology.

271. There will be no discussion here of 13.4 or 13.10, even though some interpreters use them to identify opponents, because these verses appear within a didactic section. According to our method, we cannot use affirmations in didactic sections to identify opponents.

allusion, despite the comparison in the first part of the verse. The comparison in v. 8 is between Paul's boast that he is 'of Christ' (v. 7) and what he could boast of,[272] not between what he could say (or is saying) and his 'boasting' at some earlier time.[273] He comments on the purpose of his authority to overcome the suspicion that he wants to frighten the Corinthians with his letters (10.9)[274] and to defend his prior use of apostolic authority. Since he has used it to build up, his claim to authority seems, to the opponents, to be without basis.

This verse probably shows that the opponents question Paul's apostolic authority because of the way he has used it. They see nothing of the power of apostles in his use of authority. Thus, 10.8 confirms that the opponents question Paul's apostolic authority. It also confirms that Paul and his rivals understand apostolic service differently.

11.30

Paul says in 11.30 that if he must boast,[275] he will boast only in what shows his weakness. Within this polemical section (11.21b-33), Paul is here rejecting the opponents' criteria for comparing ministries. He interprets the hardship catalog of vv. 22-29 in v. 30 so that the Corinthians do not miss the point;[276] his weakness is his evidence of apostleship. This affirmation, confirms that Paul and his rivals recognize different criteria for identifying apostles.

12.5-6

Paul's boasting in weakness surfaces again in 12.5-6. He rejects telling of visionary experiences as a criterion for apostleship, contending that

---

272. Bultmann, *The Second Letter to the Corinthians*, p. 188; Plummer, *Commentary*, p. 280; Barrett, *2 Corinthians*, p. 258; Furnish, *II Corinthians*, p. 466; Martin, *2 Corinthians*, p. 309. Oostendorp asserts that the authority Paul boasts of is that which he will use on his next visit (*Another Jesus*, p. 19).

273. Gunther contends that this verse shows that the opponents know that Paul has defended his authority in other letters (*St. Paul's Opponents*, p. 302).

274. Barrett, *2 Corinthians*, pp. 258-59.

275. Martin asserts that 'it is necessary to boast' may be a slogan of the opponents (*2 Corinthians*, p. 383). Cf. my discussion of this expression in the section on 12.1; above pp. 344-46.

276. Bultmann calls v. 30 the concluding survey of vv. 22-29 and suggests that it sets everything in vv. 22-29 'under the viewpoint of *asthenia*' (*The Second Letter to the Corinthians*, p. 217). Cf. Martin, *2 Corinthians*, p. 383.

such evidence may give a false impression.[277] He further asserts that weakness is the appropriate evidence of apostolic status.[278] This affirmation, as the last two did, confirms that Paul rejects the opponents' conception of the appropriate way of life for apostles. Paul here refuses to present evidence that they ask for and which he could supply because by submitting to their demand he would be recognizing the opponents' false criteria for evaluating apostles.

12.10

The conclusion and climax[279] of 12.1-10 comes at v. 10. Paul explains in this verse that he boasts in weakness because when he is weak he is the strongest, because that is when God's power works mightily in him.[280] In 12.10 Paul both puts forward once again his weakness as evidence of apostleship and explains for the first time in this letter why he boasts in weakness. He asserts that his weakness represents 'the effective working of the power of the crucified Christ in his ministry'.[281] This affirmation confirms that Paul's criteria for validating apostleship differ from those of his opponents.

Summary of Affirmations

All four affirmations in this letter concern Paul's weakness. Instead of seeing it as a liability, Paul rejects the opponents' criteria for evaluating apostles and boasts in the weakness seen in his troubled life, his silence about visions, and his 'thorn in the flesh'. Thus these affirmations confirm that Paul's weakness is an important issue.

Boasting also comes up often in these allusions. Paul rejects the opponents' practice of presenting evidence of apostleship by telling of spiritual exploits and successful lives. Thus he rejects both the content and

---

277. Paul is probably not implying that his rivals lie about having visions when he affirms the truth of his statement about visions. Contra Martin, *2 Corinthians*, p. 408. The polemical context would allow this interpretation if we had other evidence for it, but we do not. Similarly, Paul's reference to 'false apostles' (11.13) does not mean that his opponents lie about being apostles. This label represents Paul's evaluation of his rivals, not an accusation against their truthfulness.

278. Furnish, *II Corinthians*, p. 546.

279. See the comment of Martin, *2 Corinthians*, p. 423.

280. Plummer proposes that the γάρ ('for') of v. 10 introduces the reason that Paul rejoices in weakness (*Commentary*, p. 356). As Bultmann suggests (*The Second Letter to the Corinthians*, p. 228), 12.10c expresses the same truth as v. 9a.

281. Furnish, *II Corinthians*, p. 552.

Servants of Satan

the method they use to secure their position in Corinth. These affirmations, then, confirm that the appropriate way of life for apostles is the central issue.

Conclusion

Three related issues dominate the debate between Paul and the opponents of 2 Corinthians 10–13: (1) the appropriate way of life for apostles; (2) the proper manifestation of the Spirit in apostles; and (3) pay for apostles. All three issues concern legitimate apostleship. Therefore, Käsemann is right to identify this as the overriding concern of the letter.

These opponents have come to Corinth claiming the titles 'apostle', 'servant of Christ' and 'missionary'. With these titles they claim a special relationship with Christ and equality with or superiority to Paul. They use their Jewish heritage to claim special qualifications as teachers, but nothing suggests that they are Judaizers and there is no hint that the Mosaic Law is an issue. Likewise, there is no evidence that they have or claim any connection with Jerusalem. Finding that they are not Judaizers does not mean that their Jewishness was unimportant,[282] only that they use it to some end other than extending observance of the Law to Gentile Christians.

The Spirit-inspired way of life for apostles is the central issue. It lies at the heart of the argument about apostolic legitimation. Indeed, the problems at Corinth stem from the disagreement between Paul and his rivals over the way that the Spirit operates in apostles' lives. The opponents argue that the Spirit enables apostles to lead powerful and obviously successful lives and lifts them above hardships and humiliations. In addition, the Spirit grants visions and revelations to apostles and enables them to perform miraculous deeds ('signs, wonders, and mighty deeds').

These opponents believe that apostles, as superiors, should assume authority over churches and demand special rights. This apostolic superiority includes having forceful personalities and glorious lives. They

---

282. Richardson (*Paul's Language about God* [JSNTSup, 99; Sheffield: JSOT Press, 1994], p. 141 n. 2) seems to think that not finding these opponents to be Judaizers indicates that I downplay the importance of their claim to being Jewish. Similar to my view that apostles who use their Jewish descent to some advantage among Gentiles need not be Judaizers, see Strecker, 'Die Legitimität des Paulinischen Apostolates', p. 572.

may cite Paul's unimpressive life as evidence that he is not a true apostle and perhaps as evidence that he lacks the measure of the Spirit necessary to be an apostle. They evaluate the absence of this power in his life as evidence that he lives 'according to the flesh'.

Another part of this Spirit-endowed, impressive personality is being a good speaker. The opponents criticize Paul for being a poor speaker. There is no good evidence that the speech they 'boast' of and complain that Paul lacks is some kind of ecstatic utterance. Even their visions do not seem to have been instances of public ecstasy. Paul intimates that they tell about these visions, not that they have them in public (12.1-10. 'It is necessary to *boast*...'). The opponents may claim their speech is inspired, but it is not ecstatic speech that they demand of Paul, it is rhetorical skill. They think apostles should reflect the Spirit by being persuasive, dynamic speakers.

Beyond a commanding demeanor, the way of life these opponents approve entails recounting one's qualifications for apostleship—what Paul calls boasting. They recount their successful lives, their miraculous deeds, and their visionary experiences as evidence that the Spirit lives in them in the measure that makes them apostles. They believe this presentation of credentials is appropriate and necessary for apostles.

Another feature of the opponents' understanding of the Spirit-endowed, apostolic way of life is that apostles must exercise the right to receive financial support. Thus, the opponents use Paul's rejection of maintenance to question his apostleship and his love for the Corinthians. The opponents see pay as a congregation's acknowledgment of their apostleship and, in turn, as evidence of their apostolic status. This understanding of support makes Paul's rejection of it incomprehensible if he is truly an apostle and an apostle of the Corinthian church.

The evidence of 2 Corinthians 10–13 shows that Paul's opponents are Pneumatics.[283] We may call them Pneumatics because they emphasize manifestations of the Spirit in apostles, not because they teach some abstract belief about the Spirit that is different from Paul's. They assert that the Spirit is the source of their apostolic demeanor, practices, and manner of life. The various manifestations of the Spirit are their evidence for the legitimacy of their apostleship. They see Paul's 'weak-

---

283. The data of 2 Corinthians must determine what it means when we call the opponents Pneumatics. Information from other letters in which interpreters find Pneumatics does not necessarily contribute to our understanding of the opponents of 2 Corinthians.

ness' as evidence that he does not possess the Spirit, at least not in the measure they do. Thus, he is not a true apostle. It is this understanding of the appropriate manifestations of the Spirit in apostles that makes them opponents of Paul.

A COMPARISON OF THE OPPONENTS IN THE TWO LETTERS OF 2 CORINTHIANS

Having examined the two letters in 2 Corinthians individually, we are now in a position to determine whether the opponents of these letters are related. In chs. 1–7 the argument between Paul and his rivals focuses on the proper manifestation of divine power in apostles' lives, with the issue of the proper criteria for evaluating apostles dominating the debate. Under the rubric of criteria for apostolic status the opponents raise the issues of pay for apostles, offering proof of apostolic status, and the practice of comparing ministries. They cite financial support and carry letters of recommendation as evidence of their apostleship. They also commend themselves as apostles on the basis of their powerful lives, a practice Paul calls boasting.

The central issue of the second letter, chs. 10–13, is legitimate apostleship. The crux of the matter is the difference between Paul's and his rivals' understandings of the manifestation of the Spirit in apostles' lives, more specifically, they disagree about the appropriate way of life for Spirit-endowed apostles. Issues raised in connection with this debate include pay for apostles, spiritual gifts and experiences, and presenting evidence of apostolic status. These opponents contend that the Spirit produces in them a commanding demeanor, and the ability to lead powerful and successful lives. They offer these features of their lives, along with visionary experiences and the power to perform miracles as evidence that they possess the measure of the Spirit that makes one an apostle. They assert that apostles must present evidence to claim the rights and privileges of apostles. Paul again calls this boasting and rejects it.

It is clear that the central issue of both letters is the form of apostles' lives and that the same issues are raised in connection with this central concern. Both address the issues of pay for apostles, the practice of presenting evidence of apostolic status, and the proper criteria for evaluating apostles. Furthermore, they also approach these same issues from the same point of view. The opponents of both letters value an impressive personality and way of life and see them as manifestations of God's presence in apostles. Both groups of opponents see accepting financial support as evidence of apostolic status and try to force Paul either to accept support from the Corinthians or to admit that he has no right to it. Both also believe that apostles must present their credentials and criticize Paul for not being willing to do so. Thus, on these central issues the opponents of the two letters agree.

Since the opponents of both letters raise the same issues, approach them with the same general point of view, and come to the same positions on specific issues, we may conclude that Paul is facing the same kind of opponent in both. Furthermore, since Paul is addressing the same church in two letters written within a short time-span, we may reasonably conclude that the same group is in view in both letters.

Even though the opponents of these letters are the very same group, we must be extremely careful about attributing characteristics of the opponents of one letter to those of the other. Since there was an interval, however short, between these two letters, we must allow for change or development in some of the opponents' positions, especially if the report that occasioned the second letter comes from a time after the church had received the first. If the first letter enjoyed any sucess, the opponents would have had to react to it in order to retain their status in the community. That reaction may have entailed modifications in their positions or arguments. However, since we know that they claim the Spirit as the source of their gifts and demeanor at the time of chs. 10–13, we may reasonably conclude that they grounded their claims to the divine power that enables an impressive life in their possession of the Spirit at the time of chs. 1–7. Still, we may not transfer their claims about visions and miracle working to the earlier time because that takes us beyond the evidence of that letter.[284]

This study finds no evidence that the opponents of the letters of 2 Corinthians are Gnostics or the type of divine men Georgi hypothesizes.

---

284. Our knowledge that they claimed gifts of the Spirit at this later time may, perhaps, make it more likely that 5.13 is an allusion rather than an affirmation. However, this oblique reference remains the only possible mention of a public display of ecstatic gifts in all of 2 Corinthians. Thus, it is insufficient evidence to claim that these opponents gave ecstatic displays. The references to spiritual gifts in 10–13 do not suggest that the opponents publicly exercised ecstatic gifts. The texts say only that they relate these experiences to the Corinthians as evidence of their apostolic status. Furthermore, this passage is open to interpretations other than seeing it as a reference to ecstatic experiences. See the suggestion of Plummer (*Commentary*, pp. 171-73).

Neither is there evidence that they want Gentiles to observe some aspect of Judaism that Paul does not require. Again, this does not mean their Jewishness was unimportant, only that they used it to further a different agenda. Käsemann correctly identifies apostolic legitimation as the central issue, with the Spirit as the major point in the debate. However, the connection with Jerusalem that he suggests finds no support from 2 Corinthians. Thus, there is no basis for identifying them with any other of these proposed movements. However, the issues being debated at Corinth were current in the broader religio-philosophical environment.

First-century philosophers and propagandists debated the issues of the proper way of life and means of support for teachers[285] and propagandists. Some of them assert that a true holy person has powers beyond those of ordinary people, including a powerful and impressive way of life.[286] Such an image is found in Lucian's *Dream* 13 and Philostratus's portrayal of Apollonius. Others, however, reject that understanding of a philosopher's life. The undignified and surly demeanor of the Cynics is commonly a point in caricatures.[287] Dio Chrysostom discusses the various ways philosophers present themselves and praises Diogenes's way of life.[288] Dio also quotes Diogenes recommending a life of hardships and rejecting social conventions.[289]

285. Dio Chrysostom enters this discussion when he warns against accepting pay from the wealthy (*Discourse*, 77/80.37-39). See also the work by Musonius entitled, 'What Means of Support is Appropriate for a Philosopher?' (cited by Hock, *The Social Context of Paul's Ministry*, pp. 57-58). See Hock's discussion (*The Social Context of Paul's Ministry*, pp. 52-59) for a more complete treatment of this issue.

286. This is the view of Philostratus, as seen in his treatment of Apollonius of Tyana in the *Life of Apollonius*; cf. A.D. Nock, *Conversion: The Old and the New in Religion from Alexander the Great to Augustine of Hippo* (New York: Oxford University Press, 1933), p. 91. Dio Chrysostom also comments that a philosopher should be remarkable in everything (*Discourse* 71.1-2). See also Lucian's *Lover of Lies* (34) and his description of a philosopher as a dignified and powerful figure in contrast to the lowly artisan in *Dream* (13).

287. Lucian constantly portrays Cynics as poorly dressed and carrying a rod. See, e.g., *Fisherman* (44). Cf. Hock, *The Social Context of Paul's Ministry*, p. 56 and notes.

288. Dio Chrysostom, *Discourse*, 6.1-72. Dio includes praise of Diogenes's living outside and eating habits in this passage.

289. Dio Chrysostom, *Discourse*, 8.11-13.

This milieu could easily provoke the kind of problem that arises at Corinth, as Paul and his rivals compete for the congregation's allegiance. A primary difference between these competitors is the way they believe apostles should comport themselves. The opponents may have taken up a way of life more like that described by Lucian and Philostratus; Paul's demeanor is more like that of the Cynics.

This parallel does not indicate that Paul held a Cynic ideology or that his opponents had ideological connections with any philosophical school. The point is only that contemporaries were debating the issue of the proper way of life for propagandists and coming to positions similar to those being reached in Corinth. Paul, his rivals and the Corinthians would have been aware of these competing models. Paul argues in these letters that his way of life is the appropriate one for Christian missionaries.

Chapter 4

PAUL MAKES SOME ENEMIES—GALATIANS

Hypotheses about the opponents of Galatians continue to be produced at an amazing rate, fueled in part by E.P. Sanders's work and studies on Paul's use of rhetoric in his letters. Yet the discussion often sounds much as it did to Lagrange in 1925 when he noted that the basic debate was over whether the opponents required the law for salvation (i.e. as an entrance requirement) or as a means for perfection.[1] Recent work has, however, produced new questions and given renewed force to older questions: Is there really an attack on Paul's apostleship?[2] Do the opponents think they are in agreement with Paul?[3] Is the Spirit rather than the Law the central aspect of their teaching?[4] What is the place of eschatology in the Galatian controversy?[5] Are the opponents related to the Jerusalem community?[6] Such questions call for a reexamination of the evidence.

Before turning to individual texts within Galatians, some comments on rhetorical analysis and the epistolary genre are necessary. Much fruitful effort has been expended of late on identifying the rhetorical genre of Galatians. But we cannot begin this study by taking either the view

1. M.-J. Lagrange, *Saint Paul: Epître aux Galates* (EBib; Paris: Gabalda, 2nd edn, 1925), pp. xxxi-xxxviii.
2. Beverly R. Gaventa, 'Galatians 1 and 2: Autobiography as Paradigm', *NovT* 28 (1986), pp. 309-26; Bernard Lategan, 'Is Paul Defending his Apostleship in Galatians? The Function of Galatians 1.11-12 and 2.19-20 in the Development of Paul's Argument', *NTS* 34 (1988), pp. 411-30.
3. George Howard, *Crisis in Galatia* (SNTSMS, 35; Cambridge: Cambridge University Press, 2nd edn, 1990).
4. Charles H. Cosgrove, *The Cross and the Spirit: A Study in the Argument and Theology of Galatians* (Macon, GA: Mercer University Press, 1988), pp. viii, 2.
5. Martyn, 'Events in Galatia, pp. 160-79.
6. Robert Jewett, 'The Agitators and the Galatian Congregation', *NTS* 17 (1971), pp. 198-212.

that this letter is forensic[7] or that it is deliberative[8] because each defines the situation at Galatia more precisely than evidence permits at this point. So this decision must be postponed at least until we have examined the explicit statements about opponents. We can still draw on ancient rhetorical theorists when determining what kind of context we are in because these two species of rhetoric have many of the same parts that perform similar functions. We need not postpone our initial decision about the epistolary genre. As Hansen has shown, Galatians fits well within the genre of a letter of rebuke, beginning with its use of θαυμάζω ('I am amazed').[9] This classification does not define the situation in the ways choosing a rhetorical genre does; it only shows how seriously Paul takes the situation.

Explicit Statements

6.12-13
One of the most direct statements about the other teachers in Galatia appears in 6.12-13 where Paul says they want to circumcise the Galatians in order to make a good showing, avoid persecution, and boast. Betz identifies 6.11-18 as the *conclusio* or *peroratio* that summarizes the argument and makes an emotional impact, in part by arousing hostility toward opponents and stimulating pity for the author.[10] Kennedy sees the section simply as the epilogue that restates what has been demonstrated.[11] These rhetorical analyses parallel the epistolary conven-

---

7. This is the view of H.D. Betz, 'The Literary Composition and Function of Paul's Letter to the Galatians', *NTS* 21 (1975), pp. 353-79; *idem, Galatians: A Commentary on Paul's Letter to the Churches in Galatia* (Hermeneia; Philadelphia: Fortress Press, 1979), pp. 14-28; and James D. Hester, 'The Use and Influence of Rhetoric in Galatians 2:1-14', *TZ* 42 (1986), pp. 386-408. Richard Longenecker (*Galatians* [WBC, 41; Dallas, TX: Word Books, 1990], pp. 11-12, 184) classifies 1.6–4.11 as forensic and the remainder of Galatians as deliberative.

8. This is the view of G.A. Kennedy, *New Testament Interpretation*, pp. 145-46; Joop Smit, 'The Letter of Paul to the Galatians: A Deliberative Speech', *NTS* 35 (1989), pp. 1-26; and Robert G. Hall, 'The Rhetorical Outline for Galatians: A Reconsideration', *JBL* 106 (1987), pp. 277-87.

9. G. Walter Hansen, *Abraham in Galatians: Epistolary and Rhetorical Contexts* (JSNTSup, 29; Sheffield: JSOT Press, 1989), pp. 33-44, 53-54.

10. Betz, *Galatians*, p. 313.

11. Kennedy, *New Testament Interpretation*, p. 151. Similarly Benoit Standaert,

tion of the autographic postscript that also summarizes the main points of the letter.[12] In a letter written to combat opponents, any reference to them in such concluding remarks is likely to be very polemical.[13]

This polemical context requires us to be extremely cautious about any attribution of motives, especially if part of the section's function is to arouse hostility toward opponents. We cannot accept at face value that the opponents seek 'only' to avoid persecution or simply want to make a good showing in the flesh (v. 12). Nor can we be certain from this passage that persecution is involved with their motives at all.[14] Further, the polemical accusation in v. 13 that the opponents do not themselves keep the Law may simply be a charge that they are dishonest or not sincere in their Law-keeping,[15] just as v. 13b intends to make their

'La rhétorique antique et l'épître aux Galates', *Foi et Vie* 84 (1985), pp. 33-40 (34), and Hall, 'Rhetorical Outline', p. 286.

12. Betz, *Galatians*, p. 312. See also B.R. Gaventa, 'The Singularity of the Gospel: A Reading of Galatians', in *Pauline Theology*, I, pp. 147-59 (155); and George Lyons, *Pauline Autobiography* (SBLDS, 73; Atlanta: Scholars Press, 1985), p. 168.

13. This is especially the case if Jeffrey A.D. Weima (*Neglected Endings: The Significance of the Pauline Letter Closings* [JSNTSup, 101; Sheffield: JSOT Press, 1994], pp. 237-38) and Longenecker (*Galatians*, p. 287) are correct that Paul's letters' closings usually, but especially in the case of Galatians, recapitulate the main points of the letter. Dieter Lührmann (*Galatians: A Continental Commentary* [trans. O.C. Dean; Minneapolis: Fortress Press, 1992], p. 120) comments that 6.12-13 gives a 'polemical sketch' of the opponents.

14. So also John M.G. Barclay, *Obeying the Truth: A Study of Paul's Ethic in Galatians* (Edinburgh: T. & T. Clark, 1988), pp. 37-38; Walter Schmithals, 'Judaisten in Galatien?', *ZNW* 74 (1983), p. 55; Helmut Koester, *Introduction to the New Testament*. II. *History and Literature of Early Christianity*, p. 119, who says Paul is accusing the opponents of 'dishonesty and self-interest'. Lührmann (*Galatians*, p. 123) identifies 6.12-13 as one of the three passages from which we can learn the least about the opponents because of the way Paul assigns them intentions. However, Jewett ('The Agitators', pp. 203-207) builds his understanding of the opponents' concerns on a literalistic reading of this passage which does not take the polemic of the section into account. Jewett is followed by Longenecker (*Galatians*, pp. xcv-xcvi). Elsewhere, however, Longenecker acknowledges that this is Paul's interpretation of their behavior (*Galatians*, pp. 290-91).

15. So Barclay, *Obeying the Truth*, pp. 64-65. Francis Watson (*Paul, Judaism and the Gentiles: A Sociological Approach* [SNTSMS, 56; Cambridge: Cambridge University Press, 1986], p. 62) writes: 'Paul is not interested in the slightest in an "objective" assessment of his opponents' character; thus it is a mistake to read 6.13 as evidence that they were antinomians. He is concerned only that his converts should reject their call for integration into the Jewish community, and one way of

motives suspect. Thus, it is impossible to discern with certainty anything about their practice of the Law or their motives from 6.12-13.

These verses do show that circumcision was a central issue. It is the topic of all of 6.11-18 and the focus of the accusations in vv. 12-13. The accusation that these teachers themselves do not keep the Law (v. 13a) may intimate that they require more of the Law than circumcision, but this is not certain. Finally, vv. 12-13 indicate that the opponents are from outside the Galatian congregation, because Paul distinguishes between the Galatians and the opponents.

1.6-7

In rhetorical terms, 1.6-11(12) functions as the *exordium* which states the cause of the speech and makes the audience receptive to the speaker by speaking of oneself and one's adversaries.[16] In a letter of rebuke, the material immediately following θαυμάζω ('I am amazed') contains the reason for the author's astonishment as well as rebukes.[17] Since the beginning of Galatians fits the model of a letter of rebuke, vv. 1.6-11 (12) state the letter's occasion. These verses also set the polemical tone of the letter by interpreting the opponents' activities as disturbing the community—an accusation with political shading[18]—and subverting the gospel, as well as calling down a curse on them.

In vv. 6-7 Paul says the other teachers' message is altogether different from his, a 'different gospel' and not a gospel at all, but there is no reason to think that their gospel does not include Christ, as Walter argues.[19] Instead, given the polemical nature of the section, Paul's claim

---

doing this is to give a hostile assessment of their character'. J.D.G. Dunn (*A Commentary on the Epistle to the Galatians* [BNTC; London: A. & C. Black, 1993], p. 338) notes that this charge is 'of a piece with the intersectarian polemic characteristic of Palestinian Judaism during this period'.

16. Betz, *Galatians*, pp. 44-45. However, Hall ('Rhetorical Outline', pp. 282-83) identifies vv. 1-5 as the *exordium* and vv. 6-9 as the *propositio*. But he still sees the point as setting out the main opposition of the letter.

17. Hansen, *Abraham*, p. 33.

18. So also Dunn, *Epistle to the Galatians*, p. 43. Longenecker (*Galatians*, p. 16) plays down the political aspect of the term, but in doing so seems to slight the focus of Paul on the effect the opponents are having on the Galatians as a community.

19. Nikolaus Walter, 'Paulus und die Gegner des Christusevangeliums in Galatien', in A. Vanhoye (ed.), *L'apôtre Paul: Personnalité, style, et conception du ministère* (Leuven: Leuven University Press, 1986), p. 351.

that their teaching is not a gospel is his polemical evaluation.[20] 'Another gospel' is Paul's ironic characterization of the other teaching.[21] Verses 1.6-7 also indicate that the opponents are from outside Galatia because Paul once again distinguishes them from the Galatians, even though the rebuke is directed at the Galatians.

4.17

The explicit statement, 4.17, appears in the section comprising 4.12-20, a personal appeal[22] that emphasizes pathos.[23] Jervis identifies 4.11-20 as an apostolic parousia which appeals to 'a lost love and compliance' and re-establishes Paul's 'apostolic credibility and leadership'.[24] These verses are apologetic, but do not necessarily respond to charges as Paul confirms his position among the Galatians.[25] Still, his relationship with the Galatians is a focus here.

In 4.17 Paul says that the opponents seek the Galatians for no good purpose and that they want to shut the Galatians out. These accusations[26] caricature the opponents' behavior.[27] What they want to shut the Galatians off from is somewhat obscure, but it probably means they are

20. Hansen, *Abraham*, p. 87 sees 1.7 as primarily evaluative. Schütz (*Paul and the Anatomy of Apostolic Authority*, p. 120) also sees Paul making charges against the opponents in 1.7.

21. Betz, *Galatians*, pp. 16, 46; Hester, 'Use and Influence', p. 393 n. 22. Contra Franz Mussner (*Der Galaterbrief* [HTKNT, 9; Freiburg: Herder, 1974], p. 13) who sees this expression as a slogan of the opponents. Given that this expression is ironic characterization, Longenecker (*Galatians*, p. 15) reads too much into the different adjectives (ἕτερος and ἄλλος) used in this verse.

22. Hansen, *Abraham*, p. 53; Frank Thielman, *From Plight to Solution: A Jewish Framework for Understanding Paul's View of the Law in Galatians and Romans* (NovTSup, 61; Leiden: E.J. Brill, 1989), p. 83.

23. Kennedy, *New Testament Interpretation*, p. 150. Standaert, 'La rhétorique antique', p. 37, makes 4.8-20 the section, but gives it the same function.

24. L. Ann Jervis, *The Purpose of Romans: A Comparative Letter Structure Investigation* (JSNTSup, 55; Sheffield: JSOT Press, 1991), p. 120.

25. Hansen, *Abraham*, p. 59, also sees 4.13-16 as self-defense.

26. Cf. Hansen, *Abraham*, pp. 59, 87; Watson, *Paul, Judaism and the Gentiles*, p. 62; Smit, 'The Letter of Paul to the Galatians', p. 17. Longenecker (*Galatians*, p. 194) calls v. 17 a 'biting attack'.

27. Betz, *Galatians*, p. 21; John Buckel, 'Paul's Defense of Christian Liberty in Galatians', *Louvain Studies* 17 (1992), pp. 254-68 (257). Longenecker (*Galatians*, p. 194) notes that 4.17b is Paul's evaluation.

being separated from Paul[28] because the paragraph is about Paul's relationship with the Galatians, and he specifically says that the opponents want the Galatians to seek them.[29] Interpreting the opponents' actions in this way, Paul asserts that accepting the opponents means breaking with him. This could well be a new thought to the Galatians. Thus, 4.17 shows only that Paul interprets accepting the opponents as turning from him.

5.7-10, 12

Some of Paul's strongest statements about these teachers appear in 5.7-12. The entire paragraph is an attack on them with negative judgments about their effect on the Galatians and about their own end.[30] This polemical section's primary intent is to convince the Galatians to reject the opponents.[31]

Paul begins (vv. 7-8) by saying that the Galatians' progress has been stopped by a persuasion which is not from God. Then, after a rare word of confidence in this letter's recipients (v. 10a), Paul returns to his evaluation of the opponents' activities. Verse 10b picks up the quasi-political language of 1.7 (ταράσσοντες ['disturbing']) as Paul evaluates the effect the opponents are having, emphasizing their impact on the life of the community. In v. 12 Paul keeps the focus on the community by

28. So most other interpreters, e.g. F.F. Bruce, *The Epistle to the Galatians: A Commentary on the Greek Text* (NIGTC; Grand Rapids: Eerdmans, 1982), pp. 211-12; George S. Duncan, *The Epistle of Paul to the Galatians* (MNTC; New York: Harper & Brothers, 1934), pp. 140-41; Ronald Y.K. Fung, *The Epistle to the Galatians* (NICNT; Grand Rapids: Eerdmans, 1988), p. 200; Betz, *Galatians*, pp. 230-31. Contra Martyn ('Law-Observant Mission', pp. 315-16) who understands it to mean excluding the Galatians from salvation, and Dunn (*Epistle to the Galatians*, p. 238) who argues that it means to exclude all Gentiles except proselytes from Christianity.

29. Betz (*Galatians*, pp. 230-31) finds Paul contrasting true friends and flatterers as he contrasts himself telling them the truth (v. 16) and the opponents who seek them.

30. Dunn (*Epistle to the Galatians*, p. 273) comments that in this section Galatians is 'at its sharpest and most nerve-racking' tone.

31. Hansen (*Abraham*, p. 59) sees the section as accusatory and Barclay (*Obeying the Truth*, pp. 37-38) recognizes the polemical nature of the passage. Smit ('The Letter of Paul to the Galatians', p. 19) identifies these verses as the *indignatio*, a part of the conclusion which intends to incite hatred of one's opponents. While Smit's rhetorical analysis depends on an unlikely interpolation theory at this point, he has identified the section's function.

asserting that the opponents cause a disturbance, another word with political shading.[32] Thus, 5.7-10, 12 give us only Paul's strongly negative
evaluation of the opponents' activity.[33] We will discuss 5.11 below as
an allusion.

3.1

Our final explicit statement begins ch. 3. Verses 3.1-5 are a central
passage for the theses of Cosgrove and Lull that the Spirit is the leading
issue in Galatians. With its rebuke for foolishness, 3.1-5 follows the
conventions of a θαυμάζω or rebuke letter.[34] This section introduces the
argument of 3.1–4.11,[35] but does not seem to be polemical. Rather it is
rebuke and instruction, even if somewhat ironic, and its target is primarily the Galatians, not the opponents. So 3.1-5 is didactic, but very
closely connected to the primary issues in Galatia.

The only explicit statement about opponents in this section is 3.1
where Paul asks who has bewitched the Galatians. This is another
polemical evaluation of the opponents' work, a rhetorical device to
denigrate their message and stategies.[36] So we learn nothing specific
about the opponents from 3.1.

Summary of Explicit Statements

Explicit statements show that the opponents are from outside the Galatian congregation. The clearest feature in their teaching is that they
require circumcision. Verse 6.13 may imply that they require more of
the law than this, but we cannot be certain. Paul's thoroughly polemical

---

32. Paul's view of their activity may be clarified by his use of ἀναστατόω since
it is used in Acts 21.38 to refer to the Egyptian who caused a revolt. This could point
to how seriously Paul views their activity or to the fact that they incite the Galatians
to revolt against Paul. But the evidence is too weak and inferential to make this
latter claim with any certainty at all.

33. It is possible that v. 10b singles out a particular individual as the leader of
those who trouble the Galatians, but this is not certain and not especially probable.
See the comments of Longenecker, *Galatians*, p. 232. Especially interesting is
Dunn's view that the singular is intended 'to particularize his warning to each and
every one of the other missionaries' (*Epistle to the Galatians*, pp. 278-79).

34. Hansen, *Abraham*, p. 42.

35. Betz, *Galatians*, p. 128; Hans Hübner, 'Der Galaterbrief und das Verhältnis
von antiker Rhetorik und Epistolographie', *TLZ* 109 (1984), p. 249; Smit, 'The Letter of Paul to the Galatians', pp. 13-14.

36. See Betz, *Galatians*, p. 131, and the sources cited there.

evaluation of these teachers' activity shows that he sees them as his opponents and as dangerous. It seems possible that they try to draw the Galatians away from Paul, but while this is certainly Paul's evaluation of their activity, it may not be their goal.

Allusions

Galatians contains some statements that speak directly about the situation at Galatia, but not the opponents. If we can make a connection between these statements (5.1-6; 4.8-11; 4.21) and what we know of the opponents, we may allow them to contribute to our characterization of the opponents.

5.2-6

We identify 5.2-6 as an allusion to the opponents because these verses speak of circumcision. The section comprised of 5.1(2)-12 has often been identified as the beginning of a hortatory section,[37] but many recent analyses see it as an important part of the conclusion of the arguments that begin at 3.1.[38] Just as 5.7-12 is polemical (see above), so is 5.1(2)-6.[39] Matera asserts that the purpose of 5.1-12 is to give reasons not to accept circumcision.[40] This is clearly the emphasis in vv. 2-6. Matera also sees vv. 1-12 as parallel to 6.11-17.[41] If Matera is correct, this strengthens our judgment that 5.1(2)-12 is polemical.

In 5.2-6 Paul gives what he sees as the consequences of accepting circumcision, consequences he finds unacceptable and thinks the Galatians will too.[42] The consequences he lists are: it makes Christ of no

37. E.g. Betz, *Galatians*, p. 22; Ernest deWitt Burton, *A Critical and Exegetical Commentary on the Epistle to the Galatians* (ICC; Edinburgh: T. & T. Clark, 1921), p. 269; Duncan, *The Epistle of Paul to the Galatians*, pp. 152-53; François Vouga, 'Zur rhetorischen Gattung des Galatesbriefes', *ZNW* 79 (1988), pp. 291-92 (291); Koester, *Introduction*, p. 119.

38. So e.g. Dunn, *Epistle to the Galatians*, pp. 260-61.

39. Dunn (*Epistle to the Galatians*, p. 260) describes this section as 'almost unique within Paul's letters in its passionate forcefulness, in its polarization of choice, and in its dismissal of those opposing him'.

40. Frank J. Matera, 'The Culmination of Paul's Argument to the Galatians: Gal 5,1–6,12', *JSNT* 32 (1988), p. 83.

41. Matera, '*Culmination*', pp. 83-85.

42. Longenecker (*Galatians*, pp. 228) calls vv. 2-4 a 'litany of dire consequences'.

effect, it obliges one to keep the whole law, it alienates one from Christ and it removes one from grace. Since being obligated to the whole law is part of this list, it is one of those things Paul believes the Galatians will find unacceptable.[43] So the opponents do not urge accepting the whole law, as far as the Galatians know. Dunn rejects this reading, asserting that the opponents must require much more because circumcision is the last thing a proselyte did, not the first.[44] But his view ignores the immediate literary context of this statement in Galatians. Being 'obligated to the whole law' is here one member in the list of things Paul knows the Galatians have not understood to be part of their acceptance of these other teachers. Whether they intend to increase the demands on the Galatian Gentiles at some later time, we cannot know. But at this point they do not attempt to impose the whole Law on the Galatians.

So 5.2-6 show only that Paul rejects circumcision because he views its acceptance by Gentiles as antithetical to being associated with Christ and living by grace. Since he speaks of justification in v. 5 as a future event (the hope of δικαιωσύνης ['righteousness']), this verse does not clarify for us the opponents' view of the function of circumcision for Gentiles; it shows only that they see it as compatible with Christianity.

4.8-10

We find in 4.8-10 that the Galatians are being asked to observe certain holy days. This relates to what we know of the opponents if these festivals are from Judaism, as it seems most likely.[45] Both epistolary and rhetorical analyses find a parallel between 3.1-5 and 4.8-11, with 3.1-5

---

43. Hansen, *Abraham*, p. 91 identifies this assertion as an argument of direction which indicates where one's chosen path leads.

44. Dunn, *Epistle to the Galatians*, pp. 265-66.

45. Even though no exclusively Jewish terms are used, the overall context of Galatians makes it probable that Judaism is the source of these festivals and some festivals of Judaism would be appropriately described with some of these expressions. E.g. for the way that 'new moons' were an important element in first-century Judaism see T.C.G. Thornton, 'Jewish New Moon Festivals, Galations 4:3-11 and Colossians 2:16', *JTS* 40 (1989), pp. 97-100. Lührmann's connection between these holy days and the στοιχεῖα and thus with the 'integration of one's whole life into the operation of the world' (*Galatians*, p. 85) is completely without any basis in the text. Such an interpretation seems to rely on an unestablished connection between the opponents of Galatians and those of Colossians (see Lührmann, *Galatians*, pp. 84-85, 126).

serving as the introduction and 4.8-11 as the conclusion of an *inclusio*.[46] As the conclusion to this major portion of the letter, 4.8-11 addresses in a somewhat polemical fashion specific practices that the opponents promote.[47]

We saw above that 6.13 may imply that the opponents require more of the law than circumcision, while 5.2-6 indicates that they do not require the whole Law. 4.10 reveals that what they demand beyond circumcision includes the observance of some holy days.

The most difficult aspect of 4.8-10 is the στοιχεῖα ('elements'). This passing reference has been used as evidence that the στοιχεῖα are part of the opponents' teaching and that these opponents are related to the opponents of Colossians.[48] However, since the only other mention of the στοιχεῖα in Galatians is a reference to pre-Christian existence (4.3), they do not seem to have played any part in the opponents' teaching. As Barclay asserts, making the στοιχεῖα part of the opponents' vocabulary relies too heavily on unsupported mirror reading.[49] Verse 9, with its reference to the στοιχεῖα, is the most polemical statement in this polemical section.[50] It is Paul's evaluation of the observance of these holy days rather than a citation of part of the opponents' teaching.[51] So the mention of the στοιχεῖα is part of Paul's attempt to turn the Galatians away from the opponents;[52] it is an accusation about their teachings.

46. Hansen, *Abraham*, p. 78; Kennedy, *New Testament Interpretation*, p. 149; Smit, 'The Letter of Paul to the Galatians', pp. 13-14.

47. Betz, *Galatians*, p. 213.

48. E.g. Jewett, 'The Agitators', p. 208; E. Earle Ellis, 'Paul and His Opponents', pp. 293-95; Martyn, 'Law-Observant Mission', p. 322; Eduard Schweizer, 'Slaves of the Elements and Worshipers of Angels: Gal 4:3, 9 and Col 2:8, 18, 20', *JBL* 107 (1988), pp. 455-68 (466).

49. Barclay, 'Mirror-Reading a Polemical Letter', p. 82.

50. Cf. J. Louis Martyn, 'Apocalyptic Antinomies in Paul's Letter to the Galatians', *NTS* 31 (1985), pp. 410-24 (423-24 n. 25); Betz, *Galatians*, p. 216.

51. Cf. Betz, *Galatians*, pp. 216-17. This use of the στοιχεῖα parallels their use in Colossians where they are not part of the opponents' teaching but a polemical evaluation of such teaching. See Jerry L. Sumney, '"Those Who Pass Judgment": The Opponents of Colossians', *Bib* 74 (1993), pp. 366-88. Also see Thielman, *From Plight to Solution*, p. 82 n. 125.

52. Dunn (*Epistle to the Galatians*, pp. 228-29) asserts that Paul intends to associate the careful reckoning of the dates of Jewish holy days (as part of the 'works of the law') with the στοιχεῖα. But the text gives no attention to how these dates are reckoned. The point is more simple and polemical: Paul is making the keeping of these feasts by Gentiles equivalent to keeping pagan observances.

This allusion shows that the opponents urge the observance of holy days, but gives no basis for connecting these festivals and veneration of the στοιχεῖα.[53] Paul's use of the στοιχεῖα in connection with these holy days is, to the Galatians, a surprising and devastating evaluation of the opponents' teachings.[54]

4.21

Paul alludes to the opponents in 4.21 when he speaks of wanting to be under the law. Verse 21 introduces the allegory of Sarah and Hagar which seems to be didactic, even though written in response to the opponents.[55] While some argue that the expression 'under Law' in 4.21 shows that the opponents intend to require the whole Law,[56] others find only a characterization of their position which they themselves would reject.[57] The latter view is supported by 5.2-6. D.A. Campbell's analysis of Paul's use of prepositions with πίστις ('faith') and νόμος ('law') in Romans and Galatians indicates that such expressions probably stem from the presence of ἐκ πίστεως (by faith) in Hab. 2.4.[58] Campbell further asserts that prepositional phrases with νόμος ('law') probably developed as the antithesis of Paul's use of πίστις ('faith'), 'hence, the phrase ἐξ ἔργων νόμου ['from works of law'] may mean little more for Paul than the opposite of πίστις Χριστοῦ ['faith in/of Christ']'.[59] This

53. Contra Jewett, 'The Agitators', p. 208; Ellis, 'Paul and His Opponents', p. 293; Mussner, *Der Galaterbrief*, p. 302.

54. Linda Belleville ('"Under Law": Structural Analysis and the Pauline Concept of Law in Galatians 3:21–4:11', *JSNT* 26 [1986], pp. 53-78 [69]) comments that Paul's point is that life under the law and under the στοιχεῖα are similar experiences and have similar results. At this point in our study we would alter this statement slightly so that the parallel is between life under the opponents' teaching (rather than the law) and under the στοιχεῖα.

55. There is no basis other than unsupported mirror reading for claiming that the opponents used Gen. 17 or Isaac in their arguments, as Dunn (*Epistle to the Galatians*, pp. 243-44) and Longenecker (*Galatians*, p. 200) assert.

56. E.g. Joseph B. Tyson, '"Works of Law" in Galatians', *JBL* 92 (1973), pp. 423-31 (423); Walt Russell, 'Who Were Paul's Opponents in Galatia?', *BSac* 147 (1990), pp. 329-50 (342-43); Barclay, *Obeying the Truth*, p. 86.

57. Frederic R. Crownfield, 'The Singular Problem of the Dual Galatians', *JBL* 64 (1945), pp. 491-500 (499).

58. D.A. Campbell, 'The Meaning of Πίστις and Νόμος in Paul: A Linguistic and Structural Perspective', *JBL* 111 (1992), pp. 91-103 (100-102).

59. Campbell, 'Meaning', p. 102.

analysis also supports my view that 'under law' is Paul's characterization of the opponents' teachings.[60] In addition, I have found only circumcision and the observation of holy days to be elements of their
teaching. If 4.21 is Paul's interpretation and extension of the
opponents' teaching, it makes 6.13 clearer. They require and perhaps
keep only some of the Law.

5.11

Paul says in 5.11 that he would not continue to be persecuted if he still
preached circumcision. This verse stands within the polemical section
5.7-12 where Paul constantly refers to the opponents. Combined with
the mention of circumcision, the location of this verse shows that it is
an allusion to the opponents. For many interpreters, 5.11 indicates that
the opponents claim Paul preaches circumcision.[61] Bruce supports this
view by noting that circumcision is not mentioned in the verses around
5.11.[62] Others argue that the distinction Paul makes between Jews and
Gentiles in his teaching on circumcision has led to the charge that he is
inconsistent.[63]

This statement in 5.11 does seem to show that Paul feels he must respond to a distorted presentation of his view. Unless this is the case,
there is no reason for his denial that he preaches circumcision after the
strong language about it in 5.2.[64] The phrase 'preach circumcision' is
probably, as Betz argues, Paul's formulation, not the opponents', and is
presented as the antithesis of his common expression 'preach Christ'.[65]

---

60. See Campbell's clear comments on the meaning of this expression ('Meaning', pp. 102-103).

61. E.g. Tyson, 'Paul's Opponents in Galatia', pp. 248-49; Jewett, 'The Agitators', p. 208; Mussner, *Der Galaterbrief*, p. 12; Schmithals, 'Judaisten in Galatien?', p. 57; Watson, *Paul, Judaism and the Gentiles*, p. 55. However, Barclay
(*Obeying the Truth*, pp. 50, 79-80) argues that Paul may simply be comparing himself with his opponents.

62. Bruce, *The Epistle to the Galatians*, p. 236. Betz (*Galatians*, p. 268) comments that it is puzzling that Paul raised and dropped the subject so suddenly.

63. Jerome Neyrey, 'Bewitched in Galatia: Paul and Cultural Anthropology',
CBQ 50 (1988), pp. 72-100 (93); Marxsen, *Introduction*, p. 54; Mussner, *Der Galaterbrief*, p. 12.

64. Betz (*Galatians*, p. 269) speculates that 5.11 may be necessary because 3.28;
5.6; and 6.15 could be taken as arguments either for or against circumcision. But
this problem would be cleared up by 5.2.

65. Betz, *Galatians*, pp. 268-69.

In light of the abrupt insertion of this denial and its supporting evidence of persecution, it seems the opponents claim that Paul does preach circumcision and that the Galatians do not understand him or that he had been unclear.[66] This would allow them to gain some reception among the Galatians because they are not attacking Paul or his teaching. Since this verse intimates that the opponents claim their position is close to or the same as Paul's,[67] it is unlikely that they also attacked his apostleship.[68]

3.2-5

Cosgrove claims the didactic section 3.1-5 as the center of his argument that the Spirit is the main focus of the opponents' teaching, because this is the first place Paul refers directly to the Galatian situation.[69] But this is not a methodologically sound procedure because a letter writer's first reference to opponents may be extremely polemical and evaluative. Further, we must build a foundation of explicit statements before relying on allusions like those in 3.2-5. Even Cosgrove admits that 3.1-5 may not address the actual problem, but only the implicit assumptions that Paul sees in the opponents' argument.[70] Paul's polemical evaluation of the consequences of the opponents' teaching is not a reliable basis on which to identify what they teach.

Since 3.1-5 is primarily didactic and introduces the arguments that follow (see our discussion of 3.1 above), we must strictly limit our use of mirror exegesis. In such contexts, allusions cannot add a topic to our understanding of the opponents' teaching but only indicate direction or add details. Allusions must be part of, not just compatible with, topics already raised.[71]

Since 3.2-5 speaks of works of the law, it is an allusion to the opponents. Paul here contrasts as clearly as possible his teaching with that being heard in Galatia. The expression 'works of the Law' does not

66. Howard (*Crisis in Galatia*, p. 9) goes so far as so assert that the opponents consider Paul an ally.

67. This seems to be Betz's view in *Galatians*, p. 269.

68. It is difficult to understand how the opponents could make a convincing, to say nothing of coherent, case for their teaching if they both reject Paul's apostolic status and claim to be in agreement with him. Among others, Longenecker (*Galatians*, p. 233) asserts that the opponents do both these things.

69. Cosgrove, *The Cross and the Spirit*, pp. 39-42, 45.

70. Cosgrove, *The Cross and the Spirit*, p. 45.

71. Sumney, *Identifying Paul's Opponents*, pp. 104-105.

show that the rivals demand more of the law than we have seen, rather it is *Paul's* catchphrase description of their teaching.[72] Given the necessary limits on mirror exegesis in a didactic section and the absence of mention of the Spirit in explicit statements and other allusions, these verses cannot support the claim that the Spirit plays a central role in the opponents' teaching. Rather, it is Paul who inserts the Spirit at this point. As Räisänen comments, 3.2 is question-begging.[73] The answer to this question is not in debate, it is a rhetorical question with an obvious answer that Paul contends is determinative for the issue at hand. So neither does this passage support the claim that the opponents question the Galatians' experience of the Spirit.[74] However important the Spirit is in Paul's reponse, we have no evidence that it is a central element of the opponents' teaching.

This conclusion does not settle the issue seemingly raised in 3.3 of what the opponents see as the function of the Law. This verse has been pivotal in the debate over whether the opponents assert that the Law is necessary to enter the ranks of saved people of God[75] or argue that the law advances one's spiritual life.[76] Some interpreters also argue that this verse shows that the opponents claim to complete Paul's gospel.[77] Lull's discussion of ἐναρξάμενοι ('having begun') and ἐπιτελεῖσθε ('been completed/perfected') indicates that these terms were at times used in cultic contexts to distinguish between initial conversion and complete entry into a new religion.[78] But this does not prove that they

72. Cf. Standaert, 'La rhétorique antique', 38; Tyson, '"Works of the Law" in Galatians', p. 428; J.D.G. Dunn, 'The New Perspective on Paul', *BJRL* 65 (1983), pp. 15-122 (117-18).

73. Heikke Räisänen, *Paul and the Law* (repr.; Philadelphia: Fortress Press, 1986 [1983]), p. 189.

74. Contra Betz, *Galatians*, p. 109.

75. So John Buckel, 'Paul's Defense of Christian Liberty', p. 355; E.P. Sanders, *Paul, the Law, and the Jewish People* (Philadelphia: Fortress Press, 1983), p. 19.

76. So Ernst Baasland, 'Persecution: A Neglected Feature in the Letter to the Galatians', *ST* 38 (1984), pp. 135-50 (139); R.H. Gundry, 'Grace, Works, and Staying Saved in Paul', *Bib* 66 (1985), pp. 1-38 (8-9); Longenecker, *Galatians*, p. 103.

77. Jewett, 'The Agigators', p. 206; Peder Borgen, 'Paul Preaches Circumcision and Pleases Men', in M.D. Hooker and S.G. Wilson (eds.), *Paul and Paulinism* (London: SPCK, 1982), pp. 39-40; J. Christiaan Beker, *Paul the Apostle: The Triumph of God in Life and Thought* (Philadelphia: Fortress Press, 1980), p. 42.

78. David J. Lull, *The Spirit in Galatians* (SBLDS, 49; Chico, CA: Scholars Press, 1980), p. 51 n. 87.

functioned in this technical sense in Galatians or that Paul is using
language taken from the opponents' presentation of their teaching.[79]
Obviously the opponents see their teaching as an advance for the Galatians. But these terms demonstrate no more than this, and mirror exegesis is too unreliable to claim more.[80]

So 3.2-5 indicates only that Paul argues that the presence of the Spirit
among the Galatians demonstrates that the opponents' demands are
wrong. We cannot determine what specific function they claim for their
demands beyond improving on what the Galatians now practice.

1.8-10

Within the polemical section 1.6-11(12), vv. 8-9 assert that the Galatians are to reject any change in what they received in Paul's initial
preaching, even if it comes from an angel or Paul himself. These verses
comprise an allusion because Paul is reaffirming the message he had
previously delivered in a context in which he feels he must contend that
he still preaches what the Galatians had understood at the beginning.[81]
The invective of 1.8-10[82] rejects the opponents in the strongest possible
terms.[83] Some argue that vv. 8-9 show that Paul was *accused* of preaching circumcision,[84] but this is the wrong way to describe the opponents'
treatment of Paul. They more likely say that the Galatians misunderstand Paul's view on circumcision. As Schütz notes, the concessive sentence of vv. 8-9 indicates 'an unmistakable degree of improbability' that
Paul preaches anything other than what the Galatians understood from
his visit.[85] These verses are not evidence that Paul's authority is under
attack[86] but that his teaching is being misrepresented.

---

79. Dunn (*Epistle to the Galatians*, p. 155) remarks that concentrating on the
use of these words in cultic contexts is 'a sidetrack'.

80. So also Barclay, *Obeying the Truth*, pp. 39, 49-50. Barclay rejects mirror
reading a perfectionist theology here because no perfectionist tendencies are fought
elsewhere in Galatians.

81. Lyons (*Pauline Autobiography*, p. 126) asserts that v. 9 addresses the opponents because it uses the third person.

82. See Hall, 'Rhetorical Outline', p. 280.

83. Smit ('The Letter of Paul to the Galatians', pp. 9-10) assigns vv. 7b-9 the
purpose of arousing hostility toward opponents.

84. E.g. Paul N. Tarazi, 'The Addressees and the Purpose of Galatians', *St.
Vladimir's Theological Quarterly* 33 (1989), pp. 159-79 (176).

85. Schütz, *Paul and the Anatomy of Apostolic Authority*, p. 121.

86. So also Bernard Lategan, 'Is Paul Defending his Apostleship in Galatians?

Thus v. 10 does not reflect the charge that Paul pleases humans and gains converts by relaxing requirements, as many argue.[87] Betz's suggestion that Paul formulates this rhetorical question to set himself off from flatterers,[88] or Borgen's view that this is Paul's derogatory expression of what the opponents say positively,[89] seems more likely. Verse 10 also contributes to the development of the ethos that Paul projects in chs. 1–2.[90] Following the curse of vv. 8-9, v. 10 makes it clear that if Paul were to act as a human-pleaser (his interpretation of accepting circumcision) he would be under the curse.[91] Perhaps 'human-pleaser' is a veiled polemical evaluation of the opponents.

These verses tell us nothing new about the opponents. They do, however, strengthen our impression that Paul believes he and his gospel are being misrepresented.

2.2-9

Paul tells of his second trip to Jerusalem in 2.2-9. These verses are an allusion because they deal with circumcision. Since we have no evidence that Paul's apostleship is under attack, 2.1-10 should be read as didactic; it supplies information about Paul primarily to establish his ethos as the basis for the instruction that follows, even as he addresses issues that the opponents raise.[92]

Interpreters have discovered several characteristics of the opponents in 2.1-10, including: they are from Jerusalem,[93] they question Paul's apostleship and compare him with the Jerusalem apostles,[94] and they are of the same party as, or at least related to, the 'false brothers' of v. 4.[95]

---

pp. 416-17. Longenecker's assertion that the reference to 'an angel from heaven' shows that the opponents are 'appealing to a higher authority than Paul' (*Galatians*, p. xcv) is the extreme case of his overuse of mirror reading, this in spite of his recognition of the dangers of that technique (e.g. *Galations*, p. lxxxix).

87. E.g. Watson, *Paul, Judaism and the Gentiles*, p. 55; Mussner, *Der Galaterbrief*, pp. 12-13; Fung, *The Epistle to the Galatians*, p. 48.

88. Betz, *Galatians*, pp. 55-56.

89. Borgen, 'Paul Preaches Circumcision and Pleases Men', p. 40.

90. Kennedy, *New Testament Interpretation*, p. 148.

91. So also Crownfield, 'The Singular Problem of the Dual Galatians', p. 496.

92. So also Burton, *Galatians*, p. 76.

93. Martyn, 'Law-Observant Mission', p. 322.

94. Neyrey, 'Bewitched in Galatia', p. 98.

95. Koester, *Introduction to the New Testament*, p. 118; Daniel H. King, 'Paul and the Tannaim: A Study in Galatians', *WTJ* 45 (1983), pp. 340-70 (345). Roman

All these suggestions rely too heavily on mirror exegesis to claim any credibility, especially since the passage is a didactic section.

As Paul presents it in v. 2, the Jerusalem conference was not about his apostleship but about his gospel,[96] with circumcision as the main issue. By asserting that the Jerusalem apostles waived circumcision in Titus's case,[97] he implies that his Galatian opponents' teaching is not accepted in Jerusalem.[98] This episode also gives Paul the opportunity to call those who opposed his gospel 'false brothers' (v. 4). He no doubt intends this derogatory evaluation to rub off on his Galatian opponents.[99] But this does not mean that the two groups teach the same things, only that he wants the Galatians to view them analogously.

The discussion of 2.1-10 demonstrates that what Paul preached in Galatia was accepted in Jerusalem with no modifications. This, of course, helps establish its validity. There is insufficient evidence to assert that the opponents were telling a different version of the story. Instead, Paul uses the story to set the debate at Galatia in his own terms by introducing the theme of freedom in Christ and by opposing bondage under the law to the truth of the gospel.[100]

This passage, then, supplies nothing new about the Galatian opponents. We only see Paul insisting that he and the Jerusalem apostles rejected circumcision for Gentiles. Thus, the Galatians should reject the teachers among them.

2.15-16

The reference to works of the law indicates that 2.15-16 is an allusion. Much has been written about how 2.15-21 relates to Paul's remarks at Antioch, but recent analysis focuses on the section's rhetorical purpose rather than its relationship to the Antioch dispute. Betz identifies the

Heiligenthal ('Soziologische Implikation der Paulinischen Rechtfertigungslehre im Galaterbrief am Beispiel der "Werke des Gesetzes"', *Kairos* 26 [1984], pp. 38-51 [42]) and Gerhard Ebeling (*The Truth of the Gospel: An Exposition of Galatians* [trans. D. Green; Philadelphia: Fortress Press, 1985], p. 92) say only that the 'false brothers' and the Galatians opponents have the same views. Cf. C.K. Barrett, *Freedom and Obligation: A Study of the Epistle to the Galatians* (Philadelphia: Westminster Press, 1985), p. 15.

96. So also Gaventa, 'Autobiography as Paradigm', pp. 316-17.
97. Jewett, 'The Agitators', p. 200.
98. Similarly Lührmann, *Galatians*, p. 39.
99. Betz, *Galatians*, p. 90. Cf. Longenecker, *Galatians*, p. 51.
100. Hester, 'Use and Influence', p. 399.

section as the *propositio*,[101] but Kennedy and Smit reject this analysis because the section is argumentative.[102] Kennedy identifies 2.15-21 as an *epicheireme* which gives the conclusion of one section and introduces the argument to come.[103] This seems to be the passage's function.[104] Thus it is moderately polemical. This does not mean, however, that Paul takes up specific points that the opponents raise.

Paul opposes works of law with faith in Christ for the first time in Galatians in this passage. He formulates this antithesis to combat the opponents' joining of faith in Christ and circumcision.[105] To reject this combination Paul speaks from the perspective of Jewish Christians and their recognition that Christ is the source of their justification. But this reveals nothing new about the Galatian opponents.

3.10

The mention of 'those of the works of the Law' shows that 3.10 is an allusion. Smit identifies 3.6-14[106] as the second of three arguments within 3.1–4.7, each beginning with a comparison and a claim that Paul's view is according to the law and ending with the advantages of adhering to his teaching and with the Spirit as the sign that confirms that he is correct.[107] Since the primary function of these arguments is to give instruction, 3.6-14 is didactic.[108]

---

101. Betz, *Galatians*, p. 115; *idem*, 'In Defense of the Spirit: Paul's Letter to the Galatians as a Document of Early Christian Apologetics', in E. Schüssler Fiorenza (ed.), *Aspects of Religious Propaganda in Judaism and Early Christianity* (Notre Dame: University of Notre Dame Press, 1976), pp. 99-114 (104).

102. Kennedy, *New Testament Interpretation*, pp. 148-49; Smit, 'The Letter of Paul to the Galatians', p. 3.

103. Kennedy, *New Testament Interpretation*, p. 148.

104. So also Hall, 'Rhetorical Outline', p. 280; Buckel, 'Paul's Defense of Christian Liberty', p. 260; T.L. Donaldson, 'The "Curse of the Law" and the Inclusion of the Gentiles: Galatians 3.13-14', *NTS* 32 (1986), pp. 94-112 (97).

105. So also Dunn, 'New Perspective', p. 112, and *Epistle to the Galatians*, pp. 137-38, where he comments that Paul intends to make these two mutually exclusive.

106. Others who divide the text in this way include: Heiligenthal, 'Soziologische Implikation', p. 47; Cosgrove, *The Cross and the Spirit*, pp. 48-49; Betz, *Galatians*, p. 137.

107. Smit, 'The Letter of Paul to the Galatians', p. 14.

108. Contra Longenecker (*Galatians*, p. 116) who sees 3.10-14 as a 'vigorous attack' on the opponents.

Because of this immediate literary context, a mirror reading of 3.10 is insufficient evidence to claim that the opponents say the Galatians are under a curse if they do not submit to circumcision and observe their holy days. It is more likely that Paul introduces Deut. 27.26 because it refers to 'all' that is in the law and we have already seen that Paul believes the Galatians will find keeping the whole Law unacceptable.[109] Thus, as Burton suggested, 3.10-14 is a counter-argument from Scripture.[110] The discussion of Christ taking on the curse (vv. 13-14) builds on the Deuteronomy quotation and the points Paul makes in vv. 11-12, and thus supports his assertion that those under Law are under a curse (v. 10). So 3.10-14 contains an argument generated by Paul, not a reinterpretation of a verse that the opponents use. Even if we allow that 3.6-14 is an apologetic or polemical section, it reveals nothing of the opponents' teaching without too much reliance on mirror exegesis.

Summary of Allusions

Allusions have added significantly to what we know of the opponents' teaching. We now know that the opponents urge the observance of holy days and argue that the Galatians misunderstand Paul on the issue of circumcision. So Paul must clarify his position on circumcision. However, we have found no indications that Paul's apostleship is under attack. In addition, there is no evidence that the opponents demand observance of the law beyond circumcision and the keeping of certain holy days. In fact, Paul assumes the Galatians will be surprised and distressed to hear that the whole law follows from the opponents' current demands. Furthermore, expressions like 'works of Law' and 'under Law' are Paul's characterizations, not the opponents' words.

Affirmations

In a letter with such a singular focus, nearly every statement seems to relate to the opponents in some way. Still we can single out a few that

---

109. Dunn (*Epistle to the Galatians*, p. 169) also seems to think Paul raised the question of the curse. He argues that the topic comes up as a corollary to the talk of blessings in 3.8-9 and 14.

110. Burton, *Galatians*, p. 163. Similarly Baasland ('Persecution', p. 144) asserts that 3.1-14 begins Paul's 'chief counter-argument'. This is similar to the way Campbell ('The Meaning of Πίστις and Νόμος in Paul', p. 101 n. 30) argues that Paul uses Hab. 2.4.

more certainly address them. At the same time, we must resist extensive use of mirror exegesis on affirmations, especially those outside directly polemical contexts.

2.17-18

Our first affirmation directly follows an allusion within the polemical section 2.15-21. The passage 2.17-18 addresses issues that the opponents raise when it speaks of re-establishing the Law. Some find in v. 17 a charge that those who do not keep the law make Christ a servant of sin.[111] But this requires an unjustifiable use of mirror exegesis. It seems possible that the opponents wonder aloud about whether being a Christian allows one to ignore the Law, but v. 17 probably contains only Paul's caricature of either such questionings or his formulation of an unacceptable consequence of their views.[112]

Paul continues to draw consequences from the position Peter took at Antioch in 2.18. Paul's purpose is to sully the Galatian opponents by showing that an analogous teaching results in making Christians transgressors, thereby implying that this same implication holds for the Galatian opponents' teaching. Paul argues that Jewish Christians who begin to keep the law again show themselves to be sinners.[113] By implication he places those who accept the opponents' regulations under this same judgment. This assumption of the Law, then, amounts to denying their own experience of salvation and therefore, as he is about to mention (3.2-6), their experience of the Spirit. Thus Paul argues against the Galatian opponents by presenting Peter's actions at Antioch as an analogy to the Galatian situation, and then by drawing unacceptable consequences (vv. 17-18) from his polemical interpretation of Peter's actions. He thus implies that these same consequences follow the opponents' teaching

---

111. E.g. Betz, 'In Defense of the Spirit', p. 107; Mussner, *Der Galaterbrief*, p. 13. Cf. Longenecker, *Galatians*, p. 89.

112. Cosgrove (*The Cross and the Spirit*, p. 137) calls 2.17a a *reductio ad absurdum*. Jan Lambrecht ('Once Again Gal 2,17-18 and 3,21', *ETL* 63 [1987], pp. 148-53 [150]) limits the reference to eating with Gentiles and identifies 2.17 as an irrealis conditional sentence.

113. Hendrikus Boers ('"We Who Are by Inheritance Jews"; Not from the Gentile Sinners', *JBL* 111 [1992], pp. 273-81 [280]) argues that in 2.17-19a Paul is arguing that Jews who again take up the law and claim superiority over Gentiles in this way are condemning themselves as sinners because they have not kept the law and so have been living as Gentiles.

(vv. 15-16). Unfortunately, this gives us no further insight into what they actually teach.

3.17-18

The passage 3.17-18 refers to the opponents when it uses the expression 'from law' and centers on the relationship between the inheritance/ promise and the Law. These verses are part of 3.15-29,[114] the third argument of 3.1–4.11. Like the preceding section (3.6-14), 3.15-29 is primarily didactic.

The point of 3.15-18 is, of course, to indicate that no conditions can be added to the covenant established with Abraham, thus precluding insertion of the Law. Abraham appears here for the first time in statements that relate to the opponents. His absence in explicit statements and allusions places in serious doubt the widely held view that Abraham figured prominently in the opponents' arguments. He clearly plays a large role in Paul's argument, but this does not necessarily indicate that the opponents use him. Arguments which cite the frequent discussion of Abraham in Jewish literature are insufficient to claim that the teachers *at Galatia* use him, especially since there is no direct textual evidence that they do. Paul was also familiar with these discussions, including those with universalistic tendencies, and he could well be the one who initiates discussion of Abraham.

Cousar gives several reasons Paul would refer to Abraham in Galatians, including: (1) since Abraham is the father of Israel, Gentiles must be part of Abraham's heritage to be accepted; (2) since the Law came after Abraham, he demonstrates that the Law does not condition the promises made to him; and (3) since circumcision started with Abraham, the question 'about its continuing validity must take him into account'.[115] These are important reasons for Paul to cite Abraham whether the opponents use him or not. But Martyn argues that since Paul did not make descent from Abraham part of his preaching elsewhere, the Galatian opponents must use Abraham.[116] However, being a descendent of Abraham would be of little concern to most Gentiles when Paul initially preached to them. On the other hand, at Galatia teaching that draws on the Hebrew Scriptures had probably made these converts more aware of

---

114. Smit, 'The Letter of Paul to the Galatians', p. 14.

115. Charles B. Cousar, *Galatians* (Interpretation; Atlanta, GA: John Knox Press, 1982), p. 73.

116. Martyn, 'Law-Observant Mission', p. 319.

figures from Israel's past. Thus, being a descendant of Abraham would now be meaningful to the Galatian audience. Given our investigation of passages that more certainly refer to the opponents' teaching, it seems most probable that Paul, not the opponents, brings Abraham into the argument.[117]

This passage, then, gives us only one more way that Paul rejects the other teaching. Neither this passage nor others that refer to Abraham indicate that he was a major part of the opponents' arguments for their views. None of these passages tie Abraham to the opponents' positions but only use Abraham to argue against them.

2.11-14

Interpreters have often used 2.11-14 as evidence that the Galatian opponents require the observance of food regulations.[118] But others see this as only conjectural.[119] The expression 'those of the circumcision' and the setting of the behavior of some over against 'the truth of the gospel' (an expression Paul also uses in 2.5) show that the affirmations in 2.11-14, at least indirectly, have the Galatian opponents in view. Paul gives this episode as evidence for the truth of his teaching. It also helps establish his ethos. Following 2.1-10 in the *narratio*, 2.11-14 seems to be didactic. Some, though, identify 2.11-14 as a digression[120] which may allow it a more apologetic function. It does seem a bit more point-ed than the previous sections of chs. 1 and 2, and it leads directly into the polemic of 2.15-21. So perhaps it is apologetic. If it is, the point of

---

117. Dunn (*Epistle to the Galatians*, p. 16) acknowledges that it is unclear whether the opponents or Paul brought up Abraham at an earlier time. There seems to be no reason to say that Paul did this at some earlier time. Dunn is surely on the right track when he comments that the topic of Abraham was 'bound to polarize the range of Christian views regarding acceptability of Gentiles and to bring the issue of circumcision inescapably to the fore' (Dunn, *Epistle to the Galatians*, p. 16). But why would Paul do this in his initial preaching? It is more likely that he introduces Abraham in this dispute to make the distinctions between his views and those of the opponents as clear and as wide as possible.

118. E.g. Buckel, 'Paul's Defense of Christian Liberty', p. 255; J.D.G. Dunn, 'Works of the Law and the Curse of the Law (Galatians 3:10-14)', *NTS* 31 (1985), pp. 523-42 (525).

119. Crownfield, 'The Singular Problem of the Dual Galatians', p. 498; Bruce, *The Epistle to the Galatians*, p. 19.

120. Hall, 'Rhetorical Outline', p. 285; James D. Hester, 'The Rhetorical Structure of Galatians 1:11–2:14', *JBL* 103 (1984), pp. 223-33 (231).

the defense is Paul's gospel, not his apostleship. In this passage there is evidence only for what he understands as an attack on his gospel.[121] According to our method, affirmations in apologetic sections can only show the direction that an established issue takes or add a detail to a clear point of debate. If the passage is didactic, we cannot use its affirmations at all.

Given the required limitations on mirror exegesis, we cannot identify 'those from James' with the Galatian opponents. Furthermore, since 'works of law' is Paul's characterization of the opponents' teaching rather than their own slogan, our method does not allow us to add food laws to their agenda. This episode, then, illustrates Paul's reaction to requiring observance of regulations from the law and serves as an example that he wants the Galatians to follow, but it reveals no new element of the Galatian opponents' teaching.

Summary of Affirmations

While these affirmations add nothing new to our knowledge of the Galatian teachers, they do show some of the ways Paul responds to them. Even though others use these affirmations to add features to the opponents' teaching, we must reject this use of them because identifying elements of the opponents' teachings from these verses requires unwarranted and uncontrolled mirror reading.

Conclusion

This attempt to identify the opponents of Galatians has not dealt with every passage that previous interpreters have used to make claims about them. Our method precludes several passages because it is too uncertain that they reveal information about the opponents.

Perhaps our most surprising finding is that Abraham does not appear to be prominent in the opponents' teachings. Rather, it is Paul who makes Abraham so central. Abraham is Paul's evidence against the opponents, not the opponents' evidence for their position. Similarly, it is Paul who makes the Spirit central in the dispute. There is no evidence that the opponents question the Galatians' possession of the Spirit or that they are enthusiasts. Martyn has provided valuable insights into

---

121. As Gaventa ('Autobiography as Paradigm', p. 313) says of all of 1.16b–2.21, this episode is an illustration of Paul's response to the 'singular and exclusive nature of the gospel's claim'.

Paul's use of eschatology in Galatians and into how eschatology serves as a basis for Paul's argument.[122] But we have no reason to say that a different eschatology played a role in the opponents' teaching. There is also insufficient evidence that these opponents urge the acceptance of Jewish food laws. Paul raises this issue only in what he presents as an incident analogous to the demands that the Galatians face. If these food laws are not part of the opponents' teaching, efforts to define the situation in terms of the primary identifying characteristics of Jews may be misdirected. Another common assertion about the opponents that lacks support from the text is that they have some connection with Jerusalem.[123] Finally, they do not seem to question Paul's apostleship.

These opponents do urge circumcision and the observance of certain holy days. They also seem to claim that their teaching agrees with Paul's and that the Galatians have misunderstood Paul or perhaps that Paul's teaching has changed. Both Paul's inclusion of himself in the curse of 1.8-9 and his protest that he does not 'preach circumcision' point to this conclusion.[124] These opponents do not seem to require any more of the law than circumcision and holy days. Expressions like 'works of Law' are Paul's characterizations of their demands. It is possible that they intend to add more demands later, but there is no evidence for this. By calling for circumcision and the observance of certain holy days, they clearly call for a different kind of relationship with the Jewish Law than Paul is willing to allow. But it remains unclear exactly what that relationship is.

Unfortunately, Paul also gives no clear indication of what the opponents claim as the benefit of their teaching. There is no evidence that they question the Galatians' status as Christians or the activity of the Spirit among them. While they must hold out some advantage for their teaching to be attractive, any attempt to identify that advantage is pure

122. Martyn, 'Events in Galatia', pp. 160-79.

123. This assertion about the opponents seems to be evidence of the continuing influence of F.C. Baur's reconstruction of early Christianity with its battle between Paul and Jerusalem. This reconstruction, which most of these interpreters reject, is the strongest evidence for claiming a connection with Jerusalem for these opponents.

124. It is possible that the opponents cite certain events Paul was involved with (e.g. the Jerusalem conference or the circumcision of Timothy) to show that they are in agreement with him, but there is insufficient evidence to claim this. If they do give examples as evidence that Paul agrees with them they may well be from incidents about which we have no knowledge.

speculation. Perhaps it is full initiation, as Lull suggests, or increased presence of the Spirit or even complete identity with God's people Israel. But this investigation supports neither the view that the issue was 'getting in' nor 'staying in'.[125] To call the opponents' view perfectionist also over-draws the evidence. The problem is that there is insufficient evidence for all of these suggestions. The opponents' motivation may be a matter as simple as an attempt to enhance fellowship with law-observing Jewish Christians,[126] as it seems to have been in the analogous Antioch incident. But Paul saw more at stake in Antioch, and he sees more at stake in Galatia. What Paul makes into an issue of great theological import may be much simpler in the minds of the opponents and the Galatians prior to receiving this letter.[127] Perhaps Paul sees the issue as one that determines which religious community (Judaism or Christianity) one seeks to belong to, but the Galatians probably do not understand it in such broad terms and certainly do not understand it to mean leaving Christianity. The legacy of Baur's reconstruction should not force us to see in Galatians a conflict between Paul and a developed Jewish-Christian theology.

It is important to recognize that these Galatian teachers do not view themselves as opponents of Paul. Not only do they not attack his apostolic status, they also claim to teach the same things that he teaches. They must assert either that the Galatians misunderstood Paul or that Paul's views have evolved or perhaps that it is now time to move on to the next stage of their Christian existence, as Paul advocates for mature

125. Campbell ('The Meaning of Πίστις and Νόμος in Paul', pp. 102-103) concludes that Paul's use of prepositional phrases with νόμος in Romans and Galatians designates no specific understanding of the function of the Law. So it is not specifically opposing legalism, 'covenantal nomism' or the Law as a 'sociological boundary marker'. Boers ('"We Who Are by Inheritance Jews"', p. 278) also rejects the idea that Paul's opposition of faith and works of the Law has something specific like these proposals in mind. Rather, he argues that Paul uses works of the law to designate any 'distinguishing mark of belonging to an exclusively favored community'.

126. In a similar vein, Tyson ('Paul's Opponents', p. 250) sees the opponents' motives to be unity, though he seems to mean doctrinal unity.

127. Speaking more generally of how Paul argues, Lars Hartman ('On Reading Others' Letters', in G.W.E. Nickelsburg and G.W. MacRae (eds.), *Christians Among Jews and Gentiles* [Philadelphia: Fortress Press, 1986], pp. 137-46 [139]) asserts that it is 'Paul's tendency to develop a broad theological argument, even when he is dealing with a comparatively small or trivial matter'.

Christians. Since we have no reason to think that these opponents are trying to deceive the Galatians on this (or any other) question, they must think their teaching is consistent with Paul's. No matter how they explain the difference between their understanding of Paul and the Galatians', they do not know they are Paul's opponents until this letter arrives.

If these teachers do not perceive themselves as opponents of Paul, we must immediately ask why Paul rejects them so vigorously and condemns them so vehemently. The answer may lie in Paul's own prior experiences. From his perspective, their teaching presents an enormous danger. But beyond that, this is not the first time that Paul has faced what he sees as the same or at least an analogous danger. His vehemence is the result of his previous painful experiences (e.g. the Antioch Incident) and his equating of what he opposed on those occasions with what he sees in Galatia. This, when combined with the theological issues that he sees to be at stake (even if the Galatian teachers and their auditors do not), makes his vitriolic response understandable. And while these opponents did not understand themselves as opponents of Paul before Galatians, the harsh rejection of them may well have turned them into such.

This understanding of the opponents leaves many questions unanswered. But it gives us a firmer basis for interpreting Galatians. It also opens avenues of exploration into Paul's thought and theology when we do not see him slavishly responding to specific elements of the opponents' teaching with every sentence. With this staring point, we may be able to gain some insight into Paul's pneumatology, eschatology and soteriology as he uses them to respond to unacceptable proposals.

Chapter 5

OPPONENTS EVERYWHERE—PHILIPPIANS

Despite the common notion that Philippians is written to a church with few or no serious problems, there has been no shortage of hypotheses about opponents. Not only is there no consensus on the identity of the opponents, there is no agreement about how many different types of opponents are present or even where they are. Hypotheses have ranged from non-Christian Jews[1] and Cybele-Attis cult eunuchs[2] to Divine men,[3] Judaizers[4] and libertine Gnostics,[5] or elements of both of these latter groups.

Identifying opponents in Philippians is complicated by questions about its integrity. This is an important question because our method demands that we treat letters individually. The commonly suggested divisions of Philippians and the studies of the genre of Philippians by

---

1. P. Benoit, *Epitres de saint Paul aux Philippiens, à Philémon, aux Colossiens, aux Ephésiens* (La sainte bible de Jérusalem; Paris: Cerf, 4th edn, 1969), p. 31; J.L. Houlden, *Paul's Letters from Prison* (Philadelphia: Westminster Press, 1970), p. 103; F.W. Beare, *A Commentary on the Epistle to the Philippians* (HNTC; New York: Harper & Row, 1959), p. 24; Fred B. Craddock, *Philippians* (Interpretation; Atlanta: John Knox Press, 1985), p. 56; G.F. Hawthorne, 'Philippians, Letter to the', in Hawthorne and Martin (eds.), *Dictionary of Paul and his Letters*, pp. 707-13 (711).

2. H. Ulonska, 'Gesetz und Beschneidung: Überlegungen zu einem Paulinischen Ablösungskonflikt', in D. Koch (ed.), *Jesu Rede von Gott und ihre Nachgeschichte im frühen Christentum*, (Gütersloh: Gütersloher Verlag, 1989), pp. 314-31 (320).

3. J.-F. Collange, *The Epistle of Saint Paul to the Philippians* (London: Epworth Press, 1979), pp. 12-13.

4. J. Ernst, *Die Briefe an die Philipper, an Philemon, an die Kolosser, an die Epheser* (RNT; Regensburg: Friedrich Pustet, 1974), p. 25; Peter T. O'Brien, *The Epistle to the Philippians: A Commentary on the Greek Text* (NIGTC; Grand Rapids: Eerdmans, 1991), p. 14.

5. Schmithals, *Paul and the Gnostics*, pp. 84-85.

recent defenders of its integrity exacerbate this difficulty because these different views of its composition may lead to different understandings of various sections. For example, if Philippians 3 is a separate polemical letter, the whole of the chapter might be identified as directly engaged with opponents.[6] But if Philippians is a single letter, the material in ch. 3 might simply be another instance of that letter's use of antithetical examples with none of the chapter seen as polemical.[7]

The integrity of Philippians cannot be discussed at length here, but in the face of some substantial arguments to the contrary, several studies from differing perspectives have made a strong case in favor of its integrity. This will be the working hypothesis of the current treatment of Philippians. We will, however, take note of what difference a three-letter hypothesis would make in our identification of opponents.

In addition to recommending the letter's integrity, studies of its rhetorical species strongly indicate that Philippians is deliberative rhetoric.[8] In addition to the arguments that Watson presents for this view, the repeated use of τὸ αὐτὸ φρονεῖν ('to think the same things') and related expressions (2.2-3, 5; 3.15; 4.3) also indicates that Philippians is deliberative.[9] More specifically and from a different perspective, Stowers makes a good case for seeing Philippians as a hortatory letter of friendship.[10] While these determinations cannot prove whether Philippians

6. As it is seen by Pheme Perkins, 'Philippians: Theology for the Heavenly Politeuma', in Bassler (ed.), *Pauline Theology*, I, pp. 84-104 (98); W. Schenk, *Die Philipperbriefe des Paulus* (Stuttgart: W. Kohlhammer, 1984), p. 278. Cf. Joachim Gnilka, *Der Philipperbriefe* (Freiburg: Herder, 3rd edn, 1968), p. 184.

7. See Stanley K. Stowers, 'Friends and Enemies in the Politics of Heaven: Reading Theology in Philippians', in Bassler (ed.), *Pauline Theology*, I, pp. 105-22 (89-104). See also G.B. Caird, *Paul's Letters from Prison* (New Clarendon Bible; Oxford: Oxford University Press, 1976), pp. 130-33.

8. Duane F. Watson, 'A Rhetorical Analysis of Philippians and its Implications for the Unity Question', *NovT* 30 (1988), pp. 57-88.

9. On the use of this expression in deliberative speeches see Mitchell, *Paul and the Rhetoric of Reconciliation*, p. 69. Mitchell (*Paul and the Rhetoric of Reconciliation*, p. 141 n. 454) also notes that Phil. 2.14 is the only place outside 1 Corinthians that Paul refers to grumbling, and this in the context of contrasting 'concordant and discordant behavior'. This further supports identifying Philippians as deliberative.

10. Stowers, 'Friends and Enemies in the Politics of Heaven', pp. 107-14 and those cited at p. 107 n. 6; Michael L. White, 'Morality Between Two Worlds: A Paradigm of Friendship in Philippians', in D.L. Balch, E. Ferguson and W.A. Meeks (eds.), *Greeks, Romans, and Christians: Essays in Honor of Abraham J.*

addresses opponents, they will inform our identification of types of contexts and suggest why certain topics emerge (e.g. the theme of presence and absence[11]).

Explicit Statements

3.2-3

A section that contains an often-cited explicit statement about opponents begins at 3.1a. Since Paul sometimes uses τὸ λοιπόν ('finally') to signal a change in topic (rather than signaling the conclusion of a letter),[12] 3.1a begins the section. Furthermore, identifying the letter as a hortatory letter of friendship supports interpreting τὰ αὐτὰ (the things) in 3.1 as a reference to what follows because it is part of a common 'hortatory idiom' in such letters.[13] Within the larger section 3.1-16, vv. 1-6 make up the first sub-section.

While 3.1-6 is most often identified as polemical,[14] Stowers identifies this section as more paraenetic,[15] a type of section that is more likely in

Malherbe (Minneapolis: Fortress Press, 1990), pp. 201-15 (201, 206). Cf. Loveday Alexander, 'Hellenistic Letter-Forms and the Structure of Philippians', *JSNT* 37 (1989), pp. 87-101 (90, 94-95), for a similar identification.

11. See Stowers, 'Friends and Enemies in the Politics of Heaven', pp. 108-109.

12. See the discussion of Marvin R. Vincent, *A Critical and Exegetical Commentary on the Epistles to the Philippians and to Philemon* (ICC; Edinburgh: T. & T. Clark, 1897), p. 90.

13. Stowers, 'Friends and Enemies in the Politics of Heaven', pp. 115-16. Others who accept this reading of τὰ αὐτὰ without identifying Philippians as a hortatory letter of friendship include O'Brien, *Epistle to the Philippians*, p. 352; Vincent, *Commentary on the Epistles to the Philippians and to Philemon*, pp. 91-92; Ernest F. Scott, 'The Epistle to the Philippians: Introduction and Exegesis', *IB* XI, pp. 3-129 (73). See also Watson, 'A Rhetorical Analysis of Philippians', p. 73 n. 82.

14. Those who identify at least 3.2-11 as polemical include Ernst, *Briefe an die Philipper*, p. 89; Schenk, *Die Philipperbriefe*, pp. 278-79; B. Mengel, *Studien zum Philipperbrief* (WUNT; Tübingen: J.C.B. Mohr [Paul Siebeck], 1982), p. 260 (who comments that such a section is unexpected); Wilhelm Egger, *Galaterbrief, Philipperbrief, Philemonbrief* (Neue Echten Bibel; Würzburg: Echter Verlag, 1985), p. 65; Collange, *Paul to the Philippians*, p. 12; Gnilka, *Der Philipperbrief*, p. 184; Hawthorne, 'Philippians', p. 707; Perkins, 'Theology for the Heavenly Politeuma', pp. 98-99.

15. Stowers, 'Friends and Enemies in the Politics of Heaven', p. 116. Similarly, Ronald Russell ('Pauline Letter Structure in Philippians', *JETS* 25 [1982], pp. 295-306) sees 3.1–4.8 as exhortation.

a hortatory letter of friendship. A decision about the nature of this section depends largely on one's interpretation of the βλέπετε phrases in v. 2. Kilpatrick's brief study indicates that βλέπετε with the accusative always means, 'look at, consider', rather than 'beware'.[16] This argument from usage is often countered with the assertion that the tone of the passage is too polemical and the name-calling too insulting for βλέπετε to mean anything other than 'beware'.[17] Caird rejects this argument, asserting that the repetition and names are insufficient to outweigh 'the evidence of usage'.[18] Garland and Stowers add that those spoken of in 3.2 are given as negative examples of the attitudes Paul is promoting in the larger context.[19] However, the derogatory nature of the names and the threefold repetition seem to indicate something beyond a negative example, even though serving as such an example may be a major purpose of their mention. These are people of whom Paul has told the Philippians before and he, no doubt, included his opinion of them then. So introducing them at 3.2 does not require such an insulting reference unless he perceives them as a danger to the Philippians.[20] Still, if they serve as a negative example, Paul must assume that they have found little acceptance at Philippi. On balance, then, 3.1-6 is a somewhat polemical section that may also serve a broader hortatory purpose.

16. George D. Kilpatrick, 'ΒΛΕΠΕΤΕ, Phil 3,2', in M. Black and G. Fohre (eds.), *In Memoriam Paul Kahl* (Berlin: Alfred Töpelmann, 1968), pp. 146-48. Among those who accept this understanding we find J. Hugh Michael, *The Epistle of Paul to the Philippians* (MNTC; New York: Harper & Brothers, 1927), p. 134 and Vincent, *Commentary on the Epistles to the Philippians and to Philemon*, p. 92.

17. See Helmut Koester, 'The Purpose of the Polemic of a Pauline Fragment (Philippians III)', *NTS* 8 (1961/2), pp. 317-32 (318); Günter Klein, 'Antipaulinismus in Philippi: Eine Problemskizze', in D. Koch (ed.), *Jesu Rede von Gott*, pp. 297-313 (304).

18. Caird, *Letters from Prison*, pp. 132-33.

19. David E. Garland, 'The Composition and Unity of Philippians: Some Neglected Literary Factors', *NovT* 27 (1985), pp. 166-71; Stowers, 'Friends and Enemies in the Politics of Heaven', p. 116. See also Ernst (*Briefe an die Philipper*, pp. 91-92) who ackowledges that 3.1b may be taking up the exhortation of 2.12-18. Victor P. Furnish's interpretation of ἀσφαλές (3.1) as something 'specific' seems to support seeing those spoken of in 3.2 as a negative example ('The Place and Purpose of Philippians III', *NTS* 10 [1963/4], pp. 80-88 [84]).

20. See also Michael, *Paul to the Philippians*, p. 134.

After introducing a new topic in 3.1, Paul speaks of 'the dogs', 'evil workers' and 'mutilators'. Interpreters often use these epithets to characterize these opponents. 'Dogs' has been used to identify them as non-Christian Jews,[21] Gentiles,[22] those outside the covenant[23] and libertines.[24] But this general insult is not, as Koester notes, descriptive, but invective; its aim is solely to insult.[25] Thus we learn nothing about these 'dogs'[26] except that Paul opposes them in no uncertain terms. Such a response to them justifies Jewett's assertion that this description indicates that they are outside the Philippian community,[27] which has been spoken of quite differently throughout the letter. This insult also indicates that Paul considers these people opponents.

The second insulting name that Paul calls these opponents is 'evil workers'. Interpreters generally agree that ἐργάτας ('workers') indicates that these opponents are missionaries.[28] Koester conjectures that they use this title for themselves.[29] Several interpreters claim that this insult reveals a more particular characteristic of these opponents: for example Klijn and Lohmeyer assert that calling them evil or false apostles shows that they are non-Christian Jews.[30] Michael, however,

---

21. E. Lohmeyer, *Die Briefe an die Philipper, an die Kolosser und an Philemon* (MeyerK, 9; Göttingen: Vandenhoeck & Ruprecht, 13th edn, 1964), p. 125; Benoit, *Paul aux Philippiens*, p. 31; Beare, *Epistle to the Philippians*, p. 103; Houlden, *Paul's Letters from Prison*, p. 103.

22. K. Grayston, 'The Opponents in Phil 3', *ExpTim* 97.6 (1986), pp. 170-72 (171).

23. O'Brien, *Epistle to the Philippians*, pp. 14, 355.

24. Schmithals, *Paul and the Gnostics*, pp. 84-85.

25. Koester, 'The Purpose of the Polemic of a Pauline Fragment', pp. 319-20.

26. So also Ernst, *Briefe an die Philipper*, p. 92; Mengel, *Studien zum Philipperbrief*, p. 20; Gnilka, *Der Philipperbriefe*, p. 186; Joseph B. Tyson, 'Paul's Opponents at Philippi', *Perspectives* 3 (1976), pp. 82-95 (93).

27. Robert Jewett, 'Conflicting Movements in the Early Church as Reflected in Philippians', *NovT* 12 (1970), pp. 362-90 (385).

28. E.g. Beare, *Epistle to the Philippians*, p. 104; O'Brien, *Epistle to the Philippians*, p. 29; Schmithals, *Paul and the Gnostics*, p. 85; C.L. Mearns, 'The Identity of Paul's Opponents at Philippi', *NTS* 33 (1987), pp. 194-204 (194).

29. Koester, 'The Purpose of the Polemic of a Pauline Fragment', p. 320. So also O'Brien, *Epistle to the Philippians*, p. 355.

30. A.F.J. Klijn, 'Paul's Opponents in Philippians iii', *NovT* 7 (1964–65), pp. 278-84 (282); Lohmeyer, *Briefe an die Philipper*, p. 125. Beare (*Epistle to the Philippians*, p. 104) sees it as a parody of a term used for Christian missionaries which indicates that these opponents are Jews.

argues that ἐργάτας indicates that the opponents are Christian.[31] Drawing on the use of the same term in 2 Cor. 11.13, Schmithals argues that the same opponents are combatted in Philippians and 2 Corinthians.[32] But as it was the case with the term 'dogs', we cannot determine anything very specific about the opponents from this rather general insult. It does seem probable, however, that they are Christian missionaries of some type, given the use of this term within early Christianity.[33]

The third insult in 3.2 is κατατομήν ('mutilation'). Baumbach asserts that this is the first position-fixing designation in 3.2 and that it indicates that they require circumcision.[34] While most interpreters recognize a reference to circumcision here, Ulonska argues that it refers to castration because Paul claims circumcision for himself in the immediately following verses. Thus, Paul has eunuchs in mind.[35] If, however, these opponents require circumcision of *Gentiles*, Paul may not be claiming for himself, a Jew, precisely what he judges Gentile circumcision to be. Furthermore, since exaggerated language is common in polemical contexts and since we obviously cannot take the first insult (dogs) in any literal sense, such a reference to Gentile circumcision is not out of place here. Additionally, nothing else in the context suggests a problem with Cybele-Attis cult devotees.[36]

Caird argues that κατατομήν ('mutilation') along with the περιτομή ('circumcision') in 3.3 shows that these opponents are Jews because only Jews call themselves the circumcision.[37] This argument rests on the dubious assumption that Paul is directly echoing the opponents' language. Furthermore, Paul uses precisely this language to describe Christians in Gal. 2.12 when he speaks of 'those from James' who come to

---

31. Michael, *Paul to the Philippians*, p. 135.

32. Schmithals, *Paul and the Gnostics*, p. 85.

33. See the survey of its use in Takaaki Haraguchi, 'Das Unterhaltsrecht des frühchristlichen Verkündigers: Eine Untersuchung zur Bezeichnung ἐργάτης im Neuen Testament', *ZNW* 84 (1993), pp. 178-95.

34. Günther Baumbach, 'Die von Paulus im Philipperbrief bekämpften Irrlehrer', in K.W. Tröger (ed.), *Gnosis und Neues Testament* (Berlin: Gütersloher Mohn, 1973), pp. 293-310 (300).

35. Ulonska, 'Gesetz und Beschneidung', pp. 320-21.

36. Similarly, Grayston's conjecture that the opponents see circumcision as 'an initiatory rite…out of semi-magical belief in ritual blood-shedding' ('The Opponents in Philippians 3', p. 171) finds no support in the text.

37. Caird, *Letters from Prison*, p. 133. Cf. Beare, *Epistle to the Philippians*, p. 104.

Antioch. Thus, since Paul uses this terminology to refer to Christians, albeit Jewish Christians, who require Gentiles to observe some elements of the Law, his use of it here in Phil. 3.2-3 does not exclude the possibility that he has Christians in view.

Schmithals asserts that it is not clear whether the opponents require circumcision or only boast in their own circumcision as a sign of their superiority based on Jewish identity.[38] While there is no direct statement in the text, the paranomasia between κατατομήν ('mutilation') and περιτομή ('circumcision') makes no sense if they do not urge circumcision of Gentiles.[39] The combination of this word-play, the insulting nature of κατατομήν, and the claim to be 'the circumcision' in v. 3 makes it clear that these opponents do require Gentiles to be circumcised.

From 3.1-3a, then, we see that Paul concerns himself with opponents who are not part of the Philippian congregation. These opponents seem to be traveling Christian preachers who require Gentiles to be circumcised. It also appears that, in spite of the abusive epithets, they are making little or no headway at Philippi because Paul can present them as negative examples. We cannot specify what they claim is gained through circumcision.

1.15-18

An explicit statement about opposition to Paul appears in the first section of the body of Philippians. Most agree that this section is comprised of 1.12-26. It begins with a disclosure formula in v. 12[40] and there is a clear change in topic at v. 27.[41] Craddock sees the section as an *inclusio* with προκοπήν ('advancement') in vv. 12 and 26. The section's function is usually viewed in one of two ways: Beare, Craddock and

---

38. Schmithals, *Paul and the Gnostics*, pp. 89, 119. Cf. Gnilka, *Der Philipperbriefe*, pp. 186-87.

39. O'Brien, *Epistle to the Philippians*, p. 357; Tyson, 'Paul's Opponents at Philippi', pp. 98-90.

40. So O'Brien, *Epistle to the Philippians*, p. 86. See there his discussion of this feature and the sources he cites.

41. One exception to this division of the text is Hawthorne ('Philippians', p. 707) who sees all of 1.3-26 as thanksgiving. But the disclosure formula at v. 12 and the turn from addressing God at v. 13 count decisively against this. Scott ('The Epistle to the Philippians', p. 13) extends the section through v. 30, but the move to exhortation at v. 27 makes this division unlikely.

Gnilka see it primarily as a report about Paul's situation.[42] Similarly, Garland, O'Brien and Lohmeyer see Paul interpreting his imprisonment for the Philippians.[43] Others, however, identify the section as apologetic. Collange asserts that Paul must defend the use of his citizenship to escape martyrdom.[44] Stowers also seems to find an apologetic element here as Paul must convince both friends and enemies that this misfortune is actually good fortune.[45] Watson approaches this text quite differently. He identifies 1.3-26 as an extended *exordium*, a device used when the audience did not recognize the gravity of the exigence addressed.[46] Thus, its function is to focus the Philippians' attention on an important topic.

Verse 12, with its disclosure formula, sets out the theme of this section:[47] Paul's affairs have advanced the gospel. Verses 12-18a supply the details which support this proposition,[48] while vv. 18b-26 look to the future advance of the gospel through Paul. This theme of the advance of the gospel through Paul's adverse circumstances requires no charges against him. Interpreters can find Paul defending himself against specific charges (e.g. those Jewett finds[49]) only through unsupported mirror reading.[50] At this early point in the letter Paul may well be establishing or confirming his ethos as a basis for subsequent commands. Similarly, Watson notes that these verses establish Paul as an example for those facing opposition and so prepare for the calls to imitation in

42. Beare, *Epistle to the Philippians*, p. 28; Craddock, *Philippians*, p. 9; Gnilka, *Der Philipperbriefe*, p. 54.

43. D.E. Garland, 'Philippians 1:1-26: The Defense and Confirmation of the Gospel', *RevExp* 77 (1980), pp. 327-36 (331); O'Brien, *Epistle to the Philippians*, pp. 85-88; Lohmeyer, *Briefe an die Philipper*, p. 5. Lohmeyer, of course, finds a significantly different interpretation of that imprisonment from Garland and O'Brien.

44. Collange, *Paul to the Philippians*, p. 9. Jewett ('Conflicting Movements', pp. 365-67) also see Paul responding to criticism.

45. Stowers, 'Friends and Enemies in the Politics of Heaven', p. 114.

46. Watson, 'A Rhetorical Analysis of Philippians', p. 61.

47. Cf. Collange, *Paul to the Philippians*, p. 53.

48. Several interpreters find the beginning of a new section at v. 18b, e.g. Gnilka, *Der Philipperbriefe*, p. 60; O'Brien, *Epistle to the Philippians*, pp. 97-98; Mengel, *Studien zum Philipperbrief*, pp. 229, 232; Schenk, *Die Philipperbriefe*, pp. 141-42.

49. Jewett, 'Conflicting Movements', pp. 366-67.

50. The unreliability of this technique is again demonstrated here as Collange (*Paul to the Philippians*, p. 53) finds Paul defending himself because he has escaped martyrdom while Jewett ('Conflicting Movements', pp. 366-69) finds divine men who say Paul should not suffer.

3.17 and 4.9.[51] Watson also sees Paul eliciting the Philippians' pathos in this section by showing his willingness to sacrifice his personal desires for their good.[52] Thus, this section seems to be primarily didactic.

Verses 15-18 are an excursus[53] on the people of v. 14 who have been encouraged to preach Christ through Paul's imprisonment. In vv. 15-18a Paul speaks of some who preach out of envy and strife and want to afflict him in his imprisonment. Paul's comments about these preachers are strange because, despite their opposition to him, he says they preach Christ. This fits quite well with the theme of the advance of the gospel through Paul's adversity, but is surprising to those familiar with the relationship he posits between his apostleship and his message in 2 Corinthians. Most interpreters agree that the problem with these preachers is not doctrinal (i.e. they are not false teachers) but rather their attitude toward Paul. Some, however, find a reference here to some type of opponent known from elsewhere.[54] But all such theses rely entirely on unsupported mirror reading and verbal parallels, especially with 2 Corinthians. Any identification of these opponents in Phil. 1.15-18 with others who disagree with Paul on some significant doctrinal issue overlooks Paul's acknowledgment that these envious ones preach Christ. Paul does not allow that evaluation of Judaizers or his opponents in 2 Corinthians and his pejorative comments in 3.2-3. eliminate the possibility that the same opponents are in view in ch. 1 and ch. 3. Jewett's contention that Paul could not call them heretics because he did not found the church where both Paul and these opponents are[55] does not explain how he could say they preach Christ, it only opens the possibility that he might be reticent to call them false teachers. But even that assertion is questionable in light of Paul's report in Galatians 2 of his own conduct at Antioch, a church he did not found, or his arguing at the Jerusalem Conference. Thus, it seems that the preachers of Phil. 1.15-18a preach substantially the same message as Paul.

51. Watson, 'A Rhetorical Analysis of Philippians', pp. 64-65.

52. Watson, 'A Rhetorical Analysis of Philippians', p. 64.

53. So O'Brien, *Epistle to the Philippians*, pp. 97-98; Schenk, *Die Philipper-briefe*, pp. 141-42; Gnilka, *Der Philipperbriefe*, p. 60.

54. E.g. Russell ('Pauline Letter Structure in Philippians', p. 301) finds Judaizers; Hawthorne ('Philippians', p. 711) finds divine men or Judaizers; Jewett ('Conflicting Movements', pp. 365-69) finds divine men who reject suffering as part of Christian existence.

55. Jewett, 'Conflicting Movements', p. 366.

The basic accusation Paul makes against these opponents is that they preach from bad motives. Ernst thinks it is possible that no concrete background lies behind these statements, rather these envious preachers serve as a counter for the coming exhortation, just as such counter examples are used in some Jewish traditions and Pauline vice catalogs.[56] Stowers offers a more focused thesis, noting that vv. 15-18 use the 'typical vocabulary of friendship and enmity'.[57] He goes on to assert that the use of contrasting models is fundamental to the structure of Philippians and 'a well-known hortatory strategy'.[58] Since Paul is probably drawing on stock characterizations, it is difficult to deduce anything about these opponents from this passage. It does seem clear, however, that they are present in the city of Paul's imprisonment since he accuses them of stirring up tribulation for him while he is in chains (v. 17)[59] and since they are among those emboldened to preach (v. 14).[60] This makes it highly unlikely that Paul had spoken of them previously as he had the opponents of 3.2-3.

All we can say with certainty about those Paul speaks of in 1.15-18a is that they are Christian preachers in the city from which Paul writes who do not treat Paul as he thinks they should. Even the conjecture that these opponents are leaders in that city's congregations who feel threatened by Paul's presence and prestige[61] goes beyond the evidence. Paul acknowledges that they preach Christ and condemns only their motives, so there are no significant doctrinal differences between Paul and these preachers. This understanding of them is further supported by the difference between his treatment of these preachers and those of 3.2-3 where some doctrinal difference is involved. Thus, these are not the same people as those of 3.2-3.

56. Ernst, *Philipper*, p. 46. See also Collange, *Paul to the Philippians*, p. 57.

57. Stowers, 'Friends and Enemies in the Politics of Heaven', p. 114.

58. Stowers, 'Friends and Enemies in the Politics of Heaven', p. 115.

59. Most interpreters agree with this, however, Paul S. Minear ('Singing and Suffering in Philippi', in R.T. Fortna and B.R. Gaventa [eds.], *The Conversation Continues: Studies in Paul and John in Honor of J. Louis Martyn* [Nashville: Abingdon Press, 1990], pp. 202-19 [208-209]) thinks they are in Philippi.

60. Contra Vincent (*Commentary on the Epistles to the Philippians and to Philemon*, p. 18) who argues that the envious are not included among those emboldened.

61. So, e.g., Vincent, *Commentary on the Epistles to the Philippians and to Philemon*, p. 18.

Unless the envious of 1.15-18a are wholly fictitious (which seems unlikely) and so inserted as a contrast to true friendship, Paul has spoken of two different groups that might be labeled opponents. One group treats Paul in some way that makes him see them as opponents, but do not advocate a teaching he opposes. This group is not troubling the Philippians. The second group appears in 3.2-3a. They do propagate beliefs Paul rejects and are at least a potential danger to the Philippians.

3.18-19

Another explicit statement about opponents appears in 3.18-19 where Paul speaks of 'enemies of the cross'. This passage belongs in a hortatory section[62] which begins at 3.17 (or perhaps 3.15[63]) and runs through 4.1. The section begins with a vocative which seems to signal a break,[64] but the flow of thought moves directly from the στοιχεῖν ('hold fast to') of v. 16 to the exhortation in v. 17.[65] Despite this connection, vv. 15-16 seem more closely attached to vv. 12-14 and serve as a transition to the exhortation to imitate Paul in v. 17. This exhortation is the logical consequence of vv. 12-16 and dominates vv. 17-21. The remarks in vv. 18-19 support this exhortation by giving a counter-example, as even some who see the section as polemical seem to acknowledge.[66]

Verse 3.18 speaks of 'many' who live as 'enemies of the cross of Christ'. This expression has been used to characterize these opponents

62. Those who see at least 3.17-21 as hortatory include W. Michaelis, *Der Brief an die Philipper* (Leipzig: Deichert, 1935), p. 61; Michael, *Paul to the Philippians*, p. 167; Ernst, *Briefe an die Philipper*, p. 103; O'Brien, *Epistle to the Philippians*, p. 445. Baumbach ('Die von Paulus im Philipperbrief bekämpften Irrlehrer', p. 302) sees all of 3.12–4.1 as hortatory which builds on the eschatological reservation of 3.11. Others, however, see 2.17-21 as more polemical, e.g. Egger, *Galaterbrief, Philipperbrief, Philemonbrief*, p. 65; Schenk, *Die Philipperbriefe*, p. 279; and seemingly Beare, *Epistle to the Philippians*, pp. 135-36; and Craddock, *Philippians*, pp. 64-65.

63. Ernst (*Briefe an die Philipper*, p. 103), Schenk (*Die Philipperbriefe*, p. 279), and Vincent (*Commentary on the Epistles to the Philippians and to Philemon*, p. 111) begin the section at v. 15.

64. So Gnilka, *Der Philipperbriefe*, p. 203 and O'Brien, *Epistle to the Philippians*, p. 443.

65. So Gnilka, *Der Philipperbriefe*, p. 203; O'Brien, *Epistle to the Philippians*, p. 443; Baumbach, 'Die von Paulus im Philipperbrief bekämpften Irrlehrer', p. 304; Koester, 'The Purpose of the Polemic of a Pauline Fragment', p. 325. Collange (*Paul to the Philippians*, p. 136) sees 3.17 as a consequence of the preceding.

66. E.g. Egger, *Galaterbrief, Philipperbrief, Philemonbrief*, pp. 68-69.

as antinomians,[67] Gnostic libertines,[68] enthusiasts who understand perfection differently from Paul,[69] Gnostics who reject the soteriological significance of Jesus' death[70] and even docetists.[71] All such uses of this expression rely heavily on unsupported mirror reading or parallels in other letters. Moreover, they neglect both the expression's polemical character and its function in this context. Koester recognizes the polemical and abusive character of this verse but still uses it and v. 19 to identify specific aspects of the opponents' teaching.[72] But as Egger notes, 'enemies of the cross of Christ' is not a description of the opponents as much as an attempt to make them contemptuous.[73] This imprecise and condemnatory language is a polemical evaluation which yields nothing about these opponents. With Michael, we can see the centrality of the cross in *Paul's* theology,[74] but this does not reveal how these opponents violate it. It is probable that these 'enemies' are Christians because they are possible examples for the Philippians' lives. But it is not clear that the Philippians are threatened by these 'enemies of the cross' because Paul says simply that he has told the Philippians about them.[75] Verse 18 may even be, as Gnilka suggests, a general polemic which refers to many types of opponents[76] and not to one specific type. This expression is general enough that it may include the opponents of 3.2-11, but it is not necessarily limited to them. Our only hope for more specificity is v. 19.

67. Michael, *Paul to the Philippians*, pp. 172-73.

68. Schmithals, *Paul and the Gnostics*, p. 106; Ralph P. Martin, *Philippians*, (NCB; London: Oliphants, 1976), pp. 143-44.

69. Baumbach, 'Die von Paulus im Philipperbrief bekämpften Irrlehrer', p. 304; and seemingly O'Brien, *Epistle to the Philippians,* pp. 30, 453.

70. Robert Jewett, 'The Epistolary Thanksgiving and the Integrity of Philippians', *NovT* 12 (1970), pp. 40-53 (45); *idem*, 'Conflicting Movements', p. 378.

71. Tyson, 'Paul's Opponents at Philippi', p. 95.

72. Koester, 'The Purpose of the Polemic of a Pauline Fragment', pp. 324-28.

73. Egger, *Galaterbrief, Philipperbrief, Philemonbrief*, p. 68.

74. Michael, *Paul to the Philippians*, p. 174.

75. So Caird, *Letters from Prison*, p. 146; Benoit, *Paul aux Philippiens*, p. 18. Cf. Michaelis, *Der Brief an die Philipper*, p. 62. Contra Michael *(Paul to the Philippians*, pp. 172-73) and Jewett ('Conflicting Movements', pp. 376-77) who argue that Paul's use of the perfect tense shows that these opponents were in Philippi when Paul was. But the perfect tense shows only that Paul had spoken of them before, not that they were actually present in Philippi.

76. Gnilka, *Der Philipperbrief*, p. 212. However, he still thinks they were also present in Philippi.

Verse 19 is composed entirely of polemical evaluations of the 'enemies of the cross'. Paul says their end is destruction, their god is their belly, their glory is their shame, and they are earthly minded. Since accusations of this sort are typical of polemic generally and of Paul's polemics particularly,[77] they reveal nothing specific about the target opponents.[78] Still, interpreters have mirror read these accusations to identify these opponents as Judaizers,[79] libertines,[80] Gnostics[81] and Cybele-Attis cult eunuchs.[82] But, as Perkins comments, this use of *topoi* which is 'designed to discredit the moral character of one's opposition' renders use of these accusations to identify opponents 'absurd'.[83] Furthermore, Watson identifies v. 19 as an example of amplification which was used to 'emphasize the evil nature of opponents and arouse negative pathos against them'.[84]

The function of 3.18-19 within this hortatory context suggests that Paul needs no accurate description of some specific opponents. Rather, these polemical accusations support the preceding and following exhortations. The Philippians are to imitate Paul and those like him (v. 17) rather than others who are bad examples. These 'enemies' are a contrasting model for the behavior called for in vv. 20-21.[85] As we have noted before, such contrasts are a fundamental feature of Philippians.

77. So also Baumbach, 'Die von Paulus im Philipperbrief bekämpften Irrlehrer', p. 305 and Perkins, 'Theology for the Heavenly Politeuma', p. 91 n. 10.

78. So also Collange, *Paul to the Philippians*, p. 137; Gnilka, *Der Philipperbrief*, p. 205; Caird, *Letters from Prison*, p. 146; Baumbach, 'Die von Paulus im Philipperbrief bekämpften Irrlehrer', p. 305.

79. Mearns, 'The Identity of Paul's Opponents at Philippi', p. 198; Benoit, *Paul aux Philippiens*, p. 33; Houlden, *Paul's Letters from Prison*, p. 103; O'Brien, *Epistle to the Philippians*, p. 454.

80. Jewett, 'Epistolary Thanksgiving', pp. 45-46; *idem*, 'Conflicting Movements', pp. 378-80; Michael, *Paul to the Philippians*, pp. 175-76.

81. Schmithals, *Paul and the Gnostics*, p. 112; Martin, *Philippians*, p. 144.

82. Ulonska, 'Gesetz und Beschneidung, p. 327.

83. Perkins, 'Theology for the Heavenly Politeuma', p. 101. Perkins notes further (pp. 101-102) that while 'dogs', 'evil workers' and 'mutilators' (3.2) sound like pagan anti-Jewish slander, v. 19 sounds like Jewish slander of pagans.

84. Watson, 'A Rhetorical Analysis of Philippians', p. 75.

85. See Michaelis, *Der Brief an die Philipper*, p. 62; Egger, *Galaterbrief, Philipperbrief, Philemonbrief*, pp. 68-69; Mengel, *Studien zum Philipperbrief*, p. 274; Stowers, 'Friends and Enemies in the Politics of Heaven', p. 117.

Thus 3.18-19 tells us nothing about those spoken of except that they are Christians[86] whose lives Paul rejects as examples for the Philippians. The context and polemic allow us to say no more.

3.4b(-6)

We have already identified 3.1-6 as a somewhat polemical section that serves a hortatory purpose. In v. 4b Paul speaks of those who put their confidence in the flesh. This is, of course, another polemical judgment about their teaching. They certainly would not have characterized their view in this way and would have rejected this evaluation as much as they would being called mutilators (v. 2). The surrounding verses show that their 'confidence' rests on claims about being Jewish. It seems unlikely that these opponents are proselytes[87] because Paul seems to be matching the opponents' claims to Jewishness. His superiority comes not from being a real Jew instead of a proselyte, but from his dedication to his tradition.[88]

This passage indicates that these opponents make claims based on their Jewish credentials.[89] It does not, however, reveal what they call Gentiles to do. We cannot use mirror exegesis to specify what they demand—they obviously do not require Gentiles to become members of the tribe of Benjamin.

In addition to matching their credentials and, in the process, rejecting their claims to superiority, vv. 4-6 support the assertion of the superior value of knowing Christ (vv. 7-11).[90] Verses 4-6 show only that these opponents claim some superiority based on their Jewishness and their adherence to Jewish traditions.

---

86. Paul's exclusion of them as examples for Christians implies that they are Christians. Further, Lohmeyer (*Briefe an die Philipper*, p. 153) asserts that Paul never uses 'enemies' for unbelievers. Cf. Martin, *Philippians*, p. 143.

87. Contra Craddock, *Philippians*, p. 57; Beare, *Epistle to the Philippians*, p. 106.

88. It is unlikely that the 'dogs' have dropped from sight, as Caird claims (*Letters from Prison*, pp. 134-35) since the topic remains the same.

89. Mearns ('The Identity of Paul's Opponents at Philippi', p. 197) asserts that Paul is parodying his opponents' boasts. Cf. Ernst, *Briefe an die Philipper*, p. 94; Vincent, *Commentary on the Epistles to the Philippians and to Philemon*, pp. 94-95; Tyson, 'Paul's Opponents at Philippi', pp. 92-93.

90. O'Brien, *Epistle to the Philippians*, p. 366.

1.28

Our final explicit statement about opponents, 1.28, mentions those who are opponents of the Philippians. This statement appears in the large hortatory section[91] that begins at 1.27 and extends through at least 2.16[92] and perhaps 2.18, as many interpreters divide the passage. 1.27-30 is a sub-section within this larger unit. Verses 27b-30 explicate the exhortation of v. 27a to 'live [πολιτεύεσθε] worthy of the gospel of Christ'.[93] The preceding discussion of the advance of the gospel through Paul's imprisonment supports this exhortation, as v. 30 intimates. Thus 1.12-26 serves a purpose beyond interpreting Paul's circumstances, they provide the Philippians with a needed example.[94] Paul uses his own experience of persecution in much the same way in 1 Thessalonians.

Paul gives no specifics about the opponents here except that they disturb the Philippians. This distinguishes them from the opponents of 1.15-18a who were opponents of Paul personally. The opponents in 1.28 also comprise a different group than those of 3.2-11. However, Collange, who sees this section as part of a letter written earlier than ch. 3, argues that the same opponents are in view in both places. The difference is that by the time of the later letter the crisis has grown worse.[95] While Paul certainly views those mentioned in 3.2 as opponents of the Philippians, Collange can connect them with the opponents of 1.28 only because he understands the problem in both cases to be that they reject suffering.[96] But we have not found rejection of suffering to be an ele-

91. Nearly all interpreters recognize the hortatory nature of this passage.

92. So Craddock, *Philippians*, pp. 9, 31; Lohmeyer, *Briefe an die Philipper*, p. 5; Sigfred Pedersen, '"Mit Furcht und Zittern" (Phil. 2,12-13)', *ST* 32 (1978), pp. 1-31 (2-3). Craddock (*Philippians*, p. 31) argues that the exhortation ends at v. 16 and the autobiography resumes at v. 17. Lohmeyer (*Briefe an die Philipper*, p. 5) sees vv. 17-18 as an transition to 2.19-30.

93. Schenk, *Die Philipperbriefe*, pp. 165-66. Pedersen ('"Mit Furcht und Zittern"', p. 3) sees 1.27a as the heading for all of 1.27–2.5 and 2.12-16.

94. Seeing the close connection between Paul's circumstances and the Philippians', Scott ('The Epistle to the Philippians', p. 13) identifies all of 1.12-30 as a section on Paul's life in prison. But there is a clear turn from description of Paul's circumstances to exhortation at 1.27. This exhortation in 1.27-30 may also foreshadow the call to imitation in 3.17.

95. Collange, *Paul to the Philippians*, pp. 11, 71-72.

96. Collange, *Paul to the Philippians*, pp. 11, 71-72. Mearns ('The Identity of Paul's Opponents at Philippi', p. 194) also seems to identify those of 1.28 with the opponents of 3.2-11.

ment of the opponents' teaching in ch. 3. Furthermore, the parallel Paul draws between the Philippians' experience and his own in v. 30 indicates that the opponents of 1.28 are non-Christians.[97] Thus we must reject the connection Collange makes with the opponents of 3.2-11. Based on the parallel between Paul's and the Philippians' experiences, the opponents in 1.28 are persecutors at Philippi. We can be no more specific than this. There is no evidence here for the extreme persecution Lohmeyer finds.[98] Neither is there evidence that the persecutors are Jews,[99] or Gentiles,[100] or participants in the Imperial cult.[101] The text gives no concrete information about them.[102] It does, however, place this persecution in an eschatological context[103] which gives meaning to the Philippians' suffering, and so supports the exhortation of v. 27.

We have now encountered a third group that may be referred to as opponents, namely persecutors of the Philippian Christians. These non-Christians are not included in the usual definition of Paul's opponents; they are more generally opponents of Christianity. Nevertheless, Paul refers to them as 'opponents' of the Philippians. His remarks about these opponents add nothing to our understanding of those in 1.15-18a or 3.2-11.

Summary of Explicit Statements

Explicit statements about opponents in Philippians refer to three different groups who may be called opponents: Jewish-Christian missionaries, personal opponents of Paul in the city of his imprisonment, and persecutors of the Philippians. The Jewish-Christian missionaries require circumcision for Gentiles, but we cannot yet determine what they claim is gained by it. Paul evaluates their teaching as trusting in the flesh and recounts his Jewish credentials to match their claims to authority based on being Jewish to indicate that he fulfilled (and then rejected) the requirements they insist on. Furthermore, these traveling

97. O'Brien, *Epistle to the Philippians*, p. 153.
98. Lohmeyer, *Briefe an die Philipper*, pp. 72-77, 100.
99. As Houlden finds (*Paul's Letters from Prison*, p. 65).
100. As Michael finds (*Paul to the Philippians*, p. 69).
101. As Raymond R. Brewer finds ('The Meaning of *POLITEUESTHE* in Philippians 1:27', *JBL* 73 [1954], p. 82).
102. Ernst, *Briefe an die Philipper*, p. 61.
103. Ernst, *Briefe an die Philipper*, pp. 61-62. So also Egger, *Galaterbrief, Philipperbrief, Philemonbrief*, p. 58, who draws support for this interpretation from 1.20.

preachers have met little or no success at Philippi. Stowers may be correct that they have not even come to Philippi, though the level of the polemic makes this seem less likely.

The second group of opponents, those inflicting Paul in his imprisonment, seem to advance no teaching that differs significantly from that of Paul because he acknowledges that they preach Christ. The problem with this group is the way they treat Paul. It seems unlikely that they challenge the authenticity of his apostleship since he does not make that an issue, even though he often sees a necessary relationship between it and his gospel.

The third group, the persecutors of the Philippians, are non-Christians who trouble the congregation in some way that the Philippians perceive as persecution. Since these 'opponents' are non-Christians, they do not belong among 'Paul's opponents', understood as those who specifically oppose Paul, his teaching or Pauline Christianity as distinct from other forms of Christianity.

Finally, Paul refers to opponents generally in 3.18-19. While Paul might apply the accusations found here to the opponents of 3.2-11, he does not seem to have them (or any specific group) in mind. Rather, those of 3.18-19 are a contrasting model used as a foil to support the surrounding exhortations. Even if Paul does have the opponents of 3.2-11 in view, 3.18-19, by virtue of its polemical nature and use of *topoi*, adds nothing to our understanding of them.

To this point, finding Philippians to be a compilation would not have changed our findings because we have found two different groups of opponents of Paul even while assuming its integrity. If it is correct that ch. 3 is a separate and polemical letter, it is more likely that 3.18-19 refers to the opponents mentioned earlier in that chapter. But, as we just noted, 3.18-19 yields no evidence about the beliefs or practices of those castigated there.

Allusions

3.7-10
The reference to the law in 3.9 and Paul's assessment of his own Jewish prerogatives indicates that 3.7-9 contains an allusion to the opponents of 3.2-4. The mention of sharing the sufferings of Christ in 3.10 may allude to the persecution the Philippians are suffering at the hands of their adversaries and so has been included here. If ch. 1 is part of a

separate letter, there is no basis for seeing v. 10 as an allusion to opponents.

Verses 3.7-11 are a sub-section within 3.1-16.[104] Although some find this section to be directly polemical,[105] it seems much more likely to be an expository or didactic passage that develops the contrast in v. 7 between the things Paul valued in the past and his current evaluation of them in light of 'the knowledge of Christ Jesus' (v. 8).[106] Verses 7-11 are, then, closely related to vv. 4b-6[107] where Paul recounts his impressive Jewish credentials in the face of others who claim superiority on the basis of their Jewish heritage.[108] But in vv. 7-11 Paul is explaining his refusal to consider these advantages to be of primary importance. Since Paul is explaining his position, we identify the section as didactic.

The most obvious specific tie to the opponents of 3.2 is the reference to the law in v. 9. Here Paul equates righteousness from law (ἐκ νόμου) with one's own righteousness and contrasts those two with the righteousness from God. Several interpreters see at least v. 9 as a parenthesis.[109] Verse 9b-c explicates the 'being found' in Christ of v. 9a, while 'to know' (τοῦ γνῶναι) of v. 10 resumes the 'knowledge of Christ

---

104. Michaelis (*Der Brief an die Philipper*, pp. 55-56) finds two sub-sections in vv. 7-11. Some begin the section at v. 8 (e.g. Gnilka, *Der Philipperbrief*, p. 184; Michael, *Paul to the Philippians*, p. 144; Schmithals, *Paul and the Gnostics*, p. 91), but this makes little difference for interpretation of the passage.

105. So Klein, 'Antipaulinismus in Philippi', p. 306. Cf. Schenk (*Die Philipperbriefe*, p. 279) who sees 3.8-9 as the *argumentio* of the letter composed of 3.2–4.3, 8-9. However, even Schmithals (*Paul and the Gnostics*, p. 91) acknowledges that there are no direct statements about opponents in 3.8-11.

106. Michaelis (*Der Brief an die Philipper*, p. 55) sees the topic of 3.7-8 to be Paul's present view of his Jewish past. Cf. Perkins, 'Theology for the Heavenly Politeuma', p. 99; Michael, *Paul to the Philippians*, p. 144, O'Brien, *Epistle to the Philippians*, p. 382. Although he contends that a more polemical emphasis is present, Koester ('The Purpose of the Polemic of a Pauline Fragment', p. 322) finds vv. 9-16 to be a refutation of the possibility of 'boasting' of Jewish attributes.

107. Pierre Bonnard (*L'épître de Saint Paul aux Philippiens* [Commentaire du Noveau Testament, 10; Paris: Delachaux & Niestlé, 1950], p. 61) makes all of 4.4-11 a single section.

108. At v. 7 Paul's strategy of giving himself as an example becomes more obvious. So Egger, *Galaterbrief, Philipperbrief, Philemonbrief*, p. 65. Cf. Lohmeyer, *Briefe an die Philipper*, p. 132. Gnilka (*Der Philipperbrief*, p. 194) comments that in 3.8-9 Paul wants his case to be seen as typical.

109. E.g. Michaelis, *Der Brief an die Philipper*, p. 57.

Jesus' in v. 8.[110] The explication of being found in Christ in v. 9 returns us to the issues that Paul raised in 3.2-6. But even if this reference to righteousness has a directly polemical intent, it does little to expand our knowledge of the opponents. It cannot bear the weight O'Brien puts on it when he claims that 'my righteousness' means the opponents believe they can make a claim on God.[111] Even Koester's claim that this section indicates that the question is whether 'being in Christ' includes the Law or is irreconcilably opposed to the Law[112] is not clearly supported. There are no terminological connections sufficient to support any mirror reading of v. 9.[113] On the other hand, this reference to righteousness and the law is more significant than Caird allows when he identifies it as a 'perfunctory allusion' to a past debate.[114] Still, Perkins may be correct in that since this contrast between types of righteousness is not developed, it is not a key element in the dispute.[115] Paul's characterization of righteousness from Law (ἐκ νόμου) as '*my*' righteousness is a polemically motivated evaluation rather than an accurate description of the opponents' teaching. But it does reflect their emphasis on keeping the Law. It may intimate that they require more of the law than circumcision, but we cannot be certain of this. Paul may, instead, want to characterize their demand for circumcision in these terms to make it more unacceptable to the Philippians. This characterization also fits very well with a rejection of claims of superiority based on Jewish identity. We cannot determine from this allusion what these opponents claim is gained through circumcision, not even whether it involves initial justification or some higher achievement within Christianity.[116] Thus, this verse does little to clarify the opponents' demand for circumcision, but it does affirm that this demand is rooted in Judaism.

110. See also Klein, 'Antipaulinismus in Philippi', p. 307. Cf. Michael, *Paul to the Philippians*, p. 147.

111. O'Brien, *Epistle to the Philippians*, pp. 394-96.

112. Koester, 'The Purpose of the Polemic of a Pauline Fragment', p. 322.

113. Contra Klijn, 'Paul's Opponents in Philippians III', p. 283 and Schenk, *Die Philipperbriefe*, p. 337. Schenk claims here that there are 50 words in 3.2–4.3, 8-9 which Paul takes from the opponents.

114. Caird, *Letters from Prison*, p. 138.

115. Perkins, 'Theology for the Heavenly Politeuma', p. 99 n. 53.

116. Caird (*Letters from Prison*, pp. 138-39) claims, on the basis of Pauline usage, that v. 9 has to do with initial status. But this assertion about Pauline usage is based on prior theological judgments about Paul's use of δικαιοσύνη ('righteousness').

Paul's mention of 'the knowledge of Christ Jesus' in v. 8 is sometimes claimed as evidence that the opponents have some Gnostic concepts,[117] but nothing in the context or in the explicit statements in Philippians supports this assertion.[118] Perhaps Caird and Ernst are correct that Paul draws this expression from the Hebrew Scriptures.[119] In any case, it does not advance our knowledge of the opponents.

As we noted above, if Philippians is a unity, the explication of knowing Christ in 3.10[120] as sharing in his sufferings and being conformed to his death may allude to the opposition the Philippians face (1.28). Alternatively, it might allude to Paul's own situation of imprisonment and so again be interpreting his hardships for the Philippians. Even if 3.10 refers to the persecution the Philippians face, it does not clarify the situation in any significant way. Rather it gives persecution a positive meaning, as it does if it alludes to Paul's hardships.

Several interpreters contend that Paul is countering some type of realized eschatology in 3.10-11.[121] But this reading is not supported by explicit statements about opponents, and is based solely on unsupported mirror reading. These verses seem to have no direct polemical intent. Even Schmithals acknowledges this possibility, but then relies on both his broader reconstruction and his presupposition that Paul is not well informed in order to find a reference to opponents here.[122] Klein, without these presuppositions, comments that the resurrection motif is not prominent enough to signal any opposition.[123] Furthermore, Perkins (who rejects the integrity of the letter) notes that the description of

117. So Schmithals, *Paul and the Gnostics*, pp. 91-92.

118. So also Ernst, *Briefe an die Philipper*, p. 96; Klijn, 'Paul's Opponents in Philippians III', p. 281; Jewett, 'Epistolary Thanksgiving', p. 45.

119. Ernst, *Briefe an die Philipper*, p. 96; Caird, *Letters from Prison*, p. 137.

120. Michael (*Paul to the Philippians*, p. 148) sees 3.10 as an expansion of the last clause in 3.8. Cf. Michaelis, *Der Brief an die Philipper*, p. 57.

121. Including Koester, 'The Purpose of the Polemic of a Pauline Fragment', p. 323; Schmithals, *Paul and the Gnostics*, pp. 93-95; Gnilka, *Der Philipperbrief*, p. 197. Cf. Collange, *Paul to the Philippians*, p. 132. Mearns ('The Identity of Paul's Opponents at Philippi', p. 195) argues that 3.10 shows that the opponents give too little significance to the cross.

122. Schmithals, *Paul and the Gnostics*, p. 93.

123. Klein, 'Antipaulinismus in Philippi', pp. 308-309. See also Ernst, *Briefe an die Philipper*, p. 100. Vincent (*Commentary on the Epistles to the Philippians and to Philemon*, p. 107) remarks that the notion of a reference to a spiritual resurrection is 'entirely without support'.

knowing Christ in 3.10-11 as present suffering while anticipating resurrection recalls the hymn of ch. 2.[124] In addition, Baumbach argues that the eschatological reservation in 3.11 is a common characteristic of Pauline theology.[125] Thus, there is no basis for using 3.10-11 to describe opponents.

So 3.7-10 continues Paul's remarks about the 'dogs' and gives his present evaluation of his Jewish credentials in terms of different types of righteousness. He polemically characterizes the former righteousness as his own and as being from the Law. This seems to point to both the opponents' demand that Gentiles be circumcised and their claim to superiority based on Jewish credentials, but does not clarify what it is that they claim is gained through circumcision. Verse 8 may imply that they require more of the Law than circumcision, but we cannot be certain of this. We find no evidence in 3.8-11 for Gnostics or a realized eschatology. Rather, vv. 10-11 interpret Christian suffering in the context of the superior value of knowing Christ (in contrast to claims of superiority based on Jewish heritage) for a community that knows persecution.

Summary of Allusions

The only recognizable allusions to opponents are found in 3.7-10 and relate to the opponents of 3.2-3 who call for Gentile circumcision. This allusion confirms that these opponents claim some superiority on the basis of their Jewish heritage. Since they call for Gentile circumcision, these opponents do more than claim authority over Gentiles. They must also assert that Gentiles can enhance their Christian status in some way by participating in the privileges of the circumcised.

Affirmations

3.12-16

Interpreters often rely heavily on 3.12-16 when identifying opponents in Philippians. But since there are no explicit statements about opponents or clear allusions to specific matters raised in explicit statements and allusions in these verses, we can classify this passage's statements only as affirmations. This means they can be used only minimally to

---

124. Perkins, 'Theology for the Heavenly Politeuma', p. 99.
125. Baumbach, 'Die von Paulus im Philipperbrief bekämpften Irrlehrer', pp. 301-302.

identify opponents. Still, the call to remain in what the Philippians have attained in v. 16 may refer to the whole preceding discussion of the 'dogs' and thus mean they are to reject the opponents of 3.2-11.

The beginning of a new sub-section within 3.1-16 is signalled by the asyndeton between vv. 11 and 12.[126] Furthermore, different terminology and concepts dominate this paragraph.[127] Klein asserts, in addition, that vv. 12-15 form an *inclusio* with τετελείωμαι ('I have been perfected') and τέλειοι ('the mature/perfect').[128] The paragraph ends with v. 16 because the passage takes a new and more hortatory turn at v. 17 with the call to imitation.[129] The oppositional πλήν ('however') of v. 16, which is not continued in v. 17, also shows the clear connection of v. 16 to vv. 12-15.

Schmithals contends that 3.12-15 has an indubitably polemical aim.[130] Koester also finds a significant polemical element here, seeing all of vv. 9-16 as a refutation of boasting about 'Jewish attributes'.[131] Most interpreters identify two purposes for 3.12-16: avoiding misunderstanding of what Paul has said in the previous paragraph (or more generally his law-free gospel) and countering those who claim perfection.[132] Ernst and Stowers, however, tie the passage to the hortatory purposes of the letter and thus find no allusions to a perfectionist teaching.[133] Klein argues that vv. 12ff. are not polemical on the basis of the asyndeton at v. 12, which, he argues, shows that there is no simple continuation of the polemic. He further argues that the use of οὐχ ὅτι ('not that') in v. 12 demonstrates the passage's non-polemical nature because Paul never

126. Lohmeyer, *Briefe an die Philipper*, p. 143; Klein, 'Antipaulinismus in Philippi', p. 302.

127. Klein, 'Antipaulinismus in Philippi', p. 302.

128. Klein, 'Antipaulinismus in Philippi', p. 302.

129. Klein ('Antipaulinismus in Philippi', p. 302) seems correct in seeing v. 16 as a transition to vv. 17ff.

130. Schmithals, *Paul and the Gnostics*, pp. 93-94.

131. Koester, 'The Purpose of the Polemic of a Pauline Fragment', p. 322.

132. So, e.g., O'Brien, *Epistle to the Philippians*, p. 418; Michael, *Paul to the Philippians*, p. 155; Baumbach, 'Die von Paulus im Philipperbrief bekämpften Irrlehrer', pp. 302-303; Lohmeyer, *Briefe an die Philipper*, p. 143. Watson ('A Rhetorical Analysis of Philippians', pp. 74-75) suggests that the section was included to avoid the appearance of arrogance after the call to imitation in the previous verses.

133. Ernst, *Briefe an die Philipper*, p. 100; Stowers, 'Friends and Enemies in the Politics of Heaven', p. 109. Caird (*Letters from Prison*, p. 141) also finds no polemical intention here.

uses that expression in polemic, but rather always to avert possible misunderstanding.[134]

The connection with the preceding paragraph is an important indicator of the nature of vv. 12-16. These verses play directly off v. 11— Paul's desire to attain, if possible, the resurrection through conformity to Christ's suffering and death. Our section, then, joins the eschatological reservation of v. 11 and draws out its ethical consequences.[135] Thus, the relationship of this section to the preceding section indicates that it is primarily exposition of vv. 10-11. It is, then, a didactic section with a hortatory intent. Identifying this passage as didactic excludes not only all mirror reading but all use of affirmations to identify opponents. However, since so many interpreters find allusions to opponents here, we will give the passage some attention to determine whether their judgments are justified.

Τετελείωμαι ('I have been perfected') in 3.12 is usually identified as a slogan of some type of perfectionism.[136] All such identifications rely on both unsupported mirror reading and merely terminological parallels with material outside Philippians. There have been no explicit comments (or even vague intimations) about realized eschatology, Gnosticism, pnuematic enthusiasm or antinomianism. Thus we cannot identify τετελείωμαι in v. 12 or the τέλειοι ('those who are perfect/mature') in v. 15 as slogans of opponents.[137]

---

134. Klein, 'Antipaulinismus in Philippi', p. 310.

135. Baumbach, 'Die von Paulus im Philipperbrief bekämpften Irrlehrer', p. 302. Baumbach still finds opponents in 3.12-16, but only through parallels with 1 Corinthians.

136. E.g. O'Brien (*Epistle to the Philippians*, pp. 422-23), Mengel (*Studien zum Philipperbrief*, pp. 267-69), Tyson ('Paul's Opponents at Philippi', p. 90) and Mearns ('The Identity of Paul's Opponents at Philippi', pp. 195-96) find perfectionism related to a realized eschatology; Lohmeyer (*Briefe an die Philipper*, p. 143) sees a reference to perfectionist claims by those being persecuted; Koester ('The Purpose of the Polemic of a Pauline Fragment', pp. 322-24), Schmithals (*Paul and the Gnostics*, pp. 95-99) and Carl Holladay ('Paul's Opponents in Philippians 3', *RQ* 12 (1969), pp. 86-90) find Gnostic perfectionists; Baumbach ('Die von Paulus im Philipperbrief bekämpften Irrlehrer', pp. 302-303) and Jewett ('Conflicting Movements', pp. 373-87) find perfectionist, pneumatic enthusiasts. Michael (*Paul to the Philippians*, pp. 155-56) says on the basis of this passage that they may have antinomian tendencies.

137. Vincent (*Commentary on the Epistles to the Philippians and to Philemon*, p. 109) contends that it is superfluous to introduce opposition to any sort of perfectionism here, arguing that it is simply a contrast with 'self-righteousness'. Similarly

It may yet be possible to see Paul's use of these terms as a less direct reference to conclusions he draws about the opponents' teaching.[138] 3.15 seems to suggest the need to include all among the 'mature',[139] but even this is mirror reading.[140] Still, the overall context of ch. 3 may allow such an interpretation. If this were the case, it would indicate that the opponents were claiming to offer some advanced status within Christianity through circumcision. But this need not mean perfectionism in the sense that it includes some element of realized eschatology or moral completeness. Bonnard notes that τελείωμαι had, by the first century, passed out of use solely in mystery religions and into more common usage where it described a higher state of spirituality.[141] If Paul is using it in this general way, it may speak to the opponents' offer to the Philippians. This would be no surprise; they must offer something to make circumcision attractive, but this passage does not indicate what that is. However, Klein rejects even this connection with the opponents, arguing that vv. 12-15 address only a potential danger. This interpretation, he asserts, makes the adversative of v. 16 more understandable.[142] One other possibility exists. Paul may be making it clear that in his description of his own experience he is not distinguishing himself from the Philippians. Just as they struggle with their faith in the midst of persecution, so also Paul has not risen above that struggle or

Ernst (*Briefe an die Philipper*, p. 101) understands vv. 12-13 to be the other side of Paul giving up his Jewish past. Klijn ('Paul's Opponents in Philippians III', p. 281) goes back further and identifies a parallel between v. 12 and Paul's claim to being spotless with respect to the law in 3.6.

138. Mengel (*Studien zum Philipperbrief*, p. 267) speaks of 'perfect' and 'already attained' as Reizworte. It seems doubtful that τετελείωμαι is part of the athletic metaphor used in later verses, as Caird claims (*Letters from Prison*, p. 142).

139. Caird (*Letters from Prison*, p. 144) and O'Brien (*Epistle to the Philippians*, pp. 435-36) note that Paul's use of ὅσοι (whoever) is usually inclusive (Caird cites Rom. 6.3; Gal. 5.27) and so its use in Phil. 3.15 indicates that Paul is calling all of those addressed τέλειοι (mature/perfect). Vincent (*Commentary on the Epistles to the Philippians and to Philemon*, pp. 112-13) compares the use of τέλειοι here with πνευματικοί (pneumatics/spiritual ones) in 1 Cor. 3.1 and the use of ἅγιος (saint) to refer to all Christians. I.e. these terms do not designate those who have achieved this status, but rather all Christians who have committed themselves to this life or goal.

140. Egger (*Galaterbrief, Philipperbrief, Philemonbrief*, p. 68) acknowledges that it is not certain that some at Philippi call themselves the perfect.

141. Bonnard, *L'épître de Saint Paul aux Philippiens*, p. 67.

142. Klein, 'Antipaulinismus in Philippi', pp. 310-11.

the need to constantly conform more to the knowledge of Christ as he endures persecution. This purpose for the passage fits quite well with the following call to imitation (v. 17) and the overall hortatory inclination of Philippians.[143]

The ἀποκαλύψει ('[God] will reveal') in 3.15 is another term often used to characterize opponents. Some interpreters claim that it shows that the opponents claim to receive visions.[144] But since this interpretation rests wholly on unsupported mirror reading and sometimes on a prior broader reconstruction, it must be rejected as without basis.

Thus 3.12-16 tells us very little or nothing about the opponents. These verses give no basis for finding any type of a second front of opposition to Paul's teachings in Philippi. Neither do they suggest that the opponents of ch. 3 are Gnostics, enthusiasts, perfectionists or persons with a realized eschatology. The most one can glean is that it is possible they claim that circumcision leads to a higher level of spiritual achievement. But this minimum is almost inherently necessary in the demand for circumcision, unless some advantage for fellowship (or some similar practical purpose) is claimed. But we have not found this to be an issue in Philippians, in fact, we find nothing of what the claimed advantage was. It seems equally possible that 3.12-16 heads off any interpretation of Paul's earlier comments in the chapter that might lead the Philippians to see Paul on a level of existence that they have not attained or cannot attain. That is, Paul is clearly identifying himself with the types of spiritual struggle the Philippians encounter in order to prepare for the exhortation to imitate him that follows. This interpretation also accounts for Paul including them and himself among the τέλειοι (perfect/mature) in v. 15. In either case, we gain nothing signifi-cant about the opponents from this paragraph.

4.2-3

A possible reference to opponents appears in 4.2-3 where Paul exhorts two Philippian leaders to stop quarrelling. This is the first specific exhortation in the hortatory section 4.(1)2-9. While a few interpreters have

143. If ch. 3 is a separate letter, the last argument for this suggestion is less persuasive.

144. So, e.g., Collange, *Paul to the Philippians*, p. 135; Gnilka, *Der Philipperbrief*, p. 201; Schmithals, *Paul and the Gnostics*, pp. 101-102.

read into 4.2-3 a dispute that involves the opponents,[145] the text is too general to support any specificity about the substance of the disagreement between these two women.[146] It does seem probable that the disagreement is one that effects the life of the community since Paul raises the issue as he does.[147] It also seems a good possibility that this reference to a specific disagreement is related to the exhortation to unity in ch. 2.[148] But our method allows only explicit statements in hortatory contexts to be used as evidence for opponents. Thus, this passage tells us nothing about the opponents of either 1.15-18 or 3.2-11.

1.6, 9-11
The thanksgiving of this letter (1.3-11) contains some terms used in 3.12-16. According to our method, if no explicit statements about opponents appear in a thanksgiving, only its themes that tie directly to what we know about the opponents can be used to help identify opponents. The theme that runs through both 1.6 and 1.9-11 seems to be the continuation of growth until the parousia. The thanksgiving congratulates the Philippians for their progress, while also calling for advancement. This theme is echoed in 2.12-13 and serves as the basis for the various exhortations of the letter. It also connects well with the looking toward the future called for in 3.12-16. While 1.6, 9-11 could be seen to support the presence of some realized eschatology, we cannot use such statements in a thanksgiving to characterize opponents unless there is some clear tie to issues raised elsewhere. But this issue is not discussed anywhere else in Philippians. Perhaps 1.6, 9-11 does prepare for the instructions of 3.12-16, but we cannot specify what 3.12-16 addresses on the basis of these non-explicit statements in a thanksgiving.

---

145. E.g. Schmithals, *Paul and the Gnostics*, p. 112. Lohmeyer (*Briefe an die Philipper*, pp. 165-66) says the quarrel must have been caused by persecution.

146. So also Ernst, *Briefe an die Philipper*, p. 113. Even the more general claims that their disagreement is over religious matters (Michael, *Paul to the Philippians*, p. 189) or not over theological questions (Perkins, 'Theology for the Heavenly Politeuma', p. 91) go beyond the evidence.

147. So also O'Brien, *Epistle to the Philippians*, p. 478.

148. So Perkins, 'Theology for the Heavenly Politeuma', p. 91 n. 11, p. 97; Scott, 'The Epistle to the Philippians', pp. 106-107. Mengel (*Studien zum Philipperbrief*, p. 279) sees these women as the background for 2.1-2 and 1.27-28. N.B. Most interpreters who reject the integrity of Philippians identify 4.2-3 as part of the letter which includes 2.1-30.

Summary of Affirmations

Affirmations that may address opponents have been limited to 3.12-16; 4.2-3 and 1.6, 9-11. Several other statements in Philippians speak of the situation there (e.g. 2.1-4; 2.12-18), but these do not clearly relate to problems with opponents, just as we found no sufficient basis for a connection at 4.2-3. Thus, we do not need to deal with such passages here. Even if such instructions about unity do relate to problems caused by opponents, the most they could show is that the opponents are more successful than it appears in the rest of the letter.

The most it is possible to claim on the basis of affirmations in Philippians is that the 'dogs' of 3.2 claim some, perhaps spiritual, advantage for those who are circumcised—hardly a startling revelation. But we cannot move beyond saying that even this is just a possibility because 3.12-16 may be a safeguard to prevent the Philippians from thinking Paul has moved beyond struggling to conform to the knowledge of Christ.

Conclusion

Philippians yields evidence for three types of 'opponent'. One group is specifically called opponents of the Philippians in 1.28. These opponents, who may frighten the Philippians, are non-Christians who persecute the Philippian Christians. They seem to have no other connection to Paul and so are not opponents of Paul, per se.

The second group of opponents appear in 1.15-18. This group is present in the city of Paul's imprisonment and do not treat Paul as he thinks they should. These opponents, whom he describes as envious, seem to have no significant doctrinal differences from Paul because he acknowledges that they preach Christ. Furthermore, these opponents have not troubled the Philippians or other Pauline churches outside the city of Paul's current residence.

The third group of opponents is addressed in ch. 3. These opponents are Jewish-Christian missionaries who claim some superiority on the basis of their Jewish credentials, but Paul does not indicate what advantage(s) they claim. They also demand that Gentiles be circumcised. There is insufficient evidence to claim that they require Gentiles to keep any other elements of the Law. While the abusive epithets of 3.2 seem to indicate that Paul perceives them as a real threat, his use of them as a negative example without supporting arguments shows that they have not established a following at Philippi. Paul's references to them as ἐργάται (workers) and so missionaries indicates that they are not an isolated phenomenon but part of a movement that has troubled other Pauline churches. This seems to be the most likely reason for his violent reaction to them in 3.2.

If they are part of a larger group, this is the second such group we have encountered in Paul's letters; the opponents of 2 Corinthians were also part of a group that had come after establshing themselves at other churches. While there are some points of contact between the two groups (e.g. both emphasize their Jewish credentials), the points of commonality are too limited to see them as the same group. This becomes obvious when we note that the primary issues of 2 Corinthians (the Spirit and apostleship) play no significant role in Philippians; Paul does not even use the title apostle in the greeting of Philippians. The 'opponents' of Galatians and those of Philippians 3 have common features that are more central; both require circumcision and perhaps other elements of Judaism. But if we are correct that the teachers in Galatia did not know that their message differed from Paul's until they read Galatians, they must either not belong to the same group as the 'dogs' of Philippians 3 or they rejected the clarification of Paul's gospel set out in Galatians and hardened into an opposition party in response to that letter. If the latter option is chosen, we still cannot clarify their positions in either Philippians or Galatians on the basis of the other letter because we cannot know what their hardening toward Paul might have led them to and because Philippians, the later of the two letters, is so general. So while this process is at least possible, it does not expand our information about what views Paul opposes in either letter.

Chapter 6

THOSE WHO 'PASS JUDGMENT'—COLOSSIANS*

The century-long debate over the identity of the opponents in view in Colossians has seen little movement toward a consensus.[1] Dibelius identified the Colossian opponents as syncretists who incorporate features of a cult of the 'elements' and mystery rites into Christianity.[2] Others find a form of Jewish Gnosticism[3] or proto-gnostics.[4] Schweizer argues that they advocate ascetic practices to enable the ascent of the soul through the 'elements',[5] while Bandstra asserts that they are Jewish mystical ascetics who claim not to need a mediator to gain knowledge of God.[6] The most common element in hypotheses about these oppo-

---

* This chapter is a revision of an article that appeared in *Bib* 74 (1993), pp. 366-88.

1. See the summary of 44 different hypotheses about the opponents of Colossians: Gunther, *St. Paul's Opponents*, pp. 3-4. Cf. the examples of studies of these opponents in F.O. Francis and W.A. Meeks (eds.), *Conflict at Colossae: A Problem in the Interpretation of Early Christianity Illustrated by Selected Modern Studies* (Sources for Biblical Study, 4; Missoula, MT: SBL, 1973).

2. Martin Dibelius, 'The Isis Initiation in Apuleius and Related Initiatory Rites', in Francis and Meeks (eds.), *Conflict at Colossae*, pp. 61-122. Similarly, E.F. Scott (*The Epistles of Paul to the Colossians, to Philemon, and to the Ephesians* [MNTC; New York: Harper & Brothers, 1930], pp. 7-10) and Randall A. Argall ('The Source of a Religious Error in Colossae', *Calvin Theological Journal* 22 [1987], pp. 6-20).

3. Bornkamm, 'The Heresy of Colossians', in Francis and Meeks (eds.), *Conflict at Colossae*, pp. 123-46.

4. T.K. Abbott, *A Critical and Exegetical Commentary on the Epistles to the Ephesians and to the Colossians* (ICC; Edinburgh: T. & T. Clark, 1897), p. xlix; Roy Yates, 'Colossians and Gnosis', *JSNT* 27 (1986), pp. 49-68.

5. Schweizer, 'Slaves of the Elements and Worshipers of Angels, pp. 455-68.

6. Bandstra, 'Did the Colossian Errorists Need a Mediator?', in R.N. Longenecker and M.C. Tenney (eds.), *New Dimensions in New Testament Study* (Grand Rapids: Eerdmans, 1974), pp. 329-43.

nents is that their teaching includes some type of worship directed toward angels. But F.O. Francis rejects this, arguing that they imitate the worship angels perform rather than worshipping the angels.[7] Morna Hooker contends that there were no opponents.[8] Two recent monograph-length studies come to very different understandings of these opponents. Clinton Arnold argues that the best background for understanding the teaching of the Colossian opponents is the folk-religion of the Lycus valley.[9] To establish this background he examines ways that several terms found in Colossians are used in Asia Minor. This study proceeds much like Georgi's study of the opponents of 2 Corinthians, that is, the author identifies as key certain terms from the letter at hand and then studies in detail how those terms are used in particular contexts outside the letter. Following this investigation it is assumed that the terms meant the same thing in both contexts.[10] The problematic nature of this approach can be seen by comparing Arnold's study with the other monograph on this subject, that by Troy Martin. Beginning with parts of the method advocated in the present book, Martin identifies some important terms for understanding the Colossian teachers. Once these terms have been identified he explores at length the ways they are used among philosophers.[11] Then, like Arnold, Martin assumes that since the same terms are used by both Colossians and the other

---

7. Fred O. Francis, 'Humility and Angelic Worship in Col 2:18', in Francis and Meeks (eds.), *Conflict at Colossae*, pp. 163-96. Francis ('The Christological Argument of Colossians', in J. Jervell and W.A. Meeks [eds.], *God's Christ and his People* [Oslo: Universitetsforlaget, 1977], pp. 192-208 [192-94]) is one exception to the absence of attention to method when searching for the opponents of this letter.

8. Morna Hooker, 'Were there False Teachers in Colossae?', in B. Lindars and S.S. Smalley (eds.), *Christ and the Spirit in the New Testament* (Cambridge: Cambridge University Press, 1973), pp. 315-31. She is followed by N.T. Wright, 'Poetry and Theology in Colossians 1.15-20', *NTS* 36 (1990), pp. 444-68 (463-64).

9. Clinton E. Arnold, *The Colossian Syncretism: the Interface between Christianity and Folk Belief in Colossae* (Grand Rapids: Baker Book House, 1996).

10. See Arnold (*The Colossian Syncretism*, p. 90) for Arnold's comments to this effect.

11. Troy Martin, *By Philosophy and Vain Deceit: Colossians as a Response to a Cynic Critique* (JSNTSup, 118; Sheffield: Sheffield Academic Press, 1996). While Martin identifies the philosophy as Cynic, he was preceded in looking at philosophical schools by Richard E. DeMaris (*The Colossian Controversy: Wisdom in Dispute at Colossae* [JSNTSup 96; Sheffield: JSOT Press, 1994]) who identified the problem as a 'distinctive blend of popular Middle Platonic, Jewish, and Christian elements that cohere around the pursuit of wisdom' (p. 14).

group investigated (in Martin's case Hellenistic philosophers) the words must mean the same thing in both writings. How problematic this assumption is in this case can be seen quickly by all who began reading New Testament Greek and then turned to read philosophers or Philo for the first time. Often the same words mean rather different things in the philosophers and the New Testament. But the broader unreliability of this approach can be seen by comparing the results of Martin and Arnold. Their differences depend more on the background they investigated than the text of Colossians.[12]

Explicit Statements

2.16

We begin our search for the opponents of Colossians with the fairly clear explicit statement in 2.16. There is almost universal agreement that 2.16-23 is polemical.[13] In 2.16 the Colossians are warned not to let anyone judge them with respect to food, drink or particular holy days.[14] Interpreters generally agree that these food regulations are ascetic (cf.

---

12. For more extensive critique of this method of identifying opponents see my comments on Georgi's (and Friedrich's) use of it in *Identifying Paul's Opponents*, pp. 49-61.

13. Those who identify 2.16-23 as a distinct section and identify it as polemical include Martin Dibelius and H. Greeven, *An die Kolosser, Epheser, an Philemon* (HNT; Tübingen: J.C.B. Mohr [Paul Siebeck], 3rd edn, 1953), p. 29; Hans Conzelmann, 'Der Brief an die Kolosser', in Conzelmann *et al.*, *Die kleineren Briefe des Apostels Paulus* (Das Neue Testament Deutsch, 8; Göttingen: Vandenhoeck & Ruprecht, 1962), p. 131; Eduard Lohse, *A Commentary on the Epistles to the Colossians and to Philemon* (trans. W.R. Poehlmann and R.J. Karris; Hermeneia; Philadelphia: Fortress Press, 1971), p. 114; Peter T. O'Brien, *Colossians, Philemon* (WBC, 44; Waco, TX: Word Books, 1982), pp. 136, 138, 155. This view is opposed by Martin (*By Philosophy*, p. 35 n.1) who asserts that 2.16 is a defense of the Colossians' own practice rather than a rejection of the opponents' regulations. But the evaluation of these practices given in v. 17 shows that these are judged to be without value. This evaluation would do little to encourage the community to continue in its practice in the face of outside criticism. Furthermore, v. 16 and v. 18 seem to be somewhat parallel, each calling the Colossians to reject practices that the other teachers advocate.

14. Some argue that the indefinite τις ('anyone') (Abbott, *The Epistles to the Ephesians and to the Colossian*, p. 263; Lohse, *Colossians*, p. 114) or the present imperative (O'Brien, *Colossians*, p. 138) shows that there is a real threat to the Colossian community.

2.22). The holy days mentioned include new moons and Sabbaths, celebrations derived from Judaism.[15] But this does not necessarily indicate that Colossians opposes Judaizers.[16]

This explicit statement in 2.16 shows that the author believes the Colossians need to be warned against allowing themselves to be judged on the basis of their compliance with a regimen of food regulations and the observance of certain holy days.

2.4

In 2.4, our next explicit statement, the author warns the Colossians not to let anyone deceive them with good-sounding arguments.[17] This statement occurs in the section comprising 1.24–2.5,[18] which seems to be apologetic because the writer is establishing Paul's[19] authority over the Colossian community in preparation for his attack on the opponents.[20]

In 2.4 the author proffers an evaluation of the opponents—they deceive with good-sounding arguments. It may yield a bit more information since it begins with 'I say this…' (τοῦτο λέγω) which points to the preceding statements. I will comment on 2.2-3 as an allusion below.

2.19

Another polemical evaluation of the opponents, 2.19,[21] says that they have separated themselves from Christ. No doubt the opponents would

15. This is generally accepted for the Sabbath. For discussion of the new moon in Hellenistic Judaism see Thornton, 'Jewish New Moon Festivals', pp. 97-100.

16. So Eduard Schweizer, *The Letter to the Colossians: A Commentary* (trans. A. Chester; Minneapolis: Augsburg, 1982), p. 157; Lohse, *Colossians*, p. 115; Lohse, 'Pauline Theology in the Letter to the Colossians', *NTS* 15 (1968), pp. 211-20 (212); F.F. Bruce, 'Colossian Problems Part 3: The Colossian Heresy', *BSac* 141 (1984), pp. 195-208 (197).

17. Most interpreters recognize 2.4 as a statement about the opponents. However, Hooker ('Were there False Teachers?', p. 317) sees it as a general warning.

18. Most commentators divide the text this way, e.g. Dibelius and Greeven, *Kolosser*, p. 1; Lohse, *Colossians*, p. 68; O'Brien, *Colossians*, p. liv.

19. As with the other letters whose authorship is disputed, no position on the authorship of Colossians is being taken here.

20. Others who see this as an apologetic section include Lohse, *Colossians*, p. 68, and Ralph. P. Martin, *Colossians and Philemon* (NCB; London: Oliphants, 1974) , p. 69. Similarly, Schweizer, *Colossians*, 115, and Josef Gewiess, 'Die apologetische Methode des Apostels Paulus im Kampf gegen die Irrlehre in Kolossä', *Bibel und Leben* 3 (1962), pp. 258-70 (265).

21. So also O'Brien, *Colossians*, pp. 136, 141.

have vigorously disputed this evaluation. This statement clearly does not represent the opponents' position because they must claim to be Christian to be a threat to the Colossian church and because this evaluation is pointless if they do not claim an attachment to Christ. Given its function, this verse probably contains none of the opponents' vocabulary or concepts.[22] It shows only that the author believes the opponents' views have the gravest of consequences.

2.20-23

The statements in 2.20-23 which refer explicitly to the opponents' regulations conclude the polemical section, 2.16-23. Since v. 20b indicates that some Colossians are submitting to the regulations listed in v. 21,[23] this verse is not simply an advance warning, there are opponents in Colossae advocating these views.[24]

Verse 20a sets out a presupposition of the author's opposition to the opponents in vv. 21-22. That the Colossians died with Christ to the στοιχείων ('elements'), who are involved with living according to the δόγματα ('dogmas') of the world, is not in dispute. Both the author and the Colossians accept this.[25] What the writer must point out is that their death with Christ means that they need not heed the opponents' demands. We will say more about 'the elements' below in connection with 2.8.

The three 'don'ts' of v. 21 are examples of the types of regulations that the opponents impose and are either quotations[26] of the opponents

---

22. Contra Dibelius and Greeven (*Kolosser*, p. 36) who see σῶμα (body) as a reference to the ἀρχαί and ἐξουσίαι (principalities and powers) and so to the στοιχεῖα (elements). Instead, the image of head and body may simply echo 1.15-20. Perhaps Schweizer (*Colossians*, p. 163) is correct that the body is the church, but it seems as likely that it is simply a use of the metaphor.

23. Those who see a rebuke in v. 20b seem to hold this view. E.g. Dibelius and Greeven, *Kolosser*, p. 90; Martin, *Colossians and Philemon*, p. 90; O'Brien, *Colossians*, p. 137. However, Hooker ('Were there False Teachers?', pp. 317-18) sees v. 20b as a general warning. But her comments on v. 21 somewhat negate the force of this assertion (Hooker, 'Were there False Teachers?', p. 328).

24. Cf. Lohse, *Colossians*, p. 123.

25. So Percy, *Probleme*, p. 167; Francis, 'Christological Argument', pp. 201-202. Schweizer ('Die "Elemente der Welt"', p. 247) argues that 'died to the στοιχεῖα' is more like the expressions 'died to sin' and 'died to the Law' than like a reference to spiritual powers in the narrow sense.

26. So Martin, *Colossians and Philemon*, p. 96; O'Brien, *Colossians*, p. 137;

or irony and caricature of their demands.[27] In either case, v. 21 shows that the opponents call for some type of abstinence.

Both v. 20b and v. 22 contain polemical evaluations of the opponents' rules.[28] In v. 20b the author states that they are equivalent to living in the world, which he opposes to having died with Christ. In v. 22 he says that the opponents' commands or the objects these commands involve are of no lasting value.[29] He judges 'all such things' to be according to the commands and teachings of humans. Ἐντάλματα ('commands') and διδασκαλίας ('teachings') are not slogans of the opponents, first because they are part of the writer's critical judgment on their regulations and secondly because Isa. 29.3 determined the form of the expression.[30]

Syntactical problems make even translating v. 23 difficult[31] but the main point is clear. The author is rejecting the opponents' teachings, saying that they are without value and lead to indulgence of the flesh or are without value against the indulgence of the flesh.[32] This polemical evaluation[33] follows the pattern present in 2.21-22 of listing the sorts of

F.O. Francis, 'Visionary Discipline and Scriptural Tradition at Colossae', *Lexington Theological Quarterly* 2 (1967), pp. 71-78 (73).

27. See Lohse, *Colossians*, p. 123. Cf. Abbott, *Ephesians and Colossians*, p. 273; O'Brien, *Colossians*, pp. 137, 149-50.

28. So Percy, *Probleme*, p. 139; Gewiess, 'Die apologetische Methode', p. 269; Francis, 'Christological Argument', p. 194; Lohse, *Colossians*, p. 124.

29. O'Brien (*Colossians*, pp. 137, 150) identifies this as a criticism of the opponents.

30. Many recognize this allusion to Isa including C.F.D. Moule, *The Epistles of Paul the Apostle to the Colossians and to Philemon* (CGTC; Cambridge: Cambridge University Press, 1957), p. 151; Francis, 'Visionary Discipline', p. 73; Lohse, *Colossians*, p. 124; O'Brien, *Colossians*, p. 151.

31. On translating this verse see Bruce Hollenbach, 'Col. II.23: Which things Lead to the Fulfilment of the Flesh', *NTS* 25 (1978–79), pp. 254-61. See also the translation of vv. 20-23 proposed by Martin (*By Philosophy*, pp. 37-55) who makes much of the passage interrogative. This translation makes less difference in identifying the opponents than Martin seems to claim for it.

32. This latter understanding is that of Moule, *Epistles of Paul the Apostle*, p. 108; Percy, *Probleme*, p. 139; Schweizer, *Colossians*, p. 169.

33. Others who see polemical elements here include Werner Bieder, *Die kolossische Irrlehre und die Kirche von heute* (Theologische Studien, 33; Zürich: Evangelische Verlag, 1952), pp. 9-10; Percy, *Probleme*, p. 169; Lohse, *Colossians*, p. 126; O'Brien, *Colossians*, p. 137; W. Schmithals, 'The *Corpus Paulinum* and

demands the opponents make (v. 21) and then giving an evaluation beginning with a relative pronoun (in v. 22 ἅ ['these things']) followed by ἐστιν ('are'). This construction is also found in 2.17 (see below). Verse 23 begins with the relative pronoun ἅτινά ('such things') followed by ἐστιν ('are'). That this construction introduces a negative evaluation of the opponents' teaching is made clear in v. 23 by the use of λόγον μὲν ἔχοντα σοφίας ('having the word [sound] of wisdom').[34] Some interpreters see this phrase as evidence that the opponents call their teaching wisdom.[35] However, given the respect accorded asceticism as a manifestation of wisdom in the first century, it is probably a more general statement which says only that they appear to be wise.

The expressions 'will-worship' (ἐθελοθρησκία), 'humility' (ταπεινοφροσύνη) and 'severity to the body' (ἀφειδίᾳ σώματος) all describe the opponents' practices. The question is, are they descriptions the opponents themselves use or descriptions the author assigns? Since these things give the opponents' teaching its reputation for wisdom, the Colossians see them positively. So the opponents may have used the terms. 'Severity to the body' (ἀφειδίᾳ σώματος) is a general enough expression that it need not have been a slogan, though the opponents may have used it at times to describe their manner of life. It seems more likely that they use humility (ταπεινοφροσύνη) in some specialized sense, as we will see in connection with 2.18. That humility and severity to the body were seen as wise is clear enough, but that self-chosen or voluntarily accepted worship shows wisdom is not as obvious to modern readers. Thus some see it as a negative evaluation, meaning something like alleged piety.[36] But since the immediate context indicates that the opponents may have used the term[37] and since the Colossians view it as evidence of wisdom, the point is that they have taken on a burden beyond that of ordinary Christians which makes them superior. The exhortations of 2.16 and 18 which tell the Colossians not to allow

Gnosis', in A.H.B. Logan and A.J.M. Wedderburn (eds.), *The New Testament and Gnosis* (Edinburgh: T. & T. Clark, 1983), pp. 107-24 (117); Schweizer, *Colossians*, p. 168.

34. Schweizer, *Colossians*, p. 168.

35. Those who see this term as a slogan of the opponents include Lohse, *Colossians*, p. 126 and Schmithals, 'The *Corpus Paulinum* and Gnosis', p. 117.

36. So Bieder, *Die kolossische Irrlehre*, pp. 9-10, and Schmithals, 'The *Corpus Paulinum* and Gnosis', p. 117. Cf. Martin, *Colossians and Philemon*, p. 15.

37. Dibelius, 'Isis Initiation', p. 89; Bornkamm, 'The Heresy of Colossians', p. 134; Lohse, *Colossians*, p. 126; O'Brien, Colossians, p. 153.

anyone to pass judgment against them on the basis of regulations supports identifying this term as one used by the opponents to distinguish themselves from other Christians. No other terms in v. 23 echo the opponents' terminology.[38]

Verses 20-22 show that the opponents' teachings are at least mildly ascetic and, according to the author, incompatible with Christian existence. All we see about the 'elements' is that they are done away with in baptism[39] and are involved with δόγματα of non-Christian (ἐν κόσμῳ [in the world]) existence. We see from v. 23 that the opponents may refer to their teaching as wisdom and describe their practice as severity to the body. They more likely use the terms 'will-worship' (ἐθελοθρησκίᾳ) and 'humility' (ταπεινοθροσύνη) in their teaching.

2.17
Another explicit statement about the opponents appears in 2.17. Within the polemical section 2.16-23, this verse says that the opponents' regulations about food, drink and holy days are a 'shadow of things to come, but the reality is the body of Christ'.[40]

The form of 2.21-22 should guide our interpretation of 2.17. Both 2.17 and 2.21 contain a sample of the opponents' demands. Verse 17 begin ἅ ἐστιν (these things are), just as v. 22 does. This parallel construction suggests that v. 17 is the same type of statement as v. 22, that is, an evaluation. So v. 17 is probably not using the opponents' lan-

---

38. Contra Lohse (*Colossians*, p. 126) who sees both τιμῆ ('value') and πλησμονὴν ('gratification') as reflections of the opponents' language, but this requires too extensive a use of mirror exegesis. Abbott (*Ephesians and Colossians*, p. 276) understands πλησμονὴν to mean 'excessive indulgence' and sees it opposed to asceticism.

39. Francis ('Christological Argument', p. 197) sees 2.20 as a baptismal tradition.

40. Some see a quotation of the opponents in v. 17; others specify whether 'body of Christ' refers to what Christ did on earth (e.g. H.C.G. Moule, *The Epistles to the Colossians and to Philemon* [The Cambridge Bible for Schools and Colleges; Cambridge: Cambridge University Press, 1898], p. 110) or the church (e.g. Martin, *Colossians and Philemon*, p. 91), or see a reference to the Hebrew Scriptures in the σκιά (shadow) (e.g. Caird, *Paul's Letters from Prison*, p. 162; Eduard Schweizer, 'Christianity of the Circumcised and Judaism of the Uncircumcised: The Background of Matthew and Colossians', in R. Hamerton-Kelly and R. Scroggs (eds.), *Jews, Greeks and Christians: Religious Cultures in Late Antiquity* [Leiden: E.J. Brill, 1976], pp. 245-60 [257]).

guage, it is rather the author's evaluation of their regulations—they are transitory in comparison with 'the body of Christ'.[41]

Such detrimental evaluations reveal nothing specific about one's opponents but should not surprise us given the nature of polemic in the Hellenistic period.

2.8

Our next explicit statement, 2.8, appears in the polemical section 2.6-15.[42] The writer warns the Colossians in 2.8 not to be despoiled by philosophy and vain deceit which is according to human tradition and the στοιχεῖα τοῦ κόσμου (elements of the world) and not 'accordin to Christ'. This is another polemical evaluation.[43] Still, many interpreters find quotations of the opponents here, for example the term 'philosophy'.[44] Even if this is correct, we cannot characterize the opponents' theology on the basis of this term, as some do,[45] because it had a wide range of meanings in this period and was used by many religious groups.[46]

Some also see the term 'tradition' as a slogan of the opponents.[47] Others believe 'tradition of humans' combats their claim to a super-

41. Σῶμα ('body') may simply complete the comparison with σκιά ('shadow'). So O'Brien, *Colossians*, pp. 139-41.

42. Interpreters are divided over whether the section begins at v. 6 or v. 8 or even at v. 4, but all see the section to which v. 8 belongs as polemical.

43. So Francis, 'Christological Argument', p. 194; Gewiess, 'Die apologetische Methode', p. 268; Conzelmann 'Der Brief an die Kolosser', p. 142. Lohse (*Colossians*, p. 94) supports this view by pointing to the βλέπετε ('watch out') which often begins an admonition. Cf. Schmithals, 'The *Corpus Paulinum* and Gnosis', p. 112.

44. E.g. Abbott, *Ephesians and Colossians*, p. 246; Bornkamm, 'The Heresy of Colossians', p. 126; Dibelius and Greeven, *Kolosser*, p. 27; Bieder, *Die kolossische Irrlehre*, p. 13; Lohse, *Colossians*, p. 95; O'Brien, *Colossians*, p. 109; Roy Yates, 'Christ and the Powers of Evil in Colossians', E.A. Livingstone (ed.), *Studia Biblica 1978. III. Papers on Paul and Other New Testament Authors* (JSNTSup, 3 (Sheffield: JSOT Press, 1980), pp. 461-68 (462); A.M. Moyo, 'The Colossian Heresy in the Light of Some Gnostic Documents from Nag Hammadi', *Journal of Theology for Southern Africa* 48 (1984), pp. 30-44 (36).

45. E.g. Moule, *The Epistles to the Colossians and to Philemon*, p. 101; Francis, 'Christological Argument', p. 206; and Lohse, *Colossians*, p. 95; Martin, *By Philosophy*, pp. 28-30.

46. O'Brien, *Colossians*, p. 109. It may simply parallel 'vain deceit' and so be a criticism of the opponents, as Moule proposes (*Epistles of Paul the Apostle*, p. 90).

47. E.g. Dibelius and Greeven, *Kolosser*, p. 27; Lohse, *Colossians*, p. 96;

human source of teaching.[48] Both of these interpretations are based on mirror reading and thus are far too unreliable to use without limitations beyond those present here. 'Human tradition' is probably a general polemical evaluation of the opponents' teaching,[49] especially in light of the next phrase, to which we now turn.

One of the more difficult expressions in Colossians is στοιχεῖα τοῦ κόσμου ('elements of the world'). In 2.8 this phrase stands parallel with the preceding ('tradition of humans') and following ('not according to Christ') phrases.[50] All three are evaluations of the opponents' views.[51] The point of all three is that 'the opponents' teaching is at variance with' Christian teaching.[52]

The στοιχεῖα ('elements') appear twice in explicit statements about the opponents, here as a negative evaluation of their teaching generally and in 2.20 as the foundation for rejecting their regulations. So, there is no indication that the στοιχεῖα play a part in the opponents' teachings. In fact, the evidence suggests that they did not because, in both places that they appear, the author *assumes* that a relationship with them is bad and that this assumption needs no support.[53] This understanding of 'the elements' is confirmed by both the polemical context and the placement

O'Brien, *Colossians*, p. 110. Martin (*By Philosophy*, pp. 30-31) argues use of this language shows that the opponents are operating from within an established tradition.

48. E.g. Bieder, *Die kolossische Irrlehre*, p. 14.

49. Similarly Francis, 'Christological Argument', p. 202 and Craig A. Evans, 'The Colossian Mystics', *Bib* 63 (1982), pp. 188-205 (202). Contra Martin, *By Philosophy*, p. 30. He argues that this expression shows that the opponents rely on a tradition of a recognized school of philosophy. However, the expression 'teachings and commandments of humans' which is found in Col. 2.21 is the same type of statement that we have here in v. 8. The parallels between 2.21 and Mk 7.7 and Jer. 29.13 (LXX) show clearly that 'traditions of humans' is a polemical accusation. See Hans Hübner, *An Philemon, An die Kolosser, An die Epheser* (HNT 12; Tübingen: J.C.B. Mohr [Paul Siebeck], 1997), p. 91.

50. So Percy, *Probleme*, pp. 166-67; Francis, 'Christological Argument', p. 202; Schweizer, 'Die "Elemente der Welt" ', p. 246.

51. So Percy, *Probleme*, pp. 166-67; Francis, 'Christological Argument', pp. 202, 206. This is perhaps a change in Francis's position from his 'Visionary Discipline', p. 79, where he identified κατὰ Χριστόν ('according to Christ') as a claim of the opponents.

52. Francis, 'Christological Argument', p. 202.

53. Cf. Percy, *Probleme*, pp. 156-67; Francis, 'Christological Argument', p. 206.

of 'according to the "elements"' between 'human tradition' and 'not according to Christ'. Thus, in 2.8 involvement with 'the elements' is a polemical accusation not a citation of the opponents' language. Martin is quite right in arguing that στοιχεῖα is not necessarily pejorative,[54] even though Arnold has surfaced much evidence that indicates that they were often seen as hostile powers in the second century.[55] What shows the use of στοιχεῖα to be polemical here is its context, its place within this string of polemical, denigrating evaluations of the other teaching.

While it is doubtful that στοιχεῖα was used by the opponents, we need to consider its meaning because other features of their views may warrant reconsidering this judgment. Though the στοιχεῖα have been identified many ways,[56] the philological evidence clearly favors identifying them as the elements—earth, water, air and fire,[57] as even some who disagree with this identification admit.[58] If the στοιχεῖα are the

54. Martin, *By Philosophy*, p. 31.

55. Arnold, *Colossian Syncretism*, pp. 158-76.

56. E.g. they have been identified as: the Mosaic Law (Moule, *The Epistles to the Colossians and to Philemon*, p. 102), spiritual beings, angels, or part of the *pleroma* of later Gnosticism (Dibelius and Greeven, *Kolosser*, p. 27; Scott, *Paul to the Colossians*, p. 43; Bornkamm, 'The Heresy of Colossians', pp. 123-24; F.W. Beare, 'Colossians', *IB* XI, p. 138; Percy, *Probleme*, p. 168; Schmithals, 'The Corpus Paulinum and Gnosis', p. 118; Evans, 'The Colossian Mystics', pp. 201-202; Harold Weiss, 'The Law in the Epistle to the Colossians', *CBQ* 34 (1972), p. 303; Andrew T. Lincoln, *Paradise Now and Not Yet: Studies in the Role of the Heavenly Dimension in Paul's Thought with Special Reference to his Eschatology* [SNTSMS, 43; Cambridge: Cambridge University Press, 1981], p. 114), elementary teaching (Moule, *Epistles of Paul the Apostle*, pp. 91-92; similarly Yates, 'Colossians and Gnosis', p. 59), and astral gods who control fate (F.F. Bruce [Colossians] in E.K. Simpson and F.F. Bruce, *A Commentary on the Epistles to the Ephesians and Colossians* [NICNT; Grand Rapids: Eerdmans, 1957], pp. 167, 231; Bieder, *Die kolossische Irrlehre*, p. 21; Lohse, *Colossians*, pp. 3, 98-99; O'Brien, *Colossians*, p. 110). For a more complete review of interpretations of the 'elements' see Schweizer, 'Die Elemente', pp. 247-49 and Schweizer, 'Zur neueren Forschung am Kolosserbrief (seit 1970)', *Theologische Berichte* 5 (1976), pp. 163-91 (173-76). Since 1976 see Yates 'Colossians and Gnosis', p. 59. Still more recently Clinton E. Arnold ('Returning to the Domain of the Powers: *Stoicheia* as Evil Spirits in Galatians 4:3,9', *NovT* 38 [1996], pp. 55-76) has argued that the στοιχεῖα are evil spirits and that Paul's understanding of them is derived from the Jewish apocalyptic tradition.

57. Schweizer, *Colossians*, p. 128; Schweizer, 'Die "Elemente der Welt"', pp. 247-49; *idem*, 'Slaves of the Elements, pp. 455-66.

58. Lincoln, *Paradise Now and Not Yet*, p. 114.

four (perhaps personified[59]) elements, the phrase means something rather general like worldly teaching. Accusing the opponents of having their teaching derive from the στοιχεῖα (whether it means the elements or spiritual beings) is a good example of the type of polemical exaggeration we often find in Colossians.[60]

2.18

Our last explicit statement, 2.18, is a warning. The author exhorts the Colossians not to be condemned or robbed of their place by the opponents. Since this is the second warning about allowing themselves to be judged, it is clear that the opponents are passing judgment[61] on the basis of ascetic practices and holy days (2.16) and the things mentioned here in 2.18.[62]

The 'entering into the things he has seen' (ἅ ἑόρακεν ἐμβατεύων)[63] indicates that the opponents receive visionary experiences[64] in which they see things that are significant for their teachings. The referent of ἅ (the things) is difficult to identify because it is a neuter plural relative pronoun following two feminine nouns. Rowland cites Col. 3.6, where a list of feminine nouns is followed by a neuter plural relative that includes all of the nouns in the list, as a parallel construction.[65] Thus, 2.18 says that the opponents see humility and worship in their visions.

Ἐμβατεύων ('entering into') has been discussed at length since Dibelius identified it as a term taken from the mysteries.[66] However, the

59. These 'elements' were being personified and venerated in the first century. See Schweizer, 'Die "Elemente der Welt"', pp. 247-48. and especially the references from Philo there.

60. Gewiess ('Die apologetische Methode', p. 264) points out that Colossians often presents the opponents in their most extreme form and perhaps draws consequences from their teaching which they themselves did not surmise in order to present them in the worst light possible.

61. See Dibelius and Greeven, *Kolosser*, p. 34; Caird, *Letters from Prison*, pp. 162-63; Lohse, *Colossians*, p. 117; O'Brien, *Colossians*, pp. 136, 141; Christopher Rowland, 'Apocalyptic Visions', p. 74.

62. O'Brien, *Colossians*, pp. 141-42.

63. The previous phrase, θέλων ἐν, seems best understood as a Septuagintism for 'to delight in'. So Moule, *Epistles of Paul the Apostle*, p. 104; Lohse, *Colossians*, p. 118 n. 29 and others.

64. Schmithals, 'The *Corpus Paulinum* and Gnosis', pp. 118-19.

65. Rowland, 'Apocalyptic Visions', pp. 75-76.

66. Dibelius, 'Isis Initiation', pp. 83-84. Arnold (*Colossian Syncretism*, pp. 118-21) explicitly takes up this view, contending that it means the same thing in Colos-

evidence for this use of the term is a century later than Colossians. More contemporary evidence shows it to be a fairly general term meaning simply 'to enter'.[67] Jewish apocalyptic literature used it in connection with visionary ascent, but not as a technical term for entering the heavenly realm.[68] Given its general meaning, and apocalyptic's use of that meaning, ἐμβατεύων probably had no special meaning for the opponents, though they may well have used it when describing their visionary ascents.

The first item our author says they see in these visions is humility (ταπεινοφροσύνη), which interpreters almost universally agree is a slogan of the opponents and a reference to ascetic practices, especially fasting.[69] This view is supported by the presence of ascetic regulations in the context (v.16), by the proximity of its mention here and in 2.23 with worship,[70] and by the fact that it is seen in visions.[71] Since this humility is seen in the visions, 'of angels' (τῶν ἀγγέλων) probably modifies humility as well as worship.[72] So they see the humility of angels in their visions.

One of the most important and difficult expressions in Colossians is the 'worship of angels'. The question is of course whether the genitive is objective (worship directed toward angels) or subjective (worship that angels perform). Whichever view is taken, interpreters agree that the opponents use the phrase, 'worship of angels' (θρησκείᾳ τῶν ἀγγέλων). Arnold, however, understands the phrase to be a polemical expression formulated by the author to describe these teachers in a way that

sians that it means 70 years later (by his account of the date of Colossians) in an inscription in Phrygia. No powerful new arguments for the validity of the parallel are proffered by Arnold.

67. See Francis, 'Humility and Angelic Worship', pp. 119-21.

68. Rowland, 'Apocalyptic. Visions', p. 76. Francis ('Humility and Angelic Worship', pp. 119-21) is tempted to see it as a technical term of apocalyptic Judaism and he presses too much out of this term in 'Visionary Discipline', p. 76.

69. So e.g. Dibelius and Greeven, *Kolosser*, p. 35; Conzelmann, 'Der Brief an die Kolosser', p. 145; Percy, *Probleme*, pp. 148-49; Schweizer, *Colossians*, p. 158; Lohse, *Colossians*, p. 117; O'Brien, *Colossians*, pp. 141-42.

70. Lohse, *Colossians*, p. 118; Lincoln, *Paradise Now and Not Yet*, p. 111.

71. Rowland ('Apocalyptic Visions', p. 75) cites humility as one thing seen in heavenly ascents in apocalyptic literature.

72. O'Brien (*Colossians*, p. 142) notes that 'humility' and 'worship' are closely linked because they are joined by a single preposition.

will make them unacceptable.[73] This interesting possibility seems less likely, though by no means implausible, because this expression is part of the larger phrase that includes the preceding 'humility'. Since 'of angels' (τῶν ἀγγέλων) probably modifies both humility and worship, they most likely also stand in the same relationship to it. That is, since the genitive is subjective in relation to humility, it is subjective in relation to worship. If we had evidence in explicit statements that the opponents venerated spiritual beings, it could override this grammatical consideration or force us to rethink the relationship between humility and 'of angels' (τῶν ἀγγέλων). However, the only possible references to spiritual beings in explicit statements are the two mentions of the στοιχεῖα ('elements'). Since those passages evaluate rather than describe the opponents' teaching, there seems to be no connection between the στοιχεῖα and the angels of v. 18.[74] Finding the genitive to be subjective is supported by the attention given to the 'piety practiced by angels' in the Hellenistic world generally[75] and in Jewish writings in particular.[76]

Thus 2.18 shows that the opponents' judgments against the Colossians are based on what they call angelic humility and angelic worship. This humility, which consists of their ascetic practices, is what they see and the practice they derive from their visions. They also pride themselves on observing and perhaps participating in angelic worship. So 'will-worship' (ἐθελοθρησκίᾳ) in 2.23 probably indicates that they participate in the angelic worship they observe in their visions.[77] They then

73. Arnold, *Colossian Syncretism*, p. 95.

74. Schweizer (*Colossians*, pp. 158-59; 'Slaves of the Elements', p. 465) thinks that the Colossians worshiped angels, but also rejects identifying these angels with the στοιχεῖα. DeMaris, *Colossian Controversy*, p. 83 also refuses to identify the angels with the 'elements', but then misses the polemical thrust of their presence and identifies the στοιχεῖα as the basis for the other teaching.

75. Francis, 'Visionary Discipline', p. 77.

76. See Lincoln, *Paradise Now and Not Yet*, p. 112; Rowland, 'Apocalyptic Visions', p. 75. The argument that worship directed to angels would have produced a stronger polemic (e.g. Evans, 'The Colossian Mystics', pp. 196-97) is weak because it is an argument from silence. In addition, Schweizer ('Die "Elemente der Welt"', pp. 247-49) has shown that some Jewish writers (e.g. Philo) distinguish between polytheism and the veneration of the στοιχεῖα.

77. So also O'Brien, *Colossians*, p. 143. Contra Martin (*Colossians and Philemon*, p. 94) and Lohse (*Colossians*, p. 119 n. 36) who think that ἐθελοθρησκίᾳ ('will-worship') excludes the understanding of the 'worship of angels' as a subjective genitive.

criticize their fellow Christians for not attaining such experiences. Colossians calls such judgments the results of worldly arrogance.

Summary of Explicit Statements
Explicit statements about the opponents at Colossae indicate that they
are ascetic visionaries whose asceticism includes regulations about food
and drink and the observance of holy days, including new moons and
Sabbaths. The angelic humility they observe in their visions sets the
pattern for their ascetic manner of life, which gives them a reputation
for wisdom. It is possible, though not probable, that they use the terms
wisdom and philosophy to describe their teachings.

In these visions where the opponents observe angelic worship, they
probably also participate in it. Thus they take on an additional burden
of cultic practices and may use the term 'will-worship' (ἐθελοθρησκία)
to describe them. These cultic practices may extend to recreating the
angelic worship they see in their visions. Not only do they participate in
these cultic practices, they pass judgment against those who do not,
perhaps even criticizing them for not receiving visions. It seems likely
that they view those who reject their practices as inferior Christians
who are insufficiently spiritual to move to the next stage of spirituality.
Finally, the author of Colossians says that they present arguments for
their views which sound convincing.

The author of Colossians levels many criticisms against these opponents. He calls their views human commands and teachings, and so
denies them a divine source. He calls their regulations transitory and
says they effect the opposite of what they intend—instead of leading to
restraint, they lead to indulgence of the flesh. Their teaching is further
seen as incompatible with Christian baptism. The most devastating evaluations are that they have separated themselves from Christ and that
their teachings are dogma of the world, according to the elements of the
world (κατὰ τὰ στοιχεῖα τοῦ κόσμου), and not according to Christ.
These and other evaluations show how seriously the author views their
teachings.

Allusions

1.22-23
The most oustanding feature of Colossians 1 is the hymn in vv. 15-20.
If we have correctly outlined the opponents' teaching, it will in some
way address them. Verses 22-23 apply the hymn specifically to the

Colossians.[78] The section in which these verses appear, 1.15-23,[79] is didactic, that is it presents teaching to make a point for its own sake and is neither directly polemical nor directly apologetic. So allusions here can only confirm or clarify a point that we already know is under discussion.

The point of 1.22-23 is that the universal reconciliation wrought by Christ, which was the theme of the second half of the hymn, applies to the Colossians. Verse 22 explains what that means: they now stand holy, blameless and irreproachable before God. This is an allusion because we know the opponents are passing judgment against fellow Christians. This passing of judgment seems to be one of the author's main complaints against the opponents. Verse 22 rejects this judgment against the Colossians.

Verse 23 makes this safe and sure position of the ordinary Christian conditional, but not on ascetic regulations or visionary experiences. Rather, the condition is that they must remain firm in the teaching they had heard previously, teaching the author here identifies as the apostolic teaching by citing it as the message preached throughout the world with the result that believers are reconciled through Christ.

So 1.22-23 shows that the focus was on the opponents from the beginning of this letter. The author uses the hymn to show that the Colossians have a sure place before God while the opponents seem to claim that the Colossians lack this position. So, this assertion functions as a rebuttal of the opponents' views.

It may be in order to direct some attention to the hymn of 1.15-20 itself. Most interpreters think it was composed prior to Colossians[80] and find some additions by the Colossian author, for example 'the church' to define the meaning of the body in v. 18. Some see the list of spiritual powers in v. 16 as an insertion that addresses the Colossian situation,[81]

78. Moule, *Epistles of Paul the Apostle*, p. 58; Lohse, *Colossians*, p. 62; O'Brien, *Colossians*, p. 64.

79. So also C.F.D. Moule, *Epistles of Paul the Apostle*, pp. 58-59; Conzelmann, 'Der Brief an die Kolosser', p. 62. While v. 21 is a new beginning (so Dibelius and Greeven, *Kolosser*, p. 21; Lohse, *Colossians*, p. 62; O'Brien, *Colossians*, p. 64), this beginning serves only to mark the end of the hymnic material and the beginning of its application. The flow of thought is unbroken from v. 20 to v. 21.

80. An exception to this is O'Brien, *Colossians*, pp. 40-42.

81. So, e.g., James M. Robinson, 'A Formal Analysis of Colossians 1:15-20', *JBL* 76 (1957), pp. 270-87 (284); Schweizer, *Colossians*, p. 61; Martin, *Colossians and Philemon*, p. 56.

while other reconstructions of the original include this list of powers.[82] Given such uncertainty,[83] it seems best not to use this list of powers to identify the teaching of this letter's opponents.[84] But even if we reject this caution, there is no evidence in explicit statements that these powers play a part in the opponents' teachings. Thus we could not identify the list of beings as an allusion to the opponents' teaching about them in any case.

2.2-3

The next allusion, 2.2-3, appears in the apologetic section 1.24–2.5. The first hint that this is an allusion is the 'I say this' (τοῦτο λέγω) of 2.4. This phrase probably refers to what has just preceded it.[85] The 'that they [those who have never met Paul] might be encouraged' (ἵνα παρακλη-θῶσιν) in v. 2 supports identifying vv. 2-3 as the antecedent of 'I say this'. The παρακληθῶσιν may be an irregular form of the παρακαλῶ (I beseech you) exhortation found in Pauline and other letters of the era (e.g. those of Ignatius).[86] If so, its function would be, at least in part, 'to drive home the burden of the communication'.[87] Since a main purpose of Colossians is to refute the opponents' teaching, vv. 2-3 are likely an allusion.[88]

82. E.g. Ernst Bammel, 'Versuch zu Col 1₁₅₋₂₀', *ZNW* 52 (1961), pp. 88-95 (93); Lohse, *Colossians*, p. 44-45.

83. For a fairly extensive bibliography of the research on 1[15-20], see O'Brien, *Colossians*, pp. 31-32.

84. See also below the remarks about characteristics of christological hymns.

85. Lohse (*Colossians*, p. 83 n. 119) argues that the ἵνα (so that) shows that τοῦτο λέγω (I say this) refers to the preceding.

86. E.g. Ignatius, *Phld.* 8.2. Since it serves this purpose in letters other than those of Paul, it may serve this function whether Colossians is written by Paul or not.

87. William R. Schoedel, *Ignatius of Antioch: A Commentary on the Letters of Ignatius of Antioch* (Hermeneia; Philadelphia: Fortress Press, 1985), p. 146.

88. Even some who translate παρακληθῶσιν 'encouraged' see in it an element of warning (Lohse, *Colossians*, p. 80 n. 99; Schweizer, *Colossians*, p. 116). O'Brien, (*Colossians*, pp. 92-93) sees the main thrust of the word to be a warning. Even though it is an allusion, we cannot use mirror exegesis to identify terms or precise concepts of the opponents. Contra Gewiess ('Die apologetische Methode', p. 269) who sees 'all treasures of wisdom and knowledge' as a phrase taken over from the opponents. Similarly Andrew J. Bandstra, 'Did the Colossian Errorists Need a Mediator?', p. 340. Cf. Evans, 'The Colossian Mystics', pp. 200-201.

Furthermore, 2.2-3 says that the divine mysteries are in Christ. This seems to oppose claims about knowledge of heavenly matters gained through visions. If so, the opponents' plausible arguments mentioned in v. 4 include claims that their teaching comes from their heavenly ascents. Such an argument not only seems weighty on the surface, it is also quite difficult to refute. Thus, this allusion contains an important response to the opponents' claims to spiritual insight gained through visions.

3.1-2
Another allusion, 3.1-2, appears in the didactic section comprising 3.1-4. This section functions as the transition from the discussion of the opponents to the hortatory section of the letter.[89] While the author is no longer addressing the opponents directly, many interpreters think they are still in view.[90] Verses 1-2 seem to allude to the opponents' teaching when they mentions the 'things above'. We should not identify this expression as a slogan of the opponents,[91] but the phrase does bring us into the scene the opponents claim to see in their visions, that is, the heavens. The central feature of this vision for the Colossian writer is Christ. Perhaps this is presented in opposition to the opponents' emphasis on angelic activities. The Christian's access to the highest heaven is gained through resurrection with Christ in baptism according to 3.1.[92] The contrast between the things above and the things below may have been taken over from the opponents, but it is just as likely a contrast drawn by the author. We see the same sort of contrast in 2.8.

So 3.1-4 redefines seeking the 'things above'.[93] Instead of turning attention to visionary experiences, seeking the 'things above' here means

89. So Dibelius and Greeven, *Kolosser*, p. 40; Scott, *Paul to the Colossians*, pp. 61-62; Schweizer, *Colossians*, p. 171; O'Brien, *Colossians*, pp. 157-59. Moule (*Epistles of Paul the Apostle*, p. 110) sees 3.1-4 as the positive counterpart to 2.20-23. So he may also view it as didactic. Lohse (*Colossians*, p. 132), however, includes 3.1-4 in the hortatory section.

90. E.g. Lohse, *Colossians*, p. 132; Martin, *Colossians and Philemon*, pp. 100-101; O'Brien, *Colossians*, p. 159. Dibelius and Greeven, (*Kolosser*, p. 40) disagree, saying that there is no notice of the letter's situation here.

91. Lohse, *Colossians*, p. 132.

92. Many interpreters comment on the link between the baptism language of 3.1 and that of 2.12. E.g. Scott, *Paul to the Colossians*, p. 62; Lohse, *Colossians*, p. 132; Schweizer, *Colossians*, pp. 171, 174; O'Brien, *Colossians*, p. 158.

93. Similarly John R. Levinson, '2 Apoc. Bar. 48:42–52:7 and the Apocalyptic

that one lives the ethical life defined in 3.5–4.6. Further, 3.1-4 demonstrates that rejecting the opponents' asceticism does not entail rejecting
all ethical requirements.

The only possible information about opponents in 3.1-2 is that they
may call for the adoption of their views by identifying them as the
pursuit of heavenly things in contrast to the earthly concerns of the
average Christian. But we cannot say that even this is probable.

1.9-10

The thanksgiving of Colossians consists of 1.3-14,[94] even though vv.
12-14 also serve to introduce the hymn of vv. 15-20. We identify 1.9-10
as an allusion because it concerns not just knowledge/wisdom of spiritual matters, but also the relationship between this knowledge and the
proper way of life. We saw in explicit statements that the opponents
relate their asceticism and their knowledge of heavenly things. We also
noted that they may refer to their teaching as a form of wisdom, though
this is not certain and there is no indication that they use σοφία (wisdom) in any specialized sense or as a slogan. Still, its presence reinforces the impression that 1.9-10 is an allusion.[95]

Unlike other passages we have discussed in Colossians, the realized
aspect of Christian existence is not emphasized here. Instead, the author
prays that they will be filled with the knowledge of God's will. Later in
the letter the emphasis is on the position that the Colossians already
hold (i.e. being in Christ) which has already given them access to knowledge of God. The comments in 1.9-10 allow that they have not already
attained all the knowledge of God available to them. This seems to
leave the door open for the opponents' contention that the Colossians
need to pursue knowledge of God through ascetic regulations or heavenly ascent.

Verse 10, however, closes this opening when it specifies the purpose
of this knowledge of God as living a worthy life. To this point the opponents would agree. Then the author explains that living worthily means

Dimension of Colossians 3:1-6', *JBL* 108 (1989), pp. 93-108 (101) sees the author
redefining the 'things above' here.

94. See the above notes on 1.22-23 for those who divide the text at v. 15 and
alternatively at v. 12.

95. However, Schweizer (*Colossians*, p. 41) observes that the pair 'wisdom' and
'understanding' which is found here is known from both Jewish and non-Jewish
sources of the time.

bearing fruit in good works. Perhaps this is an unexpected turn; it is certainly far from enforced asceticism. Living worthily also includes growing in the knowledge of God in v. 10. Thus, Colossians sets out a reciprocal relationship between knowledge of God and worthy living. Knowledge enables worthy living and worthy living includes growth in knowledge of God. This seems to be the relationship the opponents assert between their asceticism and their visions and knowledge of heavenly matters. In the face of their regulations, Colossians defines worthy living as producing good works.

We gain no new information about the opponents from this allusion. We do see the author define Christian behavior differently than they do, as he does in 3.1-4 and 3.5–4.6.

Summary of Allusions

Allusions confirm that the opponents claim spiritual knowledge from their visionary experiences. They then use this source, which they claim is divine, as a powerful tool in arguing for their views. They also condemn and seem to see as sinners Christians who fail to live according to their regulations.

Affirmations

2.9-10

Our first affirmation appears in the polemical section 2.6-15. Verses 9-10 address the opponents because we know that they pass judgment against others on the basis of their superior spirituality. The author asserts in 2.9-10 that the Colossians are already complete; they need no other spiritual experiences. Many see a reference to the opponents here and identify the 'fullness' mentioned as one of their slogans.[96] While the term reflects their mentality, there is no evidence that they use it in some special sense.[97]

According to v. 9 the Colossians are to reject the opponents' teachings because everything, 'all the fullness', is in Christ.[98] Verse 9 supports the assertions of both v. 8 that the opponents' teachings are not

---

96. E.g. Dibelius and Greeven, *Kolosser*, p. 29; Bornkamm, 'The Heresy of Colossians', p. 124; Martin, *Colossians and Philemon*, pp. 80-81.

97. Scott (*Paul to the Colossians*, pp. 43-44) asserts that there is no hidden meaning in this language.

98. We need not decide the precise meaning of σωματικῶς ('bodily', v. 9) to identify the opponents.

'according to Christ' (κατὰ Χριστόν[99]) and v. 10 that the Colossians
participate in this fullness. Thus, they do not need the opponents' regulations or spiritual experiences.

Verse 10b further defines the status of Christ, calling him the head of
all 'principalities and powers' (ἀρχῆς καὶ ἐξουσίας). Since we have
found insufficient evidence to show that veneration of spiritual beings
was a problem at Colossae, we cannot assert from this affirmation that
it was.[100] Mention of these beings is better explained as an echo of the
hymn of 1.15-20.[101]

So in the face of the opponents' call for ascetic regulations as the
means to spiritual insight, the author asserts here that the Colossians
have attained fullness in Christ and need nothing else.[102]

2.13-15

Many interpreters recognize that 2.13-15 refers to the opponents, often
finding some of their vocabulary in it. But explicit statements and allusions allow us to see it only as an affirmation that addresses them less
directly. Verses 11-15 are a separate paragraph within the polemical
section 2.8-15[103] that describes the fullness mentioned in vv. 9-10.[104]
The affirmation of forgiveness in vv. 13-15 is an important counter to
the opponents' judgment against the Colossians.

Several interpreters assert that the mention of circumcision in v. 13
(when combined with its mention in v. 11) indicates that the opponents

---

99. So also O'Brien, *Colossians*, p. 103.

100. Nor is there any reason to identify them with the στοιχεῖα. Contra Dibelius
and Greeven, *Kolosser*, p. 29; Bornkamm, 'The Heresy of Colossians', p. 123;
Lohse, *Colossians*, p. 101; Edwin Lewis, 'Paul and the Perverters of Christianity',
Int 2 (1948), pp. 143-57 (152-53).

101. Lohse (*Colossians*, p. 101) and O'Brien (*Colossians*, p. 103) see this as an
echo of this hymnic material. Verse 10b may both take up the language of 1.15-20
and refer to the opponents' worship of these powers, as Lohse holds, but this seems
unlikely for the reasons given above. See below our discussion of 2.15.

102. So Moule, *Epistles of Paul the Apostle*, p. 94. Similarly O'Brien (*Colossians*, p. 113) says that these verses affirm the presence of salvation among the
Colossians.

103. So Dibelius and Greeven, *Kolosser*, p. 31; Scott, *Paul to the Colossians*,
p. 44; Martin, *Colossians and Philemon*, p. 81. O'Brien (*Colossians*, pp. 13-15) and
Lohse (*Colossians*, p. 106) see vv. 13-15 as a separate paragraph.

104. Scott, *Paul to the Colossians*, p. 44.

require circumcision.[105] However, since there are no references to circumcision in statements that more clearly refer to their practices, we cannot identify it as such.[106] The writer is probably simply using a metaphor, as he does in 2.14-15.[107]

Verse 14 says that the 'handwriting with dogmas' (χειρόγραφον τοῖς δόγμασιν) that was against us was blotted out. Many earlier interpreters identified one or more elements of the 'handwriting' with the Mosaic Law.[108] However, this word is used to refer to a statement of indebtedness in contemporary materials,[109] including Jewish literature.[110] The Apocalypse of Elijah mentions one 'handwriting' (χειρόγραφον) which contains a list of one's sins and another with a list of one's good deeds.[111] Thus this image of being indebted to God because of sins was current and is likely the meaning of the term here. Lohse suggests that the use of δογματίζω ('to submit to regulations') in 2.20 shows that the dogmas of v. 14 refer generally to the opponents' teachings.[112] Although this is possible, vv. 8-15 are not as directly polemical as the preceding verses and so is less likely. Even if Lohse is correct, we learn nothing about the opponents from this very general statement. Verse 14

105. E.g. Scott, *Paul to the Colossians*, p. 44; Percy, *Probleme*, p. 140; Lohse, *Colossians*, p. 102; Martin, *Colossians and Philemon*, p. 12; Lincoln, *Paradise Now and Not Yet*, p. 113. Dibelius and Greeven (*Kolosser*, p. 30) leave this as a possibility.

106. Weiss, ('The Law in the Epistle to the Colossians', p. 309 n. 63) raises the possibility that vv. 11-13a contain a confessional formula. Dibelius earlier noted the hymn-like character of vv. 9-12 (*Kolosser*, p. 31). If so, the language of circumcision is in the tradition rather than polemic against the opponents.

107. So Schweizer, *Colossians*, pp. 142, 157. Others who deny that the opponents demand circumcision include Abbott, *Ephesians and Colossians*, p. 250 and Schmithals, 'The *Corpus Paulinum* and Gnosis', p. 118.

108. E.g. Abbott, *Ephesians and Colossians*, p. 255; Dibelius and Greeven, *Kolosser,* p. 32; Scott, *Paul to the Colossians*, p. 46; Percy, *Probleme*, pp. 88-92; Conzelmann, 'Der Brief an die Kolosser', p. 114.

109. See Eduard Lohse, 'Χειρόγραφον', *TDNT* IX, pp. 435-36; *idem, Colossians*, p. 108, esp. n. 101; Schweizer, *Colossians*, p. 148, esp. n. 42.

110. Dibelius and Greeven, *Kolosser*, p. 31; Martin, *Colossians and Philemon*, p. 84.

111. Lincoln, *Paradise Now and Not Yet*, p. 113.

112. Lohse, *Colossians*, pp. 106-107. Martin (*Colossians and Philemon*, p. 84) also holds that δόγματα ('dogmas') here refers to the opponents' teaching.

does assert that additional regulations, and at least by implication the opponents' regulations, are invalid for Christians because they have received forgiveness through Christ's crucifixion.

In v. 15, 'principalities and powers' (τὰς ἀρχὰς κὰι τὰς ἐξουσίας) appear for the second time in affirmations. If those who see elements of a confessional formula in vv. 13c-15[113] are correct, the appearance of these beings is explained by their presence in traditional material both here and in 2.10.[114] The presence of such powers in hymnic or confessional material should not surprise us. Hengel's analysis of hymnic material in the New Testament indicates that such material often deals with the significance of Jesus' death 'for universal salvation'[115] and that Christ's subsequent exaltation often includes reference to 'the divine and worldly powers'.[116] Early hymns 'continually "narrated" and "proclaimed" anew Christ's passion, glorification, and subjection of all powers'.[117] Since the motif of overcoming spiritual powers is commonly a part of hymnic material, nothing in the Colossian situation is needed to explain their presence in 1.16, 2.15 or the echo of 1.15-20 in 2.10.

So 2.13-15 reminds the Colossians of the forgiveness they have in Christ and perhaps stresses that this forgiveness includes freedom from the opponents' teachings (δόγματα). This passage confirms that the opponents assert that the Colossians are living in sin unless they submit to the opponents' regulations.

113. E.g. Lohse, *Colossians*, p. 106; O'Brien, *Colossians*, p. 104. Lohse (*Colossians*, p. 107) sees these beings as part of the confessional material quoted in these verses. Whatever δόγματα meant in the original confession, if it was a part of one, our context excludes seeing it as the Mosaic Law. Apart from mention of the Sabbath and new moons (which may have been honored for other reasons) there has been no indication that the opponents demand compliance with the Mosaic Code.

114. We noted above that the mention of them in 2.10 seems to be an echo of the hymnic material in 1.15-20.

115. Martin Hengel, 'Hymn and Christology', in Elizabeth A. Livingstone (ed.), *Studia Biblica 1978*. III. *Papers on Paul and Other New Testament Authors* (JSNTSup, 3; Sheffield: JSOT Press, 1980), pp. 173-97 (179).

116. Hengel, 'Hymn and Christology', p. 185. Here Hengel says, 'Enthronement, authorization of the resurrected Christ and, at the same time, the homage of the divine and worldly powers, i.e. all of creation, belong to this exaltation complex.'

117. Hengel, 'Hymn and Christology', p. 193.

1.12-14

Within the thanksgiving,[118] 1.12-14 seems to address the opponents. Introducing the hymnic material,[119] vv. 12-14 assert that the Colossians have received forgiveness. This assertion anticipates the message of universal reconciliation found in 1.15-20.[120] Verses 12-14 address the opponents by dealing with forgiveness of sins in the face of their accusations of sinfulness. Verse 12 asserts that the opponents' judgments are inappropriate because God has qualified the Colossians for God's gifts.

Summary of Affirmations

Affirmations reinforce our belief that the opponents accuse the Colossians of sinning when they do not follow the prescribed regulations. Affirmations also confirm that one of the author's main concerns is to remind the Colossians that God has already qualified them to participate in God's blessings.

Conclusion

We have found that Colossians addresses a community troubled by ascetic visionaries. Their asceticism includes food and drink regulations and the observance of certain holy days, including Sabbaths and new moons. These holy days suggest that they draw on Judaism for some aspects of their teachings, but there is no evidence that they demand circumcision or other commandments from Judaism beyond these holy days. In their visions the opponents observe and probably participate in angelic humility and angelic worship. These angelic practices are the model for their ascetic regulations and perhaps their self-imposed worship, their ἐθελοθρησκία. They do not seem to have venerated spiritual beings or angels. The references to various spiritual beings are quotations of traditional material and accusations against the opponents.

---

118. So Conzelmann, 'Der Brief an die Kolosser', p. 134; Moule, *Epistles of Paul the Apostle*, pp. 47-48; especially O'Brien, *Colossians*, pp. 18-19, 25.

119. Lohse (*Colossians*, pp. 32-33) and Schweizer (*Colossians*, pp. 45-47) make vv. 12-14 part of the section that contains the hymnic material and see it as a formal introduction to this material.

120. Since these verses also introduce the hymnic material, we may allow them to supply more information about opponents than would otherwise be the case for affirmations in thanksgivings.

The asceticism of these opponents is not the extreme type described by Lucian in *The Syrian Goddess*.[121] Rather, these opponents' moderate asceticism included food and abstinence regulations that may have been in effect only on the holy days mentioned or perhaps are intended to bring visions. In the ancient world, fasting and abstaining from various pleasures or comforts were often included among the preparations one went through to receive a vision. Fasting is often found in apocalyptic Judaism as a prelude to visionary experiences (e.g. *2 Bar.* 12.5; 20.3-6; 47.2; *4 Ezra* 5.50; 6.35; cf. *4 Ezra* 9.24-27 where the abstinence is only from certain types of food). The writer does not reject these opponents because they live by a strict regimen; his complaint is that they bind these regulations on others and condemn those who do not live by them. They may also pass judgment against ordinary Christians for not having visions.

This passing of judgment is perhaps the main problem the author of Colossians has with these opponents. Allusions and affirmations show that their judgment goes beyond considering other Christians spiritually immature, it includes viewing them as sinners. The opponents claim to receive their teaching in their visions and so cite a divine, or at least heavenly, source for it. They then use this source as evidence for their views. It is possible that they use the terms 'philosophy' and 'wisdom' to describe their teaching, but these broad terms tell us nothing about them.

Criticism of these opponents permeates our letter. From the thanksgiving to the introduction of the hortatory section,[122] we find rebuttal of their views. The writer considers their error serious enough to charge that they have cut themselves off from Christ.

One criticism of the view that the opponents' teaching does not include veneration of angels is that it makes ch. 1 irrelevant to the discussion at Colossae. We have found this to be incorrect. The purpose of the hymnic material is to assure the Colossians of their place before God in Christ, especially of the forgiveness of their sins. This application fits the type of opponent we have described. The author uses the hymn, not to establish the position of Christ, but to show that the Colos-

---

121. This work is often cited by commentators to show the Colossians' familiarity with ascetic behavior and ecstatic cults.

122. Our method allows us to use only explicit statements about opponents in hortatory sections. Since we cannot use possible allusions (e.g. 3.11) in such sections to identify the opponents, we will not discussed such passages in this study.

sians' participation in Christ frees them from the opponents' regulations and charges of sinfulness.

Finally we must see if these opponents fit into any known groups of the first century. They are not Judaizers, even though they draw on some things within Judaism. Drawing on Judaism may have facilitated their reception since there had been Jewish communities in the region for at least two centuries[123] and it seems likely that this church would have included some Jews. There is no evidence that they are Gnostics, though like many groups of the first century they have elements that were later taken into Gnosticism. Neither is there evidence that they are concerned with the ascent of the soul after death or have a mystery rite.

The Colossian opponents were perhaps familiar with apocalyptic Judaism, but this is hardly unusual for early Christian communities. Some elements of the Colossian opponents' teaching are similar to those of apocalyptic Judaism, for example asceticism and attention to the worship seen in visions. But these elements are not unique to apocalyptic Judaism. So there is no wider group within which they can be securely placed.

It appears, then, that the primary problem the author of Colossians has with these opponents is neither their practices nor the content of the beliefs that led to those practices, even though he identifies them with non-Christian teaching. Rather, it is the imposition of their teachings and practices on other Christians. It is the demand that all Christians adhere to their regulations which the author rejects most strongly.

---

123. See Martin (*Colossians and Philemon*, pp. 3-4) and his citation of Josephus, *Ant.* 12.147-53. Cf. the many commentators who cite Cicero, *Or.*, 59 as evidence that there were at least 11,000 Jewish men in the region of Laodicea in the first century BCE.

Chapter 7

A WORRIED CHURCH—1 THESSALONIANS

Like most of Paul's epistles, 1 Thessalonians has produced several theories about opponents. The most common is that Paul faces accusations and charges from outside the Christian community, especially from Thessalonian Jews.[1] Others argue that Paul is opposing enthusiastic Pneumatics who quit work, call into question the sexual morality Paul advocates and question the community's local leadership and Paul.[2] Jewett and Harnisch contend that this position is grounded in a realized eschatology. Still other interpreters find the problem to be more personal attacks on Paul or complaints about his behavior, rather than some doctrinal issue.[3] But many interpreters find no opponents in 1 Thes-

---

1. A.L. Moore, *1 and 2 Thessalonians* (ConBNT; Camden, NJ: Nelson, 1969), pp. 5, 32; I. Howard Marshall, *1 and 2 Thessalonians* (NCB; Grand Rapids: Eerdmans, 1983), pp. 17, 20; James E. Frame, *A Critical and Exegetical Commentary on the Epistles of St. Paul to the Thessalonians* (ICC; Edinburgh: T. & T. Clark, 1912), pp. 9-10; William Neil, *The Epistle of Paul to the Thessalonians* (MNTC; New York: Harper, 1950), pp. xv-xvi; William Horbury, 'I Thessalonians ii:3 as Rebutting the Charge of False Prophecy', *JTS* 33 (1982), pp. 492-508 (507); D.E.H. Whiteley, *Thessalonians in the Revised Standard Version* (New Clarendon Bible; London: Oxford University Press, 1969), p. 40; John W. Bailey, 'The First and Second Epistle to the Thessalonians', *IB* XI, p. 249.

2. E.g. Gerhardt Friedrich, 'Der zweite Brief an die Thessalonicher', in *idem*, *Die Briefe an die Galater, Epheser, Philipper, Kolosser, Thessalonicher und Philemon* (NTD, 8; Göttingen: Vandenhoeck & Ruprecht, 14th edn, 1976), pp. 205, 225; Robert Jewett, *The Thessalonian Correspondence: Pauline Rhetoric and Millinarian Piety* (Facets and Foundations; Philadelphia: Fortress Press, 1986), pp. 94-106; Wolfgang Harnisch, *Eschatologische Existenz: Ein exegetischer Beitrag zum Sachanliegen von 1. Thessalonicher 4,13–5,11* (FRLANT, 110; Göttingen: Vandenhoeck & Ruprecht, 1973), pp. 27-37.

3. Jan Lambrecht, 'Thanksgivings in 1 Thessalonians 1–3', in R. Collins (ed.), *The Thessalonian Correspondence* (BETL, 87; Leuven: Leuven University Press,

salonians.[4] Some of these scholars, though, still find problems in the community related to sexual immorality, people quitting their jobs, ecstatic manifestations of the Spirit, and questions about the dead and the parousia. Mearns argues specifically that 1 Thessalonians is Paul's defense in the face of reactions to his own change from a realized eschatology to a 'second adventism'.[5] Finally, without finding opponents, Munck contends that the Thessalonians are having difficulty accepting apostolic authority.[6]

This discussion flourishes even though, or perhaps because, there are no explicit statements about opponents in 1 Thessalonians. There are, however, direct statements about the situation at Thessalonica. Our method counts such statements as allusions, but they must serve as our starting point in the search for opponents here. Yet, the absence of explicit statements about them is *prima facie* evidence that opponents are not the primary reason for this letter. Furthermore, Jewett,[7] Hughes[8] and Wuellner[9] all identify 1 Thessalonians as an example of epideictic rhetoric. Unless the praise (or blame) of the Thessalonians is directed toward their rejection (or acceptance) of opponents, this identification supports our initial impression that there are no 'opponents' in view in 1 Thessalonians. But this rhetorical species cannot be used to preclude the possibility that Paul faces opposition, nor does the absence of opponents mean that all is well.

1990), pp. 183-205 (200); Karl P. Donfried, 'The Cults of Thessalonica and the Thessalonian Correspondence', *NTS* 31 (1985), pp. 336-56 (350-51).

4.   E.g. Beda Rigaux *Saint Paul: Les épîtres aux Thessaloniciens* (EBib; Paris: J. Gabalda, 1956), p. 59; Charles Masson, *Les deux épîtres de Saint Paul aux Thessaloniciens* (Neuchâtel: Delachaux & Niestlé, 1957), p. 32; Raymond F. Collins, 'Paul as Seen Through his Own Eyes', in *idem, Studies on the First Epistle to the Thessalonians* (BETL, 66; Leuven: Leuven University Press, 1984), pp. 178-208 (184); Abraham Malherbe, '"Gentle as a Nurse": The Cynic Background to 1 Thessalonians ii', *NovT* 12 (1970), pp. 203-17.

5.   C.L. Mearns, 'Early Eschatological Development in Paul: The Evidence of II and II Thessalonians', *NTS* 27 (1981), pp. 137-57.

6.   Johannes Munck, '1 Thessalonians 1.9-10 and the Missionary Preaching of Paul', *NTS* 9 (1963), pp. 94-100 (109-110).

7.   Jewett, *Pauline Rhetoric*, p. 72.

8.   Frank W. Hughes, 'The Rhetoric of 1 Thessalonians', in *The Thessalonian Correspondence* pp. 94-116 (97).

9.   W. Wuellner, 'The Argumentative Structure of 1 Thessalonians as Paradoxical Encomium', in Collins (ed.), *The Thessalonian Correspondence*, pp. 117-36 (123-25).

Statements about the Situation

1.6-7, 9-10

The first statement about the Thessalonian situation comes in the initial thanksgiving. Regardless of whether all of 1.2–3.13 is a thanksgiving,[10] 1.2-10 is a distinct section which fulfills the usual purpose of a Pauline thanksgiving (i.e. it introduces some major themes). In rhetorical terms, 1.2-10 functions as the *exordium*[11] and so sets out themes to be expanded throughout the letter. Our statements appear in a sub-section comprising vv. 6-10 which focuses on the Thessalonians' acceptance of the gospel.[12]

According to 1.6-7, the Thessalonians had accepted Christianity joyfully in the face of affliction. Verses 9-10 indicate that the gospel they accepted included a strong eschatological component as it mentions both waiting for the Son to come and 'the wrath to come'. Paul's emphasis on the Thessalonians' acceptance of the gospel may be evidence that it has not been long since their conversion, but we cannot be certain of this. These statements within the thanksgiving speak only about the past; they give no direct information about current conditions.

3.3

Another direct statement about the Thessalonian situation occurs in 3.3. At 2.17 Paul leaves off commenting on his initial visit to Thessalonica and begins discussing events closer to the present. The major section which begins at 2.17 runs through 3.10 or 3.13. Frame understands this section as a defense of Paul's failure to return to Thessalonica, a defense

10. Those who see the thanksgiving extend through 3.10 or 3.13 include: Frame, *Epistles of St. Paul to the Thessalonians*, p. 72; Ernest Best, *A Commentary on the First and Second Epistles to the Thessalonians* (BNTC; London: A. & C. Black, 1972), pp. 64-65; Bruce C. Johanson, *To All the Brethren: A Text-Linguistic and Rhetorical Approach to 1 Thessalonians* (ConBNT; Stockholm: Almquist & Wiksell, 1987), p. 160; George Lyons, *Pauline Autobiography: Toward a New Understanding*, pp. 187-89. Those who see only 1.2-10 as the thanksgiving include Neil, *The Epistle of Paul to the Thessalonians*, p. 7 and perhaps F.F. Bruce, *1 & 2 Thessalonians* (WBC, 45; Waco, TX: Word Books, 1982), p. 11.

11. So Charles A. Wanamaker, *The Epistles to the Thessalonians: A Commentary on the Greek Text* (NIGTC; Grand Rapids: Eerdmans, 1990), p. 49; Hughes, 'The Rhetoric of 1 Thessalonians', p. 97; Wuellner, 'The Argumentative Structure', pp. 117-18. Hughes and Wuellner both begin the *exordium* at 1.1.

12. So Rigaux, *Thessaloniciens*, p. 368.

necessitated by allegations from non-Christian Jews who said Paul never planned to return.[13] Rigaux rejects this analysis, seeing the purpose of the section as exhortation rather than defense.[14] Still differently, Boers identifies the section as 'apostolic parousia'[15] and so sees it as more expository than apologetic. Those who focus on rhetorical analysis find it to be a part of the *narratio*.[16] Seeing it in this way, Wanamaker comments that its function is to make Paul present through traditional themes of friendship.[17] Thus, Wanamaker's understanding of the section's function is close to Boers's. Margaret Mitchell argues that this section employs expressions and social conventions commonly found in correspondence that involved envoys.[18] Using these conventions implies no conflict or tension between the parties, they can function primarily to affirm good relations.[19] The remarks in 2.17–3.13 seem intended to strengthen Paul's relationship with the Thessalonians by telling of his concern for them and by continuing the development of his *persona* begun in 2.1. This strengthening of their relationship, in turn, prepares for the ethical exhortation of chs. 4–5. Thus, since this section is a commonplace in epistles that involve envoys, and it prepares for the exhortation to follow, we identify it as didactic.

The comments in 3.1-3 comprise a sub-section that deals with the visit of Titus.[20] Verse 3 explains why Paul was anxious about the Thessalonians; they face 'tribulations' which Paul describes no more specifically here. Meeks asserts that there is no evidence that they amounted to persecution and that they may have been limited to hostility from the

13. Frame, *Epistles of St. Paul to the Thessalonians*, pp. 12, 124.

14. Rigaux, *Thessaloniciens*, p. 456. See also Elizabeth Struthers Malbon ('"No Need to Have Anyone Write"? A Structural Exegesis of 1 Thessalonians', *Semeia* 26 [1983], pp. 57-83 [71]) who sees a parallel between 2.17–3.10 and 4.13–5.11.

15. Hendrikus Boers, 'The Form Critical Study of Paul's Letters: 1 Thessalonians as a Case Study', *NTS* 22 (1976), pp. 140-58 (158).

16. Jewett, *Pauline Rhetoric*, p. 74; Wanamaker, *Epistles to the Thessalonians*, p. 49.

17. Wanamaker, *Epistles to the Thessalonians*, p. 133.

18. Margaret Mitchell, 'New Testament Envoys in the Context of Greco-Roman Diplomatic and Epistolary Conventions: The Example of Timothy and Titus', *JBL* 111 (1992), pp. 641-62.

19. Mitchell, 'New Testament Envoys', pp. 644-61.

20. So also Frame, *Epistles of St. Paul to the Thessalonians*, pp. 123-24; Best, *First and Second Epistles to the Thessalonians*, p. 129; Bruce, *1 and 2 Thessalonians*, pp. 58-60.

non-Christians around them.[21] Paul encourages the Thessalonians by reminding them of his warning that they, as Christians, should expect tribulation. Mention of the expectation of tribulation seems to raise once again the matter of eschatology.[22]

So 3.3 shows that some in the Thessalonian congregation feel pressured by some unspecified tribulation to abandon their Christian faith.

3.6-8, 10

Another sub-section within 2.17–3.10(13) is formed by 3.6-10.[23] This sub-section recounts the good report of Titus about the Thessalonians and continues the didactic tone of 3.1-5. Verses 6-7 indicate that good relations exist between Paul and the Thessalonians. Paul goes so far as to use εὐαγγελίζω (to 'evangelize', 'proclaim good news') to describe Timothy's report of how their faith had endured and of how they think of, love and want to see Paul.[24] Perhaps, as Best conjectures, these verses speak to worries that some might misunderstand Paul's actions or make charges against him and show that Paul is glad that such worries were unnecessary.[25] But they are not evidence that any accusations have actually been made.[26] Verses 6-7 do indicate that good relations exist between Paul and the community and that the community had not misunderstood his departure and absence. Verse 8 shows further that the Thessalonians had maintained their faith.

21. Wayne A. Meeks, *The First Urban Christians: The Social World of the Apostle Paul* (New Haven: Yale University Press, 1983), p. 174.

22. So Meeks, *The First Urban Christians*, p. 174; Munck, '1 Thessalonians 1:9-10', p. 137. Cf. W. Schrage, 'Leid, Kreuz, und Eschaton', *EvT* 34 (1975), pp. 141-75 (165).

23. Those who divide the text in this way include: Frame, *Epistles of St. Paul to the Thessalonians*, p. 130; Best, *First and Second Epistles to the Thessalonians*, p. 138; Bruce, *1 and 2 Thessalonians*, p. 65; Neil, *Epistle of Paul to the Thessalonians*, p. 66; Hughes, 'The Rhetoric of 1 Thessalonians', p. 103. However, Johanson (*To All the Brethren*, pp. 99, 103) begins the new sub-section at 3.9.

24. Earl Richard ('Early Pauline Thought: An Analysis of 1 Thessalonians', in Bassler [ed.], *Pauline Theology*, I, pp. 39-52 [45]) sees the theme in 3.6 to be the good news about the Thessalonians' faith and the relationship between the community and their missionaries.

25. Best, *First and Second Epistles to the Thessalonians*, p. 140. Munck ('1 Thessalonians 1:9-10', p. 96) traces the origin of these worries to the persecution the Thessalonians have endured.

26. Contra Friedrich (*Die Briefe*, p. 233) who says that 3.6 shows they had not listened to accusations against Paul.

Verse 10 has been the subject of much attention because Paul says that the Thessalonians' faith lacks something. Unfortunately, he is not specific about what is lacking and thus allows for nearly unlimited speculation. Many interpreters assert that 3.10 points to problems with eschatology when one notes that Paul has praised the Thessalonians' faith and love without mentioning hope, the third element of the Pauline triad.[27] Others allow that the deficiency is to be understood more broadly so that it includes all the ethical and doctrinal instruction in chs. 4–5.[28] Schnelle asserts that the 'lack' is addressed particularly by the περί (concerning) passages (4.1, 13; 5.1).[29] Marshall argues that the absence of hope in 3.6 has no significance and that 3.10 suggests no reproach. Rather, 3.10 begins a transition to the instructions of chs. 4–5, *if* the focus is on what the Thessalonians lack.[30] Similarly, Wanamaker understands 3.10 as a simple indication that the 'resocialization' of the Thessalonians into the Christian life needs to continue.[31] Since Paul is unclear about the Thessalonians' deficiency, we must, at this point, leave open the question of whether or what more specific items he may have in mind.

4.1-2

Our final explicit statement about the situation appears in 4.1, the beginning of the hortatory section 4.1-12. Paul says here that the Thessalonians' way of life is conforming to the gospel (and the commands he had given them), as it must, and he exhorts them to do so even more. This passage seems to indicate that this congregation is not involved in any serious moral deficiencies, nor are they abandoning Paul's ethical instructions. Donfried rejects this interpretation, arguing that the strong language of 4.1-9 suggests that Paul is dealing with a situation of serious immorality which developed because of the Bacchic rites so common in Thessalonica.[32] But while these verses clearly function to

27. E.g. Rigaux, *Thessaloniciens*, pp. 476, 485; Donfried, 'The Cults of Thessalonica and the Thessalonian Correspondence', p. 348.

28. Neil, *Epistle of Paul to the Thessalonians*, p. 70; Best, *First and Second Epistles to the Thessalonians*, p. 145.

29. Udo Schnelle, 'Der erste Thessalonicherbrief und die Entstehung der Paulinischen Anthropologie', *NTS* 32 (1986), pp. 202-24 (209).

30. Marshall, *1 and 2 Thessalonians*, pp. 94, 98-99.

31. Wanamaker, *Epistles to the Thessalonians*, p. 139.

32. Donfried, 'The Cults of Thessalonica and the Thessalonian Correspondence', pp. 341-42.

distinguish between Christians and others and to encourage the Thessalonians to live as Christians,[33] there is no indication that problems with sexual immorality have actually arisen; the prominence of the Bacchic rites and the Cabiri cults may have been sufficient reason for Paul to speak about these matters in vv. 1-9. In addition, our method specifies that only explicit statements can be used in hortatory sections because such sections often give instruction and encouragement about matters that pose no immediate problems. Furthermore, interpreters of 2 Thessalonians often argue that the hortatory sections of 2 Thessalonians are more emphatic and call on apostolic authority more firmly than those in 1 Thessalonians.[34] This view of 2 Thessalonians argues against understanding the wording of 1 Thess. 4.1-9 as especially strong. Therefore, without some clear reason for questioning it, we must accept Paul's stated analysis of the Thessalonians' conduct, that is, they are living faithful lives.

Summary of Direct Statements about the Thessalonian Situation
We have now examined all the statements in 1 Thessalonians that speak directly about the situation there. Not only do we find no explicit statements about opponents, but there are also no clear statements about any specific doctrinal or moral problems. It is clear that the Thessalonians are experiencing some 'tribulation' which Paul thinks poses a threat to their faith. But Paul congratulates them for their endurance, faith and love. Further, Paul is encouraged by Timothy's report of their committment to and love for him. This increases the probability that Paul does not address opponents in 1 Thessalonians. While 3.10 may express a need for further instruction in some matters, Paul does not seem to imply that these matters indicate a turning away from either him or his teaching. Since Paul does mention deficiencies in their faith and it is possible

33. So O. Larry Yarbrough, *Not Like the Gentiles: Marriage Rules in the Letters of Paul* (SBLDS, 80; Atlanta: Scholars Press, 1985), p. 81.
34. E.g. Raymond F. Collins, *Letters That Paul Did Not Write: The Epistle to the Hebrews and the Pauline Pseudepigrapha* (GNS, 28; Wilmington, DE: Michael Glazier, 1988), p. 233. In this assessment Collins is following Wolfgang Trilling's (*Der zweite Brief an die Thessalonicher* [EKKNT, 14; Neukirchen–Vluyn: Neukirchener Verlag, 1980], p. 141) comments on the 'peremptory tone' of 2 Thess. 3.6-13. Cf. Glen Holland, *The Tradition that You Received from Us: 2 Thessalonians in the Pauline Tradition* (HUT, 24; Tübingen: J.C.B. Mohr [Paul Siebeck], 1988), pp. 86-87, 90.

that these involve a lack of hope, we may seek allusions to such matters. Still, these allusions must be identified by relating them to the more direct statements about the situation.

Excursus on 2.13-16

First Thessalonians 2.13(14)-16 has been the topic of much debate, most of which has been about whether it is an interpolation.[35] However, the majority of interpreters, especially those who emphasize rhetorical analysis, treat the passage as a part of the original 1 Thessalonians.[36] Marshall even sees 2.13-16 as the climax of the first major section of the epistle.[37] Hughes identifies 2.14-16 as a use of *exempla*, a common feature in epideictic rhetoric.[38] Wuellner views it similarly as one of the items in a group of models which validates the paradoxical situation in which the Thessalonians find themselves.[39] John Hurd argues powerfully that this section fits well with Paul's common use of an ABA pattern in his epistles.[40]

Overall, it seems more probable that 2.13-16 is an original part of 1 Thessalonians. Still, since it is questionable, it is unwise to base our understanding of the situation on a disputed passage. But even if we accept it as original, it does not add appreciably to our understanding of the Thessalonian situation. It does make more clear that the tribulation that the congregation is enduring is from local sources, that is, from their own people. Frame argued that use of the Judean church's problems with fellow Jews shows that the Thessalonians' difficulties came

35. E.g. Helmut Koester, '1 Thessalonians: Experiment in Christian Writing', in F.F. Church and T. George (eds.), *Continuity and Discontinuity in Church History* (Leiden: E.J. Brill, 1979), pp. 33-44 (36); Leander E. Keck, 'The First Letter of Paul to the Thessalonians', in C.M. Laymon (ed.), *Interpreter's One Volume Commentary on the Bible* (Nashville: Abingdon Press, 1971), pp. 865-74 (868); Richard, 'Early Pauline Thought', p. 43.

36. E.g. Wanamaker, *Epistles to the Thessalonians*, p. 109; Hughes, 'The Rhetoric of 1 Thessalonians', p. 102; Wuellner, 'The Argumentative Structure', p. 130; Jewett, *Pauline Rhetoric*, p. 73; Johanson, *To All the Brethren*, p. 98.

37. Marshall, *1 and 2 Thessalonians*, p. 76.

38. Hughes, 'The Rhetoric of 1 Thessalonians', p. 102.

39. Wuellner, 'The Argumentative Structure', p. 130.

40. John Hurd, 'Paul Ahead of his Time: 1 Thess. 2:13-16', in Peter Richardson (ed.), *Antijudaism in Early Christianity. I. Paul and the Gospels* (Waterloo, ON: Wilfrid Laurier, 1986), pp. 21-36.

from Jews.[41] But this can hardly be the case since the Thessalonian church was composed primarily of Gentiles (1.9) and their difficulties come from τῶν ἰδίων συμφυλετῶν ('your own fellow-country people'). Thus 2.13-16 does not significantly advance our understanding of this letter's occasion.

Allusions

4.9

Passages that use the expression περὶ δὲ (now concerning) are among those most often cited as allusions to problems in Thessalonica.[42] Thus, the comments on brotherly love in 4.9-12 are often seen to indicate a problem or lack among the Thessalonians. Several interpreters see the use of περί ('concerning') as sufficient evidence that Paul is responding to direct questions from the Thessalonians in 4.9; 4.13; and 5.1.[43] However, as Johanson notes, περὶ δὲ often introduces new topics in Hellenistic literature without necessarily referring to questions that had been asked.[44] So this formula by itself is not sufficient to identify such remarks as responses to questions from the Thessalonians. On the other hand, Malherbe argues that 1 Thessalonians contains several other epistolary clichés that make it 'highly probable' that the Thessalonians had written to Paul.[45] Thus we must leave open the possibility that Paul has received a letter from them.

We find 4.9 within the hortatory section comprising 4.1-12.[46] As we noted in connection with 4.1-2, our method allows us to use only ex-

---

41. Frame, *Epistles of St. Paul to the Thessalonians*, pp. 13-14, 109.

42. E.g. Schnelle, 'Der erste Thessalonicherbrief', p. 209.

43. E.g. Gerd Lüdemann, 'The Hope of the Early Paul', *Perspectives*, 7 (1980), pp. 145-201 (196); Richard, 'Early Pauline Thought', p. 47; Frame, *Epistles of St. Paul to the Thessalonians*, p. 140; Graydon F. Snyder, 'Apocalyptic and Didactic Elements in 1 Thessalonians' (SBLSP; Missoula, MT: Scholars Press, 1972), pp. 233-44 (236-37).

44. Johanson, *To All the Brethren*, p. 51.

45. A.J. Malherbe, 'Did the Thessalonians Write to Paul?' in R.T. Fortna and B.R. Gaventa (eds.), *The Conversation Continues: Studies in Paul and John in Honor of J. Louis Martyn* (Nashville: Abingdon Press, 1990), pp. 246-57 (quotation on p. 255).

46. Those who see this section as hortatory include: Snyder, 'Apocalyptic and Didactic Elements', pp. 235-36; Hoffmann, *Die Toten in Christus* (Münster: Aschendorff, 1966), p. 208; Lyons, *Pauline Autobiography*, p. 181; Collins 'This is the

plicit statements in hortatory contexts to identify opponents (or here serious problems within the congregation). Friedrich and Hughes seem to understand 4.9-12 as such a section[47] and Boers asserts that 4.1-8 is composed of traditional material.[48] Thus, we cannot assert, with any certainty, that brotherly love or the issues raised in connection with it (i.e. tending one's own affairs and working) are problems at this time in Thessalonica. Kloppenberg has recently explained the presence of the various topics in vv. 9-12 as an extension of an answer to the Thessalonians' question about brotherly love. He gives the connection between brotherly love and the Dioscuri and the themes associated with brotherly love in those contexts as the rhetorical setting for the instructions in these verses.[49] Thus he finds no 'polemical thrust' here.[50] This conclusion supports our assessment that the passage is hortatory. Whether or not Kloppenberg's sketch of the setting is accurate, Paul may give these instructions to be certain that no wrong conceptions about the proper mode of behavior develop.[51]

Even if the περὶ δὲ (now concerning) of 4.9 indicates that the Thessalonians had questions that Paul addresses in 4.9-12, there is no sign that the questions reflect behavior that some Thessalonian Christians have already adopted. In any case, there do not seem to be severe problems associated with these issues.

Will of God: Your Sanctification' (1 Thess 4,3)', in *idem*, *Studies on the First Letter to the Thessalonians*, pp. 299-325 (299); Boers, 'The Form Critical Study of Paul's Letters', p. 158.

47. Friedrich, *Die Briefe*, p. 241; Hughes, 'The Rhetoric of 1 Thessalonians', p. 104.

48. Boers, 'The Form Critical Study of Paul's Letters', p. 158. Boers also asserts here that this means 4.1-8 cannot be used to describe the Thessalonian situation. Cf. Snyder, 'Apocalyptic and Didactic Elements', p. 238.

49. John S. Kloppenberg, 'ΦΙΛΑΔΕΛΦΙΑ, ΘΕΟΔΙΔΑΚΤΟΣ and the Dioscuri: Rhetorical Engagement in 1 Thessalonians 4.9-12', *NTS* 39 (1993), pp. 265-89.

50. Kloppenberg, 'ΦΙΛΑΔΕΛΦΙΑ', p. 280.

51. Neil (*Epistle of Paul to the Thessalonians*, p. 89) associates this need with the expectation of the parousia. A. Malherbe (*Paul and the Thessalonians: The Philosophic Tradition of Pastoral Care* [Philadelphia: Fortress Press, 1987], pp. 100-101) cites the Cynics as examples of philosophers who do quit their jobs to devote themselves to their new beliefs. See also Ronald Hock, *The Social Context of Paul's Ministry*, pp. 43-45.

Servants of Satan

4.13-18

Many interpreters assert that 4.13-18 addresses specific problems at Thessalonica because 4.13 also contains περί ('concerning'). Koester, however, contends that 4.13–5.11 does not address anything specific at Thessalonica. Rather, these verses are Paul's attempt to make letters a Christian medium.[52] Verses 13-18 are no longer strictly hortatory material, even though they seem to have a pastoral[53] or hortatory[54] function. This passage seems to be didactic[55] because Paul is neither defending himself nor does he seem to be attacking some other teaching.

Previous statements about the Thessalonian situation have included references to eschatology, most explicitly 1.9-10. Thus, it may be possible to identify 4.13-18 as an allusion to questions that the Thessalonians raise. Hoffmann supports this view by noting that 4.13-18 (and 5.1-11) has not only περί δὲ ('now concerning'), but is also introduced with a specific address (brothers) and ends with a concluding formula. This is excellent evidence that 4.13-18 is a discrete section, but less conclusive that it addresses a question from the Thessalonians. But other evidence does strengthen the claim that this section addresses their concerns. Paul introduces the section by explaining that he is giving this teaching so that they would not grieve over those who have died and he concludes the section saying that they are to comfort one another with this teaching. This introduction and conclusion combined with the references to the parousia in passages that address the Thessalonian situation more directly seem to show that the Thessalonians are concerned about those who have died.

There is no evidence here for a radical realized eschatology.[56] Such an interpretation can be based only in unsupported mirror reading of this and several other passages. Our method does not allow mirror reading in didactic contexts.[57] Verses 13-18 do seem to indicate that the

---

52. Koester, '1 Thessalonians: Experiment in Christian Writing', p. 40.

53. So Hughes, 'The Rhetoric of 1 Thessalonians', pp. 104-105.

54. So Hoffmann, *Die Toten in Christus*, pp. 228-29.

55. So also Wanamaker, *Epistles to the Thessalonians*, p. 167.

56. Contra Jewett, *Pauline Rhetoric*, p. 94; Harnisch, *Eschatologische Existenz*, pp. 35-51.

57. If the section is primarily hortatory, this does not change our use of mirror reading. Our method does not allow use of that technique in hortatory passages either.

Thessalonians do not understand how the dead will participate in either the parousia or the promised eschatological bliss. We can say no more about their question from the exposition found in these verses.

5.1-3

A second section on eschatology, 5.1-11, appears to be didactic with a hortatory goal of encouraging the Thessalonians to encourage one another. Once again, several interpreters assert that the περὶ δὲ ('now concerning') of 5.1 shows that Paul is addressing a question the Thessalonians raise.[58] Harnisch rejects this view and identifies 5.1-3 as a *praeteritio*, a section which often contains περί ('concerning').[59] Moore argues that 5.1-11 does not suggest a problem and was, rather, written to encourage obedience.[60] Similarly, Wanamaker sees a shift to paraenesis at 5.1, but leaves open the possibility that it addresses an issue that the Thessalonians raise.[61] It seems less probable that 5.1-3 addresses a specific question of the Thessalonians than that 4.13-18 does because discussion of the time of the parousia flows quite naturally out of the comments on the events of the parousia in ch. 4. Furthermore, 5.1-3 serves as the introduction for 5.4-11, the transition to the hortatory material of 5.12-22. Thus, while it is possible that they have questions about the time of the parousia, we cannot claim that it is probable.

Summary of Allusions

We have now reviewed all of the passages that can be identified as allusions to the Thessalonian situation based on the more direct statements about the situation. These passages indicate a probability that the Thessalonains are troubled by the death of some members of their community before the parousia. But there is no evidence that any teaching about the dead is being advocated at Thessalonica. We have also seen that it is possible, but we cannot say probable, that some are concerned about the date of the parousia.

---

58. E.g. Richard, 'Early Pauline Thought', p. 47; Lüdemann, 'The Hope of the Early Paul', p. 196; Snyder, 'Apocalytic and Didactic Elements', p. 239; Frame, *Epistles of St. Paul to the Thessalonians,* p. 140.

59. Harnisch, *Eschatologische Existenz,* pp. 52-54.

60. Moore, *1 and 2 Thessalonians,* p. 72.

61. Wanamaker, *Epistles to the Thessalonians,* pp. 176-77.

Excursus on 2.1-12 and 5.12-22

To this point we have not dealt with two passages that many use to identify opponents. These are 2.1-12 and 5.12-22. Many interpreters have
viewed 2.1-12 as an apology for Paul's ministry which he offers to
refute accusations or criticism. But no direct statements about the situation in Thessalonica raise the issue of the validity of Paul's ministry,
and our method does not allow us to use affirmations to identify opponents unless they relate directly to a known point of discussion. Thus,
according to our method, Paul's comments on his ministry cannot be
construed as good evidence that he is under attack. Furthermore James
Ware contends that the comments on imitation in ch. 1 would lead an
ancient reader to expect a characterization of the model to be imitated.
The mention of imitation in 1.5b is, in fact, followed by the characterization of receiving the gospel in affliction with joy.[62] This characterization of the model to be imitated is again taken up in 2.1-12 which
Jewett entitles, 'Clarification of apostolic example'.[63] Here Paul not
only gives himself as the model to be imitated, but also establishes his
ethos in preparation for the instruction that comes later in the epistle. It
seems most likely, therefore, that this section should be understood as
didactic rather than apologetic, especially if it is correct that 1 Thessalonians is epideictic.

This understanding of 2.1-12, then, is very similar to that of Malherbe who argues that these verses give Paul as an example to help the
Thessalonians remain faithful in persecution.[64] Thus, there is no reason
to invent charges that have been made against Paul necessitating a
defense as the reason for this section.

Interpreters often use the hortatory section 5.12-22 to identify particular problems at Thessalonica.[65] Some use these verses to argue that
some at Thessalonica have quit their jobs in anticipation of the parousia,[66] while Jewett draws on 5.19-22 to support his view that there are

62. James Ware, 'The Thessalonians as a Missionary Congregation: 1 Thessalonians 1, 5-8', *ZNW* 83 (1992), p. 127.

63. Jewett, *Pauline Rhetoric*, p. 73.

64. A. Malherbe, '"Pastoral Care" in the Thessalonian Church', *NTS* 36 (1990),
pp. 375-91 (386).

65. E.g. David Alan Black, 'The Weak in Thessalonica: A Study in Pauline
Lexicography', *JETS* 25 (1982), pp. 307-21 (318).

66. E.g. Friedrich, *Die Briefe,* p. 205; Calvin Roetzel, 'Theodidactoi and Handwork in Philo and 1 Thessalonians', in A. Vanhoye (ed.), *L'apôtre Paul: Personnalité, style, et conception du ministère* (Leuven: Leuven University Press, 1986),

conflicts over ecstatic manifestations.[67] According to our method, only explicit statements in hortatory sections are admissable as evidence about opponents. Since Paul does not explicitly say that the Thessalonians are encountering problems with the behavior mentioned in 5.12-22, we cannot use these exhortations to claim that such problems exist. Malherbe's investigation of psychogogy[68] among moral philosophers supports this treatment of 5.12-22 as it shows that instructions to minister to different types of people in different ways were common within that tradition. Thus, Paul's instructions do not necessarily single out specific groups at Thessalonica, as Black contends.[69] So 5.12-22 yields information about neither opponents nor various groups within the Thessalonian church.

Conclusion

We find, then, no opponents combatted in 1 Thessalonians. The community seems to be faithful to Paul and his gospel.[70] Paul is worried about the 'tribulation' they are enduring because he fears it may cause them to question the gospel. Timothy's report may have included information that leads Paul to say some things are lacking in their faith, but he mentions no opposition to his teachings. It seems probable that the Thessalonians do have concerns about eschatology, particularly the participation of the dead in the eschatological bliss. But there is no evidence that anyone at Thessalonica is espousing a view Paul needs to defeat; he needs only to clarify the Thessalonians' understanding. It is possible, but not as probable as the previous issue, that the Thessalonians also have questions about the time of the parousia. There is also insufficient evidence that some are quitting their jobs in expectation of the parousia or that any other matter mentioned in 5.12-22 is an actual problem.

---

pp. 324-31 (330). Best (*First and Second Epistles to the Thessalonians*, p. 230) sees this as probable.

67. Jewett, *Pauline Rhetoric*, p. 101.

68. Malherbe, '"Pastoral Care"', pp. 75-91.

69. Black, 'The Weak in Thessalonica', p. 318.

70. See H. Koester, 'Apostel und Gemeinde in den Briefen an die Thessalonicher', in D. Lührmann and G. Strecker (eds.), *Kirche* (Tübingen: J.C.B. Mohr [Paul Siebeck], 1980), pp. 287-92 for discussion of the relationship between Paul and the Thessalonians that 1 Thessalonians seems to indicate.

As we have already noted, identifying 1 Thessalonians as epideictic supports our contention that it was not written to counter opponents.[71] Those who find opponents in 1 Thessalonians must use unreliable methods, including using unsupported mirror reading in hortatory and didactic sections. Such results are too uncertain to use as a basis for either exegesis or a reconstruction of early Christian beliefs.

71. So also Wanamaker, *Epistles to the Thessalonians*, pp. 59-60.

Chapter 8

'THE DAY OF THE LORD IS HERE': OVERREALIZED ESCHATOLOGY
ARRIVES IN THESSALONICA—2 THESSALONIANS

Discussion of the opponents of 2 Thessalonians has recently been given new impetus by R. Jewett's *The Thessalonian Situation*, in which he puts forward the thesis that the opponents of 1 and 2 Thessalonians are millinarian radicals who hold an overrealized eschatology that claims special pneumatic endowment and leads them to reject authority and traditional morality. Jewett's view builds on the work of Marxsen and Schmithals who find Gnostic opponents in 2 Thessalonians.[1] Hughes rejects the connection with Gnosticism, but still finds 2 Thessalonians opposing an overrealized eschatology of the type found in Colossians and Ephesians.[2] The majority of interpreters, however, contend that 2 Thessalonians opposes teachers who proclaim that the parousia is imminent.[3] This view usually gives such an eschatological expectation as

1. Willi Marxsen, *Der zweite Thessalonicherbrief* (Züricher Bibelkommentare; (Zürich: Theologischer Verlag, 1982), pp. 42, 54; Schmithals, *Paul and the Gnostics*, pp. 123-218.

2. Frank W. Hughes, *Early Christian Rhetoric and 2 Thessalonians* (JSNTSup, 30; Sheffield: JSOT Press, 1989), pp. 85-93.

3. E.g. Ernst von Dobschütz, *Die Thessalonicher Briefe* (Göttingen: Vandenhoeck & Ruprecht, 1909), pp. 21-22; George Milligan, *St. Paul's Epistles to the Thessalonians* (London: Macmillan, 1908), p. xxxviii; Friedrich, 'Der zweite Brief an die Thessalonicher', p. 257; Wolfgang Trilling, *Untersuchungen zum zweiten Thessalonicherbrief* (Erfurter Theologische Studien, 27; Leipzig: St Benno, 1972), p. 91; C.H. Giblin, *The Threat to Faith: An Exegetical and Theological Re-examination of 2 Thessalonians 2* (AnBib, 31; Rome: Pontifical Biblical Institute Press, 1967), p. 243; Gerhardt Krodel, '2 Thessalonians', in G. Krodel (ed.), *Ephesians, Colossians, 2 Thessalonians, The Pastoral Epistles* (Proclamation Commentaries; Philadelphia: Fortress Press, 1978), pp. 87-88.

the reason some have quit their jobs[4] and make claims to special spiritual endowment. Still other interpreters find no opponents or formal opposition to Paul's teaching in view in 2 Thessalonians.[5] Holland argues that those whom 2 Thessalonians opposes believe that they represent Paul's views, and so are opponents only in the sense that the author thinks they have misunderstood Paul. Thus the author of 2 Thessalonians attacks them because they reject his or her interpretation of the Pauline tradition.[6] As we have seen so often, the various presuppositions about the date, authorship, and general reconstruction of the era are much of the reason for the disagreements about the opponents.[7] In addition, the sparcity of explicit statements and the differing views on the meaning and significance of these few also contribute to the disagreements about these opponents.

Rhetorical critics generally agree that 2 Thessalonians is deliberative rhetoric, that is, intended to persuade or dissuade an audience about a future course of action.[8] This means, further, that we may expect some polemic against views or persons whom the author hopes to dissuade the audience from following.[9] We may not, of course, allow this judgment to determine the way we read passages of 2 Thessalonians at this point.

    4.   Trilling (*Der zweite Brief an die Thessalonicher*, pp. 73-96 [140]) and B.N. Kaye ('Eschatology and Ethics in 1 and 2 Thessalonians', *NovT* 17 [1975], pp. 47-57) are exceptions to this.
    5.   E.g. Beda Rigaux, *Thessaloniciens*, p. 72; Wanamaker, *The Epistles to the Thessalonians*, p. 51; R. Russell, 'The Idle in 2 Thess. 3.6-12: An Eschatological or Social Problem?', *NTS* 34 (1988), pp. 105-19 (110).
    6.   Holland, *The Tradition that You Received*, pp. 45, 53.
    7.   As with all the disputed letters, this study will take no position on the authorship of 2 Thessalonians.
    8.   So Jewett, *Pauline Rhetoric*, pp. 82, 87; Wanamaker, *The Epistles to the Thessalonians*, p. 52; Holland, *The Tradition that You Received*, p. 6; Hughes, *Early Christian Rhetoric*, pp. 51-55. See the discussion of deliberative rhetoric in Mitchell, *Paul and the Rhetoric of Reconciliation*, pp. 23-51 for analysis of this type of speech outside the context of discussion of 2 Thessalonians.
    9.   Holland (*The Tradition that You Received*, p. 156; cf. 45, 53) asserts that 2 Thessalonians as a whole is a polemical work. Holland also seems to find 2.1-12 as one of 2 Thessalonians's polemical sections (see *The Tradition that You Received*, p. 56). Trilling, (*Untersuchungen*, p. 92), however, sees 2.1-12 as a didactic/paraenetic section.

Explicit Statements

2.1-2

Commentators generally designate 2.1-12 as the section that contains 2.1-2.[10] Some include vv. 13-17 in the primary section, but then generally see vv. 1-12 as a sub-section within this larger unit.[11] Rigaux proposes that 2.1-12 is a sub-section of 2.1–3.5, all of which is on the parousia.[12] The parallels in the line of thought between 2.13–3.5 and the thanksgiving in ch. 1[13] make this larger division of the text seem more appropriate than breaking the section at 3.1 and thus supports Rigaux's view.

Rhetorical critics divide this section somewhat differently. They generally agree that 2.1-2 is the *partitio*,[14] which states the points to be argued or lists things that will be opposed in the argument to follow in the *probatio*. There is less agreement about how far the *probatio* extends, with some seeing it as 2.3-15,[15] others extending it through

10. E.g. Marxsen, *Der zweite Thessalonicherbrief*, pp. 76-77; Masson, *Les deux épîtres de Saint Paul aux Thessaloniciens*, p. 12; Best, *First and Second Epistles to the Thessalonians*, p. 274; Bruce, *1 and 2 Thessalonians*, p. 162; Frame, *Epistles of Paul to the Thessalonians*, p. 27; Roger Aus, '2 Thessalonians', in *idem et al. 1–2 Timothy, Titus, 2 Thessalonians* (Augsburg Commentary on the New Testament; Minneapolis: Augsburg, 1984), p. 192; Trilling, *Der zweite Brief*, pp. 26, 29; Wanamaker, *Epistles to the Thessalonians*, p. 51; Milligan, *Paul's Epistles to the Thessalonians*, p. 94; von Dobschütz, *Die Thessalonicher Briefe*, p. 260; Krodel, '2 Thessalonians', p. 89; Marshall, *1 and 2 Thessalonians*, p. 184.

11. E.g. Albrecht Oepke, 'Die Briefe an die Thessalonicher', in H.W. Beyer *et al.* (eds.), *Die kleineren Briefe des Apostels Paulus* (NTD, 8; Göttingen: Vandenhoeck & Ruprecht, 9th edn, 1962), p. 156; Ivan Havener, *First Thessalonians, Philemon, Philippians, Second Thessalonians, Colossians, Ephesians* (Collegeville Bible Commentary, 8; Collegeville, MN: Liturgical Press, 1983), p. 58.

12. Rigaux, *Thessaloniciens*, pp. 644-45.

13. See J.L. Sumney, 'The Bearing of a Pauline Rhetorical Pattern on the Integrity of 2 Thessalonians', *ZNW* 81 (1990), pp. 192-204.

14. Hughes, *Early Christian Rhetoric*, p. 56; Jewett, *Pauline Rhetoric*, p. 83. However, Holland (*The Tradition that You Received*, p. 14) sees all of 2.1-17 as the *probatio*.

15. Hughes, *Early Christian Rhetoric*, p. 57; Wanamaker, *The Epistles to the Thessalonians*, p. 51.

2.17,[16] and still others including all of 2.3–3.5.[17] This last position, held by Jewett, allows 2.13–3.5 to stand as a unit, which the parallels to the thanksgiving of chapter 1 support. Thus, it seems best to see the larger unit as 2.1–3.5 with 2.1-2 and 2.13–3.5 as subsections within that larger unit. I include 2.1-2 with 2.3-12 because the former sets out the topics to be discussed in the latter. The whole of 2.1-12 is polemical because it is an attempt to overthrow the position spoken of in 2.1-2.

The topics that 2.1-2 sets out for 2.3–3.5 are the parousia and 'our being gathered to him'. Verse 2 gives the reason that our writer discusses these issues: some are saying that the Day of the Lord is present. It seems likely that the congregation has not been won over to this view because the author says only that they are being disturbed.

While some have argued that ἐνέστηκεν in v. 2 means near or imminent, its meaning from all lexical evidence is 'is present'. This statement has been interpreted several ways: (1) In spite of the meaning of the term generally, many argue that ἐνέστηκεν must mean imminent in the context of the argument in vv. 3-12;[18] (2) Others argue that 2.2c means that the Day of the Lord has begun, that is, its intial stages are in motion so that it will be culminated imminently;[19] and (3) Still others see a realized eschatology reflected here which has spiritualized the parousia by means of Gnostic beliefs.[20] Jewett finds an overrealized eschatology with a spiritualized parousia, but does not associate it with Gnosticism. These differing views are in part the result of both differing interpretations of 2.3-12 and presuppositions about the possible views of Christians at the time of the writing of 2 Thessalonians.

'The Day of the Lord is present' is usually seen as a quotation taken from the opponents. However, Marxsen rightly notes that it is a formulation of the slogan by the author of 2 Thessalonians.[21] In this polemical context, the author may restate their view in a way that makes it

16. Holland, *The Tradition that You Received*, p. 14.

17. Jewett, *Pauline Rhetoric*, p. 83.

18. E.g. von Dobschütz, *Die Thessalonicher Briefe*, p. 268; Martin Dibelius, *An die Thessalonicher I, II und die Philipper* (HNT; Tübingen: J.C.B. Mohr [Paul Siebeck], 12th edn, 1925), p. 37.

19. E.g. Krodel, '2 Thessalonians', p. 89; Havener, *First Thessalonians, Philemon, Philippians, Second Thessalonians, Colossians, Ephesians*, pp. 58-59; M.J.J. Menken, 'Paradise Regained or Still Lost? Eschatology and Disorderly Behavior in 2 Thessalonians', *NTS* 38 (1992), pp. 271-89 (285).

20. Marxsen, *Der zweite Thessalonicherbrief*, pp. 43-54.

21. Marxsen, *Der zweite Thessalonicherbrief*, pp. 42-52.

easier to refute. Thus, it may not reflect their vocabulary or even state their belief in a way that they would find acceptable. Still, since the view must be recognizable to the readers, we can see that the opposed view emphasizes the 'already' of eschatology in some way. That is, they claim to possess some aspect(s) of Christian existence that 2 Thessalonians argues will come only at the parousia.

In 2.2 the author lists possible sources for this teaching: Spirit, word or letter 'as from us' (ὡς δι' ἡμῶν). This last phrase indicates that these teachers trace their message back to Paul. Thus, these teachers are not opponents in the sense that they oppose Paul's authority, or his teaching, as they understand it.[22] However, 2 Thessalonians clearly rejects this connection to Paul's teaching.[23] While a few interpreters argue that ὡς δι' ἡμῶν ('as from us') modifies only the letter,[24] the vast majority link it with all three possible sources of the teaching mentioned in v. 2.[25] In light of the mention of Paul's previous teaching in 2.5, and especially the mention of word and letter in 2.15,[26] it seems probable that 'as from us' modifies all three. This may indicate that the author is not sure about the source of this teaching,[27] or that she or he is not well informed about the situation, or that she or he wants to exclude any possible source.[28] Such a list of possible sources is too little evidence to assert that the problem lies primarily with any one of these sources.[29] In any case, as Giblin notes, the purpose of ὡς δι' ἡμῶν is not so much the

---

22. Frame (*Epistles of Paul to the Thessalonians*, pp. 18, 242) asserts that they 'innocently attributed to Paul' their views.

23. See also Holland, *The Tradition that You Received*, pp. 45, 53.

24. Bruce, *1 and 2 Thessalonians*, p. 164; Holland, *The Tradition that You Received*, p. 44; Andreas Lindemann, 'Zum Abfassungszweck des zweiten Thessalonicherbriefes', *ZNW* 68 (1977), pp. 35-47 (37).

25. E.g. von Dobschütz, *Die Thessalonicher Briefe*, pp. 21, 266; Milligan, *Paul's Epistles to the Thessalonians*, pp. 96-97; Masson, *Saint Paul aux Thessaloniciens*, p. 94; Frame, *Epistles of Paul to the Thessalonians*, p. 246; Best, *First and Second Epistles to the Thessalonians*, pp. 278-79; Giblin, *The Threat to Faith*, p. 149; Hughes, *Early Christian Rhetoric*, p. 93.

26. See Hughes, *Early Christian Rhetoric*, pp. 77-78.

27. So Wanamaker, *The Epistles to the Thessalonians*, pp. 58, 239.

28. This would give something of the same rhetorical effect as Gal. 1.8 'though we or an angel from heaven...'

29. E.g. Marxsen (*Der zweite Thessalonicherbrief*, p. 42) argues from this verse that it is primarily a problem with the Spirit. While this may be correct, the list in 2.2 is too little evidence to support this claim.

mode of transmission as it is the authority that tracing the teaching to Paul confers.[30]

This does not necessarily mean that these teachers do not use these means (word, Spirit and letter) to advocate their teaching. Indeed, the mention of word and letter later within the argument seems to show that they use such sources to support their views. Thus, while it appears probable that the Thessalonian teachers also have recourse to utterances in the Spirit, this verse does not indicate that any one of the three sources is the primary problem.

Thus 2.1-2 shows that some at Thessalonica advocate an eschatology that emphasizes its present reality and that they argue that this eschatology is Paul's view. It seems likely that the Thessalonians have not yet been persuaded to accept this view because our author says only that she or he does not want them to be swayed or disturbed by the proclamation about the parousia or the claim that it came from Paul.[31]

3.6, 11-12

Two explicit statements about aberrant behavior at Thessalonica appear together in ch. 3. While some begin a new section at 3.1, I have argued that the previous section extends through 3.5. The section that begins at 3.6, as the vocative ἀδελφοί ('brothers') indicates, extends through v. 15.[32] Jewett's judgment that v. 16 relates to issues outside this section and so belongs to a summary of the whole letter[33] seems correct. The passage 3.6-15 is hortatory in the sense that its subject is appropriate conduct. However, it addresses a single issue and has elements of polemic. Thus it is a combination of types of context. We may, then, use more material here than we would allow in a usual hortatory section, but not as much as in other polemical sections. We may use allusions to

30. Giblin, *The Threat to Faith*, p. 149.
31. See Menken, 'Paradise Regained or Still Lost?', p. 273.
32. This is the view of most interpreters. However, these scholars end it earlier: Holland, *The Tradition that You Received*, p. 24 at v. 13; Milligan (*Paul's Epistles to the Thessalonians*, p. 84) at v. 12; Trilling (*Untersuchungen*, pp. 95, 99) at v. 12, asserting that vv. 13-15 do not refer to the ἀτάκτοι; Bruce (*1 and 2 Thessalonians*, p. 203) makes 3.6-13 a sub-section of 3.6-16. Others extend the section to include v. 16. E.g. Oepke, 'Die Briefe an die Thessalonicher', p. 184; Havener, *First Thessalonians Philemon, Philippians, Second Thessalonians, Colossians, Ephesians*, p. 63; von Dobschütz, *Die Thessalonicher Briefe*, p. 309.
33. Jewett, *Pauline Rhetoric*, p. 81.

opponents, but they must be closely tied to issues raised in explicit statements.

The clearest statement in all 2 Thessalonians about the aberrant behavior of some at Thessalonica appears in 3.11-12. According to vv. 6 and 11, the author has heard that some at Thessalonica live ἀτάκτως ('disorderly'[34]). Verse 12 further specifies that they are without jobs and are busybodies. Trilling, Marxsen and Collins contend that the remarks about the disorderly in vv. 6-12 do not reflect a real problem in the Thessalonian church. Marxsen argues that 3.6-11 intends to create a contrast to Paul's image in order to call the readers to orient themselves to Paul.[35] Trilling, followed by Collins,[36] asserts that this section is an addendum which reflects the bourgeois mentality of late New Testament writings.[37] For Trilling, the problem that vv. 6-12 address does arise occasionally within early Christianity, so the author takes this opportunity to address it even though it is not an immediate problem at Thessalonica.[38]

While even Rigaux was troubled by the abrupt introduction of this topic,[39] it seems unlikely that it is unrelated to the situation that the letter addresses. The authoritative tone of this passage has often been noted. Trilling himself finds it to be the section's dominant characteristic,[40] and this observation leads him to wonder why these verses employ such powerful persuasion.[41] This query is unanswerable if the ἀτάκτοι ('disorderly') are not a real, present problem for the recipients of 2 Thessalonians. There would be little reason to focus the entire, or the only focused part of the exhortation on a problem that did not exist.[42]

---

34. Ceslaus Spicq ('Les Thessaloniciens "inquites" etaient ils des paresseux?' *ST* 10 [1956], pp. 1-13) has demonstrated convincingly that the meaning of ἀτάκτως is disorderly, not lazy or idle.

35. Marxsen, *Der zweite Thessalonicherbrief*, pp. 55-66; 98-99.

36. Collins, *Letters That Paul Did Not Write*, pp. 235-36.

37. Trilling, *Untersuchungen*, p. 97; *idem*, *Der zweite Brief*, pp. 150-53.

38. Trilling, *Der zweite Brief*, pp. 152-53.

39. Rigaux, *Thessaloniciens*, p. 710.

40. Trilling, *Der zweite Brief*, p. 141; also Collins, *Letters That Paul Did Not Write*, p. 233. Oepke ('Die Briefe an die Thessalonicher', p. 184) calls 3.6-16 a sharp attack. Milligan (*Paul's Epistles to the Thessalonians*, p. 112) speaks of the 'severe language' found here which indicates a serious problem.

41. Trilling, *Der zweite Brief*, p. 142.

42. Wanamaker (*The Epistles to the Thessalonians*, p. 279) argues that this is a real problem because the exhortation deals with only one issue. He argues further

It is even more improbable that the strongest directly authoritative and commanding tone of the letter would be reserved for a non-existent problem. Even if it is correct that 3.6-12 expresses the ethical stance of the post-Pauline church, this is not evidence that the author did not think the ἀτάκτοι were an actual and present problem for the readers. Furthermore, Jewett argues that the discussion of those who do not work was prepared for by 1.5-10, with its mention of those who reject the Pauline tradition.[43] If this is correct, the discussion of the ἀτάκτοι was planned from the beginning of the letter and the material that precedes 3.6 prepares for this discussion in some way. In any case, the emphatic character of this passage indicates that the ἀτάκτοι were a real problem for those who received this letter.

The ἀτάκτοι seem to be a minority within the Thessalonian church because the author distinguishes them from the church as a whole in 3.11. In addition, the writer expects the church as a whole to take action against them.

In 3.12 the author defines the disorderliness of those about whom the Thessalonians are being warned: they are unwilling to work for their living and are busybodies. Describing them as ἀτάκτοι is the author's polemical evaluation, as is calling them busybodies. They would, of course, reject both of these accusatory descriptions of their behavior. They might also reject the intervening description which says that they do not work. Although most interpreters see the primary issue here to be that the ἀτάκτοι do not work, some argue that they are claiming charismatic authority or spiritual power which they use to demand pay.[44] While the reference to the Spirit in 2.2 may suggest some problem with charismatic gifts, there is insufficient evidence to connect that possibility with this statement about the disorderly. Still, the ἀτάκτοι might well reject the accusation that they do not work, especially if περιεργαζομένους ('busybodies') implies that they are active in church affairs.[45] If it does, they may think they are working at the job

(pp. 279-280) that since only one issue is addressed in this section of exhortation, the matter addressed here must have been a significant part of the reason 2 Thessalonians was written.

43. Jewett, *Pauline Rhetoric*, pp. 86-87.

44. So G. Holmberg, *Paul and Power: The Structure of Authority in the Primitive Church as Reflected in the Pauline Epistles* (Philadelphia: Fortress Press, 1978), p. 159; Holland, *The Tradition that You Received*, pp. 52-53.

45. Rigaux, *Thessaloniciens*, pp. 704-705 asserts that περιεργαζομένους indi-

appropriate for themselves when they are engaged with church matters. It does seem clear that they are not employed in the usual sense, but this does not mean that they see themselves as loafers[46] or as unemployed. Our discussion of 3.7-10 as an allusion (see below) may add some information on this point.

In 3.6 the author refers to those who live ἀτάκτως ('in a disorderly manner'). Marxsen asserts that these ἀτάκτοι and those of 3.11 are not the same people.[47] But the use of the same vocabulary in both places in such close proximity and the continuity of thought in 3.6-12 argue conclusively against this view. Further, Collins identifies 3.6-12 as an *inclusio* that uses παραγγέλλομεν ('we command') and the mention of the Lord Jesus Christ in both v. 6 and v. 12.[48] Given, then, the unity of the passage, the same people are in view.

When 3.6 accuses some Thessalonian Christians[49] of living ἀτάκτως (in a disorderly manner), it explains that this means they are not living 'according to the tradition'. Holland takes this to mean that they reject the tradition.[50] Several other interpreters assert that this reference to the tradition shows the opponents oppose Paul's authority.[51] But the assertion that they do not live 'according to the tradition' is another polemical evaluation of their behavior. Labeling their conduct as contrary to Paul's teaching immediately puts them on the defense since the community as a whole accepts Paul's authority, as the claim in 2.1-2 that

cates an active state rather than a passive one. Göran Agrell, *Word, Toil, and Sustenance* (trans. S. Westerholm; Lund: Ohlssons, 1976), pp. 117-18, also notes that περιεργαζομένους is broader than not working and refers 'more generally to an active, disobedient way of behaving'. Giblin (*The Threat to Faith*, p. 144) comments that the call to shun them in 3.6 suggests that they are troublemakers, not just economic parasites. Best (*First and Second Epistles to the Thessalonians*, p. 340) also understands calling them busybodies to be an indication that they interfere with the life of the community.

46. Contra the description of them in Trilling, *Untersuchungen*, p. 91; *Der zweite Brief*, p. 140, and Wanamaker, *The Epistles to the Thessalonians*, p. 286.

47. Marxsen, *Der zweite Thessalonicherbrief*, p. 100.

48. Collins, *Letters That Paul Did Not Write*, p. 233.

49. The use of ἀδελφοί ('brothers') indicates that they are members of the community.

50. Holland, *The Tradition that You Received*, pp. 52-53.

51. E.g. Giblin (*The Threat to Faith*, pp. 9, 142) contends that it indicates their opposition to Paul's authority or teaching. Frame (*Epistles of Paul to the Thessalonians*, p. 299) asserts that they are being deliberately disobedient and Jewett (*Pauline Rhetoric*, pp. 104-105) contends that they resist authority.

the aberrant eschatology comes from Paul demonstrates. Moreover, the author goes on in vv. 7-10 to describe just what aspect of the tradition the ἄτακτοι violate. Thus, it is improbable that the disorderly understand their behavior as contrary to Pauline teaching.

As is often noted, 2 Thessalonians makes no explicit connection between the problems with eschatology and the ἄτακτοι of 3.6, 11-12. Still, the vast majority of interpreters relate these two problems, seeing the imminence of the parousia as the reason some have left their jobs. However, Trilling and Russell reject this conclusion.[52] Jewett connects these two issues by arguing that the reference to the 'steadfastness of Christ' in 3.5 is given as the antithesis of the behavior described in 3.6-15, and thus relates the eschatology discussed in 2.1–3.5 with the problem behavior of 3.6-12.[53] This tenuous connection is insufficient by itself to support a relationship between these two issues. Arguing that the two issues belong together, Agrell asserts that the author's use of the tradition to combat both problems shows that they are related.[54] But as Russell notes, the mention of the tradition in connection with both issues shows only that both are part of the tradition, not that the two are related.[55] Menken offers the most sustained recent defense of a relationship between these two issues. He asserts first that it 'seems only logical' that two problems in such a short letter are related and then designates two primary things that indicate a connection: (1) the use of a similar three-part procedure when discussing the two: the author refers to what Paul had said when with them, appeals to their knowledge and uses apostolic tradition; (2) the mention of the ὑπομονὴν ('steadfastness') of Christ in 3.5, following its use in 1.4, appears in close proximity to the discussion of the disorderly.[56]

The question of whether there are one or two groups of opponents arises in relation to 2 Thessalonians, it seems, primarily because of the difficulty some have in reconciling an overrealized (Gnostic) eschatology with the cessation of employment. This is not sufficient cause to find two different groups of opponents. The primary reason to assign both issues (overrealized eschatology and disorderly conduct) to the

52. Trilling, *Untersuchungen*, p. 101; *idem, Der zweite Brief*, p. 140; Russell, 'The Idle in 2 Thessalonians', pp. 110-13.
53. Jewett, *Pauline Rhetoric*, p. 86.
54. Agrell, *Word, Toil, and Sustenance*, p. 117.
55. Russell, 'The Idle in 2 Thessalonians', p. 116, n. 33.
56. Menken, 'Paradise Regained or Still Lost?', pp. 271-72.

same group is that there is no indication in the text that the author is dealing with multiple groups. Only if the beliefs opposed were found to be incompatible would we need to postulate the existence of a second group. But, as we will see, this does not seem to be the case. No proof beyond this compatibility is needed and none is required of other letters to establish that there is only one group of opponents. For example, no one doubts that those who criticize Paul's strong letters in 2 Corinthians are the same opponents who commend themselves through pneumatic means.

We learn from 3.6, 11-12 that some within the Thessalonian church are behaving in ways that the author believes violate apostolic tradition. This behavior includes, but is perhaps not limited to, leaving their jobs and involving themselves in the life of the church in ways that our author sees as disruptive.[57] These statements reveal no motivation for this behavior. There is no indication in the text that those whose conduct is condemned are distinct from those who hold an overrealized eschatology. Furthermore, there is no reason to suspect that those who behave in this way reject apostolic tradition, rather our author finds non-conformity with the apostolic tradition an effective charge against them.

Summary of Explicit Statements

Explicit statements reveal two problems that disturb the church that 2 Thessalonians addresses: some at Thessalonica advocate an eschatological teaching that our author rejects, and the ἄτακτοι ('disorderly') who have left their jobs are causing problems within the community. There is no evidence that these problems arise from separate groups. The author of 2 Thessalonians sees those who proclaim the alternative eschatology as opponents whose teaching must be defeated. This eschatology focuses attention on the present as the eschatological time, and claims to experience in the present something that 2 Thessalonians sees as part of the final eschatological fulfillment. These opponents also claim that their view is Paul's view. Furthermore, since the author sees the charge that the ἄτακτοι do not live according to the tradition as an effective counter, they do not reject or challenge the authority of Paul or the Pauline tradition. So these problems develop from among people who understand themselves to be representatives of Paul's teaching.

---

57. Friedrich ('Der zweite Brief', p. 274) says they are passive where they should be active and active where they should be passive.

Allusions

1.4-5

Direct statements about the situation that do not explicitly address opponents are counted as allusions according to our method. In 1.4 Paul notes that the Thessalonians are enduring persecution and tribulation and in v. 5 that they are suffering for the kingdom of God. These remarks appear in the thanksgiving that comprises of 1.3-12.[58] Rhetorically, Wanamaker identifies 1.3-12 as the *exordium*.[59] Similarly, Jewett and Hughes see 1.1-12 as the *exordium*.[60] As Hughes notes, the functions of a thanksgiving and an *exordium* fit together well:[61] both introduce topics to be developed later. Here, 1.3-12 introduces the apocalyptic framework that serves as the basis for the argument that follows.[62] More specifically it gives the Day of the Lord an apocalyptic description[63] which will be used to counter overrealized eschatology in ch. 2.

The description in 1.4 of the Thessalonians' situation as involving 'persecution' and 'tribulation' has led to opposite understandings of the problems encountered. Aus argues that this description and its liturgical basis indicates a situation of severe persecution[64] and uses this under-

58. So most commentators, including Rigaux, *Thessaloniciens*, p. 610; Best, *First and Second Epistles to the Thessalonians*, p. 249; Bruce, *1 and 2 Thessalonians*, p. 143; Frame, *Epistles of Paul to the Thessalonians*, p. 27; Giblin, *The Threat to Faith*, p. 3; Friedrich, 'Der zweite Brief', p. 258; von Dobschütz, *Die Thessalonicher Briefe*, p. 29; Marshall, *1 and 2 Thessalonians*, p. 169.

59. Wanamaker, *The Epistles to the Thessalonians*, p. 51.

60. Jewett, *Pauline Rhetoric*, p. 79; Hughes, *Early Christian Rhetoric*, p. 51. These views reject Holland's analysis which identifies vv. 5-12 as *narratio* (*The Tradition that You Received*, p. 10). As Wanamaker notes, it is common for deliberative rhetoric not to include a *narratio* (*The Epistles to the Thessalonians*, p. 237).

61. Hughes, *Early Christian Rhetoric*, p. 52.

62. So Jewett, *Pauline Rhetoric*, p. 79; Marxsen, *Der zweite Thessalonicherbrief*, p. 52. Similarly Best, *First and Second Epistles to the Thessalonians*, p. 49.

63. So Rigaux, *Thessaloniciens*, p. 610.

64. Roger D. Aus, 'The Relevance of Isaiah 66:7 to Revelation 12 and 2 Thessalonians 1', *ZNW* 67 (1976), pp. 252-68 (263); *idem*, 'The Liturgical Background of the Necessity and Propriety of Giving Thanks According to 2 Thessalonians 1:3', *JBL* 92 (1973), pp. 432-38 (438); '2 Thessalonians', pp. 200-201. Donfried ('The Cults of Thessalonica and the Thessalonian Correspondence', p. 352) asserts that 2 Thessalonians addresses a situation of intensified persecution. Cf. Krodel, '2 Thessalonians', p. 88.

standing to support his interpretation of the eschatological problems at Thessalonica which he argues involve the claim that the Messianic Woes have begun.[65] But there is no more direct indication that this persecution is particularly severe, even if the Thessalonians experience it as extreme enough to warrant the description of the punishment of their persecutors in vv. 5-10.

Trilling asserts the opposite understanding of the persecution mentioned here. He contends that θλῖψις ('tribulation') is a broader and more general term than persecution and thus 1.4 does not refer to any specifics of a single community.[66] However, the breadth of the word θλῖψις does not signify the absence of a specific situation. Rather the term connotes a breadth of meaning that gives persecution an eschatological meaning,[67] that is, it puts their sufferings into a context that supports the position asserted in ch. 2. Thus, v. 4 indicates only that the author is pleased that the Thessalonians have been able to endure whatever persecution they have been experiencing. Perhaps it could be added, on the basis of ἀνέχεσθε ('you endure'), that this persecution is ongoing[68] but this says nothing about its severity.

2.3-7

We have already identified 2.1-12 as a polemical section. Most interpreters agree that it bears the burden of the primary argument of 2 Thessalonians. We identify vv. 3-7 as an allusion to the rejected eschatology because it follows immediately the explicit statement in v. 2, and the anacoluthon of v. 3 must be directly related to the preceding statement to be understandable. Additionally, vv. 3-7 are clearly a response to the assertion that the Day of the Lord is present.

According to vv. 3-4, the rebellion and the revelation of the person of lawlessness must precede the Day of the Lord. Our author sets this rebuttal of the claim in v. 2 in apocalyptic language that asserts that the readers will be able to recognize signs which must come before the Day of the Lord. The use of imagery from Daniel in v. 4 further confirms that the author is working within an apocalyptic framework. It is often

65. Aus, '2 Thessalonians', pp. 200-201.
66. Trilling, *Der zweite Brief*, p. 48.
67. Best, *First and Second Epistles to the Thessalonians*, p. 253.
68. Aus ('2 Thessalonians', p. 200) makes this argument.

claimed that a response from within this thought-world would be effective only against a different scheme from within the same framework,[69] thus requiring that the opponents also have an apocalyptic perspective that asserts an imminent parousia. This argument assumes that an author must meet opponents on their own ground. But it is possible that our author refutes the other view by offering a different point of view.[70] If she or he chose this means, the reorientation of the Thessalonians' viewpoint began in the thanksgiving which gave them a vested interest in maintaining a more futuristic orientation by placing their bliss and their persecutors' punishment at the last day (1.5-10).

Interpreters also argue that this passage cannot be rejecting a spiritualized, overrealized eschatology because it presupposes a futuristic fulfillment which Gnosticism rejects. Thus, since 2 Thessalonians does not argue for a future aspect of eschatology (but assumes its acceptance), the argument cannot be directed against an overrealized eschatology. Such an assessment underestimates not only the many ways that one can counter opposition but also the possible range of overrealized eschatologies, and is additionally based on a misunderstanding of Gnosticism.

First, not only is there no basis in 2 Thessalonians for a connection between the presence of the Day of the Lord as spoken of in 2.2 and Gnosticism, but there is also no necessary connection between overrealized eschatology and Gnosticism. Aune finds elements of a realized eschatology in the Gospel of John and the epistles of Ignatius of Antioch,[71] neither of which was Gnostic. The Pauline communities' experience of the Spirit in worship is another form of realized eschatology without dependence on Gnosticism.[72] New Testament scholars have long recognized the 'already' element of Paul's eschatology alongside futuristic elements. Since Paul was able to hold together a partially realized eschatology and a futurist eschatology without abandoning an

---

69. E.g. von Dobschütz, *Die Thessalonicher Briefe*, p. 268; Marshall, *1 and 2 Thessalonians*, p. 186; Wanamaker, *The Epistles to the Thessalonians*, pp. 239-40; Bruce, *1 and 2 Thessalonians*, p. 166; Best, *First and Second Epistles to the Thessalonians*, p. 276.

70. So Hughes, *Early Christian Rhetoric*, p. 57.

71. David E. Aune, *The Cultic Setting of Realized Eschatology in Early Christianity* (NovTSup, 28; Leiden: E.J. Brill, 1972), pp. 45-165. Even if John is influenced by Gnostic concepts, Ignatius is certainly no Gnostic.

72. See Aune, *The Cultic Setting of Realized Eschatology*, pp. 11-14.

apocalyptic framework, there is no reason to think that others, including those opposed in 2 Thessalonians, could not do something similar.

Secondly, the association of overrealized eschatology with Gnosticism, as we find in Schmithals and Marxsen,[73] has led interpreters to assert that an overly realized eschatology could not also have a futurist element. But even the presumption that Gnostics could not have a final day for eschatological fulfillment is incorrect. Some Gnostic systems explicitly mention the end of the material universe as the eschatological climax.[74] Other systems have a cosmology and description of the creation of the physical world that seem to presuppose that the regathering of all parts of Sophia will bring with it the end of the material world. So even some Gnostic eschatologies include future elements.

Once we recognize that some types of overrealized eschatology do not exclude some future fulfillment or even abandon an apocalyptic outlook, we may read 2.2 more straightforwardly. The writer indicates in 2.3-4 that some at Thessalonica claim an aspect of Christian experience in the present which she or he believes will not be experienced until the Day of the Lord. Once our writer has framed the rejected view as a claim that the Day of the Lord is present, she or he can refute it by arguing that the Day of the Lord has not come, which all the Thessalonians already know to be true in some sense. Since the opponents claim some aspect of Christian experience as present which our writer removes to the Day of the Lord, it is appropriate to label their view overrealized eschatology. If our author assumes belief in some future fulfillment among the opponents, it may be more accurate to designate the opponents' view as a partially realized eschatology. But we cannot be certain that the writer is working with that assumption.

3.7-10, 14

We have identified 3.6-15 as a combination of hortatory and polemical material. Since this section is partly polemical and addresses the subject of work,[75] we may identify 3.7-10 as an allusion to the 'disorderly'.

73. Marxsen, *Der zweite Thessalonicherbrief*, p. 54.

74. E.g. Valentinians. See the comments of Aune, *The Cultic Setting of Realized Eschatology*, p. 6.

75. The troubling structure of 3.6-15 may be due in part to the author's strategy. She or he seems to attempt to have the ἀτάκτοι agree with the general exhortation about being disorderly before applying it to them. Who within a church that accepts Paul's authority would understand themselves to be violators of the tradition? The

Verses 7-9 call upon the example of Paul's mission practice of working while preaching as the reason the ἀτάκτοι should be employed in normal occupations. Verse 10 then cites a previous command to further establish the point. Thus, both the direct teaching and the example of Paul are used to oppose the practices of the 'disorderly'. This use of Paul's example and teaching confirms that the church and the ἀτάκτοι accept Paul and his teaching as authoritative.

It may be significant that the example of Paul's work while preaching is the primary focus of vv. 3-10, especially since v. 9 elaborates this example by stating that Paul had the right to accept pay. As we noted above, calling them περιεργαζομένους ('busybodies') in v. 11 seems to show that the disorderly involved themselves in the life of the Christian community. Verses 3-9 may indicate, by using Paul's work while preaching as an example, that they have taken up some form of ministry for which they expect pay. While we cannot claim this as certain, it seems probable based on the emphasis in vv. 3-9 and the wording of v. 11. Following the reminder of Paul's manner of ministry, 3.10 rejects abandoning normal occupations and calls on the community not to support those who are voluntarily unemployed.

So then, 3.7-10 confirms that the Thessalonians and the 'disorderly' accept Paul's authority. These verses, along with v. 11, suggest, without giving conclusive evidence, that the 'disorderly' have given up normal daily pursuits to devote themselves to some form of Christian service (perhaps, but not necessarily, preaching or evangelizing since the example given is Paul's manner of evangelizing) for which they expect pay from the church.

There also seems to be an allusion to the opponents in 3.14 as the author speaks of those who do not obey the commands of this letter. This verse instructs the community to separate from them, thus adding weight to the commands of vv. 6-15. This injunction to the community may show some doubt in the author's mind that these commands will be obeyed, but is insufficient to argue that some question or reject Paul's authority. It does indicate that the disorderly are part of the community

---

call of v. 7 that they imitate Paul by not being ἀτάκτως leaves the troublesome behavior undefined. It is only in v. 8 that it becomes clear that one's source of income is in view. Only after it is clear that this is the issue and that laboring for the church is not a substitute for other employment does the author say in v. 11 that some of them are violating *this* tradition, i.e. are ἀτάκτοι ('disorderly').

that this letter addresses, but adds nothing more to our understanding of them.

Summary of Allusions

Allusions significantly increase our information about the situation that 2 Thessalonians addresses. According to 1.4 the Thessalonians face some type of persecution, but there is no indication that these persecutions are particulary severe.[76] Only that, whatever their nature and severity, they have eschatological significance. It is possible that 2.3-4 suggests that the opponents include some future elements in their eschatology, if the author assumes their acceptance of this point. If they do retain some future aspect in their eschatology, it may be more accurate to call their view a partially realized eschatology. Still, it is a more fully realized eschatology than that of the author of this letter. This more fully realized eschatology claims possession of some aspect(s) of Christian experience that our author sees as part of the parousia. Given the use of θλῖψις ('tribulation') in 1.4 and the comment of 2.7 that the events of the eschaton are in progress, our author places the Thessalonians' situation in an eschatological process that is moving ahead, but that has not reached its final stage. Our impression that the disorderly are actively involved in church affairs is strengthened by 3.7-10, 14. These verses also suggest that these members of the Thessalonian congregation dedicate themselves to church work while abandoning ordinary occupations.

Affirmations

2.13-17

The renewed thanksgiving of 2.13–3.5 serves as a conclusion and exhortation based on 2.1-12. Since 2.13–3.5 is so similar to an introductory thanksgiving, we can expect themes to be picked up that are important for the letter as a whole. The primary exhortative point of the passage is the importance of correct beliefs. Adhering to the right beliefs is one aspect of the obedience explicitly called for in 3.4. This understanding of maintaining the traditions clarifies the continuity between 2.13-17 and 3.1-5. The reference to Paul's previous teaching in 2.5 is picked up in v. 13 where it is said that the Thessalonians were chosen for salvation through belief in the truth. So the period begins by reaffirming the

---

76. Contra Aus, '2 Thessalonians', p. 194.

importance of correct teaching by relating it to their salvation. This assertion becomes an exhortation in v. 15 where they are commanded to hold to the teaching already received. Giblin and Holland see this exhortation as the main conclusion for 2.1-14.[77] Similarly, Marshall understands v. 15 to be exhortation that summarizes vv. 3-12.[78] It seems correct that holding to the teaching previously received and correctly understood is a central point of ch. 2. The mention of 'word' and 'letter' shows a connection between this verse and 2.2[79] which draws all of the eschatological teaching of ch. 2 into the body of tradition that they are to hold firmly. Furthermore, as Marshall comments, v. 15 indicates that they are to understand all Paul has earlier said or written in the light of the explanation given it in 2 Thessalonians 2.[80]

In 2.17 the exhortation to accept the interpretation of the tradition given in 2.3-12 is further supported by asserting that God and the Lord Jesus Christ will strengthen them 'in every good work and word'. This final expression seems to tie together the eschatological teaching and the 'disorderly' because correct teaching and proper activity (every good work) are clearly related. While 'good work' is a broad expression, it is especially appropriate to the specific problem addressed in 3.6-15.

So 2.13-17 confirms that the issue between the author of 2 Thessalonians and the opponents is the correct interpretation of Paul's teaching, as the Thessalonians are urged to accept the interpretation of the tradition given in 2.3-12. In addition, it may reflect a connection between the eschatological tradition being interpreted and the problem with the 'disorderly'.

1.5-10, 11
The passage 1.5-10, a sub-section of the thanksgiving of 1.3-12, seems to relate to the problems that the opponents cause as it describes the last judgment, part of the alternative eschatology presented in ch. 2. The primary function of this description is to comfort the persecuted by telling of their persecutors' punishment and by interpreting the Thessalonians' suffering as a sign that God is with them. Wanamaker, following

77. Giblin, *The Threat to Faith*, p. 43; Holland, *The Tradition that You Received*, p. 22.
    78. Marshall, *1 and 2 Thessalonians*, p. 209.
    79. So also Giblin, *The Threat to Faith*, p. 45, among others.
    80. Marshall, *1 and 2 Thessalonians*, pp. 209-210.

Bassler, comments that persecution is a problem for the Thessalonians because the teaching of the presence of the Day of the Lord implies to them that persecution should be over.[81] The thanksgiving, then, opposes the overrealized eschatology by interpreting the Thessalonians' own experience of suffering as consistent with the apocalyptic scheme for which the letter argues. So in a veiled way, the first argument for the letter's eschatology is that it makes the Thessalonians' own experience understandable and meaningful in ways that the opposed overrealized eschatology could not. It also draws together the parousia and the final judgment as events that occur at the same time.[82] Thus, it implicitly rejects the opponents' eschatology. It is not possible to specify anything about those who cause the Thessalonians tribulation from vv. 5-10.

At 1.11 the focus moves from the final judgment to the present. The author calls on God to prepare the Thessalonians for the eschaton by making them worthy of his call and by fulfilling 'every desire for good and work of faith'. Hughes contends that the mention of 'work of faith' refers to the command to work in ch. 3 and that 'every good purpose' implies avoiding the way the 'disorderly' live.[83] Wanamaker is less specific but also asserts that vv. 11-12 prepare for both 2.13-17 and 3.1-15.[84] Identifying 1.3-12 as an exordium supports finding references within this section to the various arguments within the document.[85] It is at least possible that v. 11 has the 'disorderly' in view. If it does, the association with being made worthy of the kingdom (v. 5) again connects the aberrant eschatology and the conduct of the disorderly. Verse 11, then, may strengthen this connection and indicate that the conduct of the 'disorderly' and the aberrant eschatology were both in view at the beginning of the letter.

3.2-4

Completing the renewed thanksgiving begun at 2.13, 3.1-5 continues to echo the concerns of chs. 1 and 2 and to reflect the [86]apocalyptic out-

81. Wanamaker, *The Epistles to the Thessalonians*, p. 222; Jouette M. Bassler, 'The Enigmatic Sign: 2 Thessalonians 1:5', *CBQ* 46 (1984), pp. 496-510 (507-509). Cf. Aus, '2 Thessalonians', pp. 200-201.

82. So also Best, *First and Second Epistles to the Thessalonians*, p. 258; Wanamaker, *The Epistles to the Thessalonians*, p. 238.

83. Hughes, *Early Christian Rhetoric*, p. 55.

84. Wanamaker, *The Epistles to the Thessalonians*, p. 51.

85. E.g. the subject of persecution in 2 Thess. 1 and here in 3.1-2.

86. Seeing 1.3-12 in rhetorical terms (as an exordium) rather than in epistolary

look explicated in those chapters. Some argue that this section does not address a specific letter situation[87] or is too general to prepare for 3.6-12.[88] Others, however, see references to opponents in the 'wicked' of v. 2[89] or their teaching as the evil that God will guard the Thessalonians against in v. 3.[90] The exhortation to obedience indicates that this passage does prepare for 3.6-12 as well as urge the acceptance of the eschatology given in ch. 2. It seems less likely, though not impossible, that the wicked of v. 2 are the opponents because they pose no threat to Paul and they use his teaching to support their position. Even if the wicked are the opponents (or the evil that God guards the Thessalonians against is the opponents' teaching), this tells us nothing new about them.

As part of the thanksgiving of 2.13–3.5, 3.3-4 is a parallel of 1.11.[91] In 1.11 God enables the Thessalonians to endure persecution and live rightly, while in 3.3-4 God enables them to obey the author's commands. This parallel strengthens the case for seeing 1.11 as a reference to the 'disorderly' because 3.3-4 have them in view as it prepares for 3.6-12. If this is correct, the problem with the disorderly was in view from the beginning of this letter.

When 3.4 gives the purpose of the Lord's faithfulness in strengthening the Thessalonians (3.3) to be that they are enabled to obey the author's commands, the author uses an expression of confidence. Olson's investigation of such expressions concludes that they are 'a persuasive technique rather than a sincere reflection of the way the writer thinks the addressees will respond to his proposals or himself'.[92] So the purpose of 3.4a is 'to undergird the letter's requests or admonitions by creating a sense of obligation through praise'.[93] This function of expres-

---

terms (as a thanksgiving) allows an interpreter to claim more detailed correspondences between the section and the arguments which follow.

87. E.g. Trilling, *Untersuchungen*, p. 95.

88. Rigaux, *Thessaloniciens*, p. 693. Rigaux even argues here that 3.3, 4, 5 are not related.

89. Hughes, *Early Christian Rhetoric*, p. 92. Havener (*First Thessalonians, Philemon, Philippians, Second Thessalonians, Colossians, Ephesians*, pp. 62-63), on the other hand, sees these opponents of Paul as fictive.

90. Holland, *The Tradition that You Received*, p. 51. Giblin (*The Threat to Faith*, p. 9) sees all of 3.1-5 to be envisioning hostility to Paul's apostleship.

91. Sumney, 'The Bearing of a Pauline Rhetorical Pattern', pp. 198-99.

92. Stanley N. Olson, 'Pauline Expressions of Confidence in his Addressees', *CBQ* 47 (1985), pp. 282-95 (295).

93. Olson, 'Pauline Expressions of Confidence', p. 289.

sions of confidence supports understanding 3.1-5 as preparation for what follows as well as conclusion for what precedes, that is, it calls for obedience to the tradition about eschatology and obedience to the command to work. Still, the passage yields no new information about the opponents.

2.7-12

I consider the statements in 2.7-12 to be affirmations within the polemical section 2.1-12 because they do not refer directly to the opponents' views. Rather, vv. 7-12 are an exposition and expansion of the apocalyptic scenario given in vv. 3-5.[94] Verses 7-12 continue to interpret the tradition that the Thessalonians already know.[95] These verses also balance the statements in vv. 3-5 about the delay of the parousia until certain events have transpired with the assurance that the process has begun.[96] This balance is necessary to maintain an apocalyptic outlook that can comfort those enduring persecution. Further, this apocalyptic outlook gives the present a positive meaning[97] as the time moving toward the parousia.

Hughes identifies the deluded of 2.11 as the opponents.[98] In a somewhat similar vein, Giblin identifies the κατέχων ('Restrainer') of 2.6 and 7 with someone in the community who is causing problems by engaging in 'pseudo-charismatic activity' like that described in vv. 9-10. Giblin further uses this passage to support his view that false prophecy is the problem at Thessalonica.[99] But even if the Restrainer is an opponent, we cannot use mirror exegesis to attribute the wonder-working of vv. 9-10 to him because there has been no more explicit evidence that such charismatic activity is a problem. In addition, it is not uncommon for an apocalyptic scenario to include false signs and miracles as part of the end time (see e.g. Mt. 24.24; Mk 13.22; Rev. 13.12-14). These activities, then, are probably an element of the apocalyptic outlook being

94. Similarly Trilling, *Untersuchungen*, p. 91. Cf. Roger D. Aus, 'God's Plan and God's Power: Isaiah 66 and the Restraining Factors of 2 Thess 2:6-7', *JBL* (1977), pp. 537-53 (548).

95. Trilling, *Untersuchungen*, pp. 89-90.

96. Marshall, *1 and 2 Thessalonians*, p. 185.

97. So Trilling, *Untersuchungen*, p. 91.

98. Hughes, *Early Christian Rhetoric*, pp. 58, 61.

99. Giblin, *The Threat to Faith*, p. 151.

developed as an alternative eschatology rather than a reflection of specific traits of the teachers of the overrealized eschatology. If vv. 9-12 do refer to the opponents in some way, v. 12 is a warning about the consequences of accepting their views and a polemical evaluation of their morality—they 'delight in unrighteousness'. Still this passage adds nothing to our knowledge of their teaching or behavior because such evaluations in polemical contexts cannot be trusted to reflect accurately an author's knowledge of opponents.

Summary of Affirmations

The affirmations that relate to these opponents confirm that the argument is over the correct interpretation of Paul's teaching. They also indicate that the opponents are the main concern of the letter. Finally, these affirmations strengthen the connection between the aberrant eschatology and the 'disorderly' by drawing matters related to both into single passages.

Conclusion

The evidence of 2 Thessalonians indicates that those viewed as opponents hold an overrealized eschatology (i.e. an eschatology more fully realized than the author's) which has led them to dedicate themselves to some form of ministry (perhaps evangelizing or preaching) and to leave their normal occupations.[100] There is no reason to separate these issues such that two groups are being addressed. Furthermore, there is no evidence to support the view that the 'disorderly' are not a real problem. Those Thessalonians who advocate the more fully realized eschatology do not see themselves as opponents of Paul or his teaching. Rather, they claim that their position is in agreement with Paul's teaching. Second Thessalonians does not specify what these opponents claim to possess as a result of their fuller participation in the New Age. While it is possible that they claim some charismatic or prophetic gift, we cannot assert that this is probable. The main point of contention in this letter is the interpretation of Paul's teaching, particularly his eschatology. The chief manifestation of the opponents' more fully realized eschatology

---

100. As Dibelius (*An die Thessalonicher*, p. 48) notes, there is insufficent evidence to assert that the problem with the disorderly in 2 Thessalonians is the same behavior as that warned against in 1 Thess. 4.11-12.

is their involvement in church affairs and their abandonment of other employment.

We also see that the community is troubled by persecution. There is insufficient evidence to argue that the persecution is particularly severe, only that the Thessalonians are having trouble understanding it. Our author supports his or her eschatological teaching by giving the Thessalonians' tribulations a positive meaning within the apocalyptic schema set out in chs. 1–2. The opponents' more fully realized eschatology may have made the persecution more difficult for the Thessalonians to understand. If so, our author makes the overrealized eschatology, not the persecution, the problem.

We have found no evidence for any libertine tendencies among these opponents. The only aberrant behavior that they display is their leaving of normal occupations. It is conceivable that the opponents are not troubled by persecution as much as others because their withdrawal from normal commerce may have removed them from many occasions in which other Christians faced persecution as they went about their normal lives which included extensive contact with non-Christians. (This is even more likely if the persecution they faced was economic and social.) The absence of persecution, in turn, could have been seen by the opponents and the suffering Thessalonians as evidence that the opponents' views were correct. This interpretation would have increased, perhaps to a crisis level, the difficulty others had understanding their persecution. But speculation about the place of persecution in the opponents' lives takes us beyond the evidence of the text.

Finally, we must see if our findings fit the world of the first century. The opponents of 2 Thessalonians seem to reflect a tendency found particularly among Cynics. Converts to Cynicism were known to leave their former occupations to become proclaimers of their new beliefs. Malherbe cites Lucian's rejection of tradespeople becoming philosophers and Dio's defense of his abandonment of normal occupations as evidence for this practice.[101] Thus there is a contemporary precedent for the type of behavior that the Thessalonian opponents display, but no reason to identify them as Cynics. Those who claim to possess or to have experienced something beyond what other Christians possess or experience would be apt to see themselves as especially well qualified

---

101. Malherbe, *Paul and the Thessalonians*, pp. 100-101.

to engage in activities pertaining to the church. The presence of some of these claimants who abandon normal occupations to devote themselves to work within the Christian community, then, fits quite well with an overrealized, or more fully realized, eschatology.

Chapter 9

THE PASTORAL EPISTLES

For the last 200 years scholars have usually studied the Pastoral Epistles as a group. This approach is contrary to the method being used to
identify the opponents in this study, because this method requires us to
treat letters individually. So our treatment of these writings must begin
with a word about the genre of 1 and 2 Timothy and Titus. Among
others, Trummer and Oberlinner assert that the Pastorals were written
as a corpus and thus there are no separate occasions for the individual
writings.[1] Similarly, Roloff contends that all three Pastoral Epistles were
written at about the same time to address the same historical situation.[2]

Such understandings of the Pastoral Epistles imply that these writings
are not truly letters, an implication recognized by these interpreters.
Roloff speaks of the epistolary form of these writings as the frame into
which smaller *Gattungen* are integrated.[3] And Oberlinner often puts the
word letters (*Briefe*) in quotation marks to signify his judgment about
their literary form.[4] But such judgments about the genre of these writings are based on the presupposition that all three address the same situation and opponents and that they are all three pseudonymous. Both of
these assumptions have been challenged from various perspectives in
recent scholarship.[5] But even if they are all pseudonymous and written

1.   Peter Trummer, 'Corpus Paulinum—Corpus Pastorale: Zur Ortung des
Paulustradition in den Pastoralbriefen', in K. Kertelge (ed.), *Paulus in den neutestamentlichen Spätschriften* (Freiburg: Herder, 1981), pp. 122-45; Lorenz Oberlinner, *Die Pastoralbriefe* (HTKNT, 11/2; Freiburg: Herder, 1994), p. xxvi.
2.   Jürgen Roloff, *Der erste Brief an Timotheus* (EKK, 15; Neukirchen–Vluyn:
Neukirchener Verlag, 1988), p. 43.
3.   Roloff, *Der erste Brief an Timotheus*, p. 48.
4.   See, e.g., Oberlinner, *Die Pastoralbriefe*, pp. xxiv-xxvi.
5.   See, e.g., Luke Timothy Johnson, 'II Timothy and the Polemic Against

as a corpus, they may address different situations and different opponents. In any case, our method does not allow judgments about authorship to intrude into the search for opponents and it requires us to treat
these writings as individual letters.[6] This chapter, then, will be divided
into three major sections, one for each of the Pastoral Epistles.

1 TIMOTHY

Most interpreters, including those who see the Pastorals as three separate letters, identify the opponents of these letters as a single group:
usually Gnostics or proto-gnostics with some relation to or tendency
toward Judaism.[7] Though there are some differences in nuance among
those who hold this view,[8] it is the dominant hypothesis. Spicq, however, finds a unified front of a different sort. He identifies the opponents
of all three Pastoral Epistles as part of a circle of converted Jews who
use rabbinic and hellenistic techniques to interpret the Hebrew Scrip-

False Teachers: A Re-examination', *JRS* 6–7 (1978–79), pp. 1-26; *idem, The Writings of the New Testament* (Philadelphia: Fortress Press, 1986), pp. 384-404 and
Jerome Murphy-O'Connor, '2 Timothy Contrasted with 1 Timothy and Titus', *RB*
98 (1991), pp. 403-18. Peter G. Bush ('A Note on the Structure of 1 Timothy', *NTS*
36 [1990], pp. 152-56 [152]) also notes that it is a methodological mistake to
assume that all three Pastoral Epistles are 'essentially the same'.

6.   Of course, if it becomes clear that these writings are not letters, then the
method being used in this study is not wholly applicable.

7.   So, e.g., Wolfgang Schenk, 'Die Pastoralbriefe in der neueren Forschung',
ANRW II, pp. 3404-38 (3427-30); Günter Haufe, 'Gnostische Irrlehre und ihre
Abwehr in den Pastoralbriefen', in K.-W. Tröger (ed.), *Gnosis und Neues Tes-
tament: Studien aus Religionswissenschaft und Theologie* (Gütersloh: Gerd Mohn,
1973), pp. 325-39; E.F. Scott, *The Pastoral Epistles* (MNTC; New York: Harper &
Brothers, 1936), pp. xxix-xxx; Martin Dibelius and Hans Conzelmann, *The Pas-
toral Epistles* (trans. P. Buttolph and A. Yarbro; Hermeneia; Philadelphia: Fortress
Press, 1972) p. 65; Roloff, *Der erste Brief an Timotheus*, p. 46; Oberlinner, *Die
Pastoralbriefe* p. xxxvii; Norbert Brox, *Die Pastoralbriefe* (RNT 7; Regensburg:
Friedrich Pustet, 1969), pp. 32-33. Along the same line, George W. Knight III (*The
Pastoral Epistles: A Commentary on the Greek Text* [NIGTC; Grand Rapids: Eerd-
mans, 1992], p. 12) sees them as opponents similar to those he finds for Colossians.

8.   E.g. Roloff (*Der erste Brief an Timotheus*, p. 46) asserts that they are not
docetists (while most find them to be docetic) and Haufe ('Gnostische Irrlehre und
ihre Abwehr in den Pastoralbriefen', p. 330) argues that there is no christological
heresy.

tures and who give prominence to the Torah.[9] Even those who maintain
the authenticity of these letters usually identify their opponents by
drawing on all three, apparently assuming they are a corpus rather than
individual writings. But a few interpreters refuse to assume that the
Pastoral Epistles are to be read as a corpus when identifying their opponents or central concerns. Murphy-O'Connor goes so far as to say that,
'Nowhere has the assumption of the unity of the Pastorals been more
pernicious than in treatments of the errors they oppose.'[10] Still, he uses
1 Timothy and Titus together and asserts that both oppose Jewish Christians who keep the dietary laws of Judaism and give speculative, but
non-gnostic, interpretations to the genealogies of Scripture.[11] Using the
same method, Müller identifies the opponents of 1 Timothy and Titus as
a group that keeps the Jewish Law, is ascetic, and includes the author of
Revelation in its circle.[12] Among those who identify the opponents of
1 Timothy without relying on 2 Timothy or Titus, several hypotheses
have emerged. Oden contends that the opponents of 1 Timothy are
proto-gnostics who believe that the material world is evil.[13] McEleney,
on the other hand, finds libertines who disparage the Law.[14] Less specifically, Luke T. Johnson identifies these opponents as ambitious elitists
from within the community.[15] Fee is more specific, arguing that they
are rogue elders of some house churches in Ephesus.[16]

9.   C. Spicq, *Saint Paul: Les épîtres pastorales* (EBib; Paris: Lecoffre, 1947),
pp. lxiv-lxx, 22.

10.   Murphy-O'Connor, '2 Timothy Contrasted with 1 Timothy and Titus',
p. 414.

11.   Murphy-O'Connor, '2 Timothy Contrasted with 1 Timothy and Titus', pp.
415-16.

12.   Ulrich B. Müller, *Zur frühchristlichen Theologiegeschichte* (Gütersloh:
Gerd Mohn, 1976), pp. 61-64.

13.   Thomas C. Oden, *First and Second Timothy and Titus* (*Int*; Louisville, KY:
John Knox Press, 1989), p. 59. Similarly, Dennis R. MacDonald, *The Legend and
the Apostle: The Battle for Paul in Story and Canon* (Philadelphia: Fortress Press,
1983), p. 56; Sharon H. Gritz, *Paul, Women Teachers, and the Mother Goddess at
Ephesus* (Lanham, MD: University Press of America, 1991), pp. 115-16.

14.   Neil J. McEleney, 'Vice Lists of the Pastoral Epistles', *CBQ* 36 (1974), pp.
203-19 (205-210).

15.   Johnson, *The Writings of the New Testament*, p. 397.

16.   Gordon Fee, *1 and 2 Timothy, Titus* (NIBC; Peabody, MA: Hendrickson,
rev. edn, 1988), pp. 7-8. Fee draws on both 1 and 2 Timothy to identify these elders'
teachings as ascetic, related to the Law, and possessing an overrealized eschatology.

Explicit Statements

1.3-4, 6-7

The opening paragraph of the body of 1 Timothy contains some explicit statements about opponents. Roloff identifies 1.1-20 as the *exordium*, which introduces the themes of the work.[17] Most interpreters, however, begin the section at v. 3, after the greeting.[18] Within the larger section, vv. 3-11 form a sub-section that directly concerns false teachers.[19] This unmistakably polemical warning against the opponents[20] serves as the background for the whole letter.[21] Since the opponents appear in the beginning and theme-setting portion of this letter and since they are handled in such polemical fashion, we may conclude that the author sees them as a serious problem.

Verse 3 states that Timothy's mission in Ephesus is to command some not to teach different things, presumably different from the teachings of Paul. These different teachings are identified in v. 4 as 'myths' and 'endless genealogies' which produce controversies. Many interpreters identify these myths and genealogies with gnostic speculation about the aeons based on Scripture, especially Genesis.[22] Others understand them

17. Roloff, *Der erste Brief an Timotheus*, pp. 50, 60.

18. E.g. Oberlinner, *Die Pastoralbriefe*, p. 8; Johnson, '2 Timothy and the Polemic Against False Teachers', p. 24; Brox, *Die Pastoralbriefe*, p. 13; Walter Lock, *A Critical and Exegetical Commentary on the Pastoral Epistles* (ICC; New York: Charles Scribner's Sons, 1924), p. 67; Benjamin Fiore, *The Function of Personal Example in the Socratic and Pastoral Epistles* (AnBib, 105; Rome: Biblical Institute Press, 1986), p. 22.

19. So Johnson, '2 Timothy and the Polemic Against False Teachers', p. 23; Bush, 'A Note on the Structure of 1 Timothy', p. 156; Robert J. Karris, 'The Background and Significance of the Polemic of the Pastoral Epistles', *JBL* 92 (1973), pp. 549-64 (551 n. 9); Spicq, *Les épîtres pastorales*, p. 19; MacDonald, *The Legend and the Apostle*, p. 56; Dibelius and Conzelmann, *The Pastoral Epistles*, p. 65; A.T. Hanson, *The Pastoral Epistles* (NCB; Grand Rapids: Eerdmans, 1982), p. 23.

20. So Karris, 'The Background and Significance of the Polemic of the Pastoral Epistles', p. 551 n. 9; MacDonald, *The Legend and the Apostle*, p. 56; Roloff, *Der erste Brief an Timotheus*, p. 60; Oberlinner, *Die Pastoralbriefe*, pp. 8-9.

21. See Bush, 'A Note on the Structure of 1 Timothy', p. 156; Lewis R. Donelson, *Pseudepigraphy and Ethical Argument in the Pastoral Epistles* (HUT, 22; Tübingen: J.C.B. Mohr [Paul Siebeck], 1986), p. 116; Roloff, *Der erste Brief an Timotheus*, p. 63.

22. E.g. Haufe, 'Gnostische Irrlehre und ihre Abwehr in den Pastoralbriefen',

to be some type of Jewish Haggadah.[23] Given the following verses, which deal with the Law, it seems likely that these myths and genealogies do refer to interpretations of the Hebrew Bible. But anything more specific than this goes beyond the evidence because of the polemical nature of both this passage as a whole and the specific language used to label their interpretations.

Calling these opponents' teachings 'myths' is a polemical move. Not only is the term myth too vague to identify with any particular ideology or type of exegesis,[24] but it is also a stock polemical characterization of the teaching of one's opponents.[25] In contemporary polemical use, designating one's opponents' teachings a myth was a polemical charge. It identified a teaching as a false or foolish story/narrative[26] or as a tale 'only the gullible believe'.[27] The point of calling their teaching myths here is not to accurately describe the opponents' teaching, but to denigrate them and create an unfavorable impression about them before saying anything specific. Another polemical move against this teaching in v. 4 is the contrast between its production of controversies (i.e. its disruption of the community) and the οἰκονομίαν (stewardship or plan) of God. In the end, all that vv. 3-4 certainly reveal about the opponents' teaching is that the author of 1 Timothy rejects it.

After contrasting the controversy-mongering of the false teachers with the pure motives of Paul's command that they desist from their speculations (v. 5), 1.6-7 returns to a polemical description of the false

pp. 329, 337; Dibelius and Conzelmann, *The Pastoral Epistles*, pp. 16-18; Roloff, *Der erste Brief an Timotheus*, p. 64; Brox, *Die Pastoralbriefe*, p. 102.

23. Spicq, *Les épîtres pastorales*, pp. 20-21; Lock, *Pastoral Epistles*, pp. xvii, 8-9; Oberlinner, *Die Pastoralbriefe*, p. 13. Müller (*Zur frühchristlichen Theologiegeschichte*, p. 59) asserts that they are allegorical interpretations of the Hebrew Bible, but without aeon speculation. Philip H. Towner (*The Goal of our Instruction: The Structure of Theology and Ethics in the Pastoral Epistles* (JSNTSup, 34; Sheffield: JSOT Press, 1989], p. 28) is yet more specific, contending that this speculative exegesis is produced to support marriage and food prohibitions.

24. Murphy-O'Connor, '2 Timothy Contrasted with 1 Timothy and Titus', p. 415.

25. Karris, 'The Background and Significance of the Polemic of the Pastoral Epistles', p. 557; Fiore, *The Function of Personal Example*, p. 199 n. 18.

26. Schenk, 'Die Pastoralbriefe in der Neueren Forschung', p. 3430; Brox, *Die Pastoralbriefe*, p. 103.

27. Knight, *The Pastoral Epistles*, p. 73.

teachers.[28] In these verses, the author says they have turned away into useless discussions (ματαιολογίαν) and want to be teachers of the Law, even though they possess no proper understanding of the things about which they speak so confidently. Calling their inquiries useless discussions or vain words is another polemical evaluation. Commenting that they have 'turned away' to these discussions probably indicates that these teachers are Christians who once agreed with the author's views, but now challenge them.

The characterization of these teachers as those who want to be teachers of the law (v. 7)[29] is without parallel in stock polemical charges. This shows that these opponents are interested in interpreting and applying the Law[30] within the Christian community. Their approach, however, is rejected by 1 Timothy. Hanson[31] goes far beyond the available evidence when he asserts that calling these opponents teachers of the Law shows that they use names from the Hebrew Bible for Gnostic aeons. Similarly, when Dibelius and Conzelmann assert that 1.7 is evidence of an interweaving of speculative and ascetic practices derived from the Bible,[32] they have exceeded the evidence. At this early point in our investigation, we cannot specify what their interpretations entail, though other passages may clarify this point. The charge that they do not understand the things they teach is another stock polemical accusation.[33]

Thus, these first explicit statements about false teachers show that they are Christians who interpret and use the Law in ways that 1 Timothy finds unacceptable. Given the mention of the Law in v. 7, it seems probable that the myths and genealogies of v. 4 are related to interpreting the Hebrew Bible.

28. Cf. Brox, *Die Pastoralbriefe*, p. 104; Oberlinner, *Die Pastoralbriefe*, p. 19.

29. Lock (*Pastoral Epistles*, p. 8) suggests that the ἑτεροδιδασκεῖν ('to teach something different') of v. 3 is a parody of νομοδιδάσκαλοι ('teachers of the Law') here.

30. Given the following discussion of the Law in vv. 8-11, Schenk's ('Die Pastoralbriefe in der Neueren Forschung', p. 3429) assertion that νόμος does not necessarily refer to the Hebrew Bible seems unlikely.

31. Hanson, *The Pastoral Epistles*, p. 58.

32. Dibelius and Conzelmann, *The Pastoral Epistles*, p. 21.

33. Fiore, *The Function of Personal Example*, p. 3 n. 5.

4.1-3

Interpreters generally agree that 4.1-5 constitutes a section that directly addresses the opponents. When the section is conceived of as larger, its expansion through v. 10[34] or v. 11[35] is intended to include the contrast between Timothy's teaching and that of the opponents. While the larger section within which 4.1-5 is embedded is understood differently, it is agreed that vv. 1-5 are a polemic against and a warning about the false teachers.[36]

In 4.1 First Timothy identifies these teachers as the eschatological enemies of God, who follow deceiving spirits and teachings of demons. This polemical description draws on a traditional topos of apocalyptic writings[37] and thus reveals nothing specific about the opponents. First Timothy's comment that they have turned from the faith confirms that they are from within the Christian community. Lock's conjecture that 'deceitful spirits' points to a pagan source for the opponents' teaching[38] misses both the disparaging purpose of these verses and the fact that this charge is borrowed from Jewish tradition.[39] This characterization intends to force the readers to dissociate themselves from the opponents' teaching.[40] Verse 2 continues this tack by describing their teaching as hypocritical false words and by characterizing their conscience as seared. Such accusations about motives are standard motifs of early Christian polemic against heresy.[41]

---

34. Donelson, *Pseudepigraphy and Ethical Argument*, p. 182.

35. Brox, *Die Pastoralbriefe*, pp. 13, 164; Oberlinner, *Die Pastoralbriefe*, p. 171.

36. So e.g. Karris, 'The Background and Significance of the Polemic of the Pastoral Epistles', p. 551 n. 9; Spicq, *Les épîtres pastorales*, p. 135; MacDonald, *The Legend and the Apostle*, p. 56; Lock, *Pastoral Epistles*, p. 46; Hanson, *The Pastoral Epistles*, p. 86; Oberlinner, *Die Pastoralbriefe*, p. 172; Roloff, *Der erste Brief an Timotheus*, pp. 218-34.

37. Roloff, *Der erste Brief an Timotheus*, pp. 218-19.

38. Lock, *Pastoral Epistles*, p. 47.

39. Karris, 'The Background and Significance of the Polemic of the Pastoral Epistles', pp. 557-58. See the comments of Andrie DuToit, 'Vilification as a Pragmatic Device in Early Christian Epistolography', *Bib* 75 (1994), pp. 403-12.

40. See DuToit, 'Vilification as a Pragmatic Device in Early Christian Epistolography', p. 412.

41. Roloff, *Der erste Brief an Timotheus*, p. 221; Brox, *Die Pastoralbriefe*, p. 166. Cf. Haufe, 'Gnostische Irrlehre und ihre Abwehr in den Pastoralbriefen', p. 336.

At 4.3, two specific teachings are attributed to the opponents: they forbid marriage and they abstain from certain foods. Fiore notes that charges of false asceticism belong to stock descriptions of opponents,[42] but in this case the specific nature of the teachings indicates that these are the author's interpretations of actual teachings. It is often claimed that these teachings are rooted in a world-denying outlook and an asceticism that either leads into or is a part of Gnosticism.[43] This understanding of the regulations on marriage and food rests almost solely on a mirror reading of 4.3b-5 where 1 Timothy asserts the goodness of the world. Such mirror reading is an inadequate basis for such a claim about these opponents. 1 Timothy responds to the opponents' prohibitions in 4.3b-5 but does not necessarily contain the mirror image of their views. This is especially true if these verses draw on traditional material.[44]

What we can say about these food regulations is, as most interpreters acknowledge, that they probably come from Jewish food laws. The attachment these teachers have to the Law (1.6-7) makes this origin for food regulations quite secure. A problem with Christians observing the Mosaic food laws cannot be excluded as a possibility by asserting that this issue had already been settled by the time of the Pastorals.[45] The presence of Ebionites through and beyond the second and third centuries and their mention in the heresiologists show that the matter of the Law and its dietary regulations continued to be debated in circles of both Jewish and Gentile Christians.[46] Some interpreters give βρῶμα its most specific meaning, meat, here and thus identify these opponents as vege-

---

42. Fiore, *The Function of Personal Example*, p. 3 n. 5.

43. E.g. Oberlinner, *Die Pastoralbriefe*, pp. 179-80; J.N.D. Kelly, *A Commentary on the Pastoral Epistles* (BNTC; London: A. & C. Black, 1963), pp. 95-96; Towner, *The Goal of our Instruction*, pp. 36-37; Müller, *Zur frühchristlichen Theologiegeschichte*, p. 65; Schenk, 'Die Pastoralbriefe in der Neueren Forschung', p. 3429; Haufe, 'Gnostische Irrlehre und ihre Abwehr in den Pastoralbriefen', pp. 330-31; Brox, *Die Pastoralbriefe*, p. 167; Roloff, *Der erste Brief an Timotheus*, p. 223; Spicq, *Les épîtres pastorales*, p. 137.

44. Both A.T. Hanson (*Studies in the Pastoral Epistles* [London: SPCK, 1968], pp. 104-108), and E.E. Ellis ('Traditions in the Pastoral Epistles', in C.A. Evans and W.F. Stinespring [eds.], *Early Jewish and Christian Exegesis* [Atlanta: Scholars Press, 1987], pp. 237-53 [238, 243]), find traditional material in these verses.

45. Towner, (*The Goal of our Instruction*, p. 36), makes this argument.

46. Both Origen *Contra Celsum* 5.60-66 and Justin *Dialogue with Trypho* 47 know of Ebionites who require Gentiles to observe the Mosaic Law.

tarians. Haufe sees a gnostic revolt as the basis for their vegetarian diet,[47] while Lane argues that their realized eschatology has led them to eat only what the resurrected Jesus ate—fish and honeycomb.[48] Again, these conjectures are based on unsubstantiated presuppositions about these opponents' theology. Thus, the probable explanation of the food regulations, based on what we know from 1.6-7, is that the opponents advocate adherence to some food laws from Judaism.

The marriage prohibition is not clearly derivable from interpretation of the Law. This prohibition is usually also understood as evidence that the opponents' world-rejecting outlook has produced an ascetic lifestyle. However, some interpreters ground the marriage prohibition on a realized eschatology that viewed marriage as inappropriate to the new age.[49] Presupposing neither gnosticism nor a realized eschatology, Lock locates the origin of this command in the teachings of the Essenes.[50] This has the advantage of not imposing unfounded presuppositions about Gnostics or a rejection of the world upon the text, but to this point we have no evidence that Essene thought influenced these opponents either. Still, the Essenes' marriage regulations demonstrate that an origin for this teaching based on interpreting the Law is possible.

MacDonald and Verner argue that these ascetic regulations are derived from the image of Paul found in some apocryphal writings. The 'Paul' of these writings encourages sexual asceticism and food prohibitions. According to MacDonald and Verner, this tradition also connected celibacy and the gift of prophecy and supported the emancipation of women, a tendency which these interpreters find opposed throughout the Pastorals.[51] To this point, we have no evidence that establishes such an origin for these opponents' teachings. Alternatively, Roloff suggests that the marriage command came from the Jesus tradition (see Mt. 19.12) and has an eschatological motivation. According to Roloff, such marriage prohibitions were known among the wandering charismatic

47. Haufe, 'Gnostische Irrlehre und ihre Abwehr in den Pastoralbriefen', p. 331. Cf. Knight, *The Pastoral Epistles*, p. 190.

48. William L. Lane, '1 Tim. IV.1-3. An Early Instance of Over-realized Eschatology?', *NTS* 11 (1965), pp. 164-67 (165-66).

49. Lane, 'An Early Instance of Over-realized Eschatology?', pp. 165-66; Towner, *The Goal of our Instruction*, pp. 37-38.

50. Lock, *Pastoral Epistles*, p. 47.

51. David C. Verner, *The Household of God: The Social World of the Pastoral Epistles* (SBLDS, 71; Chico, CA: Scholars Press, 1983), p. 178; MacDonald, *The Legend and the Apostle*, pp. 56-58.

preachers of Syria and Palestine, and these preachers were probably known in Ephesus because such teaching is present in Revelation (e.g. 14.4). Additionally, Paul was a celibate.[52] Roloff acknowledges that there is no evidence here that the marriage prohibition is grounded in a rejection of the world, yet he identifies that view as its basis because he has already identified the opponents as Gnostics.[53] A proscription against marriage could also be related to the expectation of an imminent parousia, drawing on Paul's advice in 1 Corinthians 7. Thus, given all the possible sources for such regulations,[54] we cannot assume that the opponents' marriage regulations rest on some world-denying outlook. On the basis of the evidence accumulated so far, we cannot specify the origin of this regulation without relying on insufficiently grounded speculation.

From 4.1-3 we have gleaned that these opponents advocate adhering to food regulations that probably come from the food laws of Judaism. These false teachers also advocate some regulations about marriage which 1 Timothy characterizes as a complete prohibition. In such a polemical context, we cannot take this description of their teaching as an accurate representation of what they understand themselves to teach. Nothing indicates whether these marriage regulations were intended for all adherents to their message or only some particular group (as it was among the Essenes and the wandering charismatics). After all, 1 Timothy itself imposes a marriage prohibition on 'widows'. So 1 Timothy's criticism could simply be that the opponents' marriage regulations were for the wrong or too wide a group. As 1 Timothy's own celibacy regulation for widows shows, such rules need not be based on a world-denigrating ideology.

6.20-21

The section 6.20-21 seems to constitute a separate concluding section of 1 Timothy,[55] which sums up the content of the letter by returning to

52. Roloff, *Der erste Brief an Timotheus*, p. 222.

53. Roloff, *Der erste Brief an Timotheus*, pp. 222-23.

54. The two explanations that seem most likely are that these regulations rest on Jesus traditions something like those traditions used by the Syrio-Palestinian wandering charismatics and that they are derived from an interpretation of 1 Cor. 7.

55. Those who make these verses a separate section include Spicq, *Les Epîstles Pastorales*, p. 214; Donelson, *Pseudepigraphy and Ethical Argument*, p. 163;

two central themes: holding to the Pauline teaching and rejecting the false teachers.[56] Donelson identifies v. 20 as the letter's *peroratio*,[57] while Roloff sees it as a *recapitulatio*.[58] But both understand its function to be summarizing the letter's content. As the letter began with a polemical characterization of these opponents, so it ends.[59] These verses contrast what has been passed on to Timothy with the profane, vain disputes and arguments about what is 'falsely called knowledge', teaching which has caused some to go astray.

Calling their teaching profane chatter is clearly a polemical evaluation from which we can say nothing about their views. Some earlier interpreters connected the descriptive term, 'contradictions/oppositions' (ἀντιθέσεις) with Marcion's work entitled *Antitheses*, and so identified the opponents as Marcionites. But the recognition by Colson that this term was used in rhetoric for an element of argumentation[60] has helped convince more recent readers that this is an accusation about their teaching, not a reference to Marcion's work.[61]

The part of v. 20 used most often to identify opponents is the expression, 'falsely called knowledge'. Several interpreters assert that this verse shows the opponents use the term 'gnosis' for their teaching.[62] While this is not certain,[63] it is possible and perhaps probable. Many interpreters contend that this use of the term gnosis provides convincing

Roloff, *Der erste Brief an Timotheus*, pp. 328, 371; Oberlinner, *Die Pastoralbriefe* p. 308. Brox (*Die Pastoralbrief*, p. 13) sees vv. 20-21 as a sub-section of 6.3-21.

56. So e.g. Oberlinner, *Die Pastoralbriefe*, p. 308. Cf. Ellis, 'Traditions in the Pastoral Epistles', p. 244.

57. Donelson, *Pseudepigraphy and Ethical Argument*, p. 163.

58. Roloff, *Der erste Brief an Timotheus*, pp. 328, 371.

59. Karris ('The Background and Significance of the Polemic of the Pastoral Epistles', p. 551 n. 9) identifies 6.20-21 as polemical. Cf. MacDonald, *The Legend and the Apostle*, p. 56.

60. F.H. Colson, '"Myths and Genealogies": A Note on the Polemic of the Pastoral Epistles', *JTS* 19 (1918), pp. 265-71 (268-69). Also, Karris, 'The Background and Significance of the Polemic of the Pastoral Epistles', p. 559; Spicq, *Les épîtres pastorales*, p. 215.

61. See, e.g., Kelly, *Pastoral Epistles*, p. 151; Hanson, *The Pastoral Epistles*, p. 116. Lock (*Pastoral Epistles*, p. 76) identifies the antitheses as the contrasts used in rabbinic interpretation of the Hebrew Bible.

62. So Roloff, *Der erste Brief an Timotheus*, p. 374; Towner, *The Goal of our Instruction*, p. 29; Dibelius and Conzelmann, *The Pastoral Epistles*, p. 92.

63. Scott (*The Pastoral Epistles*, p. xxx) rightly calls this expression 'ridiculing invective'.

evidence that the opponents are Gnostics.[64] Even if the opponents use
the term gnosis to describe their teaching, this is not clear evidence that
they are Gnostic. The word *gnosis* was a widely used term which could
be applied to nearly any body of religious teaching, and was applied to
many. As Spicq has commented, even Christianity was a gnosis in this
period.[65] Thus, the opponents' possible use of this word reveals nothing
about the content of their teaching.

These verses, then, yield no information about the opponents' teaching, they simply demonstrate that the author of 1 Timothy rejects it.
The presence of such a polemical section at the conclusion, as well as
the opening, demonstrates that the author views these teachers as a real
and dangerous threat. It also reinforces the impression that opposition
to this teaching is a central purpose of 1 Timothy.

6.3-5
The section that begins at 6.3 contains several exhortations. This section may extend through v. 21 so that it serves as the conclusion[66] or
peroratio of the letter. Roloff hears echoes of 1.1-20 (what he identifies
as the *proem*) in 6.3-21. For him, this confirms the latter's function as
the conclusion of the argument of the letter.[67] Those who find the section to be 6.3-21 see 6.3-10 as a sub-section. Others, however, identify
6.3-10 as a separate section.[68] It seems more probable that vv. 3-10 are
closely connected to vv. 11-21 because vv. 11-21 explicitly contrast the
man of God with those discussed in vv. 9-10. Within 6.3-10, at least
vv. 3-5 are polemic against the opponents[69] and perhaps the whole sub-

64. So Scott, *The Pastoral Epistles*, p. 83; Dibelius and Conzelmann, *The Pastoral Epistles*, p. 92; Arland J. Hultgren, *I–II Timothy, Titus* (Augsburg Commentary on the New Testament; Minneapolis: Augsburg, 1984), p. 102; Brox, *Die
Pastoralbriefe*, p. 35; Kelly, *Pastoral Epistles*, p. 150. Towner (*The Goal of our
Instruction*, pp. 29-30), however, finds a reference to realized eschatology here.

65. Spicq, *Les épîtres pastorales*, p. 216.

66. So Brox, *Die Pastoralbriefe*, p. 13; Lock, *Pastoral Epistles*, p. 4; Oberlinner, *Die Pastoralbriefe*, p. 269.

67. Roloff, *Der erste Brief an Timotheus*, pp. 49, 269.

68. Knight, *The Pastoral Epistles*, p. 249. Fee, *1 and 2 Timothy, Titus*, p. 140.
But Fee begins the section with 6.2b.

69. Dibelius and Conzelmann, *The Pastoral Epistles*, p. 65; Hanson, *The Pastoral Epistles*, p. 106; Brox, *Die Pastoralbriefe*, p. 208; Karris, 'The Background
and Significance of the Polemic of the Pastoral Epistles', p. 551 n. 9.

section should be seen as polemical.[70] Though, if it is, vv. 6-10 are much less directly polemical.

In 6.3-5 we find primarily vilification of those who advocate views contrary to those of the author.[71] Roloff's identification of these verses as an *indignatio*[72] supports this understanding. Karris notes that the polemic here is closely parallel to that used by philosophers against Sophists. Thus, it is impossible to infer anything about the opponents' teaching or conduct from 6.3-5.[73] It is important to observe that these verses focus on the opponents' motivation and character,[74] not on the content of their teaching. Such polemical accusations are intended to make these teachers unacceptable.[75] This passage exemplifies the connection 1 Timothy makes between proper teaching and the conduct of one's life. Those who hold 'different teachings' (v. 3) can be assumed, in this polemical discourse, to be immoral.

In v. 4, these opponents are charged with engaging in disputes. Rather than trying to identify these disputes as a particular kind of teaching,[76] it is best to recognize this characterization as a polemical accusation.[77]

Among other accusations about these teachers, they are charged with thinking of piety as a means to profit (v. 5). Some interpreters see this as evidence that these opponents receive pay for their teaching.[78] However, Karris asserts that the charge of greed is one of the polemical

70. So Roloff, *Der erste Brief an Timotheus*, p. 329; MacDonald, *The Legend and the Apostle*, p. 56; Oberlinner, *Die Pastoralbriefe*, p. 271; Lock, *Pastoral Epistles*, p. 4.

71. So McEleney, 'Vice Lists of the Pastoral Epistles', p. 216.

72. Roloff, *Der erste Brief an Timotheus*, pp. 326-27.

73. Karris, 'The Background and Significance of the Polemic of the Pastoral Epistles', p. 558. Fiore (*The Function of Personal Example*, p. 3 n. 5) also finds the comments about the opponents' immoral character to be stock polemical characterizations. Cf. Hanson, *The Pastoral Epistles*, p. 106.

74. As Roloff (*Der erste Brief an Timotheus*, pp. 326-27) observes.

75. Brox, *Die Pastoralbriefe*, p. 208. Johnson ('2 Timothy and the Polemic Against False Teachers', p. 24) comments that 6.2-16 is detailed slander of the opponents.

76. As Haufe does ('Gnostische Irrlehre und ihre Abwehr in den Pastoralbriefen', p. 329).

77. Karris ('The Background and Significance of the Polemic of the Pastoral Epistles', p. 553) identifies this charge as one used by philosophers against Sophists.

78. So, e.g., Kelly, *Pastoral Epistles*, p. 135. Hanson (*The Pastoral Epistles*, p. 107) sees this as possible.

topoi used by philosophers against Sophists.[79] Dibelius and Conzelmann recognize this schema but still suggest that the opponents receive
support.[80] Oberlinner argues that the point of this charge is not that they
accept pay, but that their actions are not in the service of truth.[81] We
must leave open the possibility that they accepted maintenance from
their adherents, but given the highly charged polemical atmosphere of
vv. 3-5, evidence beyond an inference from this accusation will be
needed to support this view before we accept it as probable.

Thus, 6.3-5 yields no new evidence about the opponents except the
possibility that they accept pay from their converts.

1.19b-20

A final possible explicit statement appears in 1.19b-20 where the author
writes of Hymenaeus and Alexander, Christians who have deviated
from the accepted teachings and as a result have been dealt some severe
ecclesiastical penalty; they have been 'turned over to Satan'. Verses 18-
20 constitute the last sub-section within the larger section of 1.3-20.
Verses 18-20 are best described as hortatory because they exhort Timothy to hold to Pauline teaching.[82] As is common in 1 Timothy, part of
the strategy of the exhortation is to supply contrasts—we have already
seen this technique used in 4.1-11. Hymenaeus and Alexander serve as
the negative part of this contrast: they have failed to do what the author
calls Timothy to do.

Hymenaeus and Alexander, v. 19 asserts, shipwrecked their faith because they rejected conscience. This is, again, a polemical evaluation
which gives a less than honorable motive for their departure from the
accepted teaching. Perhaps they are to be seen as examples of how
Timothy and his community are to deal with false teachers.[83] Donelson
seems to have clearly understood their function here. He contends that
1.19b-20 gives Paul's life as a paradigm which Timothy may expect to

---

79. Karris, 'The Background and Significance of the Polemic of the Pastoral
Epistles', p. 552.

80. Dibelius and Conzelmann, *The Pastoral Epistles*, p. 83. This conclusion is
based in part on Tit. 1.11. Without relying on Titus, Fee (*1 and 2 Timothy, Titus*,
p. 142) reaches a similar conclusion.

81. Oberlinner, *Die Pastoralbriefe*, p. 276.

82. Oberlinner (*Die Pastoralbriefe*, p. 50) and perhaps Roloff (*Der erste Brief
an Timotheus*, p. 50) understand the section as hortatory.

83. So Roloff, *Der erste Brief an Timotheus*, pp. 105-106.

be repeated. Thus, whatever Paul says about Hymenaeus and Alexander may be transferred to Timothy's opponents.[84] It is difficult to determine whether Hymenaeus and Alexander are among those opposed in 1 Timothy.[85] But whatever we decide about this question, these men serve as a pattern for false teachers and thus their bad conscience is a rebuke of the opponents of 1 Timothy. Hymenaeus and Alexander are probably people known to the Pauline communities who are notorious for having a disagreement with Paul which ended with Paul publicly rejecting them.[86] If these two whom Paul rejected are members of the group 1 Timothy opposes, then vv. 19-20 confirm that 1 Timothy's opponents come from within the Christian community.

We cannot, however, be certain that Hymenaeus and Alexander are among the opponents of 1 Timothy. If they are not, then 1.19b-20 contains only an allusion rather than an explicit statement about the current opponents. But even if they belong among the opponents of this letter, these verses reveal no new information about their teaching.

Summary of Explicit Statements
Explicit statements about opponents in 1 Timothy indicate that these people were members of the Christian community who propagate teachings 1 Timothy rejects. The teachings of these opponents include a call to observe the Law in ways that the author of 1 Timothy finds unacceptable for his community. Among the Mosaic laws that they believe Christians should observe are at least some of the food laws. These opponents also advocate some type of marriage regulations that are different from those 1 Timothy accepts. Thus, the author of 1 Timothy characterizes their teaching as a prohibition on marriage. In this way he identifies them as the prophesied false teachers of the last days. We also saw that it is possible, though not probable, that these opponents accept maintenance from their adherents. Finally, the amount of space devoted to them, the mention of them in both the opening and closing sections of the letter, and the level of polemic against them, all indicate that the author perceives these opponents as a genuine threat to his church(es).

84. Cf. Donelson, *Pseudepigraphy and Ethical Argument*, pp. 101-103.
85. Schenk ('Die Pastoralbriefe in der neueren Forschung', p. 3427) thinks they are.
86. This is the case whether 1 Timothy is authentic or pseudonymous. See the comments of Roloff (*Der erste Brief an Timotheus*, p. 105) and Hultgren (*I–II Timothy, Titus*, p. 62).

We have seen no evidence that these opponents are Gnostics or proto-gnostics. Neither have we found sufficient reason to designate their views as world-denying or even generally ascetic.

Allusions

1.8-11

We have already identified 1.3-11 as a polemical section.[87] Verses 8-11 can be identified as an allusion because they take up discussion of the Law after 1.6-7 says that these opponents want to be teachers of the Law. The paragraph that begins with v. 8 affirms the value of the Law when it is understood correctly. This implies that correct interpretation of the Law is at issue.

The vice list in vv. 9-10 may not be used to characterize the opponents[88] because it utilizes a traditional topos and has a polemical purpose.[89] Not only is the vice list itself a traditional form, but this vice list probably draws some of its content from the Decalogue.[90] If this is correct, its content is partially determined by the text on which it is based. An equally significant reason for not using the list's details as evidence about the opponents' behavior or teaching is that its purpose is to slander them and their teaching.[91] As Donelson observes, these

---

87. Hultgren (*I–II Timothy, Titus*, p. 56) identifies 1.8-10 as a defense of the Law and Roloff (*Der erste Brief an Timotheus*, p. 61) sees these verses as an attempt to avoid any misunderstanding of Paul's critique of the Law. But when v. 9 introduces the vice list by saying that that Law is needed because of the unrighteous, we see that 1 Timothy is still on the attack.

88. So e.g. Brox, *Die Pastoralbriefe*, p. 106; Lucinda A. Brown, 'Asceticism and Ideology: The Language of Power in the Pastoral Epistles', *Semeia* 57 (1992), p. 81.

89. See especially the comments of Brown, 'Asceticism and Ideology', pp. 77-94 (81-82). See also Murphy-O'Connor, '2 Timothy Contrasted with 1 Timothy and Titus', p. 410.

90. So Frances Young, *The Theology of the Pastoral Letters* (New Testament Theology; Cambridge: Cambridge University Press, 1994), pp. 25-26; McEleney, 'Vice Lists of the Pastoral Epistles', p. 204; Ellis, 'Traditions in the Pastoral Epistles', pp. 242-43; Hultgren, *I–II Timothy, Titus*, p. 57; Scott, *The Pastoral Epistles*, p. 10.

91. Karris, 'The Background and Significance of the Polemic of the Pastoral Epistles', pp. 553-54; Brox, *Die Pastoralbriefe*, p. 106; Oberlinner, *Die Pastoralbriefe*, p. 23.

verses intend to give the label 'vice' to everything that is not Pauline.[92] Thus, the opponents' teaching is rejected as vice because they do not interpret the Law as 1 Timothy thinks they should.[93]

Finally, v. 11 asserts that the opponents' teaching of the Law is not in accord with the Gospel. Again, all we can draw from this accusation is that 1 Timothy rejects their understanding of the Law. The closing words of v. 11 also assert Paul's commission to apostleship, a theme expanded in vv. 12-17. The mention of Paul's apostolic commission serves to give authority to 1 Timothy's interpretation of the Law.

Thus, 1.8-11 confirms that the Law's interpretation and use are central points of difference between the opponents and 1 Timothy. This passage also raises the issue of Paul's apostleship. However, his apostolic status is not defended, but rather used as evidence that 1 Timothy's views are correct. So, the mention of Paul's commission in 1.11 does not indicate that his apostleship is under attack.

4.4, 7-8

Within the polemical section 4.1-5, v. 4 alludes to the opponents' regulations about food. First Timothy rejects these directly in v. 3 and then supports that rejection in 4.4, where the text proclaims that everything created by God is good and not to be rejected if it is received with thanksgiving. This affirmation of the goodness of creation is not sufficient evidence to claim that the opponents have a world-denying outlook. Nothing in this passage or in other data in 1 Timothy allow a mirror reading of v. 4 that assigns such a view to these opponents. Rather, vv. 3b-4 constitute an argument against their food prohibitions. This is an instance of 1 Timothy developing a theological argument against his opponents. So, v. 4 contributes no new information about them.

An allusion appears in 4.7-8 within a sub-section of 4.1-10(11). Verses 6-10(11) give instructions to Timothy about how to be a good minister in the face of the threat from the opponents. These instructions,

92. Donelson, *Pseudepigraphy and Ethical Argument*, p. 166. I see no evidence that these verses indicate that these opponents disparage the Law, as McEleney ('Vice Lists of the Pastoral Epistles', p. 205) contends. Rather, they are teachers of the Law whose application of the Law must be countered.

93. Both Johnson (*Writings of the New Testament*, p. 384) and Haufe ('Gnostische Irrlehre und ihre Abwehr in den Pastoralbriefen', p. 336) see this passage as one in which 1 Timothy is making a theological point.

on the heels of the polemic of vv. 1-5, seem apologetic rather than straightforwardly hortatory. They are given as the way to defend the truth and the community[94] against the false teachers.

In 4.7-8 Timothy is told to avoid the profane myths that are characteristically told by old women, and to seek piety, which is given as the opposite of pursuing these myths.[95] I identify 4.7-8 as an allusion to the opponents because it refers to profane myths, which they were accused of propagating in 1.3-4, 6-7 and because this exhortation follows the description of their teaching in 4.1-3.[96] First Timothy's description of the opponents' teachings as 'old-wives myths' in 4.7 has led a number of interpreters to use the term 'myth' to identify the opponents' teaching in some particular way: Brox thinks it refers to Gnostic myths;[97] Lock asserts that it refers to Jewish haggadah;[98] similarly, Müller argues that it refers to allegorical interpretations of the Hebrew Bible.[99] But such uses of the term myth, as we noted in connection with 1.3-4, ignore its function in polemical discourse. Here, in 4.7, its use as a derogatory term is especially clear because it is modified by γραώδεις (old women) so that its meaning is something like 'old-wives' tales' or myths told by old women. This and similar epithets were not uncommon in the polemic of philosophers of the period.[100] Thus, as Roloff

---

94. Cp. Spicq, *Les épîtres pastorales*, p. 135; Roloff, *Der erste Briefe an Timotheus*, p. 240. Karris ('The Background and Significance of the Polemic of the Pastoral Epistles', p. 551, n. 9) identifies 4.1-7 as polemical. However, Spicq *(Les Epîtres Pastorales*, p. 140) also identifies 4.6-16 as a section of personal exhortation for Timothy. It seems quite unlikely that Kelly (*Pastoral Epistles*, p. 98) is correct that there is no effort to renounce or refute the opponents in 4.6-16.

95. Brox (*Die Pastoralbriefe*, pp. 171-72) says that the point of 4.8 is that whoever believes and lives thus, is not threatened by the heresy.

96. MacDonald (*The Legend and the Apostle*, p. 114 n. 14) asserts that 4.7-8 directly refutes the opponents.

97. Brox, *Die Pastoralbriefe*, p. 35.

98. Lock, *Pastoral Epistles*, p. xvii.

99. Müller, *Zur frühchristlichen Theologiegeschichte*, p. 59.

100. See Hanson, *The Pastoral Epistles*, p. 90; Spicq, *Les épîtres pastorales*, p. 141; Roloff, *Der erste Brief an Timotheus*, pp. 242-43; Dibelius and Conzelmann, *The Pastoral Epistles*, p. 68. Knight (*The Pastoral Epistles*, p. 195) sees this description of their teaching as sarcasm. The widespread use of this description of one's opponents' teachings means it is not possible to substantiate the idea that women were leaders among the opponents or that there was an emancipatory tendency for women among the opponents.

asserts, this evaluation of their teaching reveals nothing specific about the opponents.[101]

The contrast in vv. 7b-8 between exercise in piety and bodily exercise is sometimes seen as evidence that the opponents teach asceticism.[102] But this reading rests on mirror exegesis without sufficient support from other, more certain, information. My investigation of explicit statements uncovered no tendency toward asceticism based on some world-denying outlook. Thus, I cannot equate the bodily exercise mentioned here with some type of asceticism. (This is especially the case because v. 8 is a preformed saying.) Instead, the contrast is more vague. It intends to encourage Timothy to pursue piety because its rewards are so superior to those of bodily exercise. Any possible reference to the opponents here remains general; perhaps the value of their teaching is being compared with bodily exercise, or maybe their teaching is being characterized as bodily exercise. But even these possibilities do not allow us to declare them ascetics because the same *evaluation* could be given of observing any disputed laws from Judaism.

The final clause of v. 8 has been used to assign an overrealized eschatology to these opponents. According to Lane, when v. 8 says piety holds the promise of life both now and in the future, it shows that the opponents do not distinguish between the present and life after the parousia.[103] This is another interpretation based on insufficiently supported mirror reading. Since we have seen no more certain evidence of such teachings, this reading must be rejected. So v. 8 reveals nothing new about the opponents and only confirms that 1 Timothy finds their teachings worthless.

2.4-7

In 2.1-7 we find a section on public prayer[104] that urges the readers to pray for all people, especially governing officials, and supports this exhortation with a reminder that there is only one God. While 2.1-7 exhorts the readers to prayer, its nature is primarily didactic because it

101. Roloff, *Der erste Brief an Timotheus*, pp. 242-43.

102. So, e.g., Brox, *Die Pastoralbriefe*, pp. 172-73; Dibelius and Conzelmann (*The Pastoral Epistles*, p. 68) see this as a possibility.

103. Lane, 'An Early Instance of Over-realized Eschatology?', p. 166.

104. Brox, *Die Pastoralbriefe*, p. 13; Lane, 'An Early Instance of Over-realized Eschatology?', p. 4; Hultgren, *I–II Timothy, Titus*, p. 62. Hanson (*Studies*, p. 63) says 2.1-6 gives an outline of a prayer commonly used in public worship.

supplies teaching on how and why prayers are to be offered in their assemblies. I identify vv. 4-7 as an allusion to the opponents because the Law is central in this dispute. Verse 7 asserts that Paul has been commissioned to preach to Gentiles. In first-century Christianity, the issue of the place of Gentiles and questions about the Law were inextricably woven together. Thus, the emphasis on Paul's commission to Gentiles may indicate that the opponents are, at least secondarily, in view.

The primary function of 2.3-7 is to justify the exhortation given in 2.1 to pray for all people.[105] Verses 5-6(a), an early Christian hymn or confession,[106] are incorporated into this justification. This confession of the one God and one mediator, Christ, may well serve a double purpose. Rom. 3.29-30 and 10.12 assert that the existence of the one God over all implies that he seeks both Jews and Gentiles without respect to their ethnicity or their relationship to the Mosaic covenant. This thought seems to be in our author's mind at least by the time he writes 2.7, where there is an emphatic affirmation of Paul's commission to *Gentiles*.

Interpreters often use mirror reading to find opposition to Gnostic teachings in this passage. Oberlinner and Hanson contend that calling God the savior of all people opposes Gnostic exclusiveness.[107] Oberlinner also argues that the reference to 'the man Christ Jesus' is an antidocetic assertion.[108] Focusing on another part of the reference to Christ, Hultgren thinks the mention of Christ as mediator counters the Gnostic schema which has many intermediaries.[109] However, Lock asserts that Christ's role as mediator is mentioned to contrast Jesus with Moses.[110]

105. Oberlinner, *Die Pastoralbriefe*, p. 71. Donelson (*Pseudepigraphy and Ethical Argument*, p. 138) asserts that 2.3-4 gives God's attitude toward outsiders as the paradigm for the Christians' attitude.

106. See Ellis, 'Traditions in the Pastoral Epistles', pp. 238-39; Young, *The Theology of the Pastoral Letters*, p. 61; Brox, *Die Pastoralbriefe*, p. 128; Kelly, *Pastoral Epistles*, p. 63; Roloff, *Der erste Brief an Timotheus*, pp. 110, 120; Oberlinner, *Die Pastoralbriefe*, p. 73; Hultgren, *I–II Timothy, Titus*, p. 64; Dibelius and Conzelmann, p. 41. Hanson (*Studies*, pp. 63-64) even speculates about what branch of Christianity produced different parts of this material.

107. Oberlinner, *Die Pastoralbriefe*, pp. 72, 77; Hanson, *The Pastoral Epistles*, p. 31.

108. Oberlinner, *Die Pastoralbriefe*, pp. 74, 77.

109. Hultgren, *I–II Timothy, Titus*, p. 65. Brox (*Die Pastoralbriefe*, p. 127) says the Christology of 2.5 is distinguishing itself from Gnosticism, even if this is unconscious.

110. Lock, *Pastoral Epistles*, p. 27.

All of these mirror readings lack the support of more certain data. In addition, they add issues to the opponents' agenda on the basis of an allusion in a didactic context. According to our method, such allusions must relate directly to an issue that we already know is being raised. Bearing in mind that 2.5 is a traditional liturgical formulation, Hasler is on more firm footing when he argues that the reference to Jesus' humanity is neither anti-gnostic nor anti-docetic but is the result of the formula having developed in contact with Hellenistic Judaism.[111]

Paying more careful attention to the context than the various proposed mirror readings, Roloff asserts that 2.5-6 opposes neither pagan nor Gnostic teachings, but leads to the comments in v. 7 about the gospel bringing Jews and Gentiles together into the community of the saved.[112] Not only does this reading of vv. 5-7 help account for the emphasis on all (though the primary point is still justifying prayer for all), it also fits with the dispute over the Law that we have seen in 1 Timothy.

The vehement assertion in v. 7 that Paul is not lying is notable. Lock takes it to be evidence that Paul's authority and truthfulness have been attacked.[113] But again, this use of mirror exegesis is not supported by other evidence in this letter. Kelly asserts that Paul's vehemence about his commission to Gentiles shows that the opponents had Judaizing tendencies.[114] This may be correct since we have seen that the Law is a matter of dispute in 1 Timothy. Sampley's study of oaths in the Roman juridical system may be relevant here. He notes that taking an oath ended a case; it was considered conclusive evidence.[115] Thus, 1 Timothy may assert the truthfulness of Paul's commission to Gentiles to present unquestionable evidence in support of his interpretation of the Law. We may not use this passage to assert that the false teachers opposed the Gentile mission or denied the salvation of Gentiles who did not keep the Law as they interpreted it. This passage does confirm that the Law is at issue and that the author used the oneness of God and

111. V. Hasler, 'Ephiphanie und Christologie in den Pastoralbriefen', *TZ* 33 (1977), pp. 193-209 (204). Hanson (*Studies*, p. 63) also identifies Hellenistic-Jewish Christianity as the provenance of 4.5.

112. Roloff, *Der erste Brief an Timotheus*, p. 120.

113. Lock, *Pastoral Epistles*, p. 29.

114. Kelly, *Pastoral Epistles*, pp. 64-65.

115. J. Paul Sampley, '"Before God, I do not Lie" (Gal. I.20) Paul's Self-Defense in Light of Roman Legal Praxis', *NTS* 23 (1977), pp. 477-82.

Paul's commission to the Gentiles as evidence for his interpretation of the Law.

Summary of Allusions

Allusions reveal no new points of debate with the opponents. They do clearly confirm that the author finds their views harmful, dangerous, and contrary to a life of piety. Allusions also confirm that interpretation of the Law, perhaps especially the Gentiles' keeping of it, is the basic point of the disagreement between 1 Timothy and its opponents.

Affirmations

3.16

Many interpreters see 3.14-16 as the theological center of 1 Timothy. These verses appear at the end of the first set of instructions about the community's worship and structure. We classify this short section as didactic because it provides support to bolster the previous instructions. There are no clear allusions to the opponents in this section, but some interpreters find references to them, especially within the preformed liturgical material in 3.16.[116] Some find this hymnic material to be an attack on Gnostic beliefs, especially its references to the incarnation and the preaching of Christ in the physical realm.[117] But even some who identify the opponents as Gnostics acknowledge that there is no christo-logical debate evident in the quotation of this material.[118] Still, there may yet be a connection between 3.16 and the opponents. Oberlinner connects the second strophe of the hymn—the universal preaching about

---

116. Nearly all interpreters identify 3.16 as a preformed liturgical piece. E.g. Ellis, 'Traditions in the Pastoral Epistles', p. 238; Bush, 'A Note on the Structure of 1 Timothy', p. 156; Towner, *The Goal of Our Instruction*, pp. 28-29; Verner, *The Household of God*, p. 110; I. Howard Marshall, 'The Christian Life in 1 Timothy', *RTR* 49 (1990), pp. 81-90 (83); Eduard Schweizer, 'Two New Testament Creeds Compared: 1 Corinthians 15.3-5 and 1 Timothy 3.16', in W. Klassen and G.F. Snyder (eds.), *Current Issues in New Testament Interpretation* (New York: Harper & Row, 1962), pp. 166-77 (169); Young, *The Theology of the Pastoral Letters*, p. 61; Hanson, *Studies*, p. 5; Kelly, *Pastoral Epistles*, p. 89; Oberlinner, *Die Pastoralbriefe*, p. 152.

117. So, e.g., Bush, 'A Note on the Structure of 1 Timothy', p. 156.

118. See Haufe, 'Gnostische Irrlehre und ihre Abwehr in den Pastoralbriefen', p. 330.

Jesus—to the earlier comments about Paul's preaching to Gentiles.[119] Thus, he sees this part of the hymn as the reason it is quoted here. Hanson asserts that ὁμολογουμένως (confessedly) implies an adversative. Its use in arguments among philosophers and within *4 Maccabees* establish this point for him.[120] If Hanson is correct, Oberlinner's connection between the hymn's second strophe and the opponents' teaching gains strength.

Still, according to our method, affirmations in didactic sections cannot be used to identify opponents. Not only do they require unjustifiable use of the mirror technique, but it remains too uncertain that they actually address the opponents' teachings or conduct.

4.10

At the conclusion of the apologetic section 4.6-10(11), the author of 1 Timothy asserts that ministers (or Christians) work hard because they have set their hope on God, who is the savior of all people, especially (or particularly) those who believe. A few interpreters find this assertion of God's concern for all people to be a counter to the opponents' exclusivist ideas.[121] Some reference to the opponents' teaching may be present here if it is correct that their concern with the Law means that they question the place of Gentiles who do not keep the Law as they interpret it. If 4.10 does address such teachings, it still does not expand our understanding of the opponents' views. At most, it may confirm that 1 Timothy is concerned that their teachings contradict God's concern for all people. We cannot assert on the basis of this passage that they contend that Gentiles who do not follow their teachings are outside the community of the saved.

1.12-17

The thanksgiving in 1.12-17 focuses on the transformation of Paul from a persecutor of the church to an apostle. It gives Paul as the paradigm

---

119. Oberlinner, *Die Pastoralbriefe*, p. 168.

120. Hanson, *Studies*, pp. 21-23. Hultgren (*I–II Timothy, Titus*, pp. 76-77) finds calling the church the 'pillar and ground of the truth' an important way to speak of the church in the midst of conflicting claims. Cf. Oberlinner, *Die Pastoralbriefe*, p. 170.

121. So Kelly, *Pastoral Epistles*, p. 102, and Oberlinner, *Die Pastoralbriefe*, pp. 198-99.

for all Christians,[122] and perhaps as a sign of hope for the opponents.[123] It seems doubtful that this thanksgiving has the same function as introductory thanksgivings elsewhere in the Pauline corpus. Not only is it not in the usual position within the letter's structure for it to telegraph the letter's themes, but also its focus is exclusively on Paul, and on one aspect of his experience. Thus we identify the passage as primarily didactic; it expounds the meaning of Paul's having been entrusted with the gospel, the topic introduced in 1.11.[124]

This thanksgiving period includes two pieces of traditional material: v. 15 and v. 17.[125] Roloff rightly notes that we should not look for polemic accents in the doxology of v. 17 because it is so highly formalized.[126] The same holds true for the 'faithful saying' of v. 15.

Since this is a didactic section, we cannot use affirmations from it to identify opponents. However, its overall emphasis on Paul's transformation may well be intended, in spite of the strong polemic elsewhere, to imply that the opponents may repent.

6.6-10

Though we have unearthed no confirmation that 6.5 indicates that the opponents accept support from their adherents, we will treat the discussion of greed in 6.6-10 as an affirmation which relates to the opponents on the basis of the possibility that 6.5 introduces. Verses 6-10 belong within the polemical section 6.1-10[127] and grow out of the charge that

122. So, e.g., Brox, *Die Pastoralbriefe*, p. 13; Young, *The Theology of the Pastoral Letters*, pp. 123-24. See also Kelly, *Pastoral Epistles*, pp. 51-52; Hasler, 'Ephiphanie und Christologie in den Pastoralbriefen', p. 203.

123. Donelson, 'The Structure of the Ethical Argument in the Pastorals', *BTB* 18 (1988), pp. 108-13 (111); *idem*, *Pseudepigraphy and Ethical Argument*, pp. 101-102. Cf. Michael Wolter ('Paulus, der bekehrte Gottesfeind. Zum Verständnis von 1. Tim 1:13', *NovT* 31 [1989], pp. 48-66) who argues that this passage stops short of identifying Paul in his pre-Christian life, as an enemy of God.

124. So Oberlinner, *Die Pastoralbriefe*, p. 34.

125. Among those who identify these verses as traditional material are: Ellis, 'Traditions in the Pastoral Epistles', p. 238; Kelly, *Pastoral Epistles*, pp. 54-55; Roloff, *Der erste Brief an Timotheus*, pp. 41, 90-91; Oberlinner, *Die Pastoralbriefe*, pp. 43, 47; Hultgren, *I–II Timothy, Titus*, p. 59.

126. Roloff, *Der erste Brief an Timotheus*, p. 98.

127. Bush ('A Note on the Structure of 1 Timothy', pp. 155-56) sees 6.3-10, 17-19 as one of the two main sections against opponents in 1 Timothy.

the opponents are motivated by greed (v. 5).[128] Verse 10 attributes to greed the wandering away from the faith of some. This may again be only a polemical characterization of the opponents in this polemical context.[129] So, neither this comment in v. 10, nor the preceding remarks in vv. 6-9 on greed reveal anything about the opponents' practices. The teaching on greed in vv. 6-10 may be primarily instructions for office-holders, instructions which use the opponents as a foil to make their point emphatically.[130] Thus, even these expanded comments on greed fail to confirm that these opponents expect maintenance from their followers. So, this practice remains only a possibility.

Summary of Affirmations

This look at affirmations that seem to relate to the opponents has not dealt with every passage that previous interpreters have identified as relevant.[131] Rather, it has been limited to those statements that relate to issues raised in explicit statements and allusions. These confirmable affirmations add nothing to our knowledge of the opponents.

Conclusion about the Opponents of 1 Timothy

Our investigation indicates that the opponents of 1 Timothy were originally part of the Pauline community. It does not, however, support the idea that they were leaders of a particular community. A central purpose of 1 Timothy is to make certain that the Pauline community rejects these opponents. The main differences between the opponents and the author of 1 Timothy involve interpretation of the Law. The opponents call the community to obey the Law as they interpret it, which is different from the way 1 Timothy interprets it.

The more specific issues raised by these opponents involve food prohibitions and marriage regulations. The food laws are clearly derived

---

128. So Knight, *The Pastoral Epistles*, p. 258; Fee, *1 and 2 Timothy, Titus*, pp. 142-43.

129. So Knight, *The Pastoral Epistles*, p. 258. Fee (*1 and 2 Timothy, Titus*, pp. 142-43) sees the whole of vv. 6-10 directed against the opponents' greed.

130. See the comments of Fee (*1 and 2 Timothy, Titus*, p. 142) and Roloff (*Der erste Brief an Timotheus*, p. 327).

131. E.g. Schenk ('Die Pastoralbriefe in der neueren Forschung', p. 3429) thinks the instructions to Timothy in 5.23 to drink a little wine are anti-ascetic. Similarly MacDonald, *The Legend and the Apostle*, p. 58.

from the Law. The marriage regulations pose more of a challenge if we are seeking their origin. First Timothy characterizes their teaching as a prohibition against marriage, but the opponents may not have completely rejected marriage. First Timothy may simply be giving a polemically motivated formulation of their teaching. Since this issue is raised only once and with no elaboration, we cannot determine the purpose or basis for their teaching about marriage. Their restrictions on marriage are not sufficient evidence to claim that they see the material world as evil or advocate some sort of general asceticism. As we noted above, there are many reasons for which they may put forward restrictions on marriage for some segment of the community. The origins of such regulations that lie closest to hand are Judaism or 1 Corinthians 7. But we have no clear evidence to directly support either possibility, only the knowledge that the opponents were concerned about the Law and drew other obligations for Christians from it.

Finally, we have seen that it is possible, though we cannot say probable, that these opponents accepted maintenance from their followers. The polemical setting and background of the charges of greed that 1 Timothy makes against these opponents renders any certain judgment about their practice in this matter impossible.

We have found no evidence in 1 Timothy that these opponents are Gnostics or proto-gnostics. Nothing in 1 Timothy points to this identification. Neither did any evidence surface that shows that they hold an overrealized eschatology or propose an ascetic life to enhance prophetic activity. While it may be the case that 1 Timothy opposes emancipatory tendencies, especially for women, we have found no connection between such tendencies and the opponents. There is also no good evidence that the opponents are libertines, rather they advocate a stricter regime of food and marriage regulations (at least partially based on the Law) than 1 Timothy finds acceptable.

2 TIMOTHY

The opponents of 2 Timothy, when separated from those of the Pastoral Epistles read as a corpus, have received less attention than those of 1 Timothy. The only information from 2 Timothy that plays a significant role when the opponents of the Pastorals are treated as a group is 2.18. But a few scholars have tried to identify the false teachers of 2 Timothy independently of 1 Timothy and Titus. Murphy-O'Connor argues that the opponents of 2 Timothy have nothing to do with those of 1 Timothy and that the preoccupation of 2 Timothy is with futile debate.[132] Johnson argues that in 2 Timothy the opponents function 'entirely as contrast' to the ideal minister Timothy is exhorted to become.[133]

One reason little study has been devoted to the opponents of 2 Timothy is that little is said about them in the letter.[134] Second Timothy is very different from 1 Timothy in tone and is much more focused on a hortatory purpose, especially on the importance of remaining faithful to the gospel and Paul in both beliefs and action. Still, there are comments about opponents that indicate that they are a danger to the community that 2 Timothy addresses.

Explicit Statements

2.16-18
Second Timothy 2.14-26[135] has a clear hortatory intent; it tells Timothy how to be a good minister.[136] But these instructions are given in the context of the presence and effect of false teachers.[137] Brox even sees

132. Murphy-O'Connor, '2 Timothy Contrasted with 1 Timothy and Titus', p. 415. Müller (*Zur frühchristlichen Theologiegeschichte*, pp. 73-76) argues that those who claim the resurrection has taken place and 1 Timothy's teachers of the Law are different groups, even if both groups are opposed in all three Pastoral Epistles. Donelson ('Structure', p. 111) also acknowledges that the situation of 2 Timothy is different from that of 1 Timothy.

133. Johnson, '2 Timothy and the Polemic Against False Teachers', p. 12.

134. Lock (*Pastoral Epistles*, p. xvii) says that 2 Timothy tells the least about the opponents of any of the Pastorals.

135. Though a number of commentators end the section at v. 21 (e.g. Müller, *Zur frühchristlichen Theologiegeschichte*, p. 68; Kelly, *Pastoral Epistles*, p. 181), the exhortations of vv. 22-26. are too closely related to recommend this break. If 2.14-26 is made into two sections, the break must come after v. 19. If vv. 14-19 and 20-26 are separated sections (so MacDonald, *The Legend and the Apostle*, p. 56; Oden, *First and Second Timothy and Titus*, p. 55), they have much the same function and are very closely related.

136. Johnson ('2 Timothy and the Polemic Against False Teachers', p. 9) identifies all of 2.14–4.8 as paraenetic and sees the description of the opponents as a contrast to the positive attributes of a minister being recommended.

137. Dibelius and Conzelmann, *The Pastoral Epistles,* p. 110. Kelly (*Pastoral Epistles*, p. 181) sees 2.14-21 as a summons to avoid false teaching and Oberlinner (*Die Pastoralbriefe*, p. 90) sees those verses as a description of the right behavior in relation to the opponents and a judgment on their teaching.

the section as instructions for arguing with opponents.[138] This sustained attention to opponents seems to indicate that the section has an apologetic function, because Timothy is instructed on how he is to defend the community and the correct teaching against the opponents' influence.

The clearest statement about the opponents in this letter comes in 2.17-18. Not only are two false teachers named, but their teaching is characterized in a specific doctrinal assertion: they contend that 'the resurrection has already occurred' (v. 18). This verse gives what 2 Timothy presents as the center of the opponents' teaching.[139] Most interpreters understand this statement to mean that the opponents have a spiritualized view of the resurrection that rejects a bodily resurrection on the basis of their low view of the material world and so of bodily existence. Thus, they identify baptism as the moment of one's spiritual resurrection.[140] Most interpreters ground this understanding on the presupposition that the opponents are Gnostics. But as Murphy-O'Connor argues, v. 18's statement of their position does not justify the claim that they spiritualize all of life.[141] In fact, we must bear in mind that 2.18 is 2 Timothy's presentation of what the opponents teach. We may reasonably doubt that Hymenaeus and Philetus state their position in this way.[142] The polemical thrust of the description of their teaching at the beginning of v. 18 (they have swerved from the truth) justifies some skepticism about whether this is a direct quotation. What we can say is that these opponents claim to possess some things that 2 Timothy believes are received only at the parousia or at death. Thus, the dispute is

---

138. Brox, *Die Pastoralbriefe*, p. 245.

139. So Oberlinner, *Die Pastoralbriefe*, p. 98.

140. So, e.g., Spicq, *Les épîtres pastorales*, pp. 354-55; Müller, *Zur frühchristlichen Theologiegeschichte*, p. 70; Brox, *Die Pastoralbriefe*, p. 248; Knight, *The Pastoral Epistles*, p. 414; Lock, *Pastoral Epistles*, p. 99; Kelly, *Pastoral Epistles*, pp. 184-85; Dibelius and Conzelmann, *The Pastoral Epistles*, p. 112.

141. Murphy-O'Connor, '2 Timothy Contrasted with 1 Timothy and Titus', p. 416.

142. Oberlinner (*Die Pastoralbriefe*, pp. 99-100) admits that it is difficult to know what they mean by saying that the resurrection is past and that, in these verses, it is hard to separate stock charges from what the opponents actually teach. See above my earlier comments on the similar statement of the opponents' view in 2 Thessalonians.

about eschatology and about the conditions of life for the Christian in the present. We can say no more at this point.[143]

Verses 16-18 may indicate that these opponents are enjoying some measure of success. Verse 18 acknowledges that they are upsetting the faith of some, and v. 16 notes that many are being led into ungodliness by their teaching. Additionally, v. 17 says that their teaching spreads like gangrene.[144]

Their teaching is further characterized as profane, empty words in v. 16, a sort of teaching Timothy is exhorted to avoid. Hanson understands this evaluation of the opponents' teaching to point to descriptions of the hierarchy of aeons.[145] Knight connects the language used here with that of 1 Tim. 1.6 to assert that the opponents of both letters are the same.[146] Both of these commentators over-interpret these words which 2 Timothy uses to describe the opponents' teaching. Calling their teaching profane, empty words is a derogatory evaluation,[147] not a description of its content. As Karris points out, such charges about one's opponents' teaching is a common polemical ploy used by philosophers against Sophists.[148] So this characterization shows only that 2 Timothy rejects the opponents' teaching and wants the letter's recipients to do the same.

Finally, we should give some attention to the names Hymenaeus and Philetus. Their identity depends in part on whether 2 Timothy is pseudonymous or authentic. If it is authentic, they are persons who advocate the opposed teaching at the time of the letter's composition and are probably known to Timothy's community, at least by reputation. If 2 Timothy is pseudonymous, they are more likely people known to have opposed Paul in his life-time, perhaps as leaders of a movement Paul denounced. But either way, 2 Timothy shows no interest in them

143. Fiore (*The Function of Personal Example*, p. 3 n. 5) notes that the content of the opponents' teaching is not specific here.

144. See Oberlinner, *Die Pastoralbriefe*, p. 98. Haufe ('Gnostische Irrlehre und ihre Abwehr in den Pastoralbriefen', pp. 326-37) says these verses are evidence that these opponents belong to an organized group which has an aggressive mission.

145. Hanson, *The Pastoral Epistles*, p. 135.

146. Knight, *The Pastoral Epistles*, p. 412.

147. Brox, *Die Pastoralbriefe*, p. 248.

148. Karris, 'The Background and Significance of the Polemic of the Pastoral Epistles', p. 553.

as individuals, only as figures who represent the rejected teaching.[149] Perhaps their known bad reputation contributes to 2 Timothy's rejection of the false teaching at hand.

So 2.16-18, treveals that a teaching that 2 Timothy rejects is meeting with some success. The threat is serious enough that 2 Timothy uses derogatory characterization and perhaps an exaggerated formulation of their teaching to defeat them. The opponents' teaching involves eschatology, and particularly what eschatological blessings Christians enjoy in the present. The opponents hold that Christians do (or can) possess more of these blessings than 2 Timothy allows.[150]

2.23-26

Another explicit statement about these opponents appears in the apologetic section 2.14-26. Timothy is called to correct his opponents with gentleness, but to avoid their stupid and ignorant disputes. The controversies of v. 23 are, again, often identified with Gnostic speculations or interpretations of Scripture.[151] But as we saw in connection with 1 Timothy, such characterizations of opponents' teachings were common polemical ploys.[152] The point of such a description is to give grounds for rejecting one's opponents.[153] They are also set up here as the opposite of what a true minister is to be.[154] So this assessment of their teaching calls for a rejection of them while not saying anything about the content of their teaching.[155]

---

149. Cf. the discussion of these two people in Oberlinner, *Die Pastoralbriefe*, pp. 96-98.

150. We could speculate that their views involve a rejection of suffering as a part of the Christian life since 2 Timothy emphasizes its necessity. But this takes us beyond the evidence we have found.

151. So, e.g., Schenk, 'Die Pastoralbriefe in der neueren Forschung', p. 3429; Haufe, 'Gnostische Irrlehre und ihre Abwehr in den Pastoralbriefen', p. 329.

152. See Karris, 'The Background and Significance of the Polemic of the Pastoral Epistles', p. 553. Dibelius and Conzelmann (*The Pastoral Epistles*, p. 113) identify v. 23 as polemical.

153. Oberlinner, *Die Pastoralbriefe*, p. 114. It is unlikely that Spicq (*Les épîtres pastorales*, p. 360) is correct when he identifies these vain questions as the main feature of the heresy in 2 Timothy's view.

154. Cf. Johnson, '2 Timothy and the Polemic Against False Teachers', pp. 10-11.

155. See the comments of Brox, *Die Pastoralbriefe*, p. 251; Dibelius and Conzelmann, *The Pastoral Epistles*, p. 113.

Besides denigrating their teaching, this passage also holds out hope that they will repent. So there is something of a softening of the letter's approach to them. But the purpose of this kind treatment is to lead them to renounce their unacceptable teachings, not to allow compromise with them.

While these verses hold out hope for the opponents, they still strongly reject their views. The stock polemical characterization of their teaching adds nothing to our understanding of these opponents.

3.1-9

Karris identifies 3.1-9 as the only properly polemical section in 2 Timothy.[156] Within the larger scheme of 2 Timothy, descriptions of the opponents often serve as examples to be avoided.[157] These verses are a polemical warning about and rejection of the false teachers, as the use of vocabulary from polemic against heresy indicates.[158]

This section begins as a warning against the end-time phenomenon of the appearance of evil people. But the exhortation to avoid such people in v. 5 shows that they are already present.[159] So 2 Timothy identifies the current opponents with the evil ones of the last days. Verses 2-5(a) compose a vice list that is fairly traditional in content and uses stock characterizations. Thus, it cannot be used to identify these opponents. It is another instance of characterization intended to make the opponents despicable.[160]

Many interpreters see a move to more direct speech about the opponents at v. 5 or 6. This understanding of vv. 6-7 takes the descriptions

156. Karris, 'The Background and Significance of the Polemic of the Pastoral Epistles', p. 559. Brown ('Asceticism and Ideology', p. 81) asserts that 2 Tim. 3.15 and 1 Tim. 1.9-10 are the most polemical vice lists in the Pastorals.

157. See Johnson, '2 Timothy and the Polemic Against False Teachers', p. 11; Brown, 'Asceticism and Ideology', p. 82.

158. See Brox, *Die Pastoralbriefe*, pp. 253-54; Karris, 'The Background and Significance of the Polemic of the Pastoral Epistles', pp. 552-54; Oberlinner, *Die Pastoralbriefe*, p. 120.

159. Brox, *Die Pastoralbriefe*, p. 253; Knight, *The Pastoral Epistles*, p. 428; Gerhard Lohfink, 'Paulinische Theologie in der Rezeption der Pastoralbriefe', in K. Kertelge (ed.), *Paulus in den neutestamentlichen Spätschriften* (Freiburg: Herder, 1981), pp. 90-91; Kelly, *Pastoral Epistles*, p. 195.

160. See Brox, *Die Pastoralbriefe*, p. 256; Oberlinner, *Die Pastoralbriefe*, p. 120; Dibelius and Conzelmann, *The Pastoral Epistles*, pp. 115-16; Brown, 'Asceticism and Ideology', p. 81.

found in these verses to indicate that the opponents' locus of activity is households and that they are especially well received by women.[161] However, Karris notes that such statements about success with women were among the stock charges made against Sophists.[162] But here he accepts this characterization as having a basis in fact because he is reading the Pastoral Epistles as a group and he finds an emphasis on women in the corpus. Our method rejects reading one letter through the lens of another and so this argument carries insufficient weight to support the conclusion. Others base their acceptance of these charges against the opponents on the presupposition that the opponents are Gnostics who assert the equal authority of men and women.[163] We have no clear evidence in 2 Timothy that the opponents are Gnostics—an overrealized eschatology is not sufficient grounds to identify them as Gnostics.[164]

Rather than a sudden shift from the stock polemical characterization of the opponents to citation of their actual practices, vv. 6-7 seem to continue the polemical denunciation begun in v. 1. Knight sees vv. 6-9 as an application of the evil characteristics of the end-time ungodly to the opponents.[165] Brox argues that vv. 6-7 are an ironic and sarcastic description of the opponents intended to make them despicable. Thus, his judgment is that all of 3.1-9 is typical, polemical characteriza-tion from which no specifics about these particular opponents can be drawn.[166] The continuation of the stock polemical charges, recognized

---

161. So Kelly, *Pastoral Epistles*, pp. 195-96; Oden, *First and Second Timothy and Titus*, pp. 176-78; MacDonald, *The Legend and the Apostle*, p. 57; Dibelius and Conzelmann, *The Pastoral Epistles*, p. 116; Schenk, 'Die Pastoralbriefe in der Neueren Forschung', p. 3429; Towner, *The Goal of our Instruction*, pp. 26-27; Oberlinner, *Die Pastoralbriefe*, pp. 125-26.

162. Karris, 'The Background and Significance of the Polemic of the Pastoral Epistles', pp. 554, 560.

163. E.g. Oberlinner, *Die Pastoralbriefe*, pp. 125-26; Schenk, 'Die Pastoralbriefe in der Neueren Forschung', p. 3429.

164. See above the discussion of the relationship between realized eschatology and Gnosticism in connection with 2 Thess. 2.3-7.

165. Knight, *The Pastoral Epistles*, p. 428.

166. Brox, *Die Pastoralbriefe*, pp. 255-56. Dibelius and Conzelmann (*The Pastoral Epistles*, p. 116) also comment on the ironic nature of these verses. Oberlinner (*Die Pastoralbriefe*, p. 127) argues that the charges about the immorality of these women is not to be taken literally. Similarly, Karris ('The Background and Sig-

by Karris, make this the most probable reading of 3.6-7. We cannot completely exclude the possibility that the opponents were especially successful with women, but there is no attention given to the place of women in this letter. Only the illegitimate assumption that the Pastoral Epistles are to be read as a corpus when identifying their opponents lends support to the view that these opponents were especially successful with women. Thus it is best to understand vv. 6-7 as a continuation of the incriminating characterization begun in v. 1.

This section composed of 3.1-9 ends by comparing the present opponents with Jannes and Jambres, the magicians who, according to Jewish tradition, opposed Moses before Pharaoh. Some interpreters, using mirror exegesis, contend that these verses show that the opponents are magicians.[167] But the point of the comparison is not that the opponents are magicians. Rather, identifying the opponents with Jannes and Jambres is meant to devalue their teaching by asserting that they reject the truth.[168] It is this aspect of the earlier opponents of Moses that serves as a paradigm for the present opponents.

The strong polemic of 3.1-9 reveals nothing about the opponents' teaching. Perhaps this powerful rejection of them is intended to emphasize that the gentle treatment intended to bring them to repent (2.24-26) does not mean there is to be compromise with them. It is possible, though far from probable, that 3.6-7 indicates that these opponents do most of their teaching in households and are especially successful among women. If other evidence *in 2 Timothy* supports this idea, we may be able to see this as probable.

Summary of Explicit Statements
Our study of explicit statements in 2 Timothy reveals that the opponents of this letter advocate an overrealized eschatology. They seem to claim to possess or experience something in the present time that the author of 2 Timothy believes will be received only at the resurrection. Whether they state their views in the language of 2.18 remains questionable. So far, 2 Timothy gives no hint about the theoretical or expe-

---

nificance of the Polemic of the Pastoral Epistles', p. 560) contends that these verses cannot be used to show that the opponents are libertines.

167. So Spicq, *Les épîtres pastorales* p. lxx. Scott (*The Pastoral Epistles*, p. xvii) finds this a possibility.

168. See Brox, *Die Pastoralbriefe*, p. 256; Oberlinner, *Die Pastoralbriefe*, p. 131.

riential background of the opponents' understanding of present existence or life in the eschaton. Explicit statements also indicate that the
opposed teachers have met with some success in 2 Timothy's community. It is possible, that they were especially successful in gaining
women as adherents. But this remains very speculative because the
comments about women draw on stock polemical characterizations.

Allusions

2.14-15

The apologetic section 2.14-26 begins with a twofold exhortation to
Timothy. He is to remind the community of the faithful saying about
Christ in 2.11-13 and to charge them not to enter into disputes about
words. Such disputes are said to harm those who hear them. These disputes about words allude to the profane and empty talk of the
opponents (2.16). This is perhaps the most certain allusion to the
opponents in this letter. It is a characterization of their teachings that
again draws on the polemic of philosophers against Sophists.[169] This
polemical evaluation reveals the author's repudiation of these teachers,
but provides no clarification of their teaching.

2.20-22

Also within the apologetic section of 2.14-26, vv. 20-22 appear to be
something of a digression that alludes to the opponents. These verses
distinguish two types of vessels contained in a house, those for noble
use and those for ignoble. It seems likely, given the surrounding references to them, that the vessels for ignoble use are the opponents. Not
only is it said that these ignoble ones may purify themselves so that
they may be for noble use, but also the immediate application of the
analogy is for Timothy to aim at various virtues with a pure heart. Possessing these virtues is then immediately contrasted with the opponents'
disputations. Even though this analogy alludes to the opponents, it only
judges them ignoble, and by implication impure (v. 22). It does not
speak about their teachings or conduct any more directly and so reveals
nothing about them.

---

169. Karris, 'The Background and Significance of the Polemic of the Pastoral
Epistles', p. 553.

4.3-4

Second Timothy begins to come to its conclusion at 4.1. In 4.1-8 Timothy is exhorted to fulfill his duties as a minister in light of Paul's imminent death. In the middle of this hortatory section, Timothy is told that soon people will not want to hear sound teaching but will seek out more pleasing teachers who will desert the truth for myths. This prediction of some turning from the truth to myths may allude to the opponents.[170] As we have seen interpreters do before, many find the term myth to apply to some particular kind of false teaching.[171] But, again, it is a polemical description that reveals nothing about the teaching's content. Furthermore, according to our method, allusions in hortatory contexts cannot be used to identify opponents.

3.13

In 3.10-17 the author provides a hortatory contrast to the opponents described in preceding polemical verses.[172] Verses 10-17 give Paul's suffering as the opposite of the false teachers described in vv. 1-9 with the goal being to encourage Timothy to adhere to the teachings he had received from Paul and which are in accord with Scripture. Within this exhortation, 2 Timothy contrasts the godly who are persecuted with the evil who are deceived and deceivers. This reference to the ungodly may allude to the opponents.[173] But since this allusion appears in a hortatory section, our method does not allow us to use it the identify opponents. Even if it were to be used, it adds nothing to our knowledge of them. It is simply another rejection of them with a derogatory characterization.

170. Karris ('The Background and Significance of the Polemic of the Pastoral Epistles', p. 562), however, contends that this is not a specific reference to the opponents.

171. So, e.g., Haufe, 'Gnostische Irrlehre und ihre Abwehr in den Pastoralbriefen', p. 329; Scott, *The Pastoral Epistles*, p. 130; Lock, *Pastoral Epistles*, p. xvii.

172. Brox (*Die Pastoralbriefe*, p. 256) identifies 3.10-17 as a section which gives instructions about how to live, especially about enduring suffering with steadfastness. Similarly Knight, *The Pastoral Epistles*, p. 438. Dibelius and Conzelmann (*The Pastoral Epistles*, p. 118) see these verses as the beginning of the letter's closing exhortations.

173. So Brox, *Die Pastoralbriefe*, p. 259. Scott (*The Pastoral Epistles*, p. xvii) thinks it is possible that the mention of deceiving may point to the opponents being magicians. But this interpretation relies wholly on unsupported mirror reading.

1.15
When 1.15 identifies Phygelus and Hermogenes as two among 'all those in Asia' who turned away from Paul, it may allude to the opponents. We find in 1.8-18 a hortatory section which encourages Timothy to neither be ashamed of Paul's imprisonment nor shrink back from suffering for the Gospel. The section uses example and antithesis to strengthen its exhortation.[174] In vv. 15-18, Phygelus and Hermogenes are bad examples set in antithesis to the good example of Onesiphorus. So these persons present contrasting models to illustrate the two options before Timothy.

While it is possible the Phygelus and Hermogenes are to be counted among the opponents discussed in chs. 2 and 3, it is more probable that their desertion of Paul had to do with behavior involving his imprisonment,[175] as did Onesiphorus's good conduct. Even if they are to be identified with the opponents fought in the later parts of 2 Timothy, nothing is stated in 1.15 about their views or their conduct beyond the fact that they deserted Paul.

Summary of Allusions
Allusions to opponents in 2 Timothy primarily pronounce judgments about them. As a means of gathering information about the opponents, these allusions are rather disappointing—we gain no clarification about their teaching or conduct. These allusions do clearly serve as the antithesis to the ideal Timothy is to strive to attain.[176]

Affirmations

2.13
To this point, references to the opponents have been concentrated in 2.14–3.9, with only a few possible allusions outside this section. One other statement that may relate to the opponents is 2.13, where within the preformed 'faithful saying' of 2.11-13 we read: 'if we are faithless,

174. See Fiore, *The Function of Personal Example*, p. 23; Johnson, '2 Timothy and the Polemic Against False Teachers', p. 6; Donelson, *Pseudepigraphy and Ethical Argument*, p. 92.

175. Cf. Dibelius and Conzelmann, *The Pastoral Epistles*, pp. 65, 106; Johnson, '2 Timothy and the Polemic Against False Teachers', p. 9.

176. Cf. Johnson, '2 Timothy and the Polemic Against False Teachers', p. 12; Donelson, *Pseudepigraphy and Ethical Argument*, p. 92.

he remains faithful'. Overall, 2.1-13 is a hortatory passage that encourages Timothy to be faithful even in the midst of suffering. Within this exhortation, vv. 8-13 provide bases for Timothy's faithfulness and so are primarily instructive or didactic.

Many interpreters have difficulty finding a place within the argument of 2 Timothy for the fourth line of the hymnic piece (i.e. v. 13).[177] However, J.M. Bassler argues that it refers to the letter's opponents who have shown themselves to be faithless by turning from the truth. So, the mention of Christ's faithfulness means that God remains willing to accept them back.[178] If Bassler is correct, we have an affirmation that relates to the opponents in the verses that introduce the first explicit references to them. However, since this statement appears in a didactic section, it cannot be used to identify them. In any case, 2.13 yields no information about these faithless one.

Conclusion about the Opponents of 2 Timothy

Our investigation of 2 Timothy indicates that the opponents of this letter proclaim an overrealized eschatology. However, we cannot be precise about what they claim, even if 2.18 is a direct quotation of their teaching. All we can be certain of is that they claim to possess something that the author of 2 Timothy believes is available only at the parousia. Thus, they have a different view of Christian existence in the present than does 2 Timothy. There is no sufficient evidence to support the idea that they do not expect a future bodily resurrection. The evaluations of and polemic against these false teachers also show that they have been somewhat successful. And while it is possible that they have been particularly successful among women, the only evidence for this comes in stock polemical characterizations. Thus, this matter remains highly questionable.

It is easy to see why interpreters have so often turned to 1 Timothy and Titus to help identify the opponents of 2 Timothy. With so little solid evidence in 2 Timothy, our portrait of them remains only the

177. See the review of commentators treatment of this passage in Jouette M. Bassler, '"He remains faithful" (2 Tim 2:13a)', in Eugene H. Lovering, Jr, and Jerry L. Sumney (eds.), *Theology and Ethics in Paul and his Interpreters: Essays in Honor of Victor Paul Furnish* (Nashville: Abingdon Press, 1996), pp. 173-83 (173-79).

178. Bassler, '"He Remains Faithful"', p. 179-83.

faded outline of a vague sketch. But, we have found no evidence that links the opponents of 2 Timothy to those of 1 Timothy (and it will be the same with Titus). So we cannot fill in our dim portrait with the pallet of 1 Timothy. Thus, a fuller understanding of these opponents remains lost to us. This is true in part because combating opponents is not a primary purpose of 2 Timothy. Rather, its purpose is primarily hortatory. So our less than complete understanding of these opponents does not inhibit interpretation of this letter because they function largely as antithetical paradigms, examples of the behavior and teaching that Timothy is to avoid.

TITUS

Many identify the opponents of Titus as Gnostics,[179] again, primarily because these interpreters draw on the whole corpus of the Pastorals and try to construct a single type of opponent. They also rely heavily upon mirror reading. But others recognize some significant differences in Titus that require us to consider the opponents of this letter on their own.[180] Those who make this distinction usually find that the opponents of Titus require observance of some regulations from Judaism. Even those who identify the opponents of the Pastorals as a single front of Gnostics point to Titus as evidence that the heresy is a Jewish Gnosticism.

Explicit Statements

1.10-14, 16

Titus 1.10-16 is a section devoted wholly to the opponents. Verse 9 prepares the way for this section by referring to those who contradict sound teaching and assigning elders the task of refuting them.[181] Verses 10-16 constitute a polemical section[182] which is filled with stock polemical charges and characterizations of these opponents.

---

179. So, e.g., Scott, *The Pastoral Epistles*, p. 158; Schenk, 'Die Pastoralbriefe in der Neueren Forschung', pp. 3427-30; Kelly, *Pastoral Epistles*, p. 236; Brox, *Die Pastoralbriefe*, pp. 35, 287; Hultgren, *I–II Timothy, Titus*, p. 157.

180. Johnson, *Writings of the New Testament*, pp. 402-403; Fee, *1 and 2 Timothy, Titus*, p. 171.

181. So Fee, *1 and 2 Timothy, Titus*, pp. 175, 177.

182. So, e.g., Karris, 'The Background and Significance of the Polemic of the Pastoral Epistles', p. 551 n.9; Spicq, *Les Epîtres Pastorales*, p. 241; Verner, *The*

Verse 10 begins the section by asserting that many are insubordinate, empty-talkers and deceivers. These descriptions are general invectives that draw on charges used against Sophists.[183] Thus, they reveal little other than that the author disapproves of them. Calling them insubordinate immediately after recounting the qualifications and duties of elders, however, probably indicates that they are Christians and may suggest that they are members of the community being addressed.[184] But this latter assertion remains uncertain.[185] When v. 10 says there are many such people, this may indicate that they have enjoyed a significant amount of success.[186] Or, it may be polemical exaggeration to increase alarm about their presence.

In addition to the general invectives, v. 10 designates these people 'the circumcision'. Schenk rejects the broad consensus that sees this label as evidence that the opponents are Jewish Christians[187] or at least advocate observances from Judaism.[188] He argues that calling them Jews is another polemical characterization, just as calling them Cretans is in v. 12. Schenk asserts that this appellation had become an insult within Christianity and is used so here.[189] But this hypothesis seems very unlikely and Schenk cites no evidence for this use of labeling people Jews. Calling them 'the circumcision' at least indicates that their

Household of God, p. 178; MacDonald, *The Legend and the Apostle*, p. 114 n. 14; Hanson, *The Pastoral Epistles*, p. 175; Scott, *The Pastoral Epistles*, p. 156; Knight, *The Pastoral Epistles*, p. 295.

183. Scott, *The Pastoral Epistles,* p. 158; Karris, 'The Background and Significance of the Polemic of the Pastoral Epistles', p. 553. Lock (*Pastoral Epistles*, p. 133) notes that ματαιολόγοι was a common Jewish description of pagan worship. So the author may be suggesting that their teaching is as worthless as paganism.

184. So Hultgren, *I–II Timothy, Titus*, pp. 156-57. For the more general point see Brox, *Die Pastoralbriefe*, p. 287. Verner (*The Household of God*, p. 179) notes that the charge of insubordination is not part of traditional polemical charges.

185. Johnson (*Writings of the New Testament*, p. 403) asserts that they are outsiders.

186. So Brox, *Die Pastoralbriefe*, p. 286. Haufe ('Gnostische Irrlehre und ihre Abwehr in den Pastoralbriefen', p. 327) argues that it shows they had existed from the beginning of the addressed community.

187. Those who hold this view include: Hanson, *The Pastoral Epistles*, p. 175; Knight, *The Pastoral Epistles*, p. 297; Scott, *The Pastoral Epistles*, p. 158; Fee, *1 and 2 Timothy, Titus*, p. 177.

188. So, e.g., Brox, *Die Pastoralbriefe*, p. 287.

189. Schenk, 'Die Pastoralbriefe in der Neueren Forschung', p. 3429.

teaching involves matters drawn from Judaism and probably shows that
at least the instigators are Jewish. Though if they had been at all
successful, they will count Gentiles among their number.[190] From v. 10
we cannot determine what parts of Judaism it is that they urge Christians to observe and that Titus rejects as inappropriate for Christians.[191]

Knight contends that these characterizations in v. 10 reveal that the
opponents are morally lax.[192] But no such charge is made directly and
Knight's thesis fails to take account of the use of the polemical topoi
being used here.

The polemical characterization begun in v. 10 continues in v. 11 with
the accusations that these opponents are upsetting whole households and
are motivated by greed. Although some commentators have understood
the accusation that these teachers are literally motivated by greed[193] or
have taken it as evidence that they accept pay,[194] this is another stock
polemical charge that yields no good evidence about these teachers.[195]

When v. 11 accuses them of upsetting whole households, it may
show that they are actively engaged in soliciting followers (as we
would expect) and have been successful to some degree.[196] This charge
in no way suggests or reflects any special attention to women.[197]

Verses 12-13 identify these opponents as Cretans and therefore as
liars, cheats, beasts and lazy. Fee argues that the author intends this accusation to apply only to the false teachers rather than to all Cretans.[198]
One wonders whether such fine distinctions would be made by Cretans

190. See Kelly, *Pastoral Epistles*, p. 234. Cf. Hultgren, *I–II Timothy, Titus*,
p. 157 See the discussion of μάλιστα by T.C. Skeat, '"Especially the Parchments":
A Note on 2 Timothy iv.13', *JTS* 30 (1979), pp. 173-77, cited by Fee, *1 and 2 Timothy, Titus*, p. 183.

191. Strangely, Fee (*1 and 2 Timothy, Titus*, p. 178) asserts that the issue does
not involve circumcision, even though they are called 'the circumcision'.

192. Knight, *The Pastoral Epistles*, p. 295.

193. E.g. Spicq, *Les épîtres pastorales*, p. 242; Kelly, *Pastoral Epistles*, p. 234.

194. So, e.g., Scott, *The Pastoral Epistles*, p. 159.

195. Karris, 'The Background and Significance of the Polemic of the Pastoral
Epistles', p. 552; Hanson, *The Pastoral Epistles*, p. 175; Brox, *Die Pastoralbriefe*,
pp. 287-88.

196. Cf. Johnson, *Writings of the New Testament*, p. 403; Brox, *Die Pastoralbriefe*, p. 38; Fee, *1 and 2 Timothy, Titus*, p. 178.

197. Contra Scott, *The Pastoral Epistles*, p. 158.

198. Fee, *1 and 2 Timothy, Titus*, p. 178.

hearing such insults. In any case, it is clearly a case of polemical name-calling,[199] though we can only guess at its effectiveness if it is heard by Cretans.[200] Thus, the point is to impugn the character of these teachers.

After this name-calling, v. 14 tells Titus to avoid their Jewish myths and human commands. This reference to myths is again understood differently, depending on the assumed identity of the opponents. So Lock and Scott find a reference to Jewish haggadah,[201] while Hanson sees Gnostic theogonies.[202] Fee contends that this language refers to a phenomenon like that spoken of in 1 Tim. 1.4 because the same language is used in both places.[203] But as we have seen in connection with 1 and 2 Timothy, such a characterization of an opponents' teaching is simply a stock polemical charge which reveals nothing about the teaching's content. However, here in Titus, their myths are further specified as Jewish. This does show some connection with Judaism. This is confirmed by the earlier identification of these opponents as 'the circumcision'.

The author's calling their teachings human commands has also provoked much speculation. Hultgren takes this to mean precepts from Judaism.[204] Several others deny that these commands could be those found in Scripture because the author would not call those precepts *human* commands. Thus they must be the 'traditions of the elders' observed within Judaism, that is the halakkah.[205] Many other interpreters find these regulations to be ascetic rules, particularly those found in 1 Timothy, based on a Gnostic view of the world.[206] But this polemical evaluation of their teaching can bear the weight of none of these hypotheses. Such a description of their teaching shows only that the author of Titus rejects it and intends for the readers to do the same because it is not teaching from God, while Paul's and Titus's is (1.1-3). This limited

199. Hultgren, *I–II Timothy, Titus*, pp. 157-58.

200. Brox (*Die Pastoralbriefe*, p. 288) asserts that these verses give good reason to think that Titus was not written to Crete.

201. Lock, *Pastoral Epistles*, pp. xvii, 135; Scott, *The Pastoral Epistles*, p. 160.

202. Hanson, *The Pastoral Epistles*, p. 178.

203. Fee, *1 and 2 Timothy, Titus*, p. 180.

204. Hultgren, *I–II Timothy, Titus*, p. 158.

205. Lock, *Pastoral Epistles*, p. 135; Hanson, *The Pastoral Epistles*, p. 178.

206. So Kelly, *Pastoral Epistles*, p. 236; Scott, *The Pastoral Epistles*, p. 160; Knight, *The Pastoral Epistles*, pp. 300-301 (though without the Gnostic connection).

function is also confirmed by the next phrase in v. 14—these are commandments of those who reject the truth.

Verse 16 accuses these teachers of claiming to know God, but denying him by their deeds. Thus they are despicable people who are unable to perform any good deeds. The mention of knowing God is often cited as evidence that these teachers are Gnostics.[207] But with no more direct evidence that knowledge of God is a theme of their teaching or that any Gnostic ideas play a part in their teaching, this single statement cannot serve as evidence that these opponents are Gnostic. A more likely background is suggested by Fee. He comments that v. 16 alludes to the claim of Jews to know God, in contrast to pagans who do not.[208] Even though this fits the Jewish identity of these opponents, it remains very speculative. Claims to know God were not limited to Gnosticism or Judaism and played a significant role within the Christian tradition.[209] So this statement is not evidence of a problem with Gnosticism.

The real function of asserting that these teachers claim to know God is the polemical contrast that follows: they show that they do not know God by the way they live. Karris identifies this contrast between what they preach and what they do as another stock polemical schema used against Sophists.[210] Thus, this simply gives another reason to reject them without specifying anything about their teaching. Some interpreters, though, contend that denying God with their deeds is a reference to ascetic regulations.[211] But the following characterization of the opponents as detestable and unable to do any good work shows that the intention of v. 16 is to paint a somewhat frightening portrait of them so that the readers will reject them out of hand. This verse also makes an excellent contrast for the beginning of the next section, which urges correct behavior for various groups within the church.[212]

In spite of the amount of space devoted to the false teachers in 1.10-16, we learn little about them. They had their origin, at least, among

---

207. E.g. Brox, *Die Pastoralbriefe*, pp. 35, 290; Haufe, 'Gnostische Irrlehre und ihre Abwehr in den Pastoralbriefen', pp. 328-29.

208. Fee, *1 and 2 Timothy, Titus*, p. 182. See also Fee's comments on the absence of any suggestion of a problem with Gnosticism in all of 1.10-16.

209. See Fee, *1 and 2 Timothy, Titus*, p. 182.

210. Karris, 'The Background and Significance of the Polemic of the Pastoral Epistles', pp. 552-53.

211. Knight, *The Pastoral Epistles*, p. 303. Kelly (*Pastoral Epistles*, pp. 237-38) thinks it refers to either ascetic regulations or loose behavior.

212. See Brox, *Die Pastoralbriefe*, pp. 290-91.

Jewish Christians who require some things of Christians that the author of Titus rejects. These requirements seem to come from Judaism, but nothing more precise can be said about them at this point. (Some more specification may be possible when we examine 1.15 below as an allusion). These opponents are also identified as native Cretans rather than as teachers who have come there from outside. Thus, they are presented as a local phenomenon rather than as part of a larger movement. These verses also indicate that they have garnered a significant following.

3.9-11

The only other explicit statements about opponents appear in 3.9-11 where they are called factious people who participate in stupid controversies, genealogies, dissensions and legal disputes. The section 3.8b-11 is the closing of the body of Titus. Many interpreters begin the section at v. 9[213] but the contrast between the believers who apply themselves to good deeds and the disputatious opponents belong together.[214] This section is again clearly an attack on the opponents, and so a polemical section.

The description of the opponents given in 3.9-11 echoes that given in 1.10-16. Calling their teaching stupid argumentation is obviously a polemical evaluation that tells us nothing about it. Some have used this string of polemical evaluations to connect these teachers with the opponents of 1 Timothy because similar vocabulary is used in 1 Timothy.[215] But these rather general accusations, which include stock polemical charges, are too vague and too common to make a connection with 1 Timothy.

Several interpreters think that the genealogies mentioned in v. 9 refer to either some sort of Jewish legendary material[216] or a system of Gnostic aeons.[217] But there is insufficient evidence to support any specifica-

213. So Spicq, *Les épîtres pastorales*, p. 290; Lock, *Pastoral Epistles*, p. 150; Fee, *1 and 2 Timothy, Titus*, p. 210.

214. So Dibelius and Conzelmann, *The Pastoral Epistles*, p. 151; Hultgren, *I–II Timothy, Titus*, p. 172. Brox (*Die Pastoralbriefe*, p. 310) begins the section at the beginning of v. 8.

215. So, e.g., Spicq, *Les épîtres pastorales*, p. 298; Kelly, *Pastoral Epistles*, p. 255; Knight, *The Pastoral Epistles*, pp. 353-54.

216. E.g. Knight, *The Pastoral Epistles*, p. 353; Lock, *Pastoral Epistles*, p. 159; Murphy-O'Connor, '2 Timothy Contrasted with 1 Timothy and Titus', pp. 415-16; Spicq, *Les épîtres pastorales*, p. 298.

217. E.g. Hanson, *The Pastoral Epistles*, p. 194; Schenk, 'Die Pastoralbriefe in

tion for these genealogies beyond some sort of interpretation of the Hebrew Bible. We can specify it to that extent only because we know from 1.10-16 that the Law is under discussion.[218] Additionally, 3.9 speaks of their teaching as legal argumentation. Though Schenk asserts that this need not refer to interpretation of the Hebrew Bible,[219] the knowledge that they are Jewish Christians who are called 'the circumcision' and advocate observance of commands different from those that Titus accepts as appropriate for Christians points to a reference to the Mosaic Law in v. 9. Unfortunately, no more specifics are found here.

In v. 10, these teachers are described as factious. Spicq asserts that this vocabulary (αἱρετικὸν) shows that they are separatists who have created a faction within the community.[220] But this word had not yet taken on the technical meaning of 'heretical', even near the end of the first century (though it was headed in that direction). It did, however, seem to possess a sense of contentiousness or to designate someone who causes division. So it is another polemical characterization.

After 3.10 commissions Titus to exercise some sort of ecclesiastical discipline against these teachers if they refuse to recant, such people are called perverted, sinful and self-condemned. Again, these charges tell us only that the author of Titus rejects these teachers.

Once again, the statements about the opponents in this section are almost entirely judgments against their teachings and character. They confirm that there is a dispute about the Law, but show nothing else.

Summary of Explicit Statements
Explicit statements reveal that these opponents are Jewish–Christian teachers, or at least that their teaching is rooted in their interpretation of the Law and their origin was among Jewish Christians. They advocate that Christians observe some commands that the author of Titus thinks must be rejected. These opponents also are identified as native Cretans. Thus, they do not seem to be part of a larger movement that arrived from outside. They do seem to have enjoyed some success in the community addressed by this letter.

---

der Neueren Forschung', p. 3429; Haufe, 'Gnostische Irrlehre und ihre Abwehr in den Pastoralbriefen', p. 329.

218. See the comments of Colson, '"Myths and Genealogies"', pp. 368-69.
219. Schenk, 'Die Pastoralbriefe in der Neueren Forschung', p. 3429.
220. So Spicq, *Les épîtres pastorales*, p. 299.

Allusions

1.15

We have identified 1.10-16 as a polemical section and discussed every verse in the section except v. 15. Verse 15 is not a direct statement about the opponents as the other verses in this section are. But since the opponents are 'the circumcision' and since they instigate disputes about the Law, the references to purity in 1.15 probably allude to their teachings.[221]

Many interpreters contend that the mention of purity in v. 15 alludes to the opponents' ascetic regulations.[222] But I have found no evidence that suggests that these opponents are ascetics and, without the presupposition that they are Gnostics, no evidence of such tendencies is forthcoming. The most probable implication of these comments about purity is that they are related to their interpretation of the Law and so involve purity laws of Judaism. Hanson, however, rejects this understanding of the opponents' teaching. He contends that v. 15 could not be a reference to commands from the Hebrew Bible because their observance is no longer an issue in Christianity and that anyone who advocates such observances at the time of the writing of Titus was immediately branded a heretic.[223] Even on the assumption that Titus is pseudonymous and composed in the late first or early second century, Hanson's description of the situation within early Christianity is inaccurate. Questions about the place of the Law continued to be debated well past the first century. And while Paul's writings may seem to settle the issue for modern readers, they did not have canonical status at the time of the composition of Titus.

The Mosaic Law is the only context that the letter to Titus gives for the opponents' concern about purity. Thus, it must remain our touchstone for identifying their regulations. Many interpreters specify these

221. Nearly all interpreters recognize 1.15 as a statement about the opponents' teachings. Knight (*The Pastoral Epistles*, p. 301) seems to notice that 1.15 does not speak as directly about them as do the surrounding verses. He comments that Paul raises the purity issue because they do.

222. So, e.g., Dibelius and Conzelmann, *The Pastoral Epistles*, p. 137; Müller, *Zur frühchristlichen Theologiegeschichte*, p. 59.

223. Hanson, *The Pastoral Epistles*, p. 178.

purity laws as those involving food prohibitions in Judaism[224] and some add regulations about sex.[225] These specifications are, however, usually drawn from 1 Timothy rather than Titus. This use of another letter to identify the opponents of the primary text is methodologically unsound. Unless we can be certain that the very same opponents are in view in both letters and that they have not modified their view, such borrowing cannot be permitted. Certainty on both of these points is seldom possible, and it is impossible at this stage of my investigation. Thus, we cannot use 1 Timothy to expand our understanding of the opponents of Titus. So we are left with only the knowledge that the opponents are concerned about purity laws that are based on the Mosaic Code. It is possible that food laws were among their concerns. Indeed, given what we know of the concerns raised by Jewish Christians elsewhere, we might think it probable. But purity laws encompass a much broader spectrum of life than food prohibitions and sex regulations. Verse 15 gives us no basis to narrow the concerns of these teachers to these or any other matters or to explicitly include them among their concerns. This verse suggests only that they regard matters about purity as important, without specifying any particular areas on which they concentrate their attention.

1.9

The body of this letter begins with a description of the qualifications and duties of elders (1.5-9). It is primarily instructive and so a didactic section. In 1.9 the author says elders are to be able to refute those who contradict the truth. Since this leads directly into the polemical comments of 1.10-16, v. 9 seems to allude to the opponents. Unfortunately, it reveals only that the author's judgment against them—they contradict the truth.

2.8

In 2.7-8, Titus is exhorted to proper conduct and sound speech so that no opponent will be able to say anything evil about him. This statement appears in a hortatory section which gives instructions about conduct

---

224. So, e.g., Murphy-O'Connor, '2 Timothy Contrasted with 1 Timothy and Titus', p. 415; Fee, *1 and 2 Timothy, Titus*, p. 181; Hultgren, *I–II Timothy, Titus*, p. 158.

225. E.g. Müller, *Zur frühchristlichen Theologiegeschichte*, p. 59, and presumably all those who find ascetic tendencies here.

for various groups in the church.[226] The reference in 2.8 to opponents has been understood to refer primarily to the opponents of this letter[227] or to pagan opponents,[228] though most interpreters leave room for a secondary inclusion of the other group. Even if this comment about opponents does refer to the false teachers, it reveals only that the author thinks they may be watching Titus (or church leaders) closely to have reason to accuse him (them). But a sanction for an exhortation may intend to provide a more general basis rather than a reference to a particular group. Furthermore, our method does not allow allusions in hortatory contexts to supply information about opponents.

1.5

The first sentence in the letter's body refers to something that is defective in the churches on Crete. While some think this defect is that the congregations do not have elders,[229] others see it as an allusion to the opponents.[230] If it is an allusion to the opponents, and this remains uncertain, it yields no information about them. However, a mention of them at this point in the letter would suggest that they are a central reason for its composition.

Summary of Allusions

Allusions indicate that one area of the opponents's disputes involve purity laws of Judaism. Nothing more specific can be said about their teaching from the comments in 1.15 without illegitimately bringing in

226. So Brox, *Die Pastoralbriefe*, p. 291; Kelly, *Pastoral Epistles*, p. 238; Dibelius and Conzelmann, *The Pastoral Epistles*, p. 139; Fee, *1 and 2 Timothy, Titus*, p. 184. Knight (*The Pastoral Epistles*, p. 305) expands the section to include the theological justification for these instructions given in vv. 11-15, but sees the function of vv. 1-10 as hortatory.

227. So Brox, *Die Pastoralbriefe*, p. 296; Hultgren, *I–II Timothy, Titus*, p. 162; Knight, *The Pastoral Epistles*, p. 313; Dibelius and Conzelmann, *The Pastoral Epistles*, p. 141; Fee, *1 and 2 Timothy, Titus*, p. 189. Hanson (*The Pastoral Epistles*, pp. 242-43) leaves it more vague, identifying them as those 'ill-disposed individuals in the community itself'.

228. Lock, *Pastoral Epistles*, p. 142.

229. Hultgren, *I–II Timothy, Titus*, pp. 153-54. Perhaps also Kelly, *Pastoral Epistles*, pp. 229-30. Fee (*1 and 2 Timothy, Titus*, p. 176) seems to fit here because he thinks the defect is present because the churches had been only recently founded.

230. Johnson, *Writings of the New Testament*, p. 403; Dibelius and Conzelmann, *The Pastoral Epistles*, p. 132.

evidence from other letters.[231] So we cannot specify what particulars of
the purity code are their focus of attention. Other allusions to these
opponents yield no additional information about them.

Affirmations

3.5

Within another section of exhortation, 3.1-8a,[232] some have perceived a
statement that refers to the opponents in 3.5.[233] Given the overall context of the discussion of the Law, the rejection of righteousness based
on one's deeds in 3.5 may be an allusion to the opponents. However,
v. 5 is part of the preformed traditional material found in vv. 4-7.[234] So
the inclusion of the remark about righteousness based on one's deeds is
in the tradition rather than a formulation of this author. Still, the tradition could be quoted as part of the argument against the opponents.
But given its placement in the midst of these exhortations about appropriate conduct, its function is probably as a sanction for the ethical
instructions, that is, it gives the theological basis for righteous living.[235]
Thus, it does not seem to have the opponents in view.

Conclusions about the Opponents of Titus

Our study of the opponents of Titus reveals that they are a group of
teachers who are largely or at least originally Jewish Christians who
advocate interpretations and observances of the Law that the author of
Titus rejects. They probably give particular attention to some purity

---

231. Müller (*Zur frühchristlichen Theologiegeschichte*, p. 65) suggests that their
attention to purity laws may show a concern from Jewish Christians about contact
with pagans. Though this cannot be supported with specific evidence from Titus, if
this were their concern, it would still not help us specify what matters within the
purity code they emphasize.

232. Dibelius and Conzelmann, *The Pastoral Epistles*, p. 147. Others who see the
section as hortatory but include all of v. 8 in it include: Fee, *1 and 2 Timothy, Titus*,
p. 200; Knight, *The Pastoral Epistles*, p. 331. Similarly Kelly (*Pastoral Epistles*,
p. 248) who includes all of 3.1-11 in the section.

233. Johnson, *Writings of the New Testament*, p. 403. Perhaps Dibelius and
Conzelmann, *The Pastoral Epistles*, p. 148.

234. See Young, *The Theology of the Pastoral Letters*, p. 62.

235. Cf. Kelly, *Pastoral Epistles*, p. 251; Knight, *The Pastoral Epistles*, p. 335;
Fee, *1 and 2 Timothy, Titus*, p. 204.

regulations from Judaism, but we cannot isolate any particular laws within the purity code on which they place special emphasis. This letter presents them as a local phenomenon rather than as teachers related to some larger movement. But the author does perceive them as successful enough to comment that they upset whole households and to devote a significant portion of this letter to combating them.

CONCLUSIONS ABOUT THE OPPONENTS OF THE PASTORAL EPISTLES

This study of the Pastorals has found different types of opponents rather than a single front of opposition. The opponents of 2 Timothy stand out as significantly different from those of 1 Timothy or Titus. The opponents of 2 Timothy have an overrealized eschatology (at least by the measure of the author of that letter), which is not found opposed or discussed in either of the other two Pastoral Epistles. All we can claim with certainty about their eschatology is that they claim to possess in the present something that the author of 2 Timothy believes is available only at the parousia. This, it seems, has some effect on the way that they view Christian existence before the parousia. Their viewpoint has gained enough adherents that 2 Timothy employs strong polemical language and characterizations against them. This rather imprecise description of these opponents is all that the text yields. Perhaps we should expect no more since opposition to them does not seem to be the primary purpose of 2 Timothy. Still, we see enough to know that they are clearly distinct from the opponents of 1 Timothy or Titus because it is only in 2 Timothy that eschatology is an issue.

Our investigation of the opponents of Titus indicates that Jewish Christians have raised questions about observing at least some the purity laws of the Mosaic Code. However, we cannot isolate any particular part of the purity regulations as those with which they are most concerned. Their disputing about the Law may well include more than matters about purity, but we cannot determine what other matters of interpretation or observance they raise. Again, they seem to have been able to gather a following. Titus portrays these opponents as a local, Cretan phenomenon. So at least as far as the author of Titus cares to describe them, these opponents are not part of a larger movement.

We can give a bit more detailed description of the opponents of 1 Timothy than was possible for either 2 Timothy or Titus. The defeat of these opponents seems closer to the primary purpose of 1 Timothy than it is for either of the other two Pastoral Epistles. The central issue in dispute with the opponents of 1 Timothy is the interpretation and observance of the Law. The opponents interpret the Law in ways that 1 Timothy finds unacceptable and urge observance of some commands within it that 1 Timothy rejects as inappropriate for Christians. In particular, they advocate that Christians observe the (or some) food laws from Judaism. They also prescribe marriage regulations that 1 Timothy rejects. There is no good evidence that these rules about food and marriage are part of a larger ascetic regime that the opponents follow and advocate. Neither is there evidence that these regulations are based on a Gnostic world view or an overrealized eschatology. The injunctions about food and marriage are based on their interpretation of the Law.

So we have found a separate group of opponents in each of these letters. While two of the groups are similar, we have no evidence that they are identical or are both part of a larger movement—and some evidence to the contrary. There is also no sufficient evidence to identity any of these opponents as Gnostics. Some of the issues that they raise are found among Gnostics, but none of the central tenets of Gnosticism is combated in these letters.

Since these three letters each address different opponents, each letter addresses a somewhat different occasion. This provides some confirmation that they are indeed letters. This is so even if they were composed as a corpus. Then, it appears, the author wanted to address different sorts of problems and situations with these letters, even while 'publishing' them as a corpus. This being the case, our study of the opponents of the Pastoral Epistles also confirms that these letters must be read on their own before looking for similarities and connections.

Chapter 10

OF OPPONENTS AND 'OPPONENTS': A RECONSTRUCTION
OF THOSE OPPOSED IN THE PAULINE LETTERS

Having completed this examination of individual letters, we must now synthesize the results and take stock of what can be said about Pauline opponents.

The method used in this study has produced a spectrum of opposition to Paul, which is more diverse than that envisioned by Baur, Schmithals, Lüdemann and many others who allow a preconceived type of opponent to control their understanding of the Pauline texts and the situations they address.[1] We should note first that our study reveals that 1 Thessalonians has no opponents or competitors of Paul in view. Still, the Thessalonian Christians needed guidance from Paul as they attempted to understand and interpret their current experience with their new Christian outlook. They are, perhaps, an important paradigm for our understanding of both those whom Paul opposes and Paul's reaction to them. We have no sufficient reason to suspect that all or most of these opponents are dishonest or are intentionally leading people astray.[2] Some, though not all, were like the Thessalonians, groping their way in their new existence. They were interpreting their experience of God, received teaching, and at times Scripture to arrive at an authentic understanding and practice of Christianity.[3] These Christians were exploring the limits

1. Similarly, the reconstruction of Michael D. Goulder (*St. Paul versus St. Peter* is also too simplistic when it finds only two types of Christians (Pauline and Petrine) in early Christianity.

2. As Bauer (*Orthodoxy and Heresy in Earliest Christianity* [trans. the Philadelphia Seminar: Philadelphia: Fortress Press, 1971], p. xxvi) asserts, we should not presuppose that, in his words, heretics were morally inferior to the orthodox.

3. Gerd Theissen (*Social Reality*) comments that Christianity was a 'revolution of values' through which people acquired new possibilities for life. Their questions about how to practice Christianity included their struggles to work out the

of their new faith, and the boundaries were being drawn in reaction to them[4]—a process which would continue in earnest for several centuries. The point is not to idolize Paul's opponents as heroes of personal discovery, but to avoid envisioning them as the 'deceitful workers' that the Pauline rhetoric sometimes leads us to imagine. Paul's reaction to his opponents may be the first formulation of a teaching that drew those specific implications, whether theological, ethical, or social.[5] That does not mean that he saw those opponents as any less dangerous.

Despite our methodological insistence on identifying the opponents of each letter solely on the basis of that individual letter, we are able to make connections among certain letters and witness developments in some congregations. The deteriorating relations between Paul and the Corinthians are especially notable. At the time of 1 Corinthians, questions were being raised about Paul's position as the dominant or exclusive authority over the congregation. Paul and his apostolic credentials were being compared with other apostolic figures (and possibly local leaders) and he was not comparing favorably in the eyes of some. Paul treats this as a problem of misunderstanding appropriate standards for evaluating apostles. But beyond his rejection of their 'wisdom', which he judges to be worldly (i.e. sub-Christian), Paul attacks no theological agenda in the comparisons. Furthermore, this problem has grown up from within the congregation. Thus, 1 Corinthians provides an example of opposition to Paul's claim to authority over a congregation developing without the arrival of teachers from outside who oppose him. Perhaps such questionings should not be surprising given the reliance of Paul's churches on charisma for authority.[6]

implications of Christian faith for their relations within the community, relations with ideas from outside Christianity, and relations among the differing ethnic groups and social classes within their churches.

4.   Castelli (*Imitating Paul*, p. 46) notes that Paul's letters are 'concerned with establishing the boundaries of the group and maintaining order within the group itself, with disciplining of the body, with power relations and questions of authority'.

5.   Speaking of the Pastorals, James D.G. Dunn (*Unity and Diversity in the New Testament: An Inquiry into the Character of Earliest Christianity* [San Antonio, TX: Trinity Press International, 2nd edn, 1990], pp. 281-82) asserts that the boundaries between the acceptable and unacceptable were not yet clearly drawn. His evidence is that teachings like those being opposed are still advocated by some within the communities those letters address.

6.   Theissen (*Social Reality*, p. 262) says, 'If the personal relationship actually

By the time of 2 Corinthians 1–7, the questions and challenges have become accusations and rejection. Preachers have arrived from outside the community with letters of recommendation, which facilitated their rise to a position of influence at Corinth. These teachers claim to be apostles and compare ministries and ministers' qualifications and successes. They further claim that their presentation of evidence for their apostolic status and their comparisons with other apostles are part of the appropriate manner of life for apostles. They also cite their acceptance of maintenance as evidence of their apostleship. Overall, their view is that apostles should possess a strong, powerful, impressive presence. This demeanor, they argue, is evidence that the power of God works in them. Quite deliberately, they include Paul in their comparisons of apostolic qualifications. By their standards, he is woefully deficient and so is to be denied apostolic status. Furthermore, they intimate, Paul is not to be trusted generally, given the inconsistency between what he says and does with respect to visiting Corinth. They intend to discredit Paul and denigrate his apostleship, and thus to replace him.

This message finds ready ears at Corinth. The behavior and criteria for apostolic status and authority that these opponents advocate fits extremely well with the outlook Paul that had opposed in 1 Corinthians. Whether this was simply a fortuitous match or whether the opponents adapted their message in significant ways to the Corinthians' expectations (or some of both), we do not know. But the continuity between the problems of 1 Corinthians and 2 Corinthians 1–7 are unmistakable. We must remember, of course, that this does not indicate that the opponents were there at the earlier time, only that when they arrived they capitalized on the Corinthians' prior leanings.

Things had only gotten worse by the writing of 2 Corinthians 10–13. These same opponents, whom we now find claiming the titles missionary and 'servant of Christ', seem to have a firmer grip at Corinth. The central issue remains the appropriate way of life for apostles. By this time, they argue that their powerful and successful lives are the correct apostolic manifestation of the Spirit. The Spirit also gives them visions, revelations and miraculous powers. Beyond this, the Spirit ensures that

becomes the basic structure of a religion, if it leads people to expect that God's Spirit can be efficacious in everyone, independent of hard and fast rules, then a general readiness for individually mediated reawakenings can develop'. This model of the way a religion may develop seems relevant to the situation we encounter in 1 Corinthians.

they possess impressive speaking ability and are able to display their qualifications convincingly. They also make a point of being Jewish, perhaps claiming that this makes their understanding of God, Christianity or Scripture superior. Apostles with such credentials must, of course, receive appropriate recognition from a congregation. The apostle assumes special authority and the congregation submits; the apostle demands special rights (including maintenance), and the congregation complies. Moreover, these 'super-apostles' argue that since it is clear that Paul does not possess the appropriate manner of life, he does not possess the measure of the Spirit that makes one an apostle.

The clearest development from the letter of chs. 1–7 to that of chs. 10–13 is the explicit emphasis on the Spirit as the source of the power that these 'apostles' exhibit in their lives. Thus, the issue that Paul must address in chs. 10–13 is how the Spirit manifests itself in apostles. As we have seen, this same basic debate about the manifestation of God's presence was going on in the wider cultural milieu.

In spite of the presence of a similar debate outside Christianity, these 'servants of Satan' seem to come the closest to being the type of opponent often envisioned as the recipients of Paul's criticisms. The nearly perfect fit between their self-presentation and the Corinthians' previously expressed expectations seems too great a coincidence to be innocent. When we note their intentional exacerbation of misunderstandings between Paul and the Corinthians (by interpreting his actions in the worst possible light) and their insistence on receiving maintenance as a part of the Corinthians' recognition of them, it is difficult to view them as the honest seekers described at the beginning of this chapter. Still, they probably believed that their understanding of Christianity and its apostles was correct and that Paul's was wrong. Their tactics seem deceitful and harsh from the perspective of interpreters who read as allies of Paul, but he is no gentler with those he identifies as opponents.

This investigation of the Corinthian correspondence has vindicated reading letters individually by demonstrating that this methodological procedure does not prohibit the interpreter from seeing connections between the situations various letters address. An initial independent reading of each letter does not lead to merely isolated snap-shots between which we cannot identify links, when they exist. Thus, this method can lead to a more solidly based reconstruction of opposition to Paul.

We have also discovered an anti-Pauline movement. The Corinthian opponents were Jewish-Christian traveling missionaries who enter that church to supplant Paul. They claim some unspecified superiority on the basis of their Jewish heritage, but they do not require Gentiles to observe elements of the Mosaic Law that Paul did not require. Acknowledging that they do not require more Law observance of Gentiles is not minimizing the importance of their claim to being Jewish. It simply recognizes that not all Jewish-Christian missionaries advocated a Christianity that demanded that Gentiles keep the Law. Since Paul does not mention any other advantage that they claim by being Jewish, we must settle for knowing that they use their ethnic background as one of their qualifications for the position of authority that they claim. While this anti-Pauline mission is broader than a single church (they arrive with letters of recommendation), there is no justification for associating it with the Jerusalem church.

In Galatians we find a very different situation. Here teachers have come to Paul's church arguing that Gentiles need to be circumcised and observe certain holy days from Judaism. These seem to be the only requirements they impose beyond Paul's teaching because Paul thinks that telling the Galatians that circumcision obligates them to observe the whole Law will be an effective counter-argument. Unlike the intentional opponents in Corinth, these teachers do not seem to think that they are at odds with Paul. Rather, they apparently think their teaching is in line with his (perhaps revised) preaching. If this were not the case, Paul would not find it necessary to deny so vehemently that he 'preaches circumcision'. These teachers, then, are attempting to convince the Galatians to accept their message as either the completion of Paul's initial preaching or the correction of the Galatians' misunderstanding of Paul.

Paul reacts violently against this teaching. Such a harsh reaction does not show that Paul had previously encountered these teachers (or their compatriots within a movement) or their exact teaching before, but that he has had experiences with teaching that he considers analogous. He recounts some of these painful experiences in Galatians as part of his argument that he does not hold the views these teachers claim he does. Paul finds their view incompatible with Christianity as he understands it and so utterly rejects them and their teaching.

Galatians yields no evidence that Paul's authority or apostleship are under attack. Rather these opponents claim to agree with Paul. Similarly, there is no evidence that they are authorized or claim to be authorized by any segment of the Jerusalem church. They are Jewish, but that does not mean they claim an attachment to Jerusalem or compare Paul's credentials with those of the Jerusalem apostles. Paul's comments in Galatians 1 and 2 do not defend his apostleship in the face of attacks, but establish his ethos as one authorized by God to oppose the kind of teaching being advocated in Galatia.

The evidence of Galatians does not demonstrate that these opponents are in any way anti-Pauline. They are travelling preachers who proclaim a form of Gentile Christianity different from that which Paul preaches. This does not mean they are an *anti-Pauline* movement. At the time of their arrival in Galatia, they may have seen themselves as supplementers of Paul's earlier, less developed (and less correct) proclamation, but they do not seem to understand themselves as supplanters of Paul. If they assert that the Galatians misunderstood Paul, there is even less reason to read antagonism with Paul into their presence.

Unfortunately, Galatians gives us no clear basis for determining what these opponents claim that Gentiles gain by submitting to circumcision. *If* it is something as simple as easier association with Jewish Christians (and so no soteriological issues are involved for them),[7] Paul's circumcision of Timothy (if that tradition is as old as this dispute) could appear to be in agreement with such a policy. In any case, these opponents may see their regulations as a minor concession on the Gentiles' part.

Paul, of course, views the matter quite differently. He sees great theological issues at stake. His extreme reaction to these teachers may have won him the day in Galatia, we cannot be certain. But it does seem to have set this group of teachers against him and so won him some enemies. That is, Paul treats them as opponents/enemies, and that is what they become. It seems likely that they reacted to the polemics of Galatians by hardening their position and, of necessity, becoming anti-Pauline. These (now properly called) opponents may well become the

7.	The conduct of Cephas and Barnabas in Antioch incident shows that it is possible to adhere to the Mosaic purity code in the context of a mixed Jewish/Gentile congregation without thinking that large theological issues are at stake. If, as many interpreters now contend, Paul lost at Antioch, and if the Galatian teachers know of the incident, they may know a version of it which asserted that Paul acceded (see Dunn's list [*Galatians*, p. 130])). Again, this does not mean the opponents are dishonest, they just have heard a different interpretation (perhaps from some who do oppose Paul's views) of those events. Furthermore, our investigation does not indicate that they use the incident in their arguments, but it is possible though we cannot say probable.

movement Paul refers to as the 'dogs' in Philippians. These Philippian opponents are Jewish-Christian missionaries who require circumcision for Gentiles. While these two points are insufficient evidence to be certain that the same group is in view, it seems reasonable. The Philippian opponents' membership in a group that had troubled other Pauline churches supports this connection with the Galatian opponents. And, when Paul castigates them in Philippians, the only requirement he mentions that they impose and which he rejects is circumcision. Again, what significance they attach to it and whether they advocate adherence to any other Mosaic regulations remain unclear. Thus, Paul's focal issue is the same when he rejects the opponents of Galatians and Philippians.

Whether or not the connection between the Galatian teachers and the Philippian 'dogs' stands, Paul's comments in Philippians make it clear that the 'dogs' are part of a traveling group of Christian teachers. At least in Paul's view, they are an anti-Pauline movement. We cannot be certain that the group understood or presented itself as such. On the other hand, they enter Pauline congregations with the intent of changing those Gentiles' practice of Christianity. Thus, they do intentionally oppose Paul's teaching and assert their own authority, legitimating their claim to such a position by recourse to their Jewish descent. This combination of teaching and assertion of authority seems almost to require an attack on Paul's apostolic status. Yet, he does not mention that aspect of their presentation. Even if they do not explicitly attack his apostleship in their attempts to win over Paul's churches, they are clearly an anti-Pauline movement.

Our investigation, then, has discovered two anti-Pauline movements: the Corinthian 'super-apostles' and the Philippian 'dogs' who may have originated from the Galatian teachers. These movements are not related. Their only common feature beyond opposition to Paul is their Jewish descent. Only an unrealistic and unhistorical view of early Jewish Christianity could suppose that all Christian Jews believed all the same things[8] and so must oppose Paul for the same reasons. First-century Jewish Christianity was far too diverse to allow such a simple identification of these two groups of Pauline opponents. Furthermore, that both

---

8. See R.E. Brown, 'Not Jewish Christianity and Gentile Christianity but Types of Jewish/Gentile Christianity', *CBQ* 45 (1983), pp. 74-79, and Craig C. Hill, *Hellenists and Hebrews: Reappraising Division within the Earliest Church* (Minneapolis: Fortress Press, 1992).

groups are composed of Jews should not surprise us. After all, most Christian missionaries mentioned in the New Testament were Jewish, including Paul, Barnabas and Apollos. Jews were, of course, the first Christians and the majority of Christians for some years after Christianity's inception. Moreover, Jewish Christians were in a better position to assume the roles of leaders and teachers because of their monotheistic background, their grounding in Jewish ethics and their knowledge of Scripture. Plus, Gentile Christians found Jewish descent a convincing element of a case to establish authoritative status, if 2 Corinthians and Philippians are any indication. Thus, the claim to a Jewish heritage is no reason to identify these two anti-Pauline groups with one another, and they have nothing else in common.

This conclusion calls into question the routinely accepted thesis that Paul was rejected by 'Jewish Christianity'. Once we acknowledge the diversity among Jewish Christians, such a thesis of nearly unanimous rejection of Paul becomes less feasible. But beyond this, having leaders who are Jewish and who claim some advantage on that basis does not make a group 'Jewish-Christian'. If it did, all Pauline Christianity would be classified as 'Jewish Christianity' because Paul is a Jew and he claims advantages for Jews over Gentiles in Romans 2–3. We have found no evidence that the opponents of 2 Corinthians draw on their Jewish background to bring the Corinthians into some kind of 'Jewish Christianity' as opposed to a 'Gentile Christianity'. There were, of course, law-observant Jewish Christians, for example in Jerusalem, perhaps including James. Some of these Christians believed Gentiles needed to be circumcised and sent out missionaries to teach this, as Acts 15 shows. Furthermore, the doubts of at least some of the Christian 'Pharisees' (Acts 15.5) about Paul did not just vanish after the Jerusalem Conference, as Paul's worries about the reception of the collection from his churches demonstrates. And they probably sent out missionaries after the Conference to convert members of Paul's churches. It seems unlikely, though, that after the Jerusalem Conference such traveling evangelists/teachers could have claimed a connection with the Jerusalem church. It also seems likely that even some of those who forced the Jerusalem Conference with their opposition to the way others admitted Gentiles acknowledged Paul's apostleship and mission to the Gentiles after the Conference, even as Paul acknowledged James.

The point is that *the data of the Pauline letters* do not support finding a group attached to Jerusalem that constantly hounds Paul as he moves from one city to another.[9] We have found no connection with Jerusalem for any of the opponents to whom the Pauline letters respond. Thus, our findings, when combined with the certain absence of uniformity among Jewish Christians, indicate that the hypothesis of a pervasive opposition to Paul throughout 'Jewish Christianity' is at best significantly over-drawn. This is not to say that Paul was not a controversial figure; he clearly was. Nor does it deny that some Jewish Christians opposed his teaching and rejected his apostolic status; they certainly did. But there is insufficient evidence to claim that this rejection of Paul (particularly if it is attached to his Law-free gospel to Gentiles) was nearly as per-vasive among Christian Jews as current scholarly constructs imagine.

Still, 1 Timothy and Titus show that discussions about the place of the Law within Christianity were not unusual. Even though there is no basis to claim a connection between the opponents in view in these two letters or for either of them to be associated with a broader anti-Pauline movement, they do demonstrate that questions about the Law came up in various Gentile–Christian communities, sometimes because they were raised by Jewish Christians. One should expect nothing different since the Law was a significant part of the Scriptures of earliest Chris-tianity. First Timothy's recipients were being encouraged to observe Jewish food laws and some marriage regulations which may have been derived from interpretations of the Law. The opponents in view in Titus were Jewish Christians who seem to advocate the observance of some regulations from the Mosaic purity code. Notably, the author of Titus speaks of these opponents as a local phenomenon rather than as a part of a larger movement. So we have no basis for assigning them a place within an anti-Pauline movement. Again, what they show is that the issue of the Law was recurrent, but also that those who raised it did not necessarily frame the issue in terms of agreement with or opposition to Paul.

The kind of opposition found in Colossians is quite different from what we have seen from the members of anti-Pauline groups. The vi-sionaries in Colossae show no signs of understanding themselves to be rejecting any part of Paul's teaching. Their use of elements of Judaism seems limited to the observance of Sabbaths and new moons. Perhaps their food and drink abstinence regulations come from Judaism, but we

9.   There was of course a Jerusalem-based missionary movement, but the Pauline letters give us no reason to think that it defined itself by its opposition to Paul or that such opposition was a major part of its preaching.

cannot be certain. There is more reason to think that these regulations
are related to the visions they receive. In these visions they observe and
perhaps participate in angelic worship which becomes the basis for
their additional worship observances, their 'will-worship'. In addition to
their own participation in these rituals and observances, they have
begun to consider those who do not join them to be sinners. This
judgment of others seems to be the Colossian author's primary
objection to these visionaries. He denigrates their regulations as
worldly and ineffective, but the letter's focus is on demonstrating that
the Colossians do not need such rules or experiences to enjoy the
appropriate and saving relationship with God through Christ. The writer
(whether Paul or someone later) could hardly condemn either the more
restrictive ethic or the receiving of visions because Paul himself lived a
mildly ascetic existence (e.g. his celibacy) and was himself a visionary.
These things are not the problem, it is the imposition of them upon all
Christians and the accompanying condemnation.

Thus, these Colossian visionaries may well have seen themselves as
good followers of Paul. Colossians rejects their imposition of 'commandments' and their pride in their spiritual exploits, but does not
accuse them of revolting against Paul. We have in Colossians, then,
another example of opponents who are defined as opponents by the arrival of the letter, but do not understand themselves as Paul's opponents
before that time. This does not mean, of course, that there was no
dispute in the community about their teachings and practices, only that
they do not intentionally oppose Paul's teaching.

Those opposed in 2 Thessalonians not only do not reject Paul or his
teaching, they claim to agree with him and to possess the correct interpretation of his teaching. They contend that their more fully realized
eschatology is what Paul preaches. These Christians have quit their jobs
and dedicated themselves to ministry within the Thessalonian congregation. Perhaps they believe that their experience of the parousia blessings has prepared them to minister to their fellow-Christians in ways
beyond those who have not had or do not understand this eschatological
experience. They at least believe that their experience of eschatological
blessings qualifies them to receive the congregation's financial support
as ministers. Once again, these 'opponents' only become such after the
letter arrives. Up to that point, even if they were wrong in this, they
claim that their views are Paul's. If 2 Thessalonians is deutero-Pauline,
they may have continued to maintain their position by rejecting the

letter's authenticity. It is also possible that their reliance on their eschatological experiences could have led them to reject Paul's authority
after the letter arrived, even if Paul wrote it. But we have absolutely no
evidence to suggest a desire, or a even willingness, to disagree with
Paul.

The opponents of 2 Timothy are similar to those of 2 Thessalonians
in that they advocated an eschatology that is more fully realized than
that of the letter's author. The comments about these opponents are so
general and sparse, as well as consisting mostly of stock characterizations, that we can say little else about them. There is certainly no basis
for identifying them as Gnostics or for seeing them as a manifestation
of a larger group or movement that included those opposed in 2 Thessalonians or elsewhere in the Pauline corpus.

At this point it may be instructive to notice what Paul and his opponents do *not* argue about. We have found no major christological issues
being debated with opponents. The disputes are not about the relationship of Christ to the Father or Christ's place in the *Pleroma* or any other
cosmological scheme. We do not even find arguments from opponents
about the relationship between the earthly Jesus and the heavenly Christ
or the centrality of Christ for salvation. Neither is there evidence for
disagreements about pneumatology in the sense of the Spirit's relationship to the Father or Christ. They do not even argue over whether all
Christians possess the Spirit. There was significant debate over how the
Spirit should and does manifest itself in apostles, but not over its nature
or presence. We also did not find any arguments about the importance
of worshiping the one God or about that God's nature. Though not
connected with opponents, Paul's comments in 1 Cor. 8.7-10 indicate
that he is willing to accept henotheism for those not yet convinced that
there is only one God. Again, we have found no opponents who advocate antinomianism, though some Christians at Corinth seem to have
taken up such a position with respect to sexual matters (1 Cor. 5.1-13;
6.12-20), these beliefs are not clearly based on or related to opposition
to Paul. There was, furthermore, no debate about *whether* Gentiles
should be admitted into Christianity and no disagreement about whether
the Hebrew Bible was authoritative in the Christian community. Finally, they do not argue about Christ's role as the initiator of the New Age.

It is not that these issues had not yet been thought of; most certainly
had been. It is not that they were considered unimportant; they clearly
were important. Rather, Paul and his opponents agreed about them, at

least at a level that kept them from becoming the primary divisive issues. While complete uniformity is very doubtful, the differences were
not those that Paul saw as threatening to his churches. Thus, Paul and
his opponents have much in common.

On the other hand, Paul does argue with his opponents about the
extent to which the eschatological age has broken into the world and
what that means for Christian existence in the present. They do argue
about how to use the Hebrew Bible and what requirements from it are
incumbent on Christians, both Jews and Gentiles.[10] And there is some
dispute over the significance of Jewish descent for establishing oneself
in an authoritative position.

Paul and his opponents also argue about how the power of God is
revealed in apostles/ministers. This rather broad area is perhaps the
most widespread issue raised in conversation with opponents. In addition to being the central problem for the letters of 2 Corinthians, it also
takes in the behavior of the 'disorderly' of 2 Thessalonians. It even
encompasses the discussion about criteria for judging apostles raised in
1 Corinthians and perhaps the claims of the Philippian 'dogs' when
they raise the matter of their Jewish descent. So the struggle to establish
appropriate means of identifying legitimate authority was raised often
and not always in the context of a rejection of Paul's authority, but also
in more local manifestations such as that of 2 Thessalonians. This
shows us that at least some of those opposed were seeking ways of
living out their experience of Christ. They were seeking the appropriate
means by which to mainfest the presence of God. As we have also seen,
some found Paul's means of existence an unacceptable alternative.

One final type of dispute arises between these letters and their opponents: that of who agrees with Paul. The opponents of 2 Thessalonians
and, according to our reading, Galatians claim to teach what Paul teaches. Thus, agreement with Paul was sometimes at issue, just as some
intentionally disagreed with him.

We have now seen that those treated as opponents in the Pauline
letters take several forms. They differ in their practices, understandings
of authority, and beliefs about visionary experiences and the eschaton.
On these issues, Paul was pushed past his limits of toleration of difference. We know from his acceptance of law-abiding Jewish Christians

10. See the discussion of Hill, *Hellenists and Hebrews*, pp. 111-22, where he
argues that the issue of the Antioch incident was the obedience to the Law by Jews
when with Gentile Christians.

that he allowed some considerable range of Christian practice, but these opponents pressed him beyond those limits. Clearly Paul would not allow the imposition upon Gentiles of circumcision, keeping the Sabbath, and Jewish food regulations. For him, it seems, such demands violated God's call to Gentiles as Gentiles. Similarly, Colossians refuses to allow Christians to be condemned or judged inferior because they do not receive extraordinary visions or adhere to a regimen of even mildly ascetic regulations (which by themselves might not have been rejected). Such teachings, it seemed to him, denigrated the efficacy of being in Christ for securing and maintaining the proper relationship with God. Paul also found challenges to his authority unacceptable. His understanding of his apostolic office entailed this limit. But beyond this, Paul rejects understandings of leadership that, in his view, are detrimental to the life and growth of the community. One of his complaints against the opponents of 2 Corinthians 10–13 is that they abuse the Corinthians. Paul can allow for different sorts of apostolic comportment (see 1 Corinthians 9) but not for those that exalt the apostle at the expense of the community.

Despite our emphasis on those judged unacceptable, we have in this process also observed some permissible diversity. Paul allows for the significant differences between those law-abiding Jewish Christians and his law-free Gentile Christians. He does not even condemn the Galatian opponents for keeping the Law themselves. He allows for some different styles of apostolic manner of life, as we have just noted. And finally, Colossians does not reject the visions or even the spiritual experiences of those it opposes, only the imposition of such regulations and experiences on others. Thus, the Pauline letters do not require complete uniformity, even as they reject some differences.

I began this study with discussion of the importance of sameness within groups and how groups often perceive difference as dangerous. While Paul did not judge all difference as dangerous and unacceptable, when it was so judged he sometimes reacts vehemently. The sociological studies of groups discussed in Chapter 1 show that this is what we should expect. Moreover, Paul often finds more at stake than either the opponents or the listening congregations had recognized.[11]

11. The observations of Gager which we noted in chapter one are supported by this aspect of Paul's response to opponents. Gager ('Jews, Christians and the Dangerous Ones in Between', p. 251) asserts that it is those in leadership roles who more readily conceive of issues in terms of 'negative antitheses'.

As these Christians in Paul's communities clarified their self-understanding, it was obvious that some elements of their identity were not unique to them. Particularly, they shared a great deal with Judaism: the same God, Bible and basic morality, among other things. Not surprisingly, then, it was especially important to make their differences with Judaism as sharp as possible. It is, after all, essential that groups clearly distinguish themselves from those most like themselves if they are to survive as a group. We should not be shocked to discover that on such an important matter differences arose and the debate about the question was sharp—the identity of the group was at stake. The anti-Pauline movement seen in Philippians and perhaps born in Galatia seems to have focused on this aspect of self-definition.[12]

The other anti-Pauline group focuses its attention on another major issue for emerging groups: their structure of authority. Paul's communities were in the process of struggling with how a group with so many ethnic and social classes could and should live together. To succeed, they needed to determine what sorts of authority were necessary and how leaders were to be identified and legitimated. Charismatic gift was widely acknowledged as an important criterion, but it was open to many interpretations. The opponents of 2 Corinthians interpreted it in ways unaceptable to Paul, but quite pleasing to some at Corinth. Thus Paul is forced to define more narrowly the appropriate criteria for apostolic authority and so set an important parameter for group identity by explicating a specific understanding of leaders and their relationship to their communities.

Thus, the two clearly anti-Pauline movements focus on two different issues that bear directly on the development of the group's self-identity. In these cases the conflicts are, as we might well expect with so much at stake, rather vitriolic at times. These are just the sorts of places we might well expect to find heated debate, places where this emerging movement must make significant decisions to clarify its self-image in the context of their similarities with and yet distinction from Judaism and the surrounding culture and of their need to establish structures of

---

12. Paul is willing to use the drawing of group boundaries with other issues as well. He frames part of his argument in 1 Corinthians about criteria for apostleship in such terms by labeling 'non-Christian' the standards that they were considering and using to compare apostles. When he associates them with their former pagan existence, he implies that the use of such standards places those who use them outside the Christian group.

authority within and above their communities. Recognizing these issues as matters that bear on group self-identity and their designation of boundaries between themselves and others does not suggest that these issues are not theological. Paul's treatment of them makes them theological, even when his opponents and their potential supporters do not see so much involved.

My findings from 2 Thessalonians and Colossians point us to two other important and related conclusions. The first is that studies of Paul's opponents need to distinguish between those who oppose Paul intentionally and those whom the Pauline letters identify as enemies when those opposed did not necessarily see themselves in that position. The 'super-apostles' of 2 Corinthians and the 'dogs' of Philippians intend to oppose and defeat Paul and his teachings. These are clearly opponents of Paul. However, the visionaries of Colossians, the 'disorderly' ministers of 2 Thessalonians, and the teachers at Galatia do not intend to disagree with Paul. This is especially the case with those opposed in 2 Thessalonians; they argue that their eschatology is Paul's eschatology. They are 'opponents' only because the author of this letter judges them to be such. Such teachers may well have misunderstood Paul, but they do not understand themselves to stand in opposition to him. Since they identify themselves with Paul and his teaching, they should not be considered opponents in the same sense as those in the anti-Pauline groups.

Our second conclusion is that finding these 'opponents' who think they represent Paul and want to claim identity with Paul, or in the case of Colossians simply do not know that they disagree with him, forces us to rethink the question of Paul's standing within the early Christian church. Colossians and 2 Thessalonians, along with 1 Thessalonians and Galatians, are evidence that many first- and perhaps second-generation Christians looked to Paul as their apostolic authority. Even when they hold teachings that Paul (or his successors) reject, these 'opponents' assert their agreement with him as evidence of their correctness. Thus, while the letters give evidence for at least[13] two anti-Pauline movements, anti-Pauline sentiment does not seem to have been as widespread or pervasive as it is often assumed. Paul remains the apostolic

---

13. I say 'at least' because Paul's discussion of those who required circumcision at the Jerusalem Conference (Gal. 2.1-10) may allude to some who continued to require Gentile circumcision for admission into Christianity or for salvation after the conference.

authority for many, perhaps most, Gentile Christians and we have seen no evidence in his letters for any widespread rejection of him among Jewish Christians, especially if we are looking for evidence outside of Palestine.[14]

This study of the opponents of the individual Pauline letters and the reconstruction built from that research finds these opponents to be more diverse than previous studies of opponents across the corpus. We have found two distinct anti-Pauline movements plus other teachers who are judged unacceptable and dealt with as opposition. The teachings of this latter type of 'opponent' are firmly rejected, but it seems that the teachers themselves may sometimes be reclaimed (see e.g. the exhortations of 2 Thess. 3.12-16 and 2 Tim. 2.24-26).[15] We have also discovered through these unwitting 'opponents' who do not recognize themselves as such or want to be so understood, that scholarship's vision of widespread, pervasive anti-Pauline sentiment in early Christianity is overdrawn. Furthermore, even the notion that there was a pervasive anti-Paulinism within 'Jewish Christianity' cannot be sustained on the basis of the Pauline letters.

A correlate of this diversity of opposition to Paul, both deliberate and unintentional, is that it is too simplistic for us to identify a single issue (e.g. the Law or Judaizers) as *the* problem Paul faced throughout his ministry. Certain problems no doubt resurfaced in various places. That does not mean that a single issue or constellation of issues was the only or primary problem that Paul faced when dealing with opponents of his churches more generally. There were many issues to be settled in this early period.

The understanding of the opponents of the various Pauline letters reached by this study leaves many questions unanswered. But it provides a more secure identification of those opposed, an identification reached without allowing speculation to race beyond what the evidence of the text will bear. Thus, this study gives us a firmer basis for interpreting the letters. It also opens avenues of exploration into Paul's thought and theology when we do not see him slavishly responding to specific elements of some opponent's teaching with every sentence. With this new starting point, we may be able to gain some insight into

14. Of course, we know that such opposition developed among some Christian Jews because the Ebionites explicitly rejected his apostleship.

15. Paul seems to make no attempts to reclaim, or bring in for the first time, those in the anti-Pauline movements.

Paul's own theology as he uses (and develops) it to respond to unacceptable understandings of Christianity.

An Application of these Findings about Pauline Opponents

The rejection of the various types of opponent we have found in the Pauline letters has implications for several areas of Christian thought in the present. The most obvious connection, perhaps, involves understandings of the lives of Christian ministers and the expectations appropriate for Christians to have of them. The opponents of 2 Corinthians had an understanding of Christian ministry that was attractive then and its contemporary parallels remain attractive for many. The opponents of 2 Corinthians argued that the power of God and the Spirit of God were seen in powerful and impressive ministers and ministries. They believed God lifted them above the kinds of problems Paul faced in his life. Such ministers cut an attractive figure. Who would not want to be associated with the most impressive and confident leaders?

Today, ministers are too often judged according to criteria like those used by the Corinthians and the opponents of 2 Corinthians rather than those Paul accepts and advocates. Any development of a theology of ministry must take account of the debates at Corinth and Thessalonica. Discussion of the evidence of the presence of God in a minister's life must be a central component of any theology of ministry. If we listen in on the disputes Paul was engaged in, we find that he saw evidence of the power of God in ministers who kept their faith and led others to God in the midst of problems and weakness—not in the absence of such difficulties. In fact, in 2 Cor. 11.21b-30, Paul lists his hardships and weakness as evidence that he is a Servant of Christ. So Paul did not see strength of personality or impressive rhetorical skills as evidence that God was working through a minister. Paul even rejects glorious and extraordinary manifestations of the Spirit as the criteria by which one evaluates ministers. In 2 Cor. 12.1-10 he parodies those who claim superiority because of their spiritual experiences. He argues that the power of God is seen most clearly in ministers who are surrounded by hardship and endure with faith, not in those who claim to be above such difficulties.

As they did in the first century, the values Paul advocates and the model of ministry he supports violate current tendencies to seek those with a powerful appearance and impressive demeanor. Even before he faced these sorts of opponent, he had come to the conclusion that ministers' lives must be lives of 'weakness' rather than spectacles of success and shows of powerful gifts—whether personal or spiritual.[16] Paul gives the suffering of Christ as the model for the lives of ministers in 1 Thess. 1.6-7. In the face of teachers who claim that powerful and impressive lives are marks of true ministers, Paul asserted that such lives deflect attention from God. For Paul, the ministers who face difficulties and appear less than what some might hope are those through whom the power of God is seen most clearly. This is especially clear in 2 Cor. 4.7-12 where he contrasts the glorious gospel with the 'earthen vessels' who proclaim it. He further asserts that it is through their endurance of hardships that apostles mediate the life of Christ to their churches.

A similar perspective can be seen in the rejection of the opponents of 2 Thessalonians and 2 Timothy. The overrealized eschatologies opposed in these letters claimed some higher life based on experiences beyond those that other Christians enjoyed. These letters roundly reject such claims. So what held true for minsters also holds true for other Christians: the presence of God in one's life cannot be measured by powerful, superior interventions, but by how one maintains his or her faith through the difficulties of life. These letters reject a sort of triumphalism that has many parallels in popular theologies today, for example what one often sees from some television evangelists. A triumphalist view of Christian life that claims that Chistians are raised above problems and pain stands in sharp contrast to the point of view revealed in 2 Thessalonians and 2 Timothy. The thanksgiving of 2 Thessalonians cites its recipients' steadfastness and faith in persecution, not the absence of such trials, as the reason the author boasts of them. Second Thessalonians 1.5 goes so far as to say that endurance of persecution is evidence that God had chosen God's people well. A similar perspective is found in 2 Tim. 3.10-12. These verses give Paul's life of faithfulness as the example Timothy is to follow, adding that all who want to live a godly life in Christ will be persecuted. So 2 Thessalonians and 2 Timothy (along with 1 Corinthians and 1 Thessalonians) reject triumphalist understandings of Christian life in the present. The rejection of these sorts of opponents shows that, according to these biblical texts, God does not keep Christians (or ministers) from

16. See Jerry L. Sumney, 'Paul's "Weakness": An Integral Part of his Conception of Apostleship', *JSNT* 52 (1993), pp. 71-91.

experiencing pain and problems or rescue them when they ask. Rather, God promises to be with them in the midst of such difficulties.

We also find in these debates with opponents a rejection of the imposition on others of what some regarded as important, even necessary, in their experience of Christianity. In this respect, the opponents of Galatians, 1 Timothy, Titus and Colossians have something in common. The opponents of Galatians, 1 Timothy and Titus all seek to impose some aspect of the Law on Gentile Christians that these letters reject. These various opponents believed their practice of Christianity offerred some advantage to those who submit. These three letters reject such claims, calling on Gentiles to live Christian lives as Gentiles. Though they argue differently, Galatians, 1 Timothy and Titus all seek ways of interpreting and using the Hebrew Bible in ways appropriate to both the texts and the circumstances in which they are read.

But I have grouped them with Colossians here to make another point. Colossians opposes Christians who have extraordinary spiritual experiences and who call on others to seek those experiences through the same means. It is not the visionaries' experiences, but their judgment on those who do not follow this path that Colossians rejects. Colossians refuses to allow the experience of some and the means by which they achieve those experiences to be normative for all Christians. This is the point of the hymn of Colossians and its application in 2.16-23. Colossians asserts that its readers should not submit to the visionaries' rules and need not recieve visions to be secure in their place before God. Judgments based on such things, this text insists, are inappropriate if one is in Christ. Thus, Colossians, Galatians, 1 Timothy and Titus all oppose attempts of some Christians to impose on others their means of serving God.

Once again, similar tendencies are a constant within Christianity. There has never been a lack of movements that claim that their discipline or regimen is the key to the best or only relationship with God and to the best Christian life. It is interesting to note in this connection that Colossians does not deny the place of the regulations advocated by the opponents *for* the opponents. Opposition to the visionaries in Colossae did not include invalidating their experiences or their means of attaining them, only their insistence that this must be the paradigm for all Christians and their judgment against those who do not conform. Such openness to diverse ways of serving God and experiencing God in one's life has implications beyond ecumenical dialogue among denominations. It also bears on one's attitude toward various renewal movements within and across denominations. Colossians and Galatians leave room for differing experiences and differing patterns of life. Galatians gives evidence that differing patterns of Christian behavior can be appropriate for differing ethnic and cultural groups. This has implications for theologies of missions, as well as for acknowledging and accepting differences among Christians within a common culture. At the same time, these letters impose limits to such differences, requiring that all Christians' patterns of life, worship and belief reflect the character of God as it is seen in Christ.

The Pauline writings that were concerned with those seen as opponents were not simply interested in doctrinal purity for its own sake or with uniformity for its own sake. Rather, they were reacting to what they saw as manifestations of their religion that they understood to be inappropriate to the message of Christianity and to what it means to be a Christian and to act in accordance with Christian faith. At their core, then, they were trying to show what it meant in their time and place to be the people of God—how it was possible for them to reflect as fully as possible the character of God as it is seen in Christ. This continues to be the task of all Christians in every time and place.

BIBLIOGRAPHY

Abbott, T.K., *A Critical and Exegetical Commentary on the Epistles to the Ephesians and to the Colossians* (ICC; Edinburgh: T. & T. Clark, 1897).

Agrell, Göran, *Word, Toil, and Sustenance* (trans. S. Westerholm; Lund: Ohlssons, 1976).

Alexander, Loveday, 'Hellenistic Letter-Forms and the Structure of Philippians', *JSNT* 37 (1989), pp. 87-101.

Allo, E.B., *St. Paul, seconde épître aux Corinthiens* (EBib; Paris: Libraire Lecoffre, 1956).

Argall, Randall A., 'The Source of a Religious Error in Colossae', *Calvin Theological Journal* 22 (1987), pp. 6-20.

Arnold, Clinton E., 'Returning to the Domain of the Powers: *Stoicheia* as Evil Spirits in Galatians 4:3,9', *NovT* 38 (1996), pp. 55-76.

—*The Colossian Syncretism: The Interface between Christianity and Folk Belief in Colossae* (Grand Rapids: Baker Book House, 1996).

Aune, David E., *The Cultic Setting of Realized Eschatology in Early Christianity* (NovTSup, 28; Leiden: E.J. Brill, 1972).

Aus, Roger D., 'God's Plan and God's Power: Isaiah 66 and the Restraining Factors of 2 Thess 2:6-7', *JBL* 96 (1977), pp. 537-53.

—'The Liturgical Background of the Necessity and Propriety of Giving Thanks According to 2 Thess 1:3', *JBL* 92 (1973), pp. 432-38.

—'The Relevance of Isaiah 66:7 to Revelation 12 and 2 Thessalonians 1', *ZNW* 67 (1976), pp. 252-68.

—'2 Thessalonians', in *idem et al.*, *1–2 Timothy, Titus, 2 Thessalonians* (Augsburg Commentary on the New Testament; Minneapolis: Augsburg, 1984).

Baasland, Ernst, 'Persecution: A Neglected Feature in the Letter to the Galatians', *ST* 38 (1984), pp. 135-50.

—'Die περί-Formel und die Argumentation(ssituation) des Paulus', *ST* 42 (1998), pp. 77, 81-82.

Bailey, John W., 'The First and Second Epistle to the Thessalonians', *IB* 11 (1955), pp. 245-339.

Bailey, Kenneth, 'The Structure of I Corinthians and Paul's Theological Method with Special Reference to 4:17', *NovT* 25 (1983), pp. 152-81.

Baird, William, 'Letters of Recommendation: A Study of II Cor 3_{1-3}', *JBL* 80 (1961), pp. 166-72.

Bammel, Ernst, 'Versuch zu Col 1_{15-20}', *ZNW* 52 (1961), pp. 88-95.

Bandstra, Andrew J., 'Did the Colossian Errorists Need a Mediator?', in R.N. Longenecker and M.C. Tenney (eds.), *New Dimensions in New Testament Study* (Grand Rapids: Eerdmans, 1974), pp. 329-43.

Barclay, John M.G., 'Mirror-Reading a Polemical Letter: Galatians as a Test Case', *JSNT* 31 (1987), pp. 73-93.

—*Obeying the Truth: A Study of Paul's Ethic in Galatians* (Edinburgh: T. & T. Clark, 1988).

Barnett, P.W. ,'Opposition in Corinth', *JSNT* 22 (1984), pp. 3-17.

Barré, Michael L., 'Paul as "Eschatological Person": A New Look at 2 Cor 11.29', *CBQ* 37 (1975), pp. 500-526.

Barrett, C.K., 'Cephas and Corinth', in O. Betz, M. Hengel and P. Schmidt (eds.), *Abraham unser Vater: Juden und Christen im Gespräch über die Bibel* (Arbeiten zur Geschichte des Späatjudentums und Urchristentums; Leiden: E.J. Brill, 1963), pp. 1-12.

—'Christianity at Corinth', *BJRL* 46 (1964), pp. 269-97.

—*A Commentary on the First Epistle to the Corinthians* (HNTC; San Francisco: Harper & Row, 1968).

—*A Commentary on the Second Epistle to the Corinthians* (HNTC; New York: Harper & Row, 1973).

—*Freedom and Obligation: A Study of the Epistle to the Galatians* (Philadelphia: Westminster Press, 1985).

—'Paul's Opponents in II Corinthians', *NTS* 17 (1971), pp. 233-54.

Bassler, Jouette M., ' "He Remains Faithful" (2 Tim 2:13a)', in Eugene H. Lovering, Jr, and Jerry L. Sumney (eds.), *Theology and Ethics in Paul and his Interpreters: Essays in Honor of Victor Paul Furnish* (Nashville: Abingdon Press, 1996), pp. 173-79.

—The Enigmatic Sign: 2 Thessalonians 1:5', *CBQ* 46 (1984), pp. 496-510.

Bassler Jouette M. (ed.), *Pauline Theology. I. Thessalonians, Philippians, Galatians, Philemon* (Minneapolis: Fortress Press, 1991).

Bates, W.H., 'The Integrity of II Corinthians', *NTS* 12 (1965–66), pp. 56-69.

Bauer, Walter, *Rechtgläubigkeit und Ketzerei im ältesten Christentum* (Tübingen: J.C.B. Mohr, 2nd edn, 1964); ET: *Orthodoxy and Heresy in Earliest Christianity* (Philadelphia: Fortress Press, 1971).

Baumbach, Günther, 'Die von Paulus im Philipperbrief bekämpften Irrlehrer', in K.-W. Tröger (ed.), *Gnosis und Neues Testament* (Berlin: Gerhard Mohn, 1973), pp. 293-310.

Baur, F.C., 'Die Christuspartei in der korinthischen Gemeinde, der Gegensatz des Petrischen und Paulinischen Christentum in der ältesten Kirche, der Apostel Petrus in Rom', *Tübingen Zeitschrift für Theologie* 4 (1831), pp. 61-206.

—*Paul, The Apostle of Jesus Christ: His Life and Work, his Epistles and Doctrine* (trans. Eduard Zeller; 2 vols.; London: Williams & Norgate, 2nd edn; 1876).

Beare, F.W., 'Colossians', *IB* 11 (1955).

—*A Commentary on the Epistle to the Philippians* (HNTC; New York: Harper, 1959).

Beker, Christiaan, *Paul the Apostle: The Triumph of God in Life and Thought* (Philadelphia: Fortress Press, 1980).

Belleville, Linda, 'A Letter of Apologetic Self-Commendation: 2 Cor. 1:8–7:16', *NovT* 31 (1989), pp. 142-63.

—' "Under Law": Structural Analysis and the Pauline Concept of Law in Galatians 3:21–4:11', *JSNT* 26 (1986), pp. 53-78.

Benoit, P., *Epîtres de saint Paul aux Philippiens, à Philémon, aux Colossiens, aux Ephésiens* (La sainte bible de Jérusalem; Paris: Cerf, 4th edn, 1969).

Berger, K., 'Die implitzen Gegner: zur Methode des Erschliessens von "Gegner" in neutestamentlichen Texten', in D. Lührmann and G. Strecker (eds.), *Kirche* (Tübingen: J.C.B. Mohr [Paul Siebeck], 1980), pp. 372-400.

Bernard, J.H., *Second Epistle to the Corinthians* (The Expositor's Greek Testament; Grand Rapids: Eerdmans, repr. edn, 1974 [1897–1910]).

Best, Ernest, *A Commentary on the First and Second Epistles to the Thessalonians* (BNTC; London: A. & C. Black, 1972).

Betz, Hans Dieter, *Der Apostel Paulus und die Sokratische Tradition* (BHT, 45; Tübingen: J.C.B. Mohr [Paul Siebeck], 1972).

—*Galatians: A Commentary on Paul's Letter to the Churches in Galatia* (Hermeneia; Philadelphia: Fortress Press, 1979).

—'In Defense of the Spirit: Paul's Letter to the Galatians as a Document of Early Christian Apologetics', in E. Schüssler Fiorenza (ed.), *Aspects of Religious Propaganda in Judaism and Early Christianity* (Notre Dame: University of Notre Dame Press, 1976), pp. 99-114.

—'The Literary Composition and Function of Paul's Letter to the Galatians', *NTS* 21 (1975), pp. 353-79.

—*Paul's Apology; 2 Corinthians 10–13 and the Socratic Tradition* (Protocol of the Second Colloquy; Berkeley: Center for Hermeneutical Studies, 1975).

Bieder, Werner, *Die kolossische Irrlehre und die Kirche von heute* (Theologische Studien, 33; Zürich: Evangelischer Verlag, 1952).

—'Paulus und seine Gegner in Korinth', *TZ* 17 (1961), pp. 319-33.

Black, David Alan, *Paul, Apostle of Weakness: Astheneia and its Cognates in the Pauline Literature* (American University Studies, Theology and Religion Series, 3; New York: Peter Lang, 1984).

—'The Weak in Thessalonica: A Study in Pauline Lexicography', *JETS* 25 (1982), pp. 307-21.

Boers, Hendrikus, 'The Form Critical Study of Paul's Letters: I Thessalonians as a Case Study', *NTS* 22 (1976), pp. 140-58.

—' "We Who Are by Inheritance Jews; Not from the Gentile Sinners" ', *JBL* 111 (1992), pp. 273-81.

Bonnard, Pierre, *L'épître de Saint Paul aux Philippiens* (CNT, 10; Paris: Delachaux & Niestlé, 1950).

Borgen, Peder, 'Paul Preaches Circumcision and Pleases Men', in M.D. Hooker and S.G. Wilson (eds.), *Paul and Paulinism* (London: SPCK, 1982), pp. 37-46.

Bornkamm, Günther, *Die Vorgeschichte des sogenannten zweiten Korintherbriefes* (Sitzungsberichte der Heidelberger Akademie der Wissenschaften; Heidelberg: Carl Winter, 1961).

—'The Heresy of Colossians', in Francis and Meeks (eds.), *Conflict at Colossae*, pp. 123-46.

—'The Letter to the Romans as Paul's Last Will and Testament', in Karl P. Donfried (ed.), *The Romans Debate* (Peabody, MA: Hendrickson, 2nd edn, 1991), pp. 16-28.

Bosch, Jorge Sânchez, 'L'apologie apostolique: 2 Cor. 10–11 comme réponse de Paul à ses adversaires', in Lohse (ed.), *Verteidigung und Begründung des apostolischen Amtes*, pp. 42-64.

Brewer, Raymond R., 'The Meaning of *POLITEUESTHE* in Phil 1:27', *JBL* 73 (1954), pp. 76-83.

Brown, Lucinda A., 'Asceticism and Ideology: The Language of Power in the Pastoral Epistles', *Semeia* 57 (1992), pp. 77-94.

Brown, R.E., 'Not Jewish Christianity and Gentile Christianity but Types of Jewish/Gentile Christianity', *CBQ* 45 (1983), pp. 74-79.

Brox, Norbert, *Die Pastoralbriefe* (RNT, 7; Regensburg: Friedrich Pustet, 1969).

Bruce, F.F., 'Colossian Problems Part 3: The Colossian Heresy', *BSac* 141 (1984), pp. 195-208.

—*The Epistle to the Galatians: A Commentary on the Greek Text* (NIGTC; Grand Rapids: Eerdmans, 1982).

—*1 and 2 Corinthians* (NCB; London: Oliphants, 1971).

—*1 and 2 Thessalonians* (WBC, 45; Waco, TX: Word Books, 1982).

Buckel, John, 'Paul's Defense of Christian Liberty in Galatians', *Louvain Studies* 17 (1992), pp. 254-68.

Bultmann, Rudolf, *Exegetische Probleme des zweiten Korintherbriefe* (SymBU, 9; Uppsala: Wretman, 1947).

—*The Second Letter to the Corinthians* (trans. Roy A. Harrisville; Minneapolis: Augsburg, 1985).

Burton, Ernest deWitt, *A Critical and Exegetical Commentary on the Epistle to the Galatians* (ICC; Edinburgh: T. & T. Clark, 1921).

Bush, Peter G., 'A Note on the Structure of 1 Timothy', *NTS* 36 (1990), pp. 152-56.

Caird, G.B., *Paul's Letters from Prison* (New Clarendon Bible; Oxford: Oxford University Press, 1976).

Cambier, J., 'Connaissance charnelle et spirituelle de Christ dans 2. Cor 5.16', in A. Descamps *et al.* (eds.), *Littérature et théologie pauliniennes* (RechBib, 5; Paris: Desclée de Brouwer, 1960), pp. 72-92.

Campbell, D.A., 'The Meaning of Πίστις and Νόμος in Paul: A Linguistic and Structural Perspective', *JBL* 111 (1992), pp. 91-103.

von Campenhausen, H., *The Fathers of the Greek Church* (trans. S. Godman; New York: Pantheon, 1959).

Castelli, Elizabeth A., *Imitating Paul: A Discourse of Power* (Literary Currents in Biblical Interpretation; Louisville, KY: Westminster/John Knox Press, 1991).

Chance, J. Bradley, 'Paul's Apology to the Corinthians', *Perspectives* 9 (1982), pp. 145-55.

Classen, C. Joachim, 'St Paul's Epistles and Ancient Greek and Roman Rhetoric', in Porter and Olbricht (eds.), *Rhetoric and the New Testament*, pp. 265-91.

Collange, J.-F., *The Epistle of Saint Paul to the Philippians* (London: Epworth Press, 1979).

Collins, Raymond F., *Letters That Paul Did Not Write: The Epistle to the Hebrews and the Pauline Pseudepigrapha* (GNS, 28; Wilmington, DE: Michael Glazier, 1988).

—'Paul as Seen Through His Own Eyes', in *idem*, *Studies on the First Epistle to the Thessalonians* (BETL, 66; Leuven: Leuven University Press, 1984), pp. 175-208.

—' "This is the Will of God: Your Sanctification." (1 Thess 4,3)', in *idem*, *Studies on the First Letter to the Thessalonians* (BETL 66; Leuven: Leuven University Press, 1984), pp. 299-325.

Collins, Raymond F. (ed.), *The Thessalonian Correspondence* (BETL, 87; Leuven: Leuven University Press).

Colson, F.H., 'Μετεσχημάτισα 1 Cor. iv.6', *JTS* 17 (1915–16), pp. 379-84.

—' "Myths and Genealogies": A Note on the Polemic of the Pastoral Epistles', *JTS* 19 (1918), pp. 265-71.

Conzelmann, Hans, *A Commentary on the First Epistle to the Corinthians* (trans. J.W. Leitch; Hermeneia; Philadelphia: Fortress Press, 1975).

—'Der Brief an die Kolosser', in *idem et al.*, *Die kleineren Briefe des Apostels Paulus* (Das Neue Testament Deutsch, 8; Göttingen: Vandenhoeck & Ruprecht, 1962).

Coser, Lewis, *The Functions of Social Conflict* (Glencoe, IL: Free Press, 1956).

Cosgrove, Charles H., *The Cross and the Spirit: A Study in the Argument and Theology of Galatians* (Macon, GA: Mercer University Press, 1988).

Court, John M., 'The Controversy with Adversaries of Paul's Apostolate in the Context of his Relations to the Corinthian Congregation (2 Corinthians 12,14–13,13)', in Lohse (ed.), *Verteidigung und Begründung des apostolischen Amtes*, pp. 87-106.

Cousar, Charles B., *Galatians* (Interpretation; Atlanta: John Knox Press, 1982).

—'II Corinthians 5:17-21', *Int* 35 (1981), pp. 180-83.

Coxe, A., Cleveland, 'Introductory Note to *Irenaeus Against Heresies*', in A. Roberts and J. Donaldson (eds.), *The Apostolic Fathers with Justin Martyr and Irenaeus* (ANF; Grand Rapids: Eerdmans, 1956).

Craddock, Fred B., *Philippians* (Interpretation; Atlanta: John Knox Press, 1985).

Crownfield, Frederic R., 'The Singular Problem of the Dual Galatians', *JBL* 64 (1945), pp. 491-500.

Dahl, Nils A., 'Paul and the Church at Corinth According to 1 Corinthians 1:10–4:21', in W.R. Farmer, C.F.D. Moule and R.R. Niehbuhr (eds.), *Christian History and Interpretation* (Cambridge: Cambridge University Press, 1967), pp. 313-35.

Davies, S., 'Remarks on the Second Epistle to the Corinthians 4:3,4', *BSac* 25 (1968), pp. 23-30.

Davis, James A., *Wisdom and Spirit: An Investigation of 1 Corinthians 1:18–3:20 Against the Background of Jewish Sapiential Traditions in the Greco–Roman Period* (Lanham, MD: University Press of America, 1984).

DeMaris, Richard E., *The Colossian Controversy: Wisdom in Dispute at Colossae* (JSNTSup 96; Sheffield: JSOT Press, 1994).

Dibelius, Martin, *An die Thessalonicher I, II und die Philipper* (HNT; Tübingen: J.C.B. Mohr [Paul Siebeck], 12th edn, 1925).

—'The Isis Initiation in Apuleius and Related Initiatory Rites', in Francis and Meeks (eds.), *Conflict at Colossae*, pp. 61-122.

Dibelius, Martin, and Hans Conzelmann, *The Pastoral Epistles* (trans. P. Buttolph and A. Yarbro; Hermeneia; Philadelphia: Fortress Press, 1972).

Dibelius, Martin, and H. Greeven, *An die Kolosser, Epheser, an Philemon* (HNT, 3rd edn; Tübingen: J.C.B. Mohr [Paul Siebeck], 3rd edn, 1953).

Dobschütz, Ernst von, *Die Thessalonicher Briefe* (Göttingen: Vandenhoeck & Ruprecht, 1909).

Donaldson, T.L., 'The "Curse of the Law" and the Inclusion of the Gentiles: Galatians 3.13-14', *NTS* 32 (1986), pp. 94-112.

Donelson, Lewis R., *Pseudepigraphy and Ethical Argument in the Pastoral Epistles* (HUT, 22; Tübingen: J.C.B. Mohr [Paul Siebeck], 1986).

—'The Structure of the Ethical Argument in the Pastorals', *BTB* 18 (1988), pp. 108-13.

Donfried, Karl P., 'The Cults of Thessalonica and the Thessalonian Correspondence', *NTS* 31 (1985), pp. 336-56.

—*The Romans Debate* (Peabody, MA: Hendrickson, 2nd edn, 1991).

Duncan, George S., *The Epistle of Paul to the Galatians* (MNTC; New York: Harper & Brothers, 1934).

Dunn, James D.G., *A Commentary on the Epistle to the Galatians* (BNTC; London: A. & C. Black, 1993).

—'The New Perspective on Paul', *BJRL* 65 (1983), pp. 95-122.

—*Unity and Diversity in the New Testament: An Inquiry into the Character of Earliest Christianity* (San Antonio, TX: Trinity Press International, 2nd edn, 1990).

—'Works of the Law and the Curse of the Law (Galatians 3.10-14)', *NTS* 31 (1985), pp. 523-42.

DuToit, Andrie, 'Vilification as a Pragmatic Device in Early Christian Epistolography', *Bib* 75 (1994), pp. 403-12.

Ebeling, Gerhard, *The Truth of the Gospel: An Exposition of Galatians* (trans. D. Green; Philadelphia: Fortress Press, 1985).

Egger, Wilhelm, *Galaterbrief, Philipperbrief, Philemonbrief* (Neue Echten Bibel NT; Würzburg: Echter Verlag, 1985).

Ellis, E. Earle, 'Paul and his Opponents: Trends in the Research', in J. Neusner (ed.), *Christianity, Judaism, and Other Greco–Roman Cults: Part 1* (Leiden: E.J. Brill, 1975), pp. 264-98.

—'Traditions in 1 Corinthians', *NTS* 32 (1986), pp. 481-502.

—'Traditions in the Pastoral Epistles', in C.A. Evans and W.F. Stinespring (eds.), *Early Jewish and Christian Exegesis* (Atlanta: Scholars Press, 1987), pp. 237-53.

Engberg-Pedersen, Troels, 'The Gospel and Social Practice According to 1 Corinthians', *NTS* 33 (1987), pp. 557-84.

Ernst, J., *Die Briefe an die Philipper, an Philemon, an die Kolosser, an die Epheser* (RNT; Regensburg: Friedrich Pustet, 1974).

Evans, Craig A., 'The Colossian Mystics', *Bib* 63 (1982), pp. 188-205.

Fahy, T., 'St. Paul's "Boasting" and "Weakness" ', *ITQ* 31 (1964), pp. 214-27.

Fee, Gordon D., *1 and 2 Timothy, Titus* (NIBC; Peabody, MA: Hendrickson, rev. edn, 1988).

—*The First Epistle to the Corinthians* (NICNT; Grand Rapids: Eerdmans, 1987).

Filson, Floyd V., '2 Corinthians', *IB* 10 (1951), pp. 265-425.

Fiore, Benjamin, ' "Covert Allusions" in 1 Corinthians 1–4', *CBQ* 47 (1985), pp. 85-102.

—*The Function of Personal Example in the Socratic and Pastoral Epistles* (AnBib, 105; Rome: Biblical Institute Press, 1986).

Fitzmyer, Joseph A., 'Glory Reflected on the Face of Christ (2 Cor 3:7–4:6) and a Palestinian Jewish Motif', *TS* 42 (1981), pp. 630-44.

Forbes, Christopher, 'Comparison, Self-Praise and Irony: Paul's Boasting and the Conventions of Hellenistic Rhetoric', *NTS* 32 (1986), pp. 1-30.

—'Paul's Opponents in Corinth', *Buried History* 19 (1983), pp. 19-23.

Frame, James E., *A Critical and Exegetical Commentary on the Epistles of St. Paul to the Thessalonians* (ICC; Edinburgh: T. & T. Clark, 1912).

Francis, Fred O., 'The Christological Argument of Colossians', in J. Jervell and W.A. Meeks (eds.), *God's Christ and his People* (Oslo: Universitetsforlaget, 1977), pp. 192-208.

—'Humility and Angelic Worship in Col 2:18', in Francis and Meeks (eds.), *Conflict at Colossae*, pp. 163-96.

—'Humility and Angelic Worship in Col 2:18', *ST* 16 (1962), pp. 109-34.

—'Visionary Discipline and Scriptural Tradition at Colossae', *Lexington Theological Quarterly* 2 (1967), pp. 71-78.

Francis, Fred O., and W.A. Meeks (eds.), *Conflict at Colossae: A Problem in the Interpretation of Early Christianity Illustrated by Selected Modern Studies* (Sources for Biblical Study, 4; Missoula, MT: SBL, 1973).

Fraser, John W., 'Paul's Knowledge of Jesus: II Corinthians V.16 Once More', *NTS* 17 (1971), pp. 293-313.

Freyne, Sean, 'Vilifying the Other and Defining the Self: Matthew's and John's Anti-Jewish Polemic in Focus', in Neusner and Frerichs (eds.), *'To See Ourselves As Others See Us'*, pp. 117-43.

Friedrich, Gerhardt, *Amt und Lebensführung: Eine Auslegung 2. Kor. 6.1-10* (Biblische Studien, 39; Neukirchen–Vluyn: Neukirchener Verlag, 1963).

—'Der zweite Brief an die Thessalonicher', in Friedrich *et al.*, *Die Briefe an die Galater, Philipper, Kolosser, Thessalonicher und Philemon* (NTD, 8; Göttingen: Vandenhoeck & Ruprecht, 14th edn, 1976).

—'Die Gegner des Paulus im 2. Korintherbrief', in Betz, Hengel and Schmidt (eds.), *Abraham unser Vater*, pp. 181-215.

Fuchs, Eric, 'La faiblesse glorie de l'apostolat selon Paul: Etude sur 2 Corinthiens 10–13', *ETR* 55 (1980), pp. 231-53.

Fung, Ronald Y.K., *The Epistle to the Galatians* (NICNT; Grand Rapids: Eerdmans, 1988).

Funk, Robert W., *Language, Hermeneutics, and Word of God* (New York: Harper & Row, 1966).

Furnish, Victor P., 'The Place and Purpose of Philippians III', *NTS* 10 (1963–64), pp. 80-88.

—*II Corinthians* (AB, 32A; Garden City, NY: Doubleday, 1984).

—' "Fellow Workers in God's Service" ', *JBL* 80 (1961), pp. 364-70.

Gager, John G., 'Jews, Christians and the Dangerous Ones in Between', in S. Biderman and B.-A. Scharfstein (eds.), *Interpretation in Religion* (Leiden: E.J. Brill, 1992), pp. 249-57.

Garland, David E., 'The Composition and Unity of Philippians: Some Neglected Literary Factors', *NovT* 27 (1985), pp. 141-73.

—'Philippians 1:1-26; The Defense and Confirmation of the Gospel', *RevExp* 77 (1980), pp. 327-36.

Gaventa, Beverly R., 'Galatians 1 And 2: Autobiography as Paradigm', *NovT* 28 (1986), pp. 309-326.

—'The Singularity of the Gospel: A Reading of Galatians', in Bassler (ed.), *Pauline Theology*, I, pp. 147-59.

Georgi, Dieter, 'Der Kampf um die reine Lehre im Urchristentum als Auseinandersetzung um das rechte Verständnis der an Israel ergangenen Offenbarung Gottes', in W.P. Eckert, N.P. Levinson and M. Stöhr (eds.), *Antijudaismus im Neuen Testament?* (Munich: Chr. Kaiser Verlag, 1967), pp. 82-94.

—*Die Gegner des Paulus im 2. Korintherbrief: Studien zur religiösen Propaganda in der Spätantike* (WMANT, 11; Neukirchen–Vluyn: Neukirchener Verlag, 1964); ET: *The Opponents of Paul in Second Corinthians* (trans. H. Attridge *et al.*; Philadelphia: Fortress Press, 1986).

Gewiess, Josef, 'Die apologetische Methode des Apostels Paulus im Kampf gegen die Irrlehre in Kolossä', *Bibel und Leben* 3 (1962), pp. 258-70.

Giblin, C.H., *The Threat to Faith: An Exegetical and Theological Re-examination of 2 Thessalonians 2* (AnBib, 31; Rome: Pontifical Biblical Institute Press, 1967).

Gnilka, Joachim, *Der Philipperbrief* (Freiburg: Herder, 3rd edn, 1968).

Goulder, Michael D., *St. Paul versus St. Peter: A Tale of Two Missions* (Louisville, KY: Westminster/John Knox Press, 1994).

—'The Visionaries of Laodicea', *JSNT* 43 (1991), pp. 15-39.

Grant, Robert M., 'Charges of "Immorality" Against Various Religious Groups in Antiquity', in R. van den Broek and M. J. Vermaseren (eds.), *Studies in Gnosticism and Hellenistic Religions* (Leiden: E.J. Brill, 1981), pp. 161-70.

—'The Wisdom of the Corinthians', in S.E. Johnson (ed.), *The Joy of Study: Papers on New Testament and Related Studies Presented to Honor Frederick Clifton Grant* (New York: Macmillan, 1951), pp. 51-59.

Grayston, K., 'The Opponents in Philippians 3', *ExpTim* 97.6 (1986), pp. 170-72.

Green, William S., 'Otherness Within: Towards a Theory of Difference in Rabbinic Judaism', in Neusner and Frerichs (eds.), *'To See Ourselves as Others See Us'*, pp. 49-69.

Gritz, Sharon H., *Paul, Women Teachers, and the Mother Goddess at Ephesus* (Lanham, MD: University Press of America, 1991).

Gundry, R.H., 'Grace, Works, and Staying Saved in Paul', *Bib* 66 (1985), pp. 1-38.

Gunther, J.J., *St. Paul's Opponents and their Background: A Study of Apocalyptic and Jewish Sectarian Teachings* (NovTSup, 35; Leiden: E.J. Brill, 1973).

Hadidian, Dikran Y., 'A Case Study: 2 Cor. 5:16', in *idem* (ed.), *From Faith to Faith* (PTMS, 31; Pittsburgh: Pickwick Press, 1979), pp. 107-25.

Hafemann, Scott, 'Corinthians, Letters to the', in Hawthorne and Martin (eds.), *Dictionary of Paul and his Letters*, pp. 164-79.

—'Review of *Identifying Paul's Opponents* (Sumney)', *JBL* (1992), pp. 347-50.

—'Paul and His Interpreters', in Hawthorne and Martin (eds.), *Dictionary of Paul and His Letters*, pp. 666-79.

—' "Self-Commendaton" and Apostolic Legitimacy in 2 Corinthians: A Pauline Dialectic?', *NTS* 36 (1990), pp. 66-88.

—*Suffering and Ministry in the Spirit: Paul's Defense of his Ministry in II Corinthians 2:14–3:3* (Grand Rapids: Eerdmans, 1990).

Hall, David R., 'A Disguise for the Wise: ΜΕΤΑΣΧΗΜΑΤΙΣΜΟΣ in 1 Corinthians 4.6', *NTS* 40 (1994), pp. 143-49.

Hall, Robert G., 'The Rhetorical Outline for Galatians: A Reconsideration', *JBL* 106 (1987), pp. 277-87.

Hansen, Walter, *Abraham in Galatians: Epistolary and Rhetorical Contexts* (JSNTSup, 29; Sheffield: JSOT Press, 1989).

Hanson, A.T., *The Pastoral Epistles* (NCB; Grand Rapids: Eerdmans, 1982).

—*Studies in the Pastoral Epistles* (London: SPCK, 1968).

Haraguchi, Takaaki, 'Das Unterhaltsrecht des frühchristlichen Verkündigers: Eine Untersuchung zur Bezeichnung ἐργάτης im Neuen Testament', *ZNW* 84 (1993), pp. 178-95.

Harnisch, Wolfgang, *Eschatologische Existenz: Ein exegetischer Beitrag zum Sachanliegen von 1. Thessalonicher 4,13–5,11* (FRLANT, 110; Göttingen: Vandenhoeck & Ruprecht, 1973).

Hartman, Lars, 'Some Remarks on 1 Cor 20:1-5', *SEÅ* 34 (1974), pp. 109-20.

—'On Reading Others' Letters', in G.W.E. Nickelsburg and G.W. MacRae (eds.), *Christians Among Jews and Gentiles* (Philadelphia: Fortress Press, 1986), pp. 137-46.

Hasler, V., 'Epiphanie und Christologie in den Pastoralbriefen', *TZ* 33 (1977), pp. 193-209.

Haufe, Günter, 'Gnostische Irrlehre und ihre Abwehr in den Pastoralbriefen', in K.-W. Tröger (ed.), *Gnosis und Neues Testament: Studien aus Religionswissenschaft und Theologie* (Gütersloh: Gerd Mohn, 1973), pp. 325-39.

Havener, Ivan, *First Thessalonians, Philemon, Philippians, Second Thessalonians, Colossians, Ephesians* (Collegeville Bible Commentary, 8; Collegeville, MN: Liturgical Press, 1983).

Hawthorne, G.F., 'Philippians, Letter to the', in Hawthorne and Martin (eds.), *Dictionary of Paul and his Letter*, 1993), pp. 707-13.

Hawthorne, G.F., and R.P. Martin (eds.), *Dictionary of Paul and his Letters* (Downers Grover, IL: InterVarsity Press, 1993).

Heiligenthal, Roman, 'Soziologische Implikation der Paulinischen Rechtfertigungslehre im Galaterbrief am Beispiel der "Werke des Gesetzes"', *Kairos* 26 (1984), pp. 38-51.

Hengel, Martin, 'Hymn and Christology', in Elizabeth A. Livingstone (ed.), *Studia Biblica 1978. III. Papers on Paul and Other New Testament Authors* (JSNTSup, 3; Sheffield: JSOT Press, 1980), pp. 173-97.

Héring, Jean, *The Second Epistle of Saint Paul to the Corinthians* (trans. A.W. Heathcote and P.J. Allcock; London: Epworth Press, 1967).

Hester, James D., 'The Rhetorical Structure of Galatians 1:11–2:14', *JBL* 103 (1984), pp. 223-33.

—'The Use and Influence of Rhetoric in Galatians 2:1-14', *TZ* 42 (1986), pp. 386-408.

Hickling, C.J.A., 'Is the Second Epistle to the Corinthians a Source for Early Church History?', *ZNW* 66 (1975), pp. 284-87.

—'The Sequence of Thought in 2 Corinthians, Chapter Three', *NTS* 21 (1975), pp. 380-95.

Hill, Craig C., *Hellenists and Hebrews: Reappraising Division within the Earliest Church* (Minneapolis: Fortress Press, 1992).

Hill, Edmund, 'The Construction of Three Passages of St. Paul', *CBQ* 23 (1961), pp. 296-301.

Hock, Ronald, *The Social Context of Paul's Ministry* (Philadelphia: Fortress Press, 1980).

Hoffmann, Paul, *Die Toten in Christus* (Münster: Aschendorff, 1966).

Holladay, Carl, 'Paul's Opponents in Philippians 3', *RQ* 12 (1969), pp. 77-90.

Holland, Glenn, *The Tradition that You Received from Us: 2 Thessalonians in the Pauline Tradition* (HUT 24; Tübingen: J.C.B. Mohr [Paul Siebeck], 1988).

Hollenbach, Bruce, 'Col II.23: Which Things Lead to the Fulfilment of the Flesh', *NTS* 25 (1978–79), pp. 254-61.

Holmberg, G., *Paul and Power: The Structure of Authority in the Primitive Church as Reflected in the Pauline Epistles* (Philadelphia: Fortress Press, 1978).

Hooker, Morna D., 'Beyond the Things that Are Written? St. Paul's Use of Scripture', *NTS* 27 (1981), pp. 295-309.

—'Were there False Teachers in Colossae?', in B. Lindars and S.S. Smalley (eds.), *Christ and the Spirit in the New Testament* (Cambridge: Cambridge University Press, 1973), pp. 315-31.

Horbury, William, 'I Thessalonians ii.3 as Rebutting the Charge of False Prophecy', *JTS* 33 (1982), pp. 492-508.

Horsley, Richard A., 'Gnosis in Corinth: 1 Corinthians 8.1-6', *NTS* 27 (1979), pp. 32-51.

—'Wisdom of Word and Words of Wisdom in Corinth', *CBQ* 39 (1977), pp. 224-39.

Houlden, J., *Paul's Letters from Prison* (Philadelphia: Westminster Press, 1970).

Howard, George, *Crisis in Galatia* (SNTSMS, 35; Cambridge: Cambridge University Press, 2nd edn, 1990).

Hübner, Hans, 'Der Galaterbrief und das Verhältnis von antiker Rhetorik und Epistolographie', *TLZ* 109 (1984), pp. 241-50.

—*An Philemon, An die Kolosser, An die Epheser* (HNT, 12; Tübingen: J.C.B. Mohr [Paul Siebeck], 1997).

Hughes, Frank W., *Early Christian Rhetoric and 2 Thessalonians* (JSNTSup, 30; Sheffield: JSOT Press, 1989).

—'The Rhetoric of 1 Thessalonians', in Collins (ed.), *The Thessalonian Correspondence*, pp. 94-116.

Hughes, Philip E., *Paul's Second Epistle to the Corinthians* (NICNT; Grand Rapids: Eerdmans, 1962).

Hultgren, Arland J., *I–II Timothy, Titus* (Augsburg Commentary on the New Testament; Minneapolis: Augsburg, 1984).

Hurd, John, 'Paul Ahead of his Time: 1 Thess. 2:13-16', in Peter Richardson (ed.), *Antijudaism in Early Christianity* (Waterloo, ON: Wilfrid Laurier, 1986), pp. 21-36.

Jervis, L. Ann, *The Purpose of Romans: A Comparative Letter Structure Investigation* (JSNTSup, 55; Sheffield: JSOT Press, 1991).

Jewett, Robert, 'The Agitators and the Galatian Congregation', *NTS* 17 (1971), pp. 198-212.

—'Conflicting Movements in the Early Church as Reflected in Philippians', *NovT* 12 (1970), pp. 362-90.

—'The Epistolary Thanksgiving and the Integrity of Philippians', *NovT* 12 (1970), pp. 40-53.

—*The Thessalonian Correspondence: Pauline Rhetoric and Millinarian Piety* (FF; Philadelphia: Fortress Press, 1986).

Johanson, Bruce C., *To All the Brethren: A Text-Linguistic and Rhetorical Approach to 1 Thessalonians* (ConBNT; Stockholm: Almquist & Wiksell, 1987).

Johnson, Luke Timothy, 'II Timothy and the Polemic Against False Teachers: A Re-examination', *JRS* 6–7 (1978–79), pp. 1-26.

—*The Writings of the New Testament* (Philadelphia: Fortress Press, 1986).

Judge, E.A., 'The Social Identity of the First Christians: A Question of Method in Religious History', *JRH* 11 (1980), pp. 201-17.

Karris, Robert J., 'The Background and Significance of the Polemic of the Pastoral Epistles', *JBL* 92 (1973), pp. 549-64.

Käsemann, Ernst, 'Die Legitimität des Apostels. Eine Untersuchung zu II Korinther 10–13', *ZNW* 41 (1942), pp. 33-71.

Kaye, B.N., 'Eschatology and Ethics in 1 and 2 Thessalonians', *NovT* 17 (1975), pp. 47-57.

Keck, Leander E., 'The First Letter of Paul to the Thessalonians', in C.M. Laymon (ed.), *Interpreter's One Volume Commentary on the Bible* (Nashville: Abingdon Press, 1971), pp. 865-74.

Kelly, J.N.D., *A Commentary on the Pastoral Epistles* (BNTC; London: A. & C. Black, 1963).

Kennedy, George A., *New Testament Interpretation through Rhetorical Criticism* (Studies in Religion; Chapel Hill: University of North Carolina Press Press, 1984).

Kilpatrick, George D., 'ΒΛΕΠΕΤΕ, Phil 3,2', in M. Black and G. Fohrer (eds.), *In Memoriam Paul Kahle* (Berlin: Alfred Töpelmann, 1968), pp. 146-48.

King, Daniel H., 'Paul and the Tannaim: A Study in Galatians', *WTJ* 45 (1983), pp. 340-70.

Klein, Günter, 'Antipaulinismus in Philippi: Eine Problemskizze', in D. Koch (ed.), *Jesu Rede von Gott und ihre Nachgeschichte im frühen Christentum* (Gütersloh: Gerd Mohn, 1989), pp. 297-313.

Klijn, A.F.J., 'Paul's Opponents in Philippians iii', *NovT* 7 (1964–65), pp. 278-84.

Kloppenberg, John S., 'ΦΙΛΑΔΕΛΦΙΑ, ΘΕΟΔΙΔΑΚΤΟΣ and the Dioscuri: Rhetorical Engagement in 1 Thessalonians 4.9-12', *NTS* 39 (1993), pp. 265-89.

Knight, George W., III, *The Pastoral Epistles: A Commentary on the Greek Text* (NIGTC; Grand Rapids: Eerdmans, 1992).

Koester, Helmut, 'Apostel und Gemeinde in den Briefen an die Thessalonicher', in D. Lührmann and G. Strecker (eds.), *Kirche* (Tübingen: J.C.B. Mohr [Paul Siebeck], 1980), pp. 287-98.

—*History and Literature of the New Testament*. II. *Introduction to the New Testament* (Hermeneia; FF; Philadelphia: Fortress Press, 1982).

—'The Purpose of the Polemic of a Pauline Fragment (Philippians III)', *NTS* 8 (1961/2), pp. 317-32.

—'1 Thessalonians: Experiment in Christian Writing', in F.F. Church and T. George (eds.), *Continuity and Discontinuity in Church History* (Leiden: E.J. Brill, 1979), pp. 33-44.

Krodel, Gerhardt, '2 Thessalonians', in G. Krodel (ed.), *Ephesians, Colossians, 2 Thessalonians, The Pastoral Epistles* (Proclamation Commentaries; Philadelphia: Fortress Press, 1978), pp. 73-96.

Kuck, David W., *Judgment and Community Conflict: Paul's Use of Apocalyptic Judgment Language in 1 Corinthians 3:5–4:5* (NovTSup, 66; Leiden: E.J. Brill, 1992).

Lagrange, M.-J., *Saint Paul: Epître aux Galates* (EBib; Paris: J. Gabalda, 2nd end, 1925).

Lambrecht, Jan, 'Once Again Gal 2,17-18 and 3,21', *ETL* 63 (1987), pp. 148-53.

—'Structure and Line of Thought in 2 Cor 2,14–4,6', *Bib* 64 (1983), pp. 344-80.

—'Thanksgivings in 1 Thessalonians 1–3', in R. Collins (ed.), *The Thessalonian Correspondence* (BETL, 87; Leuven: Leuven University Press, 1990), pp. 183-205.

Lane, William L., '1 Tim. IV. 1-3. An Early Instance of Over-realized Eschatology?', *NTS* 11 (1965), pp. 164-67.

Langlois, Charles V., and Charles Seignobos, *Introduction to the Study of History* (trans. G.G. Berry; London: Gerald Duckworth, 1898).

Lategan, Bernard, 'Is Paul Defending his Apostleship in Galatians? The Function of Galatians 1.11-12 and 2.19-20 in the Development of Paul's Argument', *NTS* 34 (1988), pp. 411-30.

Levinson, John R., '2 Apoc. Bar. 48:42–52:7 and the Apocalyptic Dimension of Colossians 3:1-6', *JBL* 108 (1989, pp. 93-108.

Lewis, Edwin, 'Paul and the Perverters of Christianity', *Int* 2 (1948), pp. 143-57.

Lincoln, Andrew T., *Paradise Now and Not Yet: Studies in the Role of the Heavenly Dimension in Paul's Thought with Special Reference to his Eschatology* (SNTSMS, 43; Cambridge: Cambridge University Press, 1981).

Lindemann, Andreas, 'Zum Abfassungszweck des zweiten Thessalonicherbriefes', *ZNW* 68 (1977), pp. 35-47.

Lock, Walter, *A Critical and Exegetical Commentary on the Pastoral Epistles* (ICC; New York: Charles Scribner's Sons, 1924).

Lohfink, Gerhard, 'Paulinische Theologie in der Rezeption der Pastoralbriefe', in K. Kertelge (ed.), *Paulus in den neutestamentlichen Spätschrifte* (Freiburg: Herder, 1981), pp. 70-121.

Lohmeyer, E., *Die Briefe an die Philipper, an die Kolosser und an Philemon* (MeyerK, 9; Göttingen: Vandenhoeck & Reuprecht, 13th edn, 1964).

Lohse, Eduard, 'Χειρόγραφον', *TDNT*, IX, pp. 435-36.

—*A Commentary on the Epistle to the Colossians and to Philemon* (transl. W.R. Poehl-mann and R.J. Karris; Hermeneia; Philadelphia: Fortress Press, 1971).

—'Das kirchliche Amt des Apostels und das apostolische Amt der Kirche', in *idem* (ed.), *Verteidigung un Begründung des apostolischen Amtes* (Rome: Abtei St. Paul vor den Mauern, 1992), pp. 129-46.

—'Pauline Theology in the Letter to the Colossians', *NTS* 15 (1968), pp. 211-20.

Longenecker, Richard N., *Galatians* (WBC, 41; Dallas, TX: Word Books, 1990).

Lüdemann, Gerd, 'The Hope of the Early Paul', *Perspectives* 7 (1980), pp. 195-201.

—*Paulus, der Heidenapostel*. I. *Studien zur Chronologie* (FRLANT, 123; Göttingen: Vandenhoeck & Ruprecht, 1980); ET: *Paul, Apostle to the Gentiles: Studies in Chronology* (trans. F.S. Jones; Philadelphia: Fortress Press, 1984).

—*Paulus, der Heidenapostel*. II. *Antipaulinismus im frühen Christentum* (FRLANT, 130; Göttingen: Vandenhoeck & Ruprecht, 1983); ET: *Opposition to Paul in Jewish Christianity* (trans. M. Eugene Boring; Minneapolis: Fortress Press, 1989).

Lührmann, Dieter, *Galatians: A Continental Commentary* (trans. O.C. Dean; Minneapolis: Fortress Press, 1992).

Lull, David J., *The Spirit in Galatians* (SBLDS, 49; Chico, CA: Scholars Press, 1980).

Lyons, George, *Pauline Autobiography: Toward a New Understanding* (SBLDS, 73; Atlanta: Scholars Press, 1985).

MacDonald, Dennis R., *The Legend and the Apostle: The Battle for Paul in Story and Canon* (Philadelphia: Fortress Press, 1983).

MacMullen, Ramsay, *Roman Social Relations: 50 BC to AD 284* (New Haven: Yale University Press, 1974).

Malbon, Elizabeth Struthers, ' "No Need to Have Anyone Write"? A Structural Exegesis of 1 Thessalonians', *Semeia* 26 (1983), pp. 57-83.

Malherbe, Abraham J., 'Antisthenes and Odysseus, and Paul at War', *HTR* 76 (1983), pp. 143-73.

—'Did the Thessalonians Write to Paul?', in R.T. Fortna and B.R. Gaventa (eds.), *The Conversation Continues: Studies in Paul and John in Honor of J. Louis Martyn* (Nashville: Abingdon Press, 1990), pp. 246-57.

—' "Gentle as a Nurse": The Cynic Background to 1 Thessalonians ii', *NovT* 12 (1970), pp. 203-217.

—' "Pastoral Care" in the Thessalonian Church', *NTS* 36 (1990), pp. 375-91.

—*Paul and the Thessalonians: The Philosophic Tradition of Pastoral Care* (Philadelphia: Fortress Press, 1987).

Marshall, I. Howard, 'The Christian Life in 1 Timothy', *RTR* 49 (1990), pp. 81-90.

—*1 and 2 Thessalonians* (NCB; Grand Rapids: Eerdmans, 1983).

Marshall, Peter, 'Hybrists Not Gnostics in Corinth', *SBLSP* 23 (1984), pp. 275-87.

—'Invective: Paul and his Enemies in Corinth', in E.W. Conrad and E.G. Newing (eds.), *Perspectives on Language and Text* (Winona Lake, IN: Eisenbrauns, 1987), pp. 359-73.

—*Enmity in Corinth: Social Conventions in Paul's Relations with the Corinthians* (WUNT, 23; Tübingen: J.C.B. Mohr, 1987)

Martin, Dale, *The Corinthian Body* (New Haven: Yale University Press, 1995).

Martin, Ralph P., *Colossians and Philemon* (NCB; London: Oliphants, 1974).

—*Ephesians, Colossians, and Philemon* (Interpretation; Atlanta: John Knox Press, 1991).

—*Philippians* (NCB; London: Oliphants, 1976).

—*2 Corinthians* (WBC, 40; Waco, TX: Word Books, 1986).

Martin, Troy, *By Philosophy and Vain Deceit: Colossians as a Response to a Cynic Critique* (JSNTSup, 118; Sheffield: Sheffield Academic Press, 1996).

Martyn, J. Louis, 'Apocalyptic Antinomies in Paul's Letter to the Galatians', *NTS* 31 (1985), pp. 410-24.

—'Epistemology at the Turn of the Ages: 2 Corinthians 5:16', in W.R. Farmer, C.F.D. Moule and R.R. Niebuhr (eds.), *Christian History and Interpretation* (Cambridge: Cambridge University Press, 1967), pp. 269-88.

—'Events in Galatia: Modified Covenantal Nomism versus God's Invasion of the Cosmos in the Singular Gospel. A Response to J.D.G. Dunn and B.R. Gaventa', in Bassler (ed.), *Pauline Theology*, I, pp, 160-80.

—'A Law-Observant Mission to Gentiles: The Background of Galatians', *SJT* 38 (1985), pp. 307-24.

Marxsen, Willi, *Der zweite Thessalonicherbrief* (Züricher Bibelkommentare; Zürich: Theologischer Verlag, 1982).

—*Introduction to the New Testament: An Approach to its Problems* (trans. G. Buswell; Philadelphia: Fortress Press, 1968).

Masson, Charles, *Les deux épîtres de Saint Paul aux Thessaloniciens* (Neuchâtel: Delachaux & Niestlé, 1957).

Matera, Frank J., 'The Culmination of Paul's Argument to the Galatians: Gal 5,1-6, 12 17', *JSNT* 32 (1988), pp. 79-91.

McDonald, James I., 'Paul and the Preaching Ministry: A reconsideration of 2 Cor. 2.14-17 in its context', *JSNT* 17 (1983), pp. 35-50.

McEleney, Neil J., 'Vice Lists of the Pastoral Epistles', *CBQ* 36 (1974), pp. 203-19.

Mearns, C.L., 'Early Eschatological Development in Paul: The Evidence of I and II Thessalonians', *NTS* 27 (1981), pp. 137-57.

—'The Identity of Paul's Opponents at Philippi', *NTS* 33 (1987), pp. 194-204.

Meeks, Wayne A., *The First Urban Christians: The Social World of the Apostle Paul* (New Haven: Yale University Press, 1983).

Mengel, B., *Studien zum Philipperbrief* (WUNT; Tübingen: J.C.B. Mohr [Paul Siebeck], 1982).

Menken, M.J.J., 'Paradise Regained or Still Lost? Eschatology and Disorderly Behavior in 2 Thessalonians', *NTS* 38 (1992), pp. 271-89.

Michael, J. Hugh, *The Epistle of Paul to the Philippians* (MNTC; New York: Harper & Brothers, 1927).

Michaelis, W., *Der Brief an die Philipper* (Leipzig: Deichert, 1935).

Milligan, George, *St. Paul's Epistles to the Thessalonians* (London: Macmillan, 1908).

Minear, Paul S., 'Singing and Suffering in Philippi', in R.T. Fortna and B.R. Gaventa (eds.), *The Conversation Continues: Studies in Paul and John in Honor of J. Louis Martyn* (Nashville: Abingdon Press, 1990), pp. 202-19.

Mitchell, Margaret M., 'New Testament Envoys in the Context of Greco-Roman Diplomatic and Epistolary Conventions: The Example of Timothy and Titus', *JBL* 111 (1992), pp. 641-62.

—*Paul and the Rhetoric of Reconciliation: An Exegetical Investigation of the Language and Composition of 1 Corinthians* (HUT, 28; J.C.B. Mohr [Paul Siebeck]; Louisville, KY: Westminster/John Knox Press, 1991).

Moore, A.L., *1 and 2 Thessalonians* (ConBNT; Camden, NJ: Nelson, 1969).

Moule, C.F.D., *The Epistles of Paul the Apostle to the Colossians and to Philemon* (CGTC; Cambridge: Cambridge University Press, 1957).

Moule, H.C.G., *The Epistles to the Colossians and to Philemon* (The Cambridge Bible for
  Schools and Colleges; Cambridge: Cambridge University Press, 1898.)
Moyo, A.M., 'The Colossian Heresy in the Light of Some Gnostic Documents from Nag
  Hammadi', *Journal of Theology for Southern Africa* 48 (1984), pp. 30-44.
Müller, Ulrich B., *Zur frühchristlichen Theologiegeschichte* (Gütersloh: Gerd Mohn, 1976).
Munck, Johannes, '1 Thess. I.9-10 and the Missionary Preaching of Paul', *NTS* 9 (1963),
  pp. 94-110.
—*Paul and the Salvation of Mankind* (trans. F. Clarke; Atlanta: John Knox Press, 1977),
  p. 157.
Murphy-O'Connor, Jerome, '2 Timothy Contrasted with 1 Timothy and Titus', *RB* 98
  (1991), pp. 403-418.
Mussner, Franz, *Der Galaterbrief* (HTKNT, 9; Freiburg: Herder, 1974).
Neil, William, *The Epistle of Paul to the Thessalonians* (MNTC; New York: Harper,
  1950).
Neusner, Jacob, and Ernest S. Frerichs, 'Preface', in *idem* (eds.), *'To See Ourselves as
  Others See Us'*, pp. xi-xvi.
—(eds.), *'To see Ourselves as Other See Us'?: Christians, Jews, 'Others' in Late Antiquity*
  (Studies in the Humanities; Chico, CA: Scholars Press, 1985).
Neyrey, Jerome, 'Bewitched in Galatia: Paul and Cultural Anthropology', *CBQ* 50 (1988),
  pp. 72-100.
Nock, A.D., *Conversion: The Old and the New in Religion from Alexander the Great to
  Augustine of Hippo* (New York: Oxford University Press, 1933).
Oberlinner, Lorenz, *Die Pastoralbriefe* (HTKNT, 11/2; Freiburg: Herder, 1994).
O'Brien, Peter T., *Colossians, Philemon* (WBC, 44; Waco, TX: Word Books, 1982).
—*The Epistle to the Philippians: A Commentary on the Greek Text* (NIGTC; Grand
  Rapids: Eerdmans, 1991).
Oden, Thomas C., *First and Second Timothy and Titus* (Interpretation; Louisville, KY:
  John Knox Press, 1989).
Oepke, Albrecht, 'Die Briefe an die Thessalonicher', in H.W. Beyer *et al.* (eds.), *Die
  kleineren Briefe des Apostels Paulus* (NTD, 8; Göttingen: Vandenhoeck & Ruprecht,
  9th edn, 1962).
Olson, Stanley N., 'Pauline Expressions of Confidence in his Addressees', *CBQ* 47 (1985),
  pp. 282-95.
Omanson, Roger L., 'Acknowledging Paul's Quotations', *BT* 43 (1992), pp. 201-13.
Oostendorp, D.W., *Another Jesus: A Gospel of Jewish–Christian Superiority in II Corin-
  thians* (Kampen: Kok, 1967).
Orr, William F., and James A. Walther, *1 Corinthians* (AB, 32; Garden City, NY: Dou-
  bleday, 1976).
Osten-Sacken, Peter von der, 'Die Apologie des Paulinischen Apostolats in 1 Kor 15.1-11',
  ZNW 64 (1973), pp. 245-62.
Paulsen, Henning, 'Schisma und Häresie: Untersuchungen zu 1 Kor 11, 18.19', *ZTK* 79
  (1982), pp. 180-211.
Pearson, Birger A., *The Pneumatikos-Psychikos Terminology in 1 Corinthians* (SBLDS,
  12; Missoula, MT: SBL, 1973).
Pedersen, Sigfred, '"Mit Furcht und Zittern" (Phil. 2,12-13)', *ST* 2 (1978), pp. 1-31.
Penna, Romano, 'La presence des adversaires de Paul en 2 Cor 10–13: Approche littéraire',
  in E. Lohse (ed.), *Verteidigung und Begründung des apostolischen Amtes (2 Kor 10–
  13)* (Rome: Abtei St. Paul vor den Mauern, 1992), pp. 7-41.

Percy, Ernst, *Die Probleme der Kolosser- und Epheserbriefe* (Lund: C.W.K. Gleerup, 1946).

Perkins, Pheme, 'Philippians: Theology for the Heavenly Politeuma', in Bassler (ed.), *Pauline Theology*, I, pp. 89-104.

Plummer, Alfred, *A Critical and Exegetical Commentary on the Second Epistle of St. Paul to the Corinthians* (ICC; Edinburgh: T. & T. Clark, 1915).

Pogoloff, Stephen M., *Logos and Sophia: The Rhetorical Situation of 1 Corinthians* (SBLDS, 134; Atlanta: Scholars Press, 1992).

Porter, Frank C., 'Does Paul Claim to Have Known the Historical Jesus?', *JBL* 47 (1928), pp. 257-75.

Porter, Stanley E., 'The Theoretical Justification for Application of Rhetorical Categories to Pauline Epistolary Literature', in Porter and Olbricht (eds.), *Rhetoric and the New Testament*, pp. 100-22.

Porter, Stanley E., and Thomas H. Olbricht (eds.), *Rhetoric and the New Testament: Essays from the 1992 Heidelberg Conference* (JSNTSup, 90; Sheffield: JSOT Press, 1993).

Porton, Gary G., 'Forbidden Transactions: Prohibited Commerce with Gentiles in Earliest Rabbinism', in Neusner and Frerichs (eds.), *'To See Ourselves as Others See Us'*, pp. 317-35.

Provence, Thomas A., ' "Who is Sufficient for These Things?" An Exegesis of 2 Corinthians ii15–iii18', *NovT* 24 (1982), pp. 54-81.

Räisänen, Heikki, *Jesus, Paul, and Torah* (trans. D.E. Orton; JSNTSup, 43; Sheffield: JSOT Press, 1992).

—*Paul and the Law* (repr.; Philadelphia: Fortress Press, 1986 [1983]).

Reed, Jeffrey T., 'Using Ancient Rhetorical Categories to Interpret Paul's Letters: A Question of Genre', in Porter and Olbricht (eds.), *Rhetoric and the New Testament*, pp. 292-324.

Richard, Earl, 'Early Pauline Thought: An Analysis of 1 Thessalonians', in Bassler (ed.), *Pauline Theology*, I, pp. 39-52.

—'Polemics, Old Testament, and Theology: A Study of II Corinthians 3.1–4.6', *RB* 88 (1981), pp. 340-67.

Richardson, Neil, *Paul's Language about God* (JSNTSup, 99; Sheffield: Sheffield Academic Press, 1994).

Rigaux, Beda, *Saint Paul: Les épîtres aux Thessaloniciens* (EBib; Paris: J. Gabalda, 1956).

Robertson, A., and A. Plummer, *A Critical and Exegetical Commentary on the First Epistle of St. Paul to the Corinthians* (ICC; Edinburgh: T. & T. Clark, 1911).

Robinson, James M., 'A Formal Analysis of Colossians 1:15-20', *JBL* 76 (1957), pp. 270-87.

Roetzel, Calvin, 'Theodidactoi and Handwork in Philo and 1 Thessalonians', in A. Vanhoye (ed.), *L'apôtre Paul: Personnalité, style, et conception du ministère* (Leuven: Leuven University Press, 1986), pp. 324-31.

Roloff, Jürgen, *Der erste Brief an Timotheus* (EKKNT, 15; Neukirchen–Vluyn: Neukirchener Verlag, 1988).

Rowland, Christopher, 'Apocalyptic Visions and the Exaltation of Christ in the Letter to the Colossians', *JSNT* 19 (1983), pp. 73-83.

Rudolf, Kurt, *Gnosis* (trans. and ed. R.M. Wilson; New York: Harper & Row, 1983).

Russell, Ronald, 'The Idle in 2 Thess 3.6-12: An Eschatological or Social Problem?', *NTS* 34 (1988), pp. 105-19.

—'Pauline Letter Structure in Philippians', *JETS* 25 (1982), pp. 295-306.

Russell, Walt, 'Who Were Paul's Opponents in Galatia?', *BSac* 147 (1990), pp. 329-50.

Sampley, J. Paul, ' "Before God, I do not Lie" (Gal I.20) Paul's Self-Defense in Light of Roman Legal Praxis', *NTS* 23 (1977), pp. 477-82.

Sanders, E.P., *Paul, the Law, and the Jewish People* (Philadelphia: Fortress Press, 1983).

Schenk, Wolfgang, 'Die Pastoralbriefe in der neueren Forschung', *ANRW* II, pp. 3404-38.

—*Die Philipperbriefe des Paulus* (Stuttgart: W. Kohlhammer, 1984).

Schmithals, Walter, 'The *Corpus Paulinum* and Gnosis', in A.H.B. Logan and A.J.M Wedderburn (eds.), *The New Testament and Gnosis: Essays in Honor of Robert McL. Wilson* (Edinburgh: T. & T. Clark, 1983), pp. 107-24.

—*Gnosticism in Corinth* (trans. John E. Steely; Nashville: Abingdon Press, 1971).

—'Judaisten in Galatien?', *ZNW* 74 (1983), pp. 27-58.

—*Paul and the Gnostics* (trans. John E. Steely; Nashville: Abingdon Press, 1972).

Schneider, Bernardin, 'The Meaning of St. Paul's Antithesis "The Letter and the Spirit" ', *CBQ* 15 (1953), pp. 163-207.

Schnelle, Udo, 'Der erste Thessalonicherbrief und die Entstehung der Paulinischen Anthropologie', *NTS* 32 (1986), pp. 202-24.

Schoedel, William R., *Ignatius of Antioch: A Commentary on the Letters of Ignatius of Antioch* (Hermeneia; Philadelphia: Fortress Press, 1985).

Schrage, Wolfgang, *Der erste Brief an die Korinther, 1 Kor 1,1–6,11* (EKKNT, 7.1; Zürich: Benzinger Verlag, 1991).

—'Leid, Kreuz, und Eschaton', *EvT* 34 (1975), pp. 141-75.

Schubert, Paul, 'New Testament Study and Theology', *Religion in Life* 14 (1945), pp. 556-71.

Schüssler-Fiorenza, Elizabeth, 'Rhetorical Situation and Historical Reconstruction in 1 Corinthians', *NTS* 33 (1987), pp. 386-403.

Schütz, John Howard, *Paul and the Anatomy of Apostolic Authority* (SNTSMS, 26; Cambridge: Cambridge University Press, 1975).

Schweizer, Eduard, 'Christianity of the Circumcised and Judaism of the Uncircumcised: The Background of Matthew and Colossians', in R. Hamerton-Kelly and R. Scroggs (eds.), *Jews, Greeks and Christians: Religious Cultures in Late Antiquity* (Leiden: E.J. Brill, 1976), pp. 245-60.

—'Die "Elemente der Welt" Gal 4,3. 9; Kol 2,8. 20', in O. Böcher and K. Haacker (eds.), *Verborum Veritas* (Wuppertal: Theologischer Verlag, 1970), pp. 245-59.

—*The Letter to the Colossians: A Commentary* (trans. A. Chester; Minneapolis: Augsburg, 1982).

—'σάρξ', *TDNT*, pp. 119-51.

—'Slaves of the Elements and Worshipers of Angels: Gal 4:3, 9 and Col 2:8, 18, 20', *JBL* 107 (1988), pp. 455-68.

—'Two New Testament Creeds Compared: 1 Corinthians 15.3-5 and 1 Timothy 3.16', in W. Klassen and G.F. Snyder (eds.), *Current Issues in New Testament Interpretation* (New York: Harper & Row, 1962, pp. 166-77.

—'Zur neueren Forschung am Kolosserbrief (seit 1970)', *Theologische Berichte* 5 (1976), pp. 163-91.

Scott, Ernest F., 'The Epistle to the Philippians: Introduction and Exegesis', *IB* 11, pp. 3-130.

—*The Epistles of Paul to the Colossians, to Philemon, and to the Ephesians* (MNTC; New York: Harper & Brothers, 1930).

—*The Pastoral Epistles* (MNTC; New York: Harper & Brothers, 1936).

Sellin, Gerhard, 'Das "Geheimnis" der Weisheit und das Rätsel der "Christuspartei" (zu 1 Kor 1-4)', *ZNW* 73 (1982), pp. 69-96.

Sieber, John, 'Review of *Identifying Paul's Opponents* (Sumney)', *Int* 45 (1991), pp. 424, 426.

Simpson, E.K., and F.F. Bruce, *A Commentary on the Epistles to the Ephesians and Colossians* (NICNT; Grand Rapids: Eerdmans, 1957).

Skeat, T.C., ' "Especially the Parchments": A Note on 2 Timothy iv.13', *JTS* 30 (1979), pp. 173-77.

Smit, Joop, 'The Letter of Paul to the Galatians: A Deliberative Speech', *NTS* 35 (1989), pp. 1-26.

Smith, Jonathan Z., *Imagining Religion: From Babylon to Jonestown* (Chicago Studies in the History of Judaism; Chicago: University of Chicago Press, 1982).

—'What a Difference a Difference Makes', in Neusner and Frerichs (eds.), *'To See Ourselves as Others See Us'*, pp. 3-48.

Snyder, Graydon F., 'Apocalyptic and Didactic Elements in 1 Thessalonians' (SBLSP; Missoula, MT: Scholars Press, 1972), pp. 233-44.

Spenser, Aida B., 'The Wise Fool (and the Foolish Wise): A Study of Irony in Paul', *NovT* 23 (1981), pp. 349-60.

Spicq, C., 'Les Thessaloniciens "inquites" etaient ils des paresseux?', *ST* 10 (1956), pp. 1-13.

—*Saint Paul: Les épîtres pastorales* (EBib; Paris: Lecoffre, 1947).

Stamps, Dennis L., 'Rethinking the Rhetorical Situation: The Entextualization of the Situation in New Testament Epistles', in Porter and Olbricht (eds.), *Rhetoric and the New Testament*, pp. 193-210.

Standaert, Benoit, 'La rhétorique antique et l'épître aux Galates', *Foi et Vie* 84 (1985), pp. 33-40.

Stowers, Stanley K., 'Friends and Enemies in the Politics of Heaven: Reading Theology in Philippians', in Bassler (ed.), *Pauline Theology*, I, pp. 105-22.

Strecker, Georg, 'Die Legitimität des Paulinischen Apostolates nach 2 Korinther 10–13', *NTS* 38 (1992), pp. 566-86.

Strobel, August, *Der erste Brief an die Korinther* (ZBK; Zürich: Theologischer Verlag, 1989).

Sumney, Jerry L., 'The Bearing of a Pauline Rhetorical Pattern on the Integrity of 2 Thessalonians', *ZNW* 81 (1990), pp. 192-204.

—*Identifying Paul's Opponents: The Question of Method in 2 Corinthians* (JSNTSup, 40; Sheffield: JSOT Press, 1990).

—'Paul's "Weakness": An Integral Part of his Conception of Apostleship', *JSNT* 52 (1993), pp. 71-91.

—' "Those Who Pass Judgment": The Opponents of Colossians' *Bib* 74 (1993), pp. 366-88.

Tarazi, Paul N., 'The Addressees and the Purpose of Galatians', *St. Vladimir's Theological Quarterly* 33 (1989), pp. 159-79.

Theissen, Gerd, *Studien zur Soziologie des Urchristentums* (Tübingen: J.C.B. Mohr, 1979); ET: *Social Reality and the Early Christians: Theology, Ethics, and the World of the New Testament* (trans. M. Kohl; Minneapolis: Fortress Press, 1992).

—*The Social Setting of Pauline Christianity* (ed. and trans. J.H. Schütz; Philadelphia: Fortress Press, 1982).

—*Studien zur Soziologie des Urchristentums* (Tübingen: J.C.B. Mohr, 1979); ET: *Social Reality and the Early Christians: Theology, Ethics, and the World of the New Testament* (trans. M. Kohl; Minneapolis: Fortress Press, 1992).

Thielman, Frank, *From Plight to Solution: A Jewish Framework for Understanding Paul's View of the Law in Galatians and Romans* (NovTSup, 61; Leiden: E.J. Brill, 1989).

Thornton, T.C.G., 'Jewish New Moon Festivals, Galatians 4:3-11 and Colossians 2:16', *JTS* 40 (1989), pp. 97-100.

Thrall, Margaret E., 'Salvation Proclaimed; Part 5: 2 Corinthians 5:18-21: Reconciliation with God', *ExpTim* 93 (1981–82), pp. 227-32.

—'Super-Apostles, Servants of Christ, and Servants of Satan', *JSNT* 6 (1980), pp. 42-57.

Towner, Philip H., *The Goal of our Instruction: The Structure of Theology and Ethics in the Pastoral Epistles* (JSNTSup, 34; Sheffield: JSOT Press, 1989).

Trakatellis, Demetrias, 'Power in Weakness: Exegesis of 2 Cor. 12,1-13', in Lohse (ed.), *Verteidigung und Begrundigung des apostolischen Amtes*, pp. 65-86.

Travis, S.H., 'Paul's Boasting in 2 Cor. 10–12', *SE* 6 (1969), pp. 527-32.

Trilling, Wolfgang, *Untersuchungen zum zweiten Thessalonicherbrief* (Erfurter Theologische Studien, 27; Leipzig: St Benno, 1972).

—*Der zweite Brief an die Thessalonicher* (EKKNT, 14; Neukirchen–Vluyn: Neukirchener Verlag, 1980).

Trummer, Peter, 'Corpus Paulinum—Corpus Pastorale: Zur Ortung des Paulustradition in den Pastoralbriefen', in K. Kertelge (ed.), *Paulus in den neutestamentlichen Spätschriften* (Freiburg: Herder, 1981), pp. 122-45.

Tyson, Joseph B., 'Paul's Opponents at Philippi', *Perspectives* 3 (1976), pp. 82-95.

—'Paul's Opponents in Galatia', *NovT* 10 (1968), pp. 241-54.

—' "Works of the Law" in Galatians', *JBL* 92 (1973), pp. 423-31.

Ulonska, H., 'Gesetz und Beschneidung: Überlegungen zu einem Paulinischen Ablösungskonflict', in D. Koch (ed.), *Jesu Rede von Gott und ihre Nachgeschichte im frühen Christentum* (Gütersloh: Gütersloher Verlagshaus, 1989), pp. 314-31.

Verner, David C., *The Household of God: The Social World of the Pastoral Epistles* (SBLDS, 71; Chico, CA: Scholars Press, 1983).

Vielhauer, Philipp, 'Paulus und die Kephaspartei in Korinth', *NTS* 21 (1975), pp. 341-52.

Vincent, Marvin R., *A Critical and Exegetical Commentary on the Epistles to the Philippians and to Philemon* (ICC; Edinburgh: T. & T. Clark, 1897).

Vouga, François, 'Zur rhetorischen Gattung des Galaterbriefes', *ZNW* 79 (1988), pp. 291-92.

Walter, Nikolaus, 'Paulus und die Gegner des Christusevangeliums in Galatien', in A. Vanhoye (ed.), *L'apôtre Paul: Personnalité, style, et conception du ministère* (Leuven: Leuven University Press, 1986), pp. 351-56.

Wanamaker, Charles A., *The Epistles to the Thessalonians: A Commentary on the Greek Text* (NIGTC; Grand Rapids: Eerdmans, 1990).

Ware, James, 'The Thessalonians as a Missionary Congregation: 1 Thessalonians 1, 5-8', *ZNW* 83 (1992), pp. 126-31.

Watson, Duane F., 'A Rhetorical Analysis of Philippians and its Implications for the Unity Question', *NovT* 30 (1988), pp. 57-88.

Watson, Francis, *Paul, Judaism and the Gentiles: A Sociological Approach* (SNTSMS, 56; Cambridge: Cambridge University Press, 1986).

Wedderburn, A.J.M., 'The Problem of the Denial of the Resurrection in 1 Corinthians XV', *NovT* 23 (1981), pp. 229-41.

—*The Reasons for Romans* (Minneapolis: Fortress Press, 1991).

Weima, Jeffrey A.D., *Neglected Endings: The Significance of the Pauline Letter Closings* (JSNTSup, 101; Sheffield: JSOT Press, 1994).

Weiss, Hans-Friedrich, 'Gnostische Motive und antignostische Polemik in Kolosser- und im Epheserbrief', in K.-W. Tröger (ed.), *Gnosis und Neues Testament* (Gütersloh: Gerd Mohn, 1980), pp. 311-24.

Weiss, Harold, 'The Law in the Epistle to the Colossians', *CBQ* 34 (1972), pp. 294-314.

Wellborn, L.L., 'A Conciliatory Principle in 1 Cor. 4:6', *NovT* 29 (1987), pp. 320-46.

White, L. Michael, 'Morality Between Two Worlds: A Paradigm of Friendship in Philippians', in D.L. Balch, E. Ferguson and W.A. Meeks (eds.), *Greeks, Romans, and Christians: Essays in Honor of Abraham J. Malherbe* (Minneapolis: Fortress Press, 1990), pp. 201-15.

Whiteley, D.E.H., *Thessalonians in the Revised Standard Version* (New Clarendon Bible; London: Oxford University Press, 1969).

Willis, Wendell, 'An Apostolic Apologia? The Form and Function of 1 Corinthians 9', *JSNT* 24 (1985), pp. 33-48.

—'The "Mind of Christ" in 1 Corinthians 2,16' *Bib* 70 (1989), pp. 110-22.

Wilson, Jack H., 'The Corinthians Who Say There Is No Resurrection of the Dead', *ZNW* 59 (1968), pp. 90-107.

—'Gnosis at Corinth', in M.D. Hooker and S.G. Wilson (eds.), *Paul and Paulinism* (London: SPCK, 1982), pp. 102-14.

Wilson, R.M., 'How Gnostic were the Corinthians?', *NTS* 19 (1972–73), pp. 65-74.

Windisch, Hans, *Der zweite Korintherbrief* (Göttingen: Vandenhoeck & Ruprecht,1924).

Wire, Antoinette Clark, *The Corinthian Women Prophets: A Reconstruction through Paul's Rhetoric* (Minneapolis: Fortress Press, 1990).

Wisse, F., 'The Use of Early Christian Literature as Evidence for Inner Diversity and Conflict', in C.W. Hedrick and R. Hodgson, Jr (eds.), *Nag Hammadi, Gnosticism, and Early Christianity* (Peabody, MA: Hendrickson, 1986), pp. 177-90.

Wolff, Christian, *Der erste Brief des Paulus an die Korinther*. II. *Auslegung der Kapitel 8–16* (THNT, 7.2; Berlin: Evangelische Verlagsanstalt, 1982).

Wolter, Michael, 'Paulus, der bekehrte Gottesfeind. Zum Verständnis von 1. Tim 1:13,', *NovT* 31 (1989), pp. 48-66.

Wright, N.T., 'Poetry and Theology in Colossians 1.15-20', *NTS* 36 (1990), pp. 444-68.

Wuellner, W., 'The Argumentative Structure of 1 Thessalonians as Paradoxical Encomium', in Collins (ed.), *The Thessalonian Correspondence*, pp. 117-36.

Yarbrough, O. Larry, *Not Like the Gentiles: Marriage Rules in the Letters of Paul* (SBLDS, 80; Atlanta: Scholars Press, 1985).

Yates, Roy, 'Christ and the Powers of Evil in Colossians', in E.A. Livingstone (ed.), *Studia Biblica 1978: III. Papers on Paul and Other New Testament Authors* (JSNTSup, 3; Sheffield: JSOT Press, 1980), pp. 461-68.

—'Colossians and Gnosis', *JSNT* 27 (1986), pp. 49-68.

Young, Frances, *The Theology of the Pastoral Letters* (New Testament Theology; Cambridge: Cambridge University Press, 1994).

INDEXES

INDEX OF REFERENCES

OLD TESTAMENT

NEW TESTAMENT

JOURNAL FOR THE STUDY OF THE NEW TESTAMENT
SUPPLEMENT SERIES